Computational Intelligence in Analytics and Information Systems

Volume 2

Advances in Digital Transformation, Selected Papers from CIAIS-2021

Computational Intelligence in Analytics and Information Systems, 2-volume set

Hardback ISBN: 978-1-77491-142-6
Ebook ISBN: 978-1-00333-263-3
Paperback ISBN: 978-1-77491-143-3

Volume 1: Data Science and AI, Selected Papers from CIAIS-2021

Hardback ISBN: 978-1-77491-144-0
Ebook ISBN: 978-1-00333-231-2
Paperback ISBN: 978-1-77491-145-7

Volume 2: Advances in Digital Transformation, Selected Papers from CIAIS-2021

Hardback ISBN: 978-1-77491-146-4
Ebook ISBN: 978-1-00333-236-7
Paperback ISBN: 978-1-77491-147-1

Computational Intelligence in Analytics and Information Systems

Volume 2

*Advances in Digital Transformation,
Selected Papers from CIAIS-2021*

Edited by
Parneeta Dhaliwal, PhD
Manpreet Kaur, PhD
Hardeo Kumar Thakur, PhD
Rajeev Kumar Arya, PhD
Joan Lu, PhD

APPLE
ACADEMIC
PRESS

First edition published 2024

Apple Academic Press Inc.
1265 Goldenrod Circle, NE,
Palm Bay, FL 32905 USA
760 Laurentian Drive, Unit 19,
Burlington, ON L7N 0A4, CANADA

CRC Press
6000 Broken Sound Parkway NW,
Suite 300, Boca Raton, FL 33487-2742 USA
4 Park Square, Milton Park,
Abingdon, Oxon, OX14 4RN UK

© 2024 by Apple Academic Press, Inc.

Apple Academic Press exclusively co-publishes with CRC Press, an imprint of Taylor & Francis Group, LLC

Library and Archives Canada Cataloguing in Publication

Title: Computational intelligence in analytics and information systems / edited by Hardeo Kumar Thakur, PhD, Manpreet Kaur, PhD, Parneeta Dhaliwal, PhD, Rajeev Kumar Arya, PhD, Joan Lu, PhD.
Names: Thakur, Hardeo Kumar, editor. | Kaur, Manpreet (Lecturer in computer science), editor. | Dhaliwal, Parneeta, editor. | Arya, Rajeev, 1985- editor. | Lu, Zhongyu, 1955- editor.
Description: First edition. | Includes bibliographical references and index. | Contents: Volume 2. Advances in digital transformation, selected papers from CIAIS-2021.
Identifiers: Canadiana (print) 20230146627 | Canadiana (ebook) 20230146694 | ISBN 9781774911426 (set ; hardcover) | ISBN 9781774911433 (set ; softcover) | ISBN 9781774911464 (v. 2 ; hardcover) | ISBN 9781774911471 (v. 2 ; softcover) | ISBN 9781003332367 (v. 2 ; ebook)
Subjects: LCSH: Computational intelligence. | LCSH: Information technology.
Classification: LCC Q342 .C66 2023 | DDC 006.3—dc23

Library of Congress Cataloging-in-Publication Data

....

CIP data on file with US Library of Congress

....

ISBN: 978-1-77491-146-4 (hbk)
ISBN: 978-1-77491-147-1 (pbk)
ISBN: 978-1-00333-236-7 (ebk)

About the Editors

 **Parneeta Dhaliwal, PhD,** has over 16 years of experience in teaching and research. Presently, she is working as Associate Professor in the Department of Computer Science and Technology, Manav Rachna University, India. She is also working as Head of the Research Cluster of Computing (RCC) to facilitate students in their research and innovative projects.

 **Manpreet Kaur, PhD,** is working as an Associate Professor in the Department of Computer Science and Technology, Manav Rachna University, India. She has more than 14 years of teaching and research experience. She is currently working in the domains of machine learning, deep learning, and natural language processing. She is a Senior Member, IEEE (USA).

 **Hardeo Kumar Thakur, PhD,** is working as an Associate Professor in the Department of Computer Science and Technology of Manav Rachna University (MRU), Faridabad, India. He has more than 10 years of teaching and research experience in leading institutions of India. He earned his PhD (Computer Engineering) from the University of Delhi in 2017 in the field of data mining. His current research interests are data mining, dynamic graph mining, machine learning and big data analytics.

 **Rajeev Kumar Arya, PhD,** is currently an Assistant Professor with the Department of Electronics and Communication Engineering at National Institute of Technology, Patna, India. His current research interests are in wireless communication, soft computing techniques, cognitive radio, signal processing, communication systems, and circuits design.

Joan Lu, PhD, is a Professor in the Department of Computer Science and the Research Group Leader of Information and System Engineering (ISE) in the Centre of High Intelligent Computing (CHIC) at the University of Huddersfield, United Kingdom, having previously been team leader in the IT Department of the publishing company Charlesworth Group.

Contents

Najneen, Manish Kumar Mukhija, and Satish Kumar

Pradeep Kumar Sharma and S. S Tyagi

Neeru Ahuja and Pradeep Kumar Bhatia

Contributors

Amara Aditya
University of Petroleum & Energy Studies (UPES), Bidholi, Dehradun, India

Deepshikha Agarwal
Computer Science & Engg & Information Tech, Amity University Lucknow Campus, Lucknow, India

Himanshu Agarwal
Computer Science & Engineering Department, Punjabi University, Patiala, Punjab, India

Krishna Kant Agarwal
ABES Institute of Technology, Ghaziabad, India

Mayank Agarwal
Gurukula Kangri (Deemed to be University), Computer Science & Engineering Department, Haridwar, Uttarakhand, India

Riya Aggarwal
Department of Computer Science and Engineering, Amity University, Noida, Uttar Pradesh, India

Neeru Ahuja
Department of Computer Science and Engineering, Guru Jambheshwar University of Science and Technology, Hisar, India

Junaid Ali
Department of Mechanical Engineering, Indian Institute of Technology Madras, Tamil Nadu, India

Sazid Ali
Department of Computer Science & Engineering, Adamas University, Kolkata, India

Alpana
Department of Computer Science and Technology, Manav Rachna University, Faridabad, Haryana, India

Chaman Prakash Arya
Scientific Analysis Group, Defence Research and Development Organisation, Delhi, India

Sumit Bansal
Gurukula Kangri (Deemed to be University), Computer Science & Engineering Department, Haridwar, Uttarakhand, India

Abhishek Barve
JD College of Engineering and Technology, Nagpur, India

Pradeep Kumar Bhatia
Department of Computer Science and Engineering, Guru Jambheshwar University of Science and Technology, Hisar, India

Amit Bhatnagar
Research Scholar, School of Computer Science & Applications, IFTM University, Moradabad, India

Hanu Bhardwaj
Department of Computer Science & Technology, Manav Rachna University, Faridabad, India

Harshal Bhoyar
JD College of Engineering and Technology, Nagpur, India

Satish Chand
School of Computer and Systems Sciences, Jawaharlal Nehru University, New Delhi, India

Dharamendra Chouhan
Department of Computer Science and Engineering, University Visvesvaraya College of Engineering, Bangalore, India

Aninda Chowdhury
Department of Computer Science & Engineering, Adamas University, Kolkata, India

Sonika Dahiya
Department of Computer Science and Engineering, Delhi Technological University, Delhi, India

P. Damodharan
Department of Computer Engineering, Marwadi University, Rajkot, Gujarat

Anwesha Das
Department of Computer Science & Engineering, Adamas University, Kolkata, India

Jaly Dasmahapatra
Department of Computer Science & Engineering, College of Haldia Institute of Technology, West Bengal, India

Mili Dasmahapatra
Department of Computer Science & Engineering, Adamas University, Kolkata, India

Debojit Dhali
Department of Computer Science & Engineering, Adamas University, Kolkata, India

Niloy Dev
Department of Computer Science & Engineering, Adamas University, Kolkata, India

Sapna Gambhir
Department of Computer Engineering, J.C. Bose University of Science & Technology, YMCA, Faridabad, India

Nayan Garain
Department of Computer Science & Engineering, Adamas University, Kolkata, India

Nancy Girdhar
Department of Computer Science and Engineering, Amity University, Noida, Uttar Pradesh, India

Anjana Gosain
University School of Information & Communication Technology, Guru Gobind Singh Indraprastha University, Delhi, India

Akshi Goswami
Department of Computer Engineering, J.C. Bose University of Science & Technology, YMCA, Faridabad, India

Mrinal Goswami
Department of Systemics, University of Petroleum & Energy Studies, Bidholi, Dehradun, India

Anu Gupta
Department of Computer Science and Applications, Panjab University, Chandigarh, India

Ganesh Gupta
Department of Computer Science and Engineering, G L Bajaj Institute of Technology and Management, Greater Noida, India

Mukesh Kumar Gupta
Suresh Gyan Vihar University, Jaipur, India

Gaurav Habad
JD College of Engineering and Technology, Nagpur, India

B. Harsoor
Department of Information Science and Engineering, Poojya Dodappa Appa College of Engineering, Kalaburagi, India

Vivek Jaglan
Graphic Era Hill University, Dehradun, India

Parkhi Jain
Department of Computer Engineering, J.C. Bose University of Science & Technology, YMCA, Faridabad, India

Satbir Jain
Department of Computer Engineering, Netaji Subhas University of Technology, New Delhi, India

Tanuj Joshi
Department of Mechanical Engineering, Amity University, Gurugram, India

Preet Kanwal
Department of Computer Science, SGGS College, Chandigarh, India

L. Kavyashree
Department of Computer Science and Engineering, University Visvesvaraya College of Engineering, Bangalore, India

Saurabh Kharwar
Microelectronics and VLSI Lab, Electronics and Communications Engineering, National Institute of Technology Patna, Patna, India

Vansh Khera
Department of Mechanical Engineering, Rajasthan Technical University, Kota, India

Gaurav Kshirsagar
JD College of Engineering and Technology, Nagpur, India

Krishan Kumar
Suresh Gyan Vihar University, Jaipur, India

Rajiv Kumar
Department of Computer Science and Engineering, Chandigarh University, Gharuan, Punjab, India

Satish Kumar
Department of Computer Science, Arya Inst. of Engg. & Tech., Jaipur, Rajasthan, India

S. P. Ajith Kumar
Research Scholar, Manav Rachna University, Faridabad, Haryana, India
Lecturer – Selection Grade, Bhai Parmanand Institute of Business Studies, New Delhi, India

S. M. Dilip Kumar
Department of Computer Science and Engineering, University Visvesvaraya College of Engineering, Bangalore, India

Anamika Maurya
School of Computer and Systems Sciences, Jawaharlal Nehru University, New Delhi, India

Madhvendra Misra
Department of Management Studies, Indian Institute of Information Technology, Allahabad, India

Ritam Mukherjee
Department of Computer Science & Engineering, Adamas University, Kolkata, India

Manish Kumar Mukhija
Department of Computer Science, Arya Inst. of Engg. & Tech., Jaipur, Rajasthan, India

Rajib Nag
Department of Computer Science & Engineering, Adamas University, Kolkata, India

Diana Nagpal
Department of Computer Science and Engineering, Chandigarh University, Gharuan, Punjab, India

Najneen
Department of Computer Science, Arya Inst. of Engg. & Tech., Jaipur, Rajasthan, India

Ritu Nigam
Division of Computer Engineering, University of Delhi (Netaji Subhas Institute of Technology),
New Delhi, India

M. Thurai Pandian
Department of Computer Science and Technology, Manav Rachna University, Faridabad, India

Jyoti Pruthi
Department of Computer Science & Technology, Manav Rachna University, Faridabad, India

Ram Ratan
Scientific Analysis Group, Defence Research and Development Organisation, Delhi, India

Harish Rohil
Department of Computer Science & Applications, Chaudhary Devi Lal University, Sirsa, India

Anju Saha
University School of Information and Communication Technology, GGSIP University, New Delhi, India

Sameer
Department of Computer Science & Applications, Chaudhary Devi Lal University, Sirsa, India

Firdous Shamim
Department of Computer Science & Engineering, Adamas University, Kolkata, India

Pradeep Kumar Sharma
Department of Computer Engineering, MR International Institute of Research and Studies, Faridabad,
Haryana, India

Vivek Sharma
Department of Computer Science and Engineering, G L Bajaj Institute of Technology and Management,
Greater Noida, India

J. Shreyas
Department of Computer Science and Engineering, University Visvesvaraya College of Engineering,
Bangalore, India

Arvind Kumar Shukla
School of Computer Science & Applications, IFTM University, Moradabad, India

Riya Sil
Department of Computer Science & Engineering, Adamas University, Kolkata, India

Deepika Singh
University School of Information and Communication Technology, GGSIP University, New Delhi, India

Jaswinder Singh
Department of Computer Science and Applications, Panjab University, Chandigarh, India

Kuldeep Singh
Department of Management Studies, Indian Institute of Information Technology, Allahabad, India

Sangeeta Singh
Microelectronics and VLSI Lab, Electronics and Communications Engineering, National Institute of Technology Patna, Patna, India

Anudruti Singha
Department of Biomedical Engineering, School of Electronics Engineering, Vellore Institute of Technology, Vellore, India

Srikant Sonekar
JD College of Engineering and Technology, Nagpur, India

Kruti Sontakke
JD College of Engineering and Technology, Nagpur, India

N. N. Srinidhi
Department of Computer Science and Engineering, University Visvesvaraya College of Engineering, Bangalore, India

S. Suma
Department of Information Science and Engineering, Poojya Dodappa Appa College of Engineering, Kalaburagi, India

Rohit Tanwar
Department of Systemics, University of Petroleum & Energy Studies, Bidholi, Dehradun, India

Hardeo Kumar Thakur
Department of CST, Manav Rachna University, Faridabad, Haryana, India

Parul Tomar
Department of Computer Engineering, J.C. Bose University of Science & Technology, YMCA, Faridabad, India

S. S. Tyagi
Department of Computer Engineering, MR International Institute of Research and Studies, Faridabad, Haryana, India

P. K. Udayaprasad
Department of Computer Science and Engineering, University Visvesvaraya College of Engineering, Bangalore, India

Neelam Verma
Scientific Analysis Group, Defence Research and Development Organisation, Delhi, India

Jitendra Yadav
Department of Management Studies, Indian Institute of Information Technology, Allahabad, India

Veenu Yadav
Amity University, Lucknow, India

Abbreviations

ACO	ant colony optimization
AES	Advanced Encryption Standard
AI	artificial intelligence
AIML	Artificial Intelligence Mark-up Language
ANN	artificial neural network
API	application programming interface
ASiNR	armchair silicene nanoribbon
ASPP	atrous spatial pyramid pooling
AT	assistive technologies
AWS	Amazon Web Services
BABoK	Business Analyst Body of Knowledge
BER	bit error rate
BIoT	blockchain technology incorporated with IoT
BNLP	Bengali Natural Language Processing
BSM	BSMOTE
CC	cloud computing
CCC	city command center
CDAS	centralized doctor appointment system
CFCM	credibilistic fuzzy c-means
CNN	convolutional neural network
CNN	condensed nearest neighbor
CT	completion time
DBSRA	Dictionary-Based Search by Removing Affix
DC-SVM	double-coupling support vector machines
DDoS	distributed denial of service
DES	data encryption standard
DFT	density functional theory
DOFCM	density-oriented FCM
DOIFCM	density oriented intuitionistic fuzzy C-means
DOS	density of states
DS	dice score
ds	delay-sensitive
DTNs	delay-tolerant networks
DVCS	distributed version control system

EDES-ACM	Enigma Diagonal Encryption Standard Access Control Model
EF	Fermi level
Eff-MANet	efficient multiple-scale attention network
EM	expectation maximization
ET	execution time
ETSA	execution time-based Sufferage algorithm
FAQs	frequently asked questions
FCM	fuzzy-C-means
FCNs	fully convolutional networks
FIFA	Fédération Internationale de Football Association
FN	false negative
FNN	feed-forward artificial neural network
FP	false positive
GA	genetic algorithm
GCE	Google Compute Engine
GNG	growing neural gas
GSA	gravitational search algorithm
HERO	Hierarchical Exponential Region Organization
HH	heuristic algorithm
HMM	hidden Markov model
HPG	hypertext probabilistic grammar
HTTPS	hypertext transfer protocol secure
IaaS	infrastructure as a service
ICCC	integrated command and control center
ICT	communication technology infrastructure
ID	intellectual disability
IDD	India driving dataset
IDD Lite	India Driving Lite Dataset
IFCM	intuitionistic FCM
IFE	intuitionistic fuzzy entropy
IOC	International Olympic Committee
IoT	internet of things
IP	intellectual property
IPS	indoor positioning framework
IR	infrared
JI	Jaccard index
JSON	JavaScript object notation
js	jitter-sensitive

LDA	local density approximation
LDA	Latent Dirichlet Allocation
LEI	link estimation indicator
LEO	low Earth orbit
ls	loss-sensitive
MAC	media access control
MANETs	mobile ad hoc networks
MBFD	modified best-fit decreasing
MIoU	mean intersection over union
ML	machine learning
MLP	multilayer perceptron
MPI	magnetic particle inspection
MPNs	message passing networks
NCL	Neighborhood Cleaning Rule
NDR	negative differential resistance
NETCONF	network configuration protocol
NLI	natural language interface
NLP	natural language processing
NLTK	natural language toolkit
NSGA-II	non-dominated sorting genetic algorithm-II
NS2	network simulator tool
NX	Nexus
O-LEADM	on-demand link and energy aware dynamic multipath
ONF	Open Networking Foundation
OpenCV	open-source computer vision
OppIoT	opportunistic internet of things
OSS	open source software
OSS	one-sided selection
PaaS	Platform as a Service
PCB	propagation criterion bias
PCPID	The President's Committee for People with Intellectual Disabilities
PFCM	possibilistic FCM
PID	principal ideal domain
Ps	success probability
PSA	privacy and security agents
PTR	packet transmission rate
PUC	pollution under control
PWS	personalized Web search

P3P	Privacy preference Project
PII	personally identifiable information
QKD	quantum key distribution
QoS	quality-of-service
QT	quality threshold
RAM	random access memory
RCGAPC	real coded genetic algorithm for path coverage
RDBMS	relational database management system
ReLU	rectifier activation function
RF	random forest
RNN-LSTM	long-short term memory recurrent neural network
RPC	remote procedure call
RPL	routing protocol for low-power and lossy network
RPSA	random priority scheduling algorithm
RR	rectification ratio
RREQ	route request packet header
RRR	reverse rectification ratio
RSPA	random scheduling priority algorithm
RSS	received signal strength
RUS	random undersampling
RWP	random waypoint model
SANE	security architecture for enterprise network
SaaS	Software as a Service
SC	social connect
SCM	Smart Cities Mission
SDIoT	software-defined internet of things
SDN	software-defined networking
SGNG	supervised growing neural gas algorithm
SLA	service level agreement
SM	SMOTE
Social OppIoTs	social opportunistic IoT networks
SOM	self-organizing map
SONs	social opportunistic networks
SOP	security operations procedures
STE-AMM	secret twisted encryption-based access mechanism model
SVM	support vector machine
SVMC	support vector machine classification
TC	transportation company
TCAM	ternary content addressable memory

TCP	Transmission Control Protocol
Tk	Tk-Links
TL	transfer learning
TP	true positive
TTS	text-to-speech
UI	user interface
UNIBOT	University Chatbot
URL	universal resource locators
VCS	Version control system
VMs	virtual machines
WHO	World Health Organization
XaaS	anything as a service
XML	Extensible Markup Language
XMPP	Extensible Messaging and Presence Protocol
YOLO	You Only Look Once
ZSiNR	zigzag silicene nanoribbon

Preface

Digital transformation refers to adopting digital technology for transforming businesses or services, by replacing manual processes with digitization or replacing earlier digital technology with newer digital replica. Digital solutions enable innovation and better efficiency via automation, rather than just enhancing and supporting traditional techniques. The enhancements in the digital world impact not only individual businesses but also the society, such as government, media, health care, art, and science. Digital transformation is a reality because of the development and merging of various smart technologies such as internet of things (IoT), real-time analytics, computing, sensors, and embedded systems.

The new applications of IoT has highly eased and improved our lifestyle. IoT describes a network of physical objects with embedded sensors and application software for exchange of data with various other devices and systems through the internet. The upcoming technological advancements are the outcome of development of novel network technologies. Networks may vary based on the transmission medium, allotted bandwidth, protocols for network traffic management, network size, network topology, traffic control mechanisms, and organizational intent. In our day-to-day lives, devices with embedded software solutions are being used. This has resulted in vast expansion in the domain of software engineering in recent years. It involves, phase-wise approach of programming, verifying, testing, followed by debugging.

The scope of this book involves discussion of new technological advancements in various application areas of IoT, network technologies, and software engineering. Predictive analytics on real-time data from various domains have helped to ease the life of humans and provided timely solutions to various problems.

THE PURPOSE OF THE BOOK

The primary objective of this edited book is to have a qualitative discussion on the state-of-the-art developments and unsolved open issues in the field of computational intelligence. The main focus is on the empirical, theoretical, and application perspective of the introduction of computational intelligence in software engineering, networks, and smart technologies. The achievement of such a goal implies the research contribution by young and dynamic researchers and experts from industry and academia in the above domains. It helps in assisting the reviewing, identifying and developing efficient approaches and systems using emerging technologies to support their effective operations.

This book provides knowledge as a survey and critical review of the state-of-the-art techniques, identifying the advantages and limitations of each. In addition to this, various proposed novel approaches in IoT, wireless networks, traffic monitoring, and new techniques for software testing are shared. This book shares vast experiences of many researchers and, as such, is an archive suggesting future directions for health care stakeholders, decision makers, and software developers in identifying applicable approaches in order to enhance, automate, and develop effective solutions to resolve critical problems.

WHO SHOULD READ THE BOOK

The audience may vary from researchers doing research in multidisciplinary areas of health care, software development, network technologies, and IoT. The readers may be academicians, people working in research labs in industry, or students with an engineering background who might be interested in working in these varied domains. The book is of high value as an addition to the review papers, it also discusses novel approaches covering the latest smart technologies. It discusses various advanced technologies for traffic control. The book provides vital information for researchers working to develop smart cities. Our book is of interest to researchers focusing on applications of digital transformation in varied domains.

ORGANIZATION OF THE BOOK

Thirty-four self-contained chapters, authored by researchers with expertise in their field of work, are part of this book. These chapters are selected papers presented in the International Conference on "Computational Intelligence in Analytics and Information Systems (CIAIS-2021)," held on April 2–3, 2021 at Manav Rachna University, Faridabad, India. The papers were selected based on the double blind review process through the Easy-chair Conference Management System.

The book is organized into three sections, each section focusing on a different domain of research work. Broadly, the book has been organized as follows:

- Section I: Smart Technologies includes 16 chapters.
- Section II: Computational Intelligence in Network Technologies includes 11 chapters.
- Section III: Computational Intelligence in Software Engineering includes 7 chapters.

A brief introduction to each of the chapters is as follows:

In Chapter 1, Kuldeep Singh et al. present a two-stage approach; first, a theoretical model is constructed using factors taken from various research papers in the context of information sharing on social media. Second, expert mining is performed through an Expert Opinion Survey. Through this, it was realized that if Wipro implements SC (communication services for social connect) and taps into a market that would be a combination of social networking services and e-commerce platforms, then Wipro could provide many services from a single platform, such as messaging, video sharing, video chat, and voice calling.

In Chapter 2, Riya Aggarwal et al. attempt to summarize types of disability, current trends, and dual nature of various technologies in creating opportunities and raising barriers in the lives of disabled people. Overall, this paper discusses research surveys covering different assistive technologies and their limitations with some future directions.

In Chapter 3, Sazid Ali et al. carry out a relevant survey about the recent works and technologies in the field of robotics that is targeted towards the purpose of water-waste management.

In Chapter 4, Amara Aditya et al. work on city command centers in Indian smart cities and highlight the features of a smart city where its applications are in banking and finance, conventional and renewable energy, housing, health care, water and waste management, transport, including the need for a city command center (CCC) in a smart city. Various CCCs that are already implemented in Indian cities have been listed.

In Chapter 5, Akshi Goswami et al. propose a vehicle pollution detection system using IoT that works with the intention of improving the environment and to develop a mechanism that will put a control and will monitor the levels of emissions from vehicles. Different technologies have been used to build a POC for the same.

In Chapter 6, Sapna Gambhir et al. introduce a new computing paradigm by CISCO, that is, Fog Computing, that acts as an intermediate layer between cloud and the IoT devices. The main idea to introduce fog computing is to provide a solution to all those problems being faced by cloud while handling IoT data. Fog computing just complements Cloud as we need both Cloud and Fog to handle the data that arises from IoT devices. Comparison analysis of cloud and fog computing is done along with details of each concept.

In Chapter 7, Ganesh Gupta et al. perform a study of the various predictions and clustering methodologies of machine learning to design an efficient and robust technique to solve recent issues in the machine learning domain. The system studied the feature selection problem in clustering on dynamic data. The study plans for combining the fused Lasso regularization in the proposed technique of sparse feature selection, an evolutionary feature selection formulation to identify clusters and shared features in time-varying data simultaneously.

In Chapter 8, Diana Nagpal and Dr. Rajiv Kumar present a brief understanding of human action recognition (HAR), that is, sensor-based and vision-based HAR. The best techniques such as decision trees, K-nearest neighbor have been reviewed for HAR. The results obtained by every technique and the sort of dataset they have utilized are introduced. Also, deep learning neural network strategies are depicted; for example, artificial neural network, recurrent neural network, and convolutional neural network and their analyses have also been introduced.

In Chapter 9, Deepshikha Agarwal discusses an application of IoT in transportation for making it intelligent with the autonomous detection of accidents happening between vehicles on the road. This system is proposed because of the underlying poor working of the accident management system, particularly in India. When an accident happens, human help is not offered due to police enquiries and the long procedures involved. Medical help is available only after the police is informed by phone. In case of large delays, the injured people may often lose their lives. To deal with this situation, the intelligent transportation method uses IoT to eradicate human intervention and directly informs the suitable authority without any delay.

In Chapter 10, Srikant Sonekar et al. present a brief overview of the technologies that can develop intelligent spectacles. These spectacles for accident prevention can be worn and they interact with the user through voice object detection techniques, updating the user with the latest weather or traffic updates and helping during navigation. These spectacles can reduce accident rates and overcome the difficulty incurred in previous glasses.

In Chapter 11, Saurabh Kharwar and Sangeeta Singh investigated the structural, electronic, and quantum transport properties of one atom thick Al and P substitutionally co-doped armchair silicene nanoribbon (ASiNR) using density functional theory based on first principles method.

In Chapter 12, S. Dahiya and A. Gosain develop a novel clustering approach that merges intuitionistic fuzzy set theory to improve cluster computation with density-oriented outlier detection, resulting into a robust clustering algorithm—Density Oriented Intuitionistic Fuzzy C Means (DOIFCM). Performance of DOIFCM is compared with the performance of other clustering algorithms such as FCM, Credibilistic FCM (CFCM), Possibilistic FCM (PFCM), Intuitionistic FCM (IFCM), and Density-Oriented FCM (DOFCM), and the experimental results prove that DOIFCM has high efficacy in the outlier contaminated data.

In Chapter 13, Jitendra Yadav et al. focus on mining the spectator comments on Reddit concerning the discussions of blockchain adoption in eSports to unearth the hidden semantic structures through document clustering and topic modeling. One of the most common procedures in machine learning and natural language processing are topic models. The study finds that the spectator's willingness toward blockchain inclusion has vastly increased.

In Chapter 14, Deepika Singh et al. propose an algorithm that combines wCM metric to access the difficulty level of the datasets and then accordingly oversamples the minority class data points and undersamples the majority class data points. Experimental results for 23 real-world datasets demonstrate that the algorithm improves sensitivity for the minority class without much affecting the specificity for the majority class.

In Chapter 15, Rajib Nag et al. perform a survey that aims to preserve a log-file of the significant researches performed to date on e-health care and discuss the technologies used. Further, the authors confer their proposed model, termed advaity.in. It is an Indian online health care web application that provides several e-health care facilities, including online doctor's consultation, medical tests facilities, and medical services for patients as well as vendors in a single platform.

In Chapter 16, Junaid Ali et al. perform a comparative analysis of various machine learning techniques for image processing (with computer vision) to choose the best possible model for MPI machine.

In Chapter 17, Sameer and Harish Rohil did a comparative study to establish a proposed Secret Twisted Encryption-based access mechanism model (STE-AMM) and Enigma Diagonal Encryption Standard Access

Control Model (EDES-ACM). Also, a study of the existing mechanism of data sharing in effective methods to enhance the security of data sharing in cloud environments is also done. The proposed scheme is evaluated and validated with the existing method.

In Chapter 18, Krishan Kumar et al. propose a system that can maintain anonymity of individuals and reveal partial information to get benefits of personalization as well. The proposed system is using well-defined protocols and implemented on proxy level with privacy protection.

In Chapter 19, S. P. Ajith Kumar and Hardeo Kumar Thakur conduct a survey on routing techniques like First Contact, Direct Delivery, Spray and Wait, Epidemic, PROPHET, MLPROPH, KNNR, CAML, GMMR, and RLProbh to send data from source to destination in Opportunistic IoT Network, tabulated description with routing algorithms and limitations. The performance of some routing protocols in Opportunistic IoT Network are equated with each other by using performance-calculating elements like average hop count, number of messages delivered, average buffer occupancy time, average delay, and time to live field.

In Chapter 20, Chaman Prakash Arya et al. study various translation polynomials by varying modulus polynomials for various bias parameters of the S-boxes constructed. The reported new results indicate that the AES can be implemented to achieve dynamic encryption for real applications of information security.

In Chapter 21, Suma S and Bharati Harsoor propose an on-demand link and energy aware dynamic multipath (O-LEADM) routing scheme for MANETs. The proposed scheme discovers node link quality by a link estimation indicator (LEI), which decides whether a link is stable or unstable. O-LEADM scheme selects neighbor nodes by determining nodes residual energy and makes multipath routing decisions by maintaining link stability, reliability, and prolonged network lifetime.

In Chapter 22, Amit Bhatnagar and Arvind Kumar Shukla provide a process to solve a real-time transportation problem that is basically related to the organization. For this, an optimized multi-server queuing model was used to find the optimum number of unloading and loading service centers and minimum total cost of the ready product. An attempt was made to achieve effective and minimum cost of the ready product for the organization.

In Chapter 23, M. Thurai Pandian and P. Damodharan study the different assaults and the clustering mechanism of the RFID framework. The paper gives a proposal to improve the security from the attacks and furthermore improve the presentation of the correspondence between the RFID tags and the readers.

In Chapter 24, Dharamendra Chouhan et al. propose an ant-inspired traffic-aware quality of service routing scheme for SDIoT network. Simulation of the proposed solution is done in MATLAB, and the proposed solution is found to reduce the end-to-end delay by 5%, jitter by 4%, and packet loss by 7%.

In Chapter 25, Ritu Nigam and Satbir Jain utilize a feed-forward artificial neural network to improve an existing protocol named BBFT and proposed the ML-BBFT algorithm. Simulation results through one simulator demonstrate that the proposed ML-BBFT performs superior to MLProph and ProPhet on various performance metrics like delivery probability, overhead ratio, average latency, and average buffer time.

In Chapter 26, Anamika Maurya and Satish Chand suggest a new approach by using a global and a local context block on high-level features for capturing global and multiscale contextual knowledge, respectively. Thereafter, they used a channel-wise attention block to weigh multi-scale higher-level features. This strategy enhances the feature representation of specific semantics by improving channel dependencies.

In Chapter 27, Veenu Yadav proposes a model designed for a quantum channel to improve the performance of QKD protocol satellite-based communication under problem-environmental noise, adversary attacks, and atmospheric turbulence.

In Chapter 28, Jaly Dasmahapatra et al. study the existing education-based interactive automated agents and discuss the various techniques for educational-based agents. A basic model of an education-based interactive automated agent is designed by applying an artificial neural network that focuses on communication to provide a suitable answer.

In Chapter 29, Jaswinder Singh et al. use GitHub, an online platform for software hosting, as a case study to identify the issues that arise at various levels of the data extraction process for performing empirical research on open source software projects. The GitHub interface provides automated retrieval of data as well as manual inspection is applied on the test case repository to understand the issues in the data extraction process.

In Chapter 30, Hanu Bhardwaj and Jyoti Pruthi focus on the former stage for data warehouse requirements engineering, that is, an "early information" phase wherein relevant information for making decisions is identified. Early information requirements engineering defines targets as pairs $<B, I>$ where B represents organizational aspect and I is a business indicators' set. Targets are organized as a hierarchy that provides a complete specification of that has to be achieved by a top-level target.

In Chapter 31, Sumit Bansal et al. try to devise a new algorithm—Random Priority Scheduling Algorithm (RPSA)—that focuses on the drawbacks of starvation and cost. Starvation is defined as too much accomplishment of high-priority task on a regular basis and overlooking priority tasks resulting in disuse of cloudlet servers in inadequate proportion.

In Chapter 32, Najneen et al. propose a novel greedy heuristic approach RAFI for having minimal test sets across versions. RAFI is found to be faster as compared with the algorithms with exponential running time and is almost 1000 times faster as compared to the existing greedy approaches. The proposed technique has the same reduction rate in comparison to various greedy methods.

In Chapter 33, Pradeep Kumar Sharma and S. S. Tyagi present SDN-based framework to show how SDN provides improvised automation and security and centralized control for policy enforcement. The various possible automation techniques in traditional networks and their limitations are also discussed.

In Chapter 34, Neeru Ahuja and Pradeep Kumar Bhatia propose an approach that implemented path testing that traverses the most critical path of the program considering it as the maximum. Weights are assigned to paths that play a major role in GA and improve testing efficiency.

Committees of the International Conference on "Computational Intelligence in Analytics and Information Systems (CIAIS-2021)," April 2–3, 2021, Manav Rachna University, Faridabad, India

Chief Patrons
Dr. Prashant Bhalla,
President, Manav Rachna Educational Institutions

Dr. Amit Bhalla,
Vice President, Manav Rachna Educational
Institutions

Patron
Prof. I. K. Bhatt,
Vice Chancellor, Manav Rachna University

Executive Chairs
Prof. Sangeeta Banga,
Dean Academics, Manav Rachna University

Prof. Pradeep K. Varshney,
Dean Research, Manav Rachna University

Prof. Shruti Vashisht,
Dean Students Welfare, Manav Rachna
University

General Chairs
Prof. Anjana Gosain,
University School of Information Communication
Technology, Guru Gobind Singh Indraprastha
University, New Delhi, India

Prof. Rajkumar Buyya,
The University of Melbourne, Australia

Prof. Joan Lu,
School of Computing and Engineering,
University of Huddersfield, London, UK

Organizing Chair
Prof. Hanu Bhardwaj,
Head, Department of Computer Science &
Technology, Manav Rachna University

Dr. Jyoti Pruthi,
Associate Head, Department of Computer
Science & Technology, Manav Rachna University

Secretary
Prof. Susmita Ray,
Professor, Department of Computer Science &
Technology, Manav Rachna University

Dr. Rajeev Arya,
Assistant Professor, NIT, Patna

Convener
Dr. Hardeo Kumar Thakur,
Associate Professor, Department of Computer
Science & Technology

Dr. Manpreet Kaur,
Associate Professor, Department of Computer
Science & Technology

Dr. Parneeta Dhaliwal,
Associate Professor, Department of Computer
Science & Technology

ADVISORY BOARD

Dr. Gurpreet Singh Lehal, Head, AI and Data
Science Research Centre, Punjabi University,
Punjab, India

Joan Lu, Prof. Department of Computer Science
School of Computing and Engineering Centre
for Planning, Autonomy and Representation of
Knowledge, University of Huddersfield, London

Dr. Nathaniel G Martin, Emiretus Faculty,
University of Rochester, New York, USA

Prof.(Dr.) S. S. Aggarwal, Emiretus Scientist CEERI/CSIR, Advisor CDAC-Noida, Director General KIIT Group of Colleges, India

Dr. Dvln Somayajulu, National Institute of Technology, Warangal 506004, Telangana, India

Prof. S.C. Sharma, IIT Roorkee, India

Dr. Upasana Singh, University of Natal, South Africa

Dr. A R Abdul Razak, BITS Pilani, Dubai Campus, Dubai

Dr. Bhanu Prasad, Florida A&M University, USA

Dr. Abhinav Dhall, Associate Professor, IIT Ropar, Punjab, India

Rajkumar Buyya, The University of Melbourne, Australia

Dr. Anand Gupta, Associate Professor, Netaji Subhas Institute of technology, Dwarka, New Delhi, India

Dr. MPS. Bhatia, Professor, Netaji Subhas Institute of Technology, Dwarka, New Delhi, India

Dr. Satish Chand, Professor, Jawahar Lal Nehru University, New Delhi, India

Dr. Alok Gupta, Founder & CEO, Pyramid Cyber Security & Foresnsic (P) Ltd. New Delhi, India

Dr. Anjana Gossain, Professor, Indraprastha University, New Delhi, India

Dr. Saurabh Pandey, IIT Patna, India

Dr Vasudha Bhatnagar, Professor, Delhi University, India

Dr. Kiran Kumar Pattanaik, Associate Professor Department: Information Technology, IIIT Gwalior, India

Prof. Sanjay Kumar Dhurandher, Professor and Head IT, NSUT, India

TECHNICAL PROGRAM COMMITTEE

Dr. Xiao-Zhi Gao, School of Computing, University of Eastern Finland, Kuopio 70210, Finland

Dr. Sansar Singh Chahuan, Professor, Galgotias University, Greater Noida, Uttar Pradesh, India

Dr. Sanjeev Pippal, Professor, Galgotias University, Greater Noida, Uttar Pradesh, India

Dr. Sapna Gambhir, JC BOSE YMCA University, India

Dr. Neelam Duhan, JC BOSE YMCA University, India

Dr. Samayveer Singh, Assistant Professor, NIT, Jalandhar, Punjab, India

Dr. Rashmi Agarwal, JC BOSE YMCA University, India

Dr. Sudhanshu Kumar Jha, Assistant Professor, Allahabad University, Uttar Pradesh, India

Dr. Sirshendu Sekhar Ghosh, Assistant Professor, NIT, Jamshedpur, Jharkhand, India

Dr. A.K. Mohapatra, Associate Professor, Indira Gandhi Delhi Technical University, Delhi, India

Dr. Vimal Bibhu, Associate Professor, Amity university, Uttar Pradesh, India

Dr. Suneet Gupta, Assistant Professor, Bennett University, Noida, Uttar Pradesh, India

Dr. Geeta Rani, G.D. Goenka University, Gurugram, Haryana, India

Dr. Vidhi Khanduja, Sal Educational Campus, Saltier, Gujarat, India

Dr. V Kumar Assistant Professor, NIT Jamshedpur, Jharkhand, India

Dr. Niraj Kumar Singh, Assistant Professor, BIT Jagdeep Kaur Meshra, Ranchi, Jharkhand, India

Dr. Durgesh Singh, Assistant Professor, BIT Meshra, Ranchi, Jharkhand, India

Dr. Anil Kumar Yadav, Assistant Professor, Jaypee University, Guna, Madhya Pradesh, India

Dr. Shiv Prakash, Assistant Professor, Allahabad University, Uttar Pradesh, India

Dr. Vishal Goyal, Associate Professor, Punjabi University Patiala, Punjab, India

Dr. Vishal Gupta, Assistant Professor, Punjab University, Chandigarh, India

Dr. Parminder Singh Professor and Head, Guru Nanak Engineering College, Ludhiana, Punjab, India

Dr. Akashdeep, Assistant Professor, Punjab University, Chandigarh, India

Dr. Vinay Chopra, Associate Professor, DAV Institute of Engineering and Technology, Jalandhar, Punjab, India

Dr. Ashima Assistant professor, Thapar Institute of Technology, Patiala, Punjab, India

Monika Oberoi Application Development Lead, Shell, Bangalore India

Dr. Ashish Payal Assistant Professor, USICT, Guru Gobind Singh Inderprastha University, Delhi, India

Jaspreeti Singh Assistant Professor, USICT, GGSIPU, Delhi, India

Dr. Manuj Assistant Professor, University of Delhi India

Dr. Pinaki Chakraborty Assistant Professor, Netaji Subhas Institute of Technology, Dwarka, New Delhi, India

Dr. Badal Soni Assistant Professor, NIT Silchar, India

Dr. Sunil Kumar Singh, Assistant Professor, Mahatma Gandhi Central University, Bihar, India

Dr. Vipin Kumar, Assistant Professor, Mahatma Gandhi Central University, Bihar, India

Dr. Jagdeep Kaur, Assistant Professor, NIT Jalandhar, India

Mohit, PhD research scholar, Dayalbagh University, Uttar Pradesh, India

Mala Saraswat, Associate Professor, ABES Engineering College, Ghaziabad, Uttar Pradesh, India

Priti Bansal, Assistant Professor, Netaji Subhas Institute of Technology, Dwarka, New Delhi, India

Rohit Beniwal, Assistant Professor, Delhi Technological University, New Delhi, India

Dr. Dileep Kumar Yadav, Assistant Professor, Galgotia University, Greater Noida, Uttar Pradesh India

Dr. Pranav Dass, Assistant Professor, Galgotia University, Greater Noida, Uttar Pradesh, India

Dr. Arun Kumar, Assistant Professor, Galgotia University, Greater Noida, Uttar Pradesh, India

Dr. Navjot Singh, Assistant Professor, NIT, Allahabad, Uttar Pradesh, India

Sh. Nitin Gupta, Assistant Professor, NIT Hamirpur, Uttar Pradesh, India

Dr. Lokesh Chouhan, Assistant Professor, NIT Hamirpur, Uttar Pradesh, India

Dr. Amit Gaurav, Assistant Professor, Galgotia College of Engineering and Technology, Greater Noida, Uttar Pradesh, India

Dr. Lokesh Kumar Sharma, Assistant Professor, Galgotia College of Engineering and Technology, Greater Noida, Uttar Pradesh, India

Dr. Vikram Bali, Professor, J.S.S. Academy of Technical Education, Noida, Uttar Pradesh, India

Nemi Chandra Rathore, Assistant Professor, Central University of South Bihar, India

Dr. Rajeev Kumar Arya, Assistant Professor, NIT, Patna, Bihar, India

Dr. Vivek Sharma, Assistant Professor, Amity School of Engineering and Technology, Delhi, India

Dr. Aruna Malik Assistant Professor, Galgotia University, Greater Noida, Uttar Pradesh India

Dr. Vikas Chaydhary NIT, Kurukshetra, Haryana India

Dr. Rajeev Garg Cpa Global, Noida, Uttar Pradesh India

Deevyankar Agarwal Assistant Professor, HCT, Muscat, UAE India

Dr. Manish Kumar Singh Associate Professor, GCET, Greater Noida, Uttar Pradesh India

Dr. Satyajee Srivastava Assistant Professor, Galgotias University, Greater Noida, Uttar Pradesh India

Dr. Rishav Singh, Assistant Professor, Bennett University, Noida, Uttar Pradesh, India

Dr. Upasana Pandey, Associate Professor, IMS Engineering College, Ghaziabad, Uttar Pradesh, India

Dr. Anshu Bhasin, Assistant Professor, I. K. Gujral Punjab Technical University, Punjab

Dr. Abhilasha Singh, Assistant Professor, Amity University Noida, Uttar Pradesh

Dr. Yogesh Kumar, Associate Professor, Chandigarh Group of Colleges, Landran, Punjab

Dr. Amit Singhal, Professor-Department of CSE, RKGIT Ghaziabad Uttar Pradesh

Dr. Navneet Kaur, Assistant Professor, Baba Banda Singh Bahadur Engg College Fatehgarh Sahib

Dr. Bharti Sharma, Associate Professor and Academic Head Department of Computer Application, DIT University, Dehradun Uttarakhand, India

Ms. Poonam Chaudhary, Assistant Professor,
North Cap University, Gurugram, Haryana

PUBLISHING COMMITTEE

Dr. Mrinal Pandey (Chair)
Dr. Sachin Lakra (Co chair)
Dr. Sanjay Singh
Ms. Mamta Arora
Ms. Riya Sapra
Mr. Ram Chatterjee
Ms. Anupriya Sharma
Ms. Alpana

Session Track Committee:
Dr. M. Thurian Pandian, Associate Professor
(Chair)
Ms. Gunjan Chindwani
Ms. Urmila Pilania
Ms. Gaganjot Kaur
Ms. Priyanka Gupta

Sponsorship Committee:
Dr. Parneeta Dhaliwal (Chair)
Ms. Hanu Bhardwaj (Co-Chair)
Dr. Susmita Ray
Mr. Ankur Kumar Aggarwal
Ms. Priyanka Gupta

Media and Marketing Committee:
Dr. Prinima Gupta (Chair)
Ms. Nikita Taneja (Co-Chair)
Ms. Gunjan Chindwani
Ms. Bharti Jha
Mr. Manoj Kumar
Ms. Anupriya Sharma
Ms. Shreya Malhotra
Finance Committee:
Dr. Jyoti Pruthi (Chair)
Mr. Agha Imran Hussain (Co-Chair)
Mr. Narender Gautam
Ms. Priyanka Gupta
Mr. Anup Singh Khuswaha

Program Committee:
Ms. Neelu Chaudhary (Chair)
Ms. Gaganjot (Co-Chair)
Ms. Meena Chaudhary
Ms. Sarika Gambhir
Ms. Shailja Gupta
Mr. Narender Kumar

Student Committee:
Ravi Prakash (Developer)
Parikshit Sharma (Designer)
Sanchit Bajaj (Developer & Designer)
Harsh Mittal (Developer & Designer)

PART I
Smart Technologies

CHAPTER 1

Communication Services for Social Connect: A Proposed Market for Wipro

KULDEEP SINGH, MADHVENDRA MISRA, and JITENDRA YADAV

Department of Management Studies, Indian Institute of Information Technology, Allahabad, India

ABSTRACT

Today, most consumers use social media as a trusted platform to share and receive information and opinions about any firm's offerings. Such communication helps both parties. It enables the consumer and the organization to create and maintain a relationship and manage their expectations of each other. This study focuses on addressing some new opportunities for Wipro. The study has been undertaken using a two-stage approach; first, a theoretical model is constructed using factors taken from various research papers in the related context. Second, expert mining has been performed through an expert opinion survey. Through this, it was realized that if Wipro implements SC (communication services for social connect) and taps into a market that would be a combination of social networking services and e-commerce platforms, then Wipro could provide many services from a single platform such as messaging, video sharing, video chat, and voice calling. Apart from these, Wipro could also provide e-commerce services using the same platform.

Computational Intelligence in Analytics and Information Systems, Volume 2: Advances in Digital Transformation, Selected Papers from CIAIS-2021. Parneeta Dhaliwal, PhD, Manpreet Kaur, PhD, Hardeo Kumar Thakur, PhD, Rajeev Kumar Arya, and Joan Lu (Eds.)

1.1   INTRODUCTION

In the current business scenario, most countries have transformed from a traditional way of gaining knowledge to being techno-centric. With this, the nurturing of social connectedness through various communication services has become essential in many people's lives. It provides an ongoing and effective exchange of people's experiences with their friends, peer groups, community, and various other associates.[1] Although in the current scenario, businesses are using social media to develop communication with their customers and other stakeholders, earlier research did not provide significant output to offer new insights about how an organization can develop its own social connect (SC) platform in the social communication environment. This study discusses the potential opportunities for Wipro Ltd. in the field of communication services for becoming more socially connected.[2]

Wipro Ltd., an Indian IT service corporation, started its journey as an oil factory in 1945.[3,4] During the late 1980s, Wipro entered the IT sector as a flagship company of the Wipro group, providing various services, such as:

- ➤ Professional IT services.
- ➤ Product engineering.
- ➤ Technology infrastructure services.
- ➤ Business process outsourcing.
- ➤ Consulting services.
- ➤ Business solutions.

Wipro InfoTech's significant areas of operations include India, the Middle East, and the Asia-Pacific region. Wipro's phenomenal success is the outcome of the inculcation of a strong and unique work culture characterized by *The Spirit of Wipro* concept.[5] This concept is built on the below values:

- Intensity to win.
- Acting with sensitivity.
- Unyielding integrity.

Wipro's digital drive empowers a more resilient future for its customers and communities. When an organization expands into innovative techno-logical progress, the resulting business perspective often provides firms with new opportunities and brings change to the current organizational structure. Therefore, socially connected communication has bright prospects for trans-forming Wipro in profitable ways and building a more adaptive transforma-tive enterprise.

1.2 HISTORICAL PERSPECTIVE

Wipro is a company known for seeking new opportunities whenever they become available. Wipro still plans to succeed by taking advantage of such opportunities. We can see this by reviewing Wipro's past. For example, since the 1980s, Wipro shifted its focus from the manufacturing of vegetable and refined oils to new business opportunities in the IT and computing industry.[6]

To examine the literature related to communication services, this study used VOSviewer software.[7,8] VOSviewer provided coword mapping results of keywords, abstracts, and title terms for 1079 related research articles in the form of a cluster diagram. Figure 1.1 represents the results of the relationship network image for different keywords and their association. Furthermore, to know the variables that could be important while deciding whether to enter into a new market, this study searched the previous literature through Web of Science journals. After applying the Boolean search method, this study obtained 85 research papers that further screened down to 38 based on title and abstract screening. Finally, this process provided us with eight factors (See Table 1.1). The results from these search criteria show that significant research has been done in this domain. However, this study provides the first of its kind theoretical model that could help an established organization diversify its old market and aim at a new demand related to communication services, especially for SC.

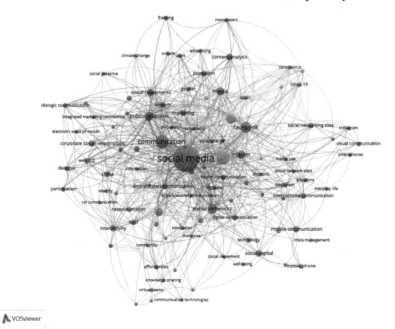

FIGURE 1.1 Cowords mapping.

TABLE 1.1   List of Variables with References.

S. No.	Variable	References
1	Cost	Reed,1993[9]; Mwai, Kiplang, & Gichoya, 2014[10]; Low, 1997[11]
2	Competitors	Wu, 2014[12]; Chen, 2000[13]; Zier, Fischer, and Brockners, 2004[14]
3	Channel	Huang and Symonds, 2009[15]; Elkela, Kokkonen, Heikki Nikali, 2005[16]; Lim, Traazil, and Ramaseshan, 2006[17]
4	Size	Reid, 2005[18]; Sobol and Klein, 2009[19]; Numata, Lei, and Iwashita, 1996[20]
5	Technology	Viterbi, 1994[21]; Antonelli, 1998[22]; Thong et. al., 2011[23]
6	Advertising	Tripathi and Siddiqui, 2008[24]; Cauberghe and Pelsmacker, 2006[25]; Roberts and Ko, 2001[26]
7	Customer relation	Jia and Yan, 2005[27]; Sun and Lau, 2007[28]; Graessler, 2003[29]; Buellingen and Woerter, 2004[30]
8	Retail Partners	Nizam, Kumar, and Jayaraman, 2012[31]; Singh, 2012[32]; Bhatt, 2013[33]

To analyze Wipro's history, we need to look at the 1966–1992 period when Wipro diversified its product line into heavy-duty industrial cylinders and mobile hydraulic cylinders.[34] During 1994–2000, Wipro again diversified with a new product line known as Super Genius Personal Computers. In 2002, Wipro became a software technology and service company. In 2008, Wipro started a clean energy business with Wipro Eco-Energy and in 2016, Wipro announced that it was buying Appirio, a cloud services company, for $500 million.

Therefore, we can say that the race is still on for Wipro because innovation is a factor that affects any business organization's thinking process to go into a new market. However, sometimes businesses do not know where to begin. Whether developing more creative strategies or thinking outside the box, these are rarely achievable by practical advice alone.

We have explored some signs that address Wipro's new opportunities arising from the external environment which Wipro can use to enter into the modern market. The main sign is that Wipro already has many assets in terms of the IT and technology dimensions plus a chain of buyers related to present goods and services provided by Wipro.

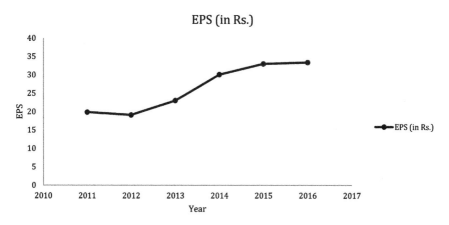

Note: Equity shares of par value Rs 2 each
FIGURE 1.2   EPS analysis of Wipro Ltd.

If we look at Wipro's annual reports from the last 6 years, we can see that their profit and number of shareholders have increased every year (see Figs. 1.2 and 1.3). This shows that Wipro is financially strong and is ready to enter into a new market. For new opportunities, we have to see an unoccupied territory and also think strategically beyond the boundaries of competition across substitute industries, across strategic groups, buyer groups, across complementary product and service offerings, and even across time.

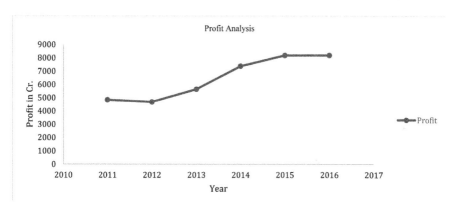

FIGURE 1.3   Profit analysis of WIPRO Ltd.

1.3   EXPERT MINING

In this study, we used an expert opinion survey through which we realized that if Wipro launches its SC platform, which could be a combination of social networking services and e-commerce services, then Wipro could provide many services from a single platform, such as messaging, video sharing, video chat, and voice calling. Apart from these, Wipro could also provide e-commerce services from the same platform. No other Indian organization offers social networking services with e-commerce services on a single platform.

Now the questions arise that if Wipro launches its SC business then:

Who would the customers be?
What process should Wipro follow to become a brand in the SC market?
When should it launch?
Where should it start – globally or from a smaller segment at first?
How – what strategic approach should they follow?

We used descriptive research to find the answers to the above questions. For this, we did *cross-sectional research* in which we asked a sample of 20 people these questions. In the group, 10 were Ph.D. research scholars at IIIT, Allahabad, and the others were final year MBA students pursuing their management degrees at the Indian Institute of Information Technology, Allahabad. Both types of respondents provided us with a clear view of the picture, which states that:

Wipro is already a successful business organization with a perfect chain of buyers. If the business is related to communication services for social connection, the customers would be different. For e-commerce, there would be a need for business customers to use Wipro's SC platform to sell their products and services. On the other hand, for social connectedness, the customers would be the final buyers or users.

1.4   THEORETICAL MODEL

To start the business in the communication service sector, it is necessary to develop a theoretical model suggesting the factors and enablers needed when entering into a new market (see Fig. 1.4). For this, the authors have developed a theoretical model through a strategic literature review of various marketing papers.[35,36]

FIGURE 1.4 A theoretical model for entering into a new market.

There are five main variables (cost, competitors, channel, size, and technology) that could help Wipro analyze whether to go into this new market or not. It is also essential to explore other moderate variables (advertising, customer relations, and retail partners) when assessing how to emerge as a brand in this new market.

> ➤ The business launch could take place at any time as today's digitalization is on-trend for Indian business organizations.
> ➤ As Wipro is already working in the information and technology sector, it would be good to start this new business on a global level.
> ➤ The strategic approach for Wipro is as follows: It could use its already-established market for creating an awareness of this new business. This would help Wipro to capture a wider market area in the initial stages.

1.5 DISCUSSION

Whenever business organizations become aware of the emergence of innovation or new technology, many desire to adapt themselves according to the emerging opportunities and value creation.[37,38] If such knowledge helps an organization to become innovative through a particular new mode of change, then that organization would be likely to adopt that technology to gain the benefits of such progress.

Researchers have examined some factors that are important for an organization to successfully embrace innovation for expansion, improved reputation, and better organizational performance. Few of them are related to the macroenvironment that could have an effect on firm operations, stakeholders' behavior, and future performance.[39-41] Other considerations could be the organization's internal factors which may include top management commitment, the organization's vision and support, and horizontal and vertical coordination between the firm's internal stakeholders. These micro- and macro-determinants create an environment for an organization to decide whether to adopt the new innovative methods and technologies for the firm's success.

The reason for entering the new market as discussed is that it would be a unique opportunity for Wipro by which it would be able to increase its profitability and also increase its market share. For proof of this, we can look at Wipro's past reports. They show that whenever Wipro decided to go into a new market, their market share and profitability increased simultaneously. We can, therefore, say that there is a positive relationship between entering into a new market and Wipro's profitability and market share rate.

1.6 CONCLUSION

We believe that this is the first study to provide a theoretical model for an established organization about whether to decide to enter a new market. The study, through the use of expert mining and analysis, found that in the existing business scenario the adoption and use of digital communication platforms (such as social media) are crucial for organizations to expand their market reach. However, this study is not without limitations. Only eight factors were taken into consideration for developing the model. Future researchers could take more variables to provide better insight into creating a new market strategy. Identification, prioritization, and relationships among the various environmental factors with the organizational growth can be done in future studies. Such research could propose a strategic prescription for established firms (such as Wipro) and also for startups as digital social communication has become an intrinsic attribute to B2C communication.

KEYWORDS

- **communication services**
- **e-commerce**
- **expert opinion mining**
- **social connect**
- **survey**
- **Wipro**

REFERENCES

1. Yadav, J.; Misra, M.; Singh, K. Sensitizing Netizen's Behavior Through Influencer Intervention Enabled by Crowdsourcing – A Case of Reddit. *Behav. Inf. Technol.* **2021**, 1–12.

2. Chatzkel, J. Establishing a Global KM Initiative: The Wipro Story. *J. Knowl. Manag.* **2004**, *8* (2), 6–18. https://doi.org/10.1108/13670410529073.

3. Purohit, M. A Study on–Employee Turnover in IT Sector with Special Emphasis on Wipro and Infosys. *IOSR J. Bus. Manag.* **2016**, *18* (4), 47–51.

4. Rao, B.; Mulloth, B. Building A Global Brand: The Case of Wipro. In *PICMET'07-2007 Portland International Conference on Management of Engineering & Technology*; IEEE, 2007; pp. 1372–1385.

5. Broekstra, G.; de Blot, P. Deep Leadership in Spirit-Driven Business Organizations. In *Handbook of Spirituality and Business*; Palgrave Macmillan: London, 2011; pp. 295-304.

6. Mazumder, T. Training Trends Over the Last Decade-The Wipro Experience. *NHRD Netw. J.* **2010**, *3* (3), 29–32.

7. Van Eck, N. J.; Waltman, L. Text Mining and Visualization Using VOSviewer. **2011**, *arXiv preprint arXiv:1109.2058.*

8. Young, F. W. *Multidimensional Scaling: History, Theory, and Applications*; Psychology Press, 2013.

9. Reed, D.P. The Cost Structure of Personal Communication Services. *IEEE Commun. Mag.* **1993**, *31* (4), 102–108.

10. Mwai, N. W.; Kiplang' at, J.; Gichoya, D. Application of Resource Dependency Theory and Transaction Cost Theory in Analysing Outsourcing Information Communication Services Decisions. *Electron. Lib.* **2014**.

11. Low, C. Integrating Communication Services. *IEEE Commun. Mag.* **1997**, *35* (6), 164-169.

12. Wu, J. Cooperation with Competitors and Product Innovation: Moderating Effects of Technological Capability and Alliances with Universities. *Ind. Market. Manag.* **2014**, *43* (2), 199–209.

13. Chen, Y. Strategic Bidding by Potential Competitors: Will Monopoly Persist?. *J. Ind. Econ.* **2000**, *48* (2), 161–175.

14. Zier, L.; Fischer, W.; Brockners, F. Ethernet-Based Public Communication Services: Challenge and Opportunity. *IEEE Commun. Mag.* **2004**, *42* (3), 88–95.

15. Huang, R. Y.; Symonds, J. Mobile Marketing Evolution: Systematic Literature Review on Multi-Channel Communication and Multi-Characteristics Campaign. In *2009 13th Enterprise Distributed Object Computing Conference Workshops*; IEEE, 2009; pp. 157-165.

16. Elkela, K.; Kokkonen, T.; Nikali, H. Consumers on the Road from E-Communication to E-Shopping. In *Managing Business in a Multi-Channel World: Success Factors for E-Business*; IGI Global, 2005; pp. 69–88.

17. Lim, L. L. K.; Traazil, L.; Ramaseshan, B. The Stimulus Factors and Consumers' Relevance Treatment of Multimedia Messaging Services. *Int. J. Technol. Market.* **2006**, *1* (3), 265–282.

18. Reid, M. Performance Auditing of Integrated Marketing Communication (IMC) Actions and Outcomes. *J. Advert.* **2005**, *34* (4), 41–54.

19. Sobol, M. G.; Klein, G. Relation of CIO Background, IT Infrastructure, and Economic Performance. *Inf. Manag.* **2009**, *46* (5), 271–278.

20. Numata, J.; Lei, B.; Iwashita, Y. Information Management for Knowledge Amplification in Virtual Enterprise. In *IEMC 96 Proceedings. International Conference on Engineering and Technology Management. Managing Virtual Enterprises: A Convergence of Communications, Computing, and Energy Technologies*; IEEE, 1996; pp. 281–285.

21. Viterbi, A. J. The Evolution of Digital Wireless Technology from Space Exploration to Personal Communication Services. *IEEE Trans. Veh. Technol.* **1994**, *43* (3), 638–644.

22. Antonelli, C. Localized Technological Change, New Information Technology and the Knowledge-Based Economy: The European Evidence. *J. Evolution. Econ.* **1998**, *8* (2), 177–198.

23. Thong, J. Y. L.; Venkatesh, V.; Xu, X.; Hong, S.-J.; Tam, K. Y. Consumer Acceptance of Personal Information and Communication Technology Services. *IEEE Trans. Eng. Manag.* **2011**, *58*, (4), 613–625.

24. Tripathi, S. N.; Siddiqui, M. H. Effectiveness of Mobile Advertising: The Indian Scenario. *Vikalpa.* **2008**, *33* (4), 47–60.

25. Cauberghe, V.; De Pelsmacker, P. Opportunities and Thresholds for Advertising on Interactive Digital TV: A View from Advertising Professionals. *J. Interact. Advert.* **2006**, *7* (1), 2–23.

26. Roberts, M. S.; Ko, H. Global Interactive Advertising: Defining What We Mean and Using What We have Learned. *J. Interact. Advert.* **2001**, *1* (2), 18–27.

27. Jia, S.; Yan, H. Empirical Analysis on the Forming Model of Customer Loyalty: The Case Study of Mobile Communication Service. In *Proceedings of ICSSSM'05. 2005 International Conference on Services Systems and Services Management, 2005;* IEEE, 2005; vol. 1, pp. 133–137.

28. Sun, Z.; Lau, S. K. Customer Experience Management in E-Services. In *E-Service Intelligence*; Springer: Berlin, Heidelberg, 2007, pp. 365–388.

29. Graessler, I. Impacts of Information Management on Customized Vehicles and After-Sales Services. *Int. J. Comput. Integr. Manuf.* **2003**, *16* (7-8), 566–570.

30. Buellingen, F.; Woerter, M. Development Perspectives, Firm Strategies and Applications in Mobile Commerce. *J. Bus. Res.* **2004**, *57* (12), 1402–1408.

31. Nizam, B. H. A.; Kumar, S.; Kumar, P.; Jayaraman, T. R. Profiting from IDM Innovations: Learning from Amazon.com and iTunes. In *Understanding the Interactive Digital Media Marketplace: Frameworks, Platforms, Communities and Issues*; IGI Global, 2012; pp. 76–88.

32. Singh, N. P. Operational Strategies of Ethnic Mobile Virtual Network Operators. *Int. J. Interdiscip. Telecommun. Netw.* **2012**, *4* (1), 1–30.

33. Bhatt, P. R. HTC Corporation: A Different Kind of Leadership of Cher Wang. *South Asian J. Bus. Manag. Cases.* **2013**, *2* (2), 217–228.

34. Ramanaiah, G.; Xavier, P. A Study on Offer Rejection (Abort Rate) at Wipro Technologies Ltd. *Manag. Labour Stud.* **2012**, *37* (1), 61–71.

35. Helfert, G.; Ritter, T.; Walter, A. Redefining Market Orientation from a Relationship Perspective. *Eur. J. Market.,* **2002**.

36. Roberts, J. H. Developing New Rules for New Markets. *J. Acad. Market. Sci.* **2000**, *28* (1), 31.

37. Yadav, J.; Misra, M.; Goundar, S. An Overview of Food Supply Chain Virtualisation and Granular Traceability Using Blockchain Technology, *Int. J. Blockchains Cryptocurr.* **2020**, *1* (2), 154.

38. Yadav, J.; Misra, M.; Goundar, S. Autonomous Agriculture Marketing Information System Through Blockchain: A Case Study of e-NAM Adoption in India. In *Blockchain Technologies, Applications and Cryptocurrencies*; World Scientific, 2020; pp. 115–138.

39. Singh, K.; Misra, M. Linking Corporate Social Responsibility (CSR) and Organizational Performance: The Moderating Effect of Corporate Reputation. *Eur. Res. Manag. Bus. Econ.* **2021**, *27*(1), 100139.

40. Singh, K.; Misra, M. Linking Harmonious CSR and Financial Inclusion: The Moderating Effects of Financial Literacy and Income. *Singap. Econ. Rev.* **2020**, 1–22.

41. Singh, K.; Misra, M. Corporate Social Responsibility and financial inclusion: Evaluating the Moderating Effect of Income. *Manager. Decis. Econ.* **2021**, 1-22, https://doi.org/10.1002/mde.3306.

CHAPTER 2

Assistive Technology as a Potential Aid for Disability and Health: A Critical Analysis

RIYA AGGARWAL[1], NANCY GIRDHAR[1], and ALPANA[2]

[1]*Department of Computer Science and Engineering, Amity University, Noida, Uttar Pradesh, India*

[2]*Department of Computer Science and Technology, Manav Rachna University, Faridabad, Haryana, India*

ABSTRACT

In the past few decades, there has been an enormous advancement in the field of technology. The Internet of Things (IoT) and assistive technologies (AT) have emerged as a promising area with application in a variety of domains, involving healthcare. Technology has a tremendous potential to boost the excellence of life for people suffering from a variety of disabilities. As per the statement of World Health Organization, about 15% of the human population is suffering from some form of infirmity. Millions of people with disabilities face problems in getting medicines due to the current pandemic situation (COVID-19), but this pandemic pop-up the importance of digital accessibility and acts as a source of both inclusion and barriers for disabled people. Artificial intelligence, assistive technology, and the IoT have opened various techniques and processes to alleviate the problems experienced by

Computational Intelligence in Analytics and Information Systems, Volume 2: Advances in Digital Transformation, Selected Papers from CIAIS-2021. Parneeta Dhaliwal, PhD, Manpreet Kaur, PhD, Hardeo Kumar Thakur, PhD, Rajeev Kumar Arya, and Joan Lu (Eds.)

disabled individuals as a result of their endless miseries. Although IoT-based healthcare devices provide a number of benefits to disabled individuals, these technologies also give rise to various security and privacy concerns. This paper attempts to summarize the types of disability, the current trends, and the dual nature of various technologies in creating opportunities, and raising barriers in the lives of disabled people. Overall, this paper will discuss research surveys covering different assistive technologies and their limitation with some future directions.

2.1 INTRODUCTION

Over 2 billion people, or 37.5% of the global population, are suffering from various types of disability. Throughout the world, disability incorporates a vast range of disorders, namely sensory, cognitive, psychological, or chronic. According to World Health Organization (WHO), approx. 1.3 billion people, or roughly 17% of the global population, are disturbed by total visual impairment and partial blindness. Nearly 6% of the worldwide population of about 466 million people are influenced by deafness and hearing misfortune. Two hundred million people, or about 2.6% of the earth's population, have an IQ below 75 which is considered as an intellectual disability (ID). Seventy-five million people, approximately 1% of the total population, need a wheelchair in their day-to-day life. According to a survey report in 2018 by WHO, it is estimated that globally there are more than one billion disabled individuals who require assistive devices. Still, just 10% of them have access to the technology they require. By 2030, such a large number would have been added, pushing the overall population to 2 billion. According to the full evaluation of current worldwide AT demands, 970 million people require glasses or low vision aids. Seventy-five million people use wheelchairs, while 150 million require mobility aids. On the other hand, prosthetics and orthotics are required for 35 million people, while hearing aids are required for 94 million people and cognitive aids are required for 150 million people.[1-3]

The percentage of people with special needs has risen dramatically across the world. In response to these needs, new assistive technologies have been developed to create ease for disabled people. In the present technology-driven age, and with movements like Digital India, made in India, artificial intelligence for accessibility, and smart cities, individuals with disabilities cannot be overlooked.[4,5] In a while, when this technology is at the core of building new smart innovated technologies, what can be done to confirm that disabled individuals' condition is improved and not intensified, and how can everybody's requirements be carried into consideration. As we watch out for progress into the future, the transhumanism program can still grow: from the creation of crutch for the disabled to robotic exoskeletons, from the wheelchairs to smart stair-climbing wheelchairs, from prosthetics special switches or pointing devices to cochlear or electronic implants, from assistive devices like hearing aids to self-driving cars, lift ware, dot (world's first braille smartwatch), helmet for the blind, smart home, driverless vehicle, bright sign gloves, and many more. However, the world of innovative technology is gradually advancing to become more comprehensive and universally accessible. Through its evolution from sign languages in 1620 to the driverless vehicle, assistive technology (AT) has transformed the lifestyle of people with physical disabilities. Individuals who are less mobile and live alone can benefit from IoT smart home gadgets such as connected speakers, microwaves, boilers, and indoor regulators. In any case, while we might be scarily near having robots controlling the working environment and by now have driverless vehicles being assessed on the streets, accessibility for the disabled still is not reasonably there yet. While several useful devices have been designed, such as mobility scooters for those with mobility issues, these designs still have many flaws and a long way to go. Assistive augmentation seeks to address both sensory ability and impairment as part of a technology's usefulness in a holistic manner. AT can become more socially acceptable, attracting less unnecessary attention, and changing misconceptions about assistive devices. Technology is continuously improving and proving to be a game-changing aspect for people with disabilities.[6-8] This paper briefly discusses the different types of disabilities, assisting technology (AT), IoT, and the influence of COVID-19 on people with disabilities. Also, the recent trends and dual nature of technology in creating opportunities and raising barriers in the life of disabled people have been briefly discussed in this research.

2.2   BACKGROUND AND SURVEY

Many studies on the issue of disability and technology have been conducted on a daily basis. AT is becoming more prominent at a rapid pace. The problem of disability is different in different countries. This section covers a variety of impairments, IoT-based assistive devices, and the influence of COVID-19 on disabled people, as well as related research.

2.2.1   DISABILITY

"Dis" + "ability" combined to form "disability," where "dis" (meaning "without") and "ability" (meaning "capability"). Disability in brief is outlined as the inability to do some activities or unable to perform certain daily life tasks due to physical, cognitive, mental impairments. Disability is classified into many types, such as cognitive, intellectual, physical, sensory, and mental illness.[3,4]

2.2.1.1   COGNITIVE DISABILITY

It is the most prevalent form of impairment. According to "The Diagnostic and Statistical Manual of Mental Disorders-IV," it is a nebulous term for describing individuals having trouble in learning new things, poor planning or problem-solving capacity, lack of self-care skills, such as dressing, bathing, and feeding yourself, etc.[7]

2.2.2   INTELLECTUAL DISABILITY

According to the "President's Committee for People with Intellectual Disability," the terms mental retardation and IDs are synonymous.[8] During a survey, it is projected that there are 7–8 million people in the USA, including children, which is 1 in 10 families who suffer IDs. Approximately (3–5%) 1.5 million Americans experiencing some type of ID like Autism, down syndrome, Alzheimer, etc.,[9] dyslexia, dysgraphia, and dyscalculia are some of the common examples of learning disabilities. Dementia is a type of brain disorder and a general term for memory loss and thinking abilities.[10]. About 4.5 million people in America are suffering from AD, which includes 10% of those over the age of 65, with 50% of those aged 85 and up. According to a research, the number of persons affected by this disease might reach 16 million by 2050.[11,12]

2.2.3   PHYSICAL DISABILITY

Disabilities like visual impairment, hearing loss, mobility impairment, etc., are referred to as physical disabilities. People with physical disabilities find it difficult to perform specific daily life tasks that the rest of the world finds easy, like walking, eating, climbing the stairs, running, reading, hearing, and many more. Individuals with physical impairments now have a variety of gadgets to select from that meet their unique needs and give them a sense of freedom.[5,6]

2.2.4   VISIBLE AND INVISIBLE DISABILITY

The main motive behind understanding the distinction between the two is knowledge about what is classified as a visible impairment and what invisible impairments are. There are many disabilities that we sense as visible and disabilities that we think of as invisible. If we see someone using devices like a wheelchair, hearing aid, or walking stick, it is obvious that they have a disability. However, not all impairments are visible to the ordinary individual. Physical disabilities are mainly visible disabilities because they are visible to an average person through the naked eye. Developmental disabilities or cognitive disabilities are sometimes hard to notice and sometimes not even visible to an average person with their naked eye. If a person has an invisible disability, it may affect how the individual thinks, hears, expresses herself/ himself, or interacts with others. Anxiety, depression, brain injuries, autism, cystic fibrosis, sadness, and other chronic diseases are examples of invisible disabilities. According to a US Census Bureau survey in 2002, it is estimated that approximately 96% of people who are suffering from a disability have a disease that is not visually recognizable. It is approximate that about 10% of individuals in the USA have a medical illness that could be considered an invisible disability. It is also estimated that about 70% of people have an invisible disability in the UK.[13]

In several interviews, disabled employees said, "Until I tell them, folks don't realize that I have a disability," implying that many individuals with disabilities living their daily lives without exposing their status as handicapped or the impairment from which they suffer intellectually, physically, or socially. There are countless internal barriers to be overcome. In 2011, a survey was done in which it was found that 88% of Canadians with invisible disabilities had an unfavorable opinion of disclosing their disability.[14] Despite the fact that the present COVID-19 crisis has a massive impact on crippled individuals.

2.3   IMPACT OF COVID-19 ON DISABLED PEOPLE

The WHO proclaimed the explosion of a harmful disease, COVID-19, in March 2020. They announced it to be a pandemic, as per the rate of spread and scale of its transmission. WHO said that people with disabilities and other chronic illnesses like diabetes, asthma, and other respiratory problems are at a higher risk of suffering from COVID-19. COVID-19 crisis and lockdown (declared by the government) are generating unbearable barriers in people with disabilities' daily lives. Disabled people are at exceptionally high risk during the COVID-19 crisis. Millions of people with disabilities face problems in getting medicines due to this pandemic but this pandemic pop-up the importance of digital accessibility and acts as a source of both inclusion and barriers for disabled people. During the COVID-19 global pandemic, people with disabilities are suffering from some significant challenges like lockdown and social isolation. Many individuals have been compelled to stay at home for extended periods of time due to social distancing regulations, only leaving the house for basics and depending on delivery and other digital infrastructure services. Most of these changes had the potential of improving the accessibility of work and education and other services. Most of the time, these services are dependent on the availability of digital technologies increases the disadvantages. Maintaining their assistive devices during lockdown is rough. Even though lockdown is necessary to avoid the spread of COVID-19, many houses are expected to become nurseries and schools quickly. This can be extremely challenging for families of people with disabilities or people living in poverty and inappropriate housing condition. As the pandemic going on, we think there is a need to understand that these new policies like lockdown, social distancing, virtual classes, home deliveries, social isolation came during the pandemic have both positive and negative impacts. The ultimate objective for all of us should be to understand how the present health crisis has revealed possibilities to improve previous employment, education, and social practice in order to create a more inclusive society. New research on COVID-19 shows that this pandemic leads to an increase in psychological distress in people with cognitive disabilities. Some of the behaviors, such as maintaining distance (physical and social), impact their economic life, make the standard population's mental health worse with many long- and short-term consequences. The research on this pandemic concludes that disabled people are finding it difficult to access their proper medical supplies, which is getting more challenging. Social isolation is making the condition of disabled people worse. People with some other disabilities are scared to have an appointment with doctors, which may directly affect their health. In this situation, the technologies like AT and IoT will make life easier for disabled people.[15]

2.4 ASSISTIVE TECHNOLOGY (AT) AND DEVICES

A term is coined explicitly for the type of technology that assists people or makes daily life tasks easier and feasible for disabled people, and that term is known to be AT. The US Government signed the AT Act on October 25, 2004. The first AT policy, the Technology-Related Assistance for People with Disabilities Act, was passed into law by the US Congress in 1988. It was the first formal document defining AT, assistive devices, and services. Another formal document was passed in 2012, defining AT as any gadget, piece of tool, service, or platform that enables individuals with impairments to fully engage in daily activities. As the name suggests, AT is a technology whose work is to assists individuals either one has disability or trouble doing simple tasks. AT might be something as necessary or low-tech as a copyholder or wrist support, or more complicated and hi-tech as a driver-less vehicle or electric wheelchair. Without AT, 77% of individuals with a disability would be helpless to deal with themselves, hold important work, or leave their homes to join parties, however. In contrast, many individuals with disabilities report that using AT has greatly enhanced their quality of life, depth of change in their satisfaction, self-confidence, flexibility, and security. Day by day, people with disabilities face many hindrances and chal-lenges in using assistive devices for their impairment. The other major factor is the affordability and accessibility of high-worth assistive products, which is a significant challenge for several individuals with disabilities. When we consider barriers to accessibility, many of us believe in physical barriers, like a person who manages a wheelchair not having the option to enter a public shop because there is no ramp. The truth of the matter is that there are various obstacles to the use of AT. Some are visible or noticeable while many are invisible or unseen. According to the findings of a survey from 2002 to 2004 by World Health, the major cause is financial constraints for people with disabilities, through gender and age groups, who did not get essential health services in low-income countries. The survey estimated that for 51 countries, 32–33% of disabled men and women could not manage the cost of medicinal services and contrasted with 51–53% of people without disabilities. According to the World Health Survey, facts and figures exposed a significant difference between males and females with disabilities and individuals without disabilities. This is based on the attitudinal, basic, and structure concentration barriers in accessing treatment. Based on the recent research and survey in Uttar Pradesh and Tamil Nadu, India, it is retrieved that cost (70.5%), shortage of facilities in the district (52.3%), and transport

(20.5%) were the leading barriers to using health care services, but on the other hand, assistive devices that were previously unavailable, too expensive, or too heavy-handed to fulfill the requirements of handicapped people are now inexpensive, efficient, and suitable. Devices like adaptive tools (utensils, keyboards, or switches), eye trackers, mobility aids (wheelchairs, walkers, orthotic devices), voice recognition software or virtual assistants (Siri, Alexa, Google Assistant), Xbox adaptive controller (for gamers with disabilities), Amazon Echo, and the smart speaker are proven to be a life-changing gadget in the lives of people with disabilities. However, Alexa echo is the brightest example and answer to how AT can be beneficial for people with disabilities. The echo can read daily news for an individual with low vision, perform necessary mathematical calculations, set alarms and reminders, perform simple searches, and update them about the city's temperature without moving hands or moving positions. iPhone 12 pro max for the blind, the freshly launched iPhone 12 pro max has a LiDAR scanner that enables a visually impaired individual to identify how close other people are and for people facing common vision issues. It is mainly used to measure the distance between the individual and the object present in front of them in a room to prevent a blind from an accident. These are some brilliant innovations of technology for disabled people. Few more examples of assistive devices are for mobility, we have walking aids, wheelchairs, canes, crutches, Orthoses, Prostheses, walkers or walking frames, prosthetics, clubfoot brace; for vision, we have eyeglasses, tactile devices, magnifiers, magnifying software for computers, communication cards, spectacles, GPs app for walking poles; for hearing: hearing aids, closed captioning devices, hearing loops, signaling products, etc. Below mentioned some of the barriers stated by UNICEF: lack of product awareness, services, lack of family participation, poor financial management, inaccessible settings, shortage of governance (including legislation, regulations, and national programs), lack of products, human resources, and financial limitations.[16] Emerging IoT-enabled assistive devices will make life better for disabled individuals.

2.5 INTERNET OF THINGS (IOT) FOR DISABLED PEOPLE

In IoT applications for disabled users, a tremendous amount of healthcare records must be assembled and examined. The Internet of Things (IoT) is nothing more than a tool for making remote monitoring in the healthcare industry possible. It is described as a system of physical or technological devices that use connectivity to permit data exchange. It has also increased patient commitment and satisfaction as doctors' interactions have become more comfortable and more efficient. It helps in reducing healthcare costs and improving treatment results. It is connecting more and more innovative devices day by day, and by 2025, we are set out toward a world that will have more than 64 billion IoT gadgets. Researchers are beginning to investigate the significant role that IoT plays in people with disabilities' lives for accessibility, but some practical and genuine applications already exist. From web-associated prosthetics to smart shoes that vibrate to guide the wearer on the right path, numerous IoT gadgets and administrations have been intended to improve the lives of individuals with disabilities. IoT technology includes wearable devices like smartwatches, and this device can translate contents like emails or texts into Braille or read them aloud. Wearable IoT technologies, like the Apple watch, will improve the physical well-being of people with disabilities. Additionally, wearable GPS mobiles, linked with mobile phones, help parents to detect their children with intellectual disabilities. IoT brought various user benefits along with some challenges. IoT presents several significant challenges, including privacy and security. Inadequate device updates, unavailability of useful and healthy security protocols, users' lack of knowledge are among the famous challenges that IoT is still confronting. IoT-supported connected devices to store user data, including confidential information that offers concerns about data security. The growing fame and usage of IoT in our lives give rise to various security issues. The biggest problem is privacy concern that makes IoT users vulnerable to cyber-assaults and leaking of personal information. In IoT, devices are interrelated or connected with various hardware and software, so there are understandable chances of spreading confidential information through unapproved control. Many of the devices transfer the users' records like name, address, date of birth, healthcare information, bank account details, and more without encryption. A great IoT innovation like smart home connections incorporates a hacker's capability to find whether anyone is present in-home or not. Unlock someone's front door, deactivate their security alarms, or control electronic appliances, including camera-empowered devices which could be utilized to keep an eye on people in their own homes. Ransomware assaults have already influenced some hospitals and medical clinics, which reveals the capability of hackers to encode confidential data or medical records. The distributed denial of service assault in 2016, which impacted numerous IoT services and devices around the world, was proof and a wake-up call that security attacks and concerns are real. In 2018, as per the survey of NETSCOUT, the estimated time for an IoT device to be hacked is only 5 min when the device is connected to the internet. Some more research derived are given below. Wessels et al.[14] reviewed the existing research on the underutilization of available AT. The authors compared factors like personal factors, environmental factors, and social factors on the nonuse of assistive devices. Agree et al. [15] reviewed the most recent data on the utility of assistive products and technology and the growing importance of digital technologies in the lives of people with disabilities. Moser et al.[16] proposed the study to deliver devices and resources to examine the evolution of AT for disabled people. Wise et al.[17] investigated various factors affecting child disability. Also, how preventive and therapeutic technologies affecting childhood disability had been discussed. Zubillaga et al.'s[18] study investigated how technology might be used to help students with impairments succeed academically. Carnevale et al.[19] showed the role of emerging future technologies in the life of disabled people. It examined how robotic technologies in the assistive and healthcare field lead to the improved human condition. Petrie et al.[20] introduced findings of a systematic review on advanced technologies for older and disabled people. Some other researches have also been done to find assistive technologies for disabled people.[21,22]

2.6 RESULTS AND DISCUSSION

Overall results show that many scholars have taken a shot at the usage and improvisation of AT for a considerable population of all ages having some impairment. Still, not much literature and survey are presented on the visible and invisible disabilities and barriers confronted by the disabled in India. Research and studies show that a lack of awareness and unavailability of repair/maintenance services, accessibility, and affordability are hindrances between the disabled and technology. According to a survey, various tech giants are working hard to improve accessibility. In 2018, internet giants such as Facebook, Microsoft, Adobe, Google, and Oath announced an accessibility initiative to include disabled people. The results and interviews showed that intellectual and learning disability is among the highest prevalence and was 33.2% encountered in more than thousands of children. From throwing out of school to unequal employment and social exclusion to the largest minority, this increased violence on people with disabilities continues to be demonstrated through the glaring hole in existing opportunities for disabled people. The results show that there is a need to improve the assistive methods for enhancing the disabled life.

2.7 CONCLUSION AND FUTURE WORK

This paper discusses the different aspects of disability and AT. The theme of this research is to find different technologies as a solution to abolish disability and whether these technologies play a game-changing role or not. By conducting surveys, it has been concluded that still, the world is struggling with the inclusion of individuals with a disability. However, as technology plays a dual and perplexing role in the lives of disabled individuals, there is a lack of understanding of how technology has evolved and how it emerges to be a game-changing component for disability. With the help of AT's new tools and services, a new hope has been emerged to motivate people and made them overcome their fear and challenges. In this paper, several barriers to technology use were discussed. The approach focused on some significant parts like AT and IoT. AT has long been recognized as both a blessing and a curse for disabled people. Further research in AT is highly encouraged as IoT, and AT is multidisciplinary area of study, and revolutionizing the industries nowadays. For future researchers, the fundamental question for the study is how we want AT to evolve, not how it will evolve.

REFERENCES

1. Federici, S.; Bracalenti, M.; Meloni, F.; Luciano, J. V. World Health Organization Disability Assessment Schedule 2.0: An International Systematic Review. *Disabil. Rehabil.* **2017**, *39*(23), 2347–2380.
2. Munthali, A. C. *A Situation Analysis of Persons with Disabilities in Malawi*; 2011.
3. Rosenbaum, P.; Stewart, D. The World Health Organization International Classification of Functioning, Disability, and Health: A Model to Guide Clinical Thinking, Practice and Research in the Field of Cerebral Palsy. *Semin. Pediatr. Neurol.* **2004**, *11*(*1*), 5–10, WB Saunders.
4. Kavale, K. A.; Forness, S. R. What Definitions of Learning Disability Say and Don't Say: A Critical Analysis. *J. Learn. Disabil.* **2000**, *33*(3), 239–256.
5. Lupton, D.; Seymour, W. Technology, Selfhood and Physical Disability. *Soc. Sci. Med.* **2000**, *50*(12), 1851–1862.
6. Bateni, H.; Maki, B. E. Assistive Devices for Balance and Mobility: Benefits, Demands, and Adverse Consequences. *Arch. Phys. Med. Rehabil.* **2005**, *86*(1), 134–145.
7. Sutton, R.; Barto, A. *The Diagnostic and Statistical Manual of Mental Disorders, IV*; American Psychiatric Association: Washington, DC, 1994.

8. Posey, V. Challenges Facing Older Adults with Intellectual Disabilities. *Research Digest No. 1. CASAS-Comprehensive Adult Student Assessment Systems (NJ1);* 2005.

9. Armstrong, T. Neurodiversity: Discovering the Extraordinary Gifts of Autism, ADHD, Dyslexia, and Other Brain Differences. *ReadHowYouWant;* 2010.

10. Leys, D.; Hénon, H.; Mackowiak-Cordoliani, M. A.; Pasquier, F. Poststroke Dementia. *Lancet Neurol.* **2005,** *4*(11), 752–759.

11. Agree, E. M. The Potential for Technology to Enhance Independence for Those Aging with a Disability. *Disabil. Health J.* **2014,** *7*(1), S33–S39.

12. Gregor, P.; Sloan, D.; Newell, A. F. Disability and Technology: Building Barriers or Creating Opportunities? *Adv. Comput.* **2005,** *64*, 283-346.

13. Foley, A.; Ferri, B. A. Technology for People, Not Disabilities: Ensuring Access and Inclusion. *J. Res. Spec. Educ. Needs.* **2012,** *12*(4), 192–200.

14. LOPresti, E. F.; Bodine, C.; Lewis, C. Assistive Technology for Cognition: Understanding the Needs of Persons with Disabilities. *IEEE Eng. Med. Biol. Mag.* **2008,** *27*(2), 29–39.

15. Isyanto, H.; Arifin, A. S.; Suryanegara, M. Design and Implementation of IoT-Based Smart Home Voice Commands for Disabled People Using Google Assistant. *In 2020 International Conference on Smart Technology and Applications (ICoSTA);* 2020, 1–6.

16. Alam, T. mHealth Communication Framework using blockchain and IoT Technologies. *Int. J. Sci. Technol. Res.* **2020,** 9(6).

17. Glushkova, T.; Stoyanov, S.; Popchev, I. Internet of Things Platform Supporting Mobility of Disabled Learners. *Int. J. Bioautom.* **2019,** *23*(3), 355.

18. Rodrigues, J.; Cardoso, A. Blockchain in Smart Cities: An Inclusive Tool for Persons with Disabilities. *IEEE In 2019 Smart City Symposium Prague (SCSP);* 2019, 1-6.

19. Frauenberger, C. Disability and Technology: A Critical Realist Perspective. *In Proceedings of the 17th International ACM SIGACCESS Conference on Computers & Accessibility;* 2015, 89–96.

20. Goggin, G. Disability and Digital Inequalities: Rethinking Digital Divides with Disability Theory; Taylor & Francis, 2017.

21. Aqel, M. O. A. et al. Review of Recent Research Trends in Assistive Technologies for Rehabilitation. *2019 International Conference on Promising Electronic Technologies (ICPET), Gaza City, Palestine;* 2019, pp. 16–21, doi: 10.1109/ICPET.2019.00011.

22. LoPresti, E. F.; Bodine, C.; Lewis, C. Assistive Technology for Cognition [Understanding the Needs of Persons with Disabilities], *IEEE Eng. Med. Biol. Mag.* **2008,** *27* (2), 29–39, doi: 10.1109/EMB.2007.907396.

23. http://mospi.nic.in/sites/default/files/publication_reports/Disabled_persons_in_India_2016.pdf

24. Velayutham, B.; Kangusamy, B.; Joshua, V.; Mehendale, S. The Prevalence of Disability in Elderly in India–Analysis of 2011 Census Data. *Disabil. Health J.* **2016,** *9*(4), 584–592.

25. https://cc.careersportal.ie/mce/plugins/filemanager/files/DH/AHEAD%20 Disability%203rd%20Level%20PARTICIPATION%202014%20-%20Feb%20 2015%20Report.pdf.

CHAPTER 3

A Study on a Water-Body-Based Robotics Waste Management System

SAZID ALI, FIRDOUS SHAMIM, RITAM MUKHERJEE, ANWESHA DAS, ANINDA CHOWDHURY, and RIYA SIL

Department of Computer Science & Engineering, Adamas University, Kolkata, India

ABSTRACT

The increase of waste material in water bodies has become an alarming threat to nature. Nevertheless, waste management has also been a challenging task for years. Though there have been plenty of technological advancements, yet no large-scale impact has been observed in the domain of waste management. Water waste is a subdomain of waste management that deals with waste present in water bodies like the sea, ocean, etc. It is essential to comprehend the aspects that lead to the generation of water waste, the nature of the waste that is to be dealt with, and highlight the issues faced while dealing with the large-scale treatment of water bodies. For better understanding, in this paper, the authors have performed a relevant survey about the recent works and technologies in the field of robotics that is targeted toward the purpose of water-waste management.

3.1 INTRODUCTION

The amount of waste generated[1] by humans has increased drastically over the years since the onset of industrialization and staggering urbanization.[2] The

Computational Intelligence in Analytics and Information Systems, Volume 2: Advances in Digital Transformation, Selected Papers from CIAIS-2021. Parneeta Dhaliwal, PhD, Manpreet Kaur, PhD, Hardeo Kumar Thakur, PhD, Rajeev Kumar Arya, and Joan Lu (Eds.)

ever-increasing amount of waste materials is mainly dealt with by throwing away these wastes into places that are far away from populated areas or burnt in incinerators.[3] But this process has led to the cause and contribution of pollution. Various alternatives are adopted to mitigate such issues which include bioremediation, plasma gasification, and waste hierarchy[4,5] that again consists of reduce, reuse, recycle, etc. But to apply such methods, wastes have to be transported to landfills and incinerators.

The water waste referred to in this paper covers the definition of surface water pollution[6] that are present in water bodies like river, lake, sea, and ocean. Types of pollutants or waste materials that are of primary concern are plastic bodies, marine debris, oil spills that are known to cause vital damage to the aquatic ecosystem, and many other physical objects which pollute these water bodies. An intensive study has been done by the ocean health index[7] on marine waste which has shown many contributing factors such as sources from land, ocean vessel, and many others. It gives a thorough study report on the components of pollution, their contribution, and also talks about the impacts in brief. The reports show the pressing matters that need to address the water waste.

Robotics has been playing a massive role in different sectors that include industrial, medical, and household sectors. Management of waste is another such sector in which robots have been playing a vital role over the past few decades. Some of the works related to waste management include tackling the issue of E-waste[8] using a collaborative robot and human–robot interaction. The latter takes such an approach due to the financial inconvenience of manual operations and lack of uniformity in devices. Apart from E-wastes, robotics is also used in handling, identifying, processing, sorting, and repackaging hazardous wastes. The works discussed above are postmeasures that are performed after the collection of waste materials. Still, the main issue that remains is the collection of waste materials effectively and systematically. To eradicate this issue, a better approach has been achieved that is the usage of swarm of robots[9] that works together. The research illustrates how swarms can be effectively deployed and used to manage wastes in urban areas.

In this paper, the authors have tried to actively survey and compare the solution and works involved in the collection of water waste.[10] The structure of this survey paper is as follows: In Section 3.2, the reasons why water waste collection is an issue have been discussed. In Section 3.3, a survey has been made on various research works that address the issues related to waste-water management. Section 3.4 shows a detailed comparison of the related research works based on specific parameters. Lastly, Section 3.5 concludes the paper and also explores its future scope of work.

3.2 ORIGIN OF THE WORK

According to a study by Chris Clarke,[11] it has been found that there is a contradiction to a popular belief of ocean plastics that consists of intact plastic bottles and bags are not how the majority of the plastic garbage is in the oceans. The big plastic bodies have been broken down by small critters, seawater corrosion, and ultraviolet lights from the sun into 1 cm and smaller-sized microplastics. These microplastics amount to around 92% and above of the total plastics that are found in the oceans. Most of these wastes are present below the surface level of the oceans rather than the surface itself. Their concentration zones or pocket formation depends upon various factors. From recent researches, it has been derived that microplastics are spread over the ice cores, ocean bottom, and throughout the vertical length of the ocean.[12] Hence from here, one can get a clear view of how plastic is a matter of massive concern. But oceans being such huge water body is difficult to clean up. Devices that would be used to work have to deal with waves of an average height of 3 m, which are very common. Another issue that the devices have to face is biofouling, a phenomenon where bacteria and diatoms create a biofilm on rigid floating bodies that provide habitat for protozoans and algae which in-turn attracts organisms such as sponges, mollusks, and crustaceans leading to an increase in weight of hundreds of kilograms per square meter of the surfaces that are submerged.

According to research by Zahugi et al.,[13] oil spills cost billions of dollars and a lot of time to clean. Traditionally, oil spills consist of floating barriers that enclose the oil from everywhere, after which it is lifted from the water by boats to be transported away which usually takes a lot of time and is very expensive. These play a major role in the spread of oil spills to a wider range in turbulent waters, causing havoc and massive damage to its surrounding aquatic ecosystem.

River plastic cleaning also has its challenges in cleaning prospects. The water current in rivers places a challenge on floating robots. Common issues include being washed away and having their batteries drained up fast. Solutions also have to take the fauna into care and not deteriorate it. There are also various water vessels to mind for in a river.

3.3   LITERATURE SURVEY

In this section, the authors have discussed various technologies in the field of waste collections and management from water, including robotic solutions like manually operated, autonomous, and swarm robots. A brief discussion has been done in this section that includes summarizing the details of open-source and product-ready solutions and also lists several shortcomings in those solutions.

3.3.1   OIL SPILL CLEANING UP USING SWARM OF ROBOTS

Zahugi et al.[13] proposed a swarm robotic technology, which aims to collect oil spills on the surface of the water. Each swarm robot has all its components enclosed in waterproof packaging. The main parts of the robot are the GPS module, transceiver module, digital compass, microcontroller, voltage regulator, LCD, motor driver IC, and many more. The swarm bots[14] offer control in both autonomous and remote-control mode. Swarms interact with the base station periodically using messages that monitor the bots using these messages. The working area of the bots has a boundary that can be defined long of four points forming a rectangular area.

In the proposed system, the swarm bots have only one ultrasonic sensor for sensing their environment. The obstacle detection and avoidance fail to achieve their task during autonomous behavior.

3.3.2   UNDERWATER ROBOTICS: SURFACE CLEANING TECHNICS, ADHESION AND LOCOMOTION SYSTEMS

Albitar et al.[15] proposed the concept of crawling techniques in an aqua cleaning bot. The bot performs its movement by shrinking and extension-legged arms using standard motors and vacuum suction cup automation. This study focuses on the stability of the bot to fight in different situations for movement and the circumstances for attaining adequate adherence between the bot and the aqua surface. Stability analysis helps in the estimation of the optimal amount of force required by each suction cup. This analysis enables better control of the balancing force helping in different locomotion in times when suction cups are off.

The paper presents the design of the crawling bot but not the computational implementation of the project. Computational implementation of the bot will help in understanding the mechanism better.

3.3.3   UNMANNED FLOATING WASTE COLLECTING ROBOT

Abir Akib et al.[16] present the prototype design of a robot which consists of two propellers, fixed with two DC motors, a Bluetooth control system to manage the robot from distance, a robotic hand for collecting the savage, a conveyor belt to lead the savage to the collector box, and a sensor for preventing the box from overloading. As it is a floating cleaning bot so it will act as a protector to the aquatic life. The use of well-sealed circuitry in the battery saves the electronic components from water and unfolds the scope of renewable solar energy.

Being a remote-controlled robot, it is operated manually. There is no reliable rate of communication.

3.3.4   INNOVATIVE DESIGN OF AN UNDERWATER CLEANING ROBOT WITH A TWO-ARM MANIPULATOR FOR HULL CLEANING

Hachicha et al.[17] present ARM ROV, an underwater ship frame cleaning bot fixing two manipulator arms to a vehicle at a distance. The central part of the robot depends on the active strength concern occurred by the coupling force between arms and the central part. To resolve the issue in the central part, kinematic and dynamic models were introduced using Khalil–Kleifinger and Newton–Euler methods, respectively. This bot is speedy, shippable, and more structured using two manipular arms, and cleaning is done using pressurized water jet technology.

The navigation speed of the robot should be increased and the consumption of fuel must be reduced.

3.3.5   WASTE SHARK: AN AUTONOMOUS CATAMARAN TO REMOVE FLOATING PLASTIC DEBRIS IN PORTS AND HARBORS

German Research Center for artificial intelligence GmbH of Robotics Innovation Center[18] presents an aqua drone that removes plastic and floating debris from the surface of water bodies. Waste shark is specifically designed to collect floating water waste from the ports and harbors. The modes of operation of this bot are fully autonomous and manual, it works on lidar-enabled anticollision algorithms.

3.3.6   *OCEAN CLEANUP SYSTEM 001: AN AUTONOMOUS FLOATING PLASTIC CAPTURE SYSTEM THAT ACCUMULATES FLOATING PLASTIC*

The ocean cleanup[19] system is designed to capture millimeter-sized plastic to large debris and relies on waves, currents, and winds to navigate the patches. As it is a passive device, it depends on the ocean and winds to direct the garbage into it. The device is anchored to slow it down which results in it being slower than the floating garbage while the garbage flows into it. The system autonomously moves around in the garbage patch for extended periods while retaining its catch in the center of the system. Once it gets full, it sends a signal for a garbage collecting boat to collect the gathered pile of plastic.

The solution is modeled around a notion of ocean plastic that is not entirely correct as mentioned here. The device can catch only plastic at only 3 m depth.

3.3.7   *OCEAN CLEANUP INTERCEPTOR: A 100% SOLAR-POWERED DEVICE THAT COLLECTS RIVER PLASTIC*

The interceptor[20] is a floating garbage collector placed strategically in the middle of a river. The garbage is funneled toward the interceptor by guides placed on both sides of the river. The interceptor has conveyor belts that pick the garbage from the water and places them in bins inside the interceptor. When the interceptor is full, a boat comes and replaces the garbage containers. The solution is designed keeping in mind the local fauna and water vessel locomotion.

3.3.8   *A WATER SURFACE CLEANING ROBOT: A FLOATING BOT THAT CLEANS GARBAGE*

The robot[21] developed is cost-effective, robust, and durable. The removal of waste is carried out by a motor-driven arm that has a net attached to the end of it. The lower section of the belt is placed below the surface water level to take out floating weeds. The bot uses Xbee Pro S2C as a communication module for controlling it. An Arduino UNO acts as the controller for the motors and arm manipulator. The bot has a carrying capacity of 20 kg and an average operation time of 1 h.

The bot is manually controlled and does not have an autonomous mode of operation. The robot is not tested in open ocean waters.

3.3.9   SUPERHYDROPHOBIC CU MESH COMBINED WITH A SUPER OLEOPHILIC POLYURETHANE SPONGE FOR OIL SPILL ADSORPTION AND COLLECTION

This paper[22] presents the simulator for soaking and collecting the oil from water which consists of a small box having superhydrophobic copper webbing immersed for a minute in the corrosive and organic solvent and super hydrophilic polyurethane sponge. This simulator helps in the absorption of different types of oils excluding water and the sponge can be squeezed off for collecting the oil and can be reused.

3.3.10   COCORO—THE SELF-AWARE UNDERWATER SWARM

This paper[23] introduces the combinational flexible, extensive, authentic concept of biological-based movement and collection technique which is named as CoCoRo swarm underwater system. The autonomous underwater vehicles are self-ware, self-controlled, and self-guided in the context of swarm robotics.

3.3.11   SENSE AND AVOID RADAR FOR MICRO/NANO ROBOTS

This paper[24] introduces the concept of the environment-influenced nonscanning micro/nano radar used for recognizing and avoiding systems. It helps in calculating the distances detecting and tracking the low elevation targets in the ground, marine, and air.

3.3.12   OBSTACLE DETECTION AND AVOIDANCE FOR AN AUTONOMOUS SURFACE VEHICLE USING A PROFILING SONAR

This paper[25] introduces innovative learning for identifying and avoiding barriers by self-controlled surface machines using sonar. The vehicle removed the possible barriers by returning echoes and it proposed a survey scheme for sonar. Since it confirms that sonar is helpful to avoid obstacles, more works are needed for the betterment of spinning and modulation of the vehicle.

3.3.13 *WIRELESS SENSOR AND NETWORKING TECHNOLOGIES FOR SWARMS OF AQUATIC SURFACE DRONES*

This paper[26] introduces the swarm of water surface drones with wireless sensor and networking technologies. The objective of the project is to carry out marine tasks such as sea-border guarding and circumstances or nature monitoring keeping the cost cheaper XBee modules with DigiMesh Protocol has been used. It stretches in a range of hundreds of meters.

3.3.14 *SURFACE TENSION DRIVEN WATER STRIDER ROBOT USING CIRCULAR FOOTPADS*

This study introduces a new aqua strider insect-influenced robot,[27] named STRIDE II. It makes the use of circular footpads having a common axis and elliptical spinning legs are fixed developed and the static and dynamic forces are established. Circular footpads lead to the gain in the payload by 4. The elliptical path movement of the propeller leg provides more propulsion force.

3.3.15 *UW MORSE—THE UNDERWATER MODULAR OPEN ROBOT SIMULATION ENGINE*

This paper[28] shows the simulation of the underwater robot which can be used for the development of a control system designing of a path, risk administration, and evaluating in a secure practical circumstance. The adaptable environment of MORSE acknowledges the user to build the miniature creating new robots and circumstances and also adjoin sensors and control interfaces. The simulation mechanism made the faster, easier, cheaper, and easy-going alternative for ocean tests.

3.4 SURVEY RESULTS

Based on the above survey, the authors of this paper have created a table to highlight the comparison between the parameters of the existing bots and their respective solutions.

TABLE 3.1 Comparison Between Different Solutions of Water Waste Collection.

Parameters	Existing solutions							
	Oil spill cleaning up using swarm of robots	In water surface cleaning robot	Unmanned floating waste collecting robot	ARM ROV	Waste shark	Ocean cleanup 001	Ocean cleanup interceptor	A water surface cleaning robot
Waste storage	–	–	10 kg	–	350 kg	–	50 m³	16 kg
Waste type	Oil spills	Biofouls, floating	Floating solid	Biofouls	Floating solid	–	Floating solid	Floating solid
Locomotion	Active	Passive	Passive	Active	Active	Passive	Passive	Active
Range	1.4 km	–	3000 cm²	–	5 km	–	–	1.2–3.2 km
Number of bot	Multi	1	1	1	1	1	1	1
Power source	Solar	–	Battery	Battery	Battery	Battery	Solar	Battery
Operation area	Sea-coastline	Sea	Canals, ponds, rivers, & oceans	Hull cleaning ships in ocean	Semiconfined water surface	Ocean	River	Sea, ocean, and river
Mode of operation	Both	Autonomous	Manual	Manual	Both	Autonomous	Autonomous	Manual
Source of propulsion	Propeller	Motors	2 × propellers	6 × thrusters	2 × electric thruster	–	–	Propeller

3.5 CONCLUSION

Water waste is a terrific matter of concern in both local and global territories. In this paper, the authors have mentioned some of the most vital challenges of waste clearance in the sea or ocean.[29] Authors have also collected utmost related works on waste management since 2010 onward to do an intensive study on them. A lot of research addresses have been executed on this issue over the time span of 10 years. The current research work and trends of technology used in water waste cleaning are observed. Among these research works done to date, very few have been successful enough for the cause. In this paper, the use of swarm robotics has been observed that can provide a cost-effective way and simple yet effective solution. Swarms bot is simple alone like an ant but as a group can clean the garbage by chipping away small segments of the total waste in an area efficiently. Thus, it would also reduce the time and complexity to clean the water waste. Therefore, it can be concluded that swarm is a prime candidate of strategy to control the connected system of garbage cleaning bots[30] autonomously with a predetermined goal. The authors have planned to explore and extend the idea and possibilities of swarm robotics in the near future as effective measures for cleaning water waste.

KEYWORDS

- **waste management**
- **water waste**
- **robotics**
- **surface water waste**
- **swarm**
- **autonomous mode**

REFERENCES

1. Jambeck, J. R.; Geyer, R.; Wilcox, C.; Siegler, T. R.; Perryman, M.; Andrady, A.; Law, K. L. Plastic Waste Inputs from Land into the Ocean. *Science* **2015,** *347* (6223), 768–771.
2. Faniran, O. O.; Caban. G. Minimizing Waste on Construction Project Sites. *Eng. Constr. Archit. Manag.* **1998,** *5* (2), 182–188.

3. Awomeso, A. J.; Taiwo, A. M. Waste Disposal and Pollution Management in Urban Areas: A Workable Remedy for the Environment in Developing Countries. *Am. J. Environ. Sci.* **2010,** *6* (1), 26–32.
4. Gupta, C.; Prakash, D. Novel Bioremediation Methods in Waste Management. In *Waste Management*; 2020. pp. 1627–1643.
5. Mazzoni, L.; Janajreh, I. In *Plasma Gasification of Municipal Solid Waste with Variable Content of Plastic Solid Waste for Enhanced Energy Recovery*, 2016 International Renewable And Sustainable Energy Conference (IRSEC), 2016.
6. Esrey, S. A. Water, Waste, and Well-Being: A Multicountry Study. *Am. J. Epidemiol.* **1996,** *143* (6), 608–623.
7. Trash Pollution. (N.D.) [Online]. March 4 2021, http://www.oceanhealthindex.org/methodology/components/trash-pollution
8. Renteria, A.; Alvarez-De-Los-Mozos, E. Human-Robot Collaboration as a New Paradigm in Circular Economy for WEEE MANAGEMENT. *Procedia Manuf.* **2019,** *38,* 375–382.
9. Yogeswaran, M.; Ponnambalam, S. G. Swarm Robotics: An Extensive Research Review. In *Advanced Knowledge Application In Practice*; 2010. doi:10.5772/10361
10. Koop, S. H.; Van Leeuwen, C. J. The Challenges of Water, Waste and Climate Change in Cities. *Environ. Dev. Sustain.* **2016,** *19* (2), 385–418.
11. Clarke, C. 6 Reasons that Floating OCEAN Plastic CLEANUP Gizmo is a Horrible Idea [Online], March 4, 2021. https://www.kcet.org/redefine/6-reasons-that-floating-ocean-plastic-cleanup-gizmo-is-a-horrible-idea
12. Benton, D. Cleaning up the Oceans is Not a Solution to the Plastic Problem [Online], March 7, 2021.https://greenallianceblog.org.uk/2017/03/14/cleaning-up-the-oceans-is-not-a-solution-to-the-plastic-problem/
13. Zahugi, E. M.; Shanta, M. M.; Prasad, T. V. Oil Spill Cleaning up Using Swarm of Robots. *Adv. Comput. Inform. Technol.* 2013, 215–224.
14. Dorigo, M.; In *Swarm-Bot: An Experiment in Swarm Robotics. Proceedings 2005 IEEE Swarm Intelligence Symposium,* 2005. SIS 2005. doi:10.1109/Sis.2005.1501622
15. Albitar, H.; Dandan, K.; Ananiev, A.; Kalaykov, I. Underwater Robotics: Surface Cleaning Technics, Adhesion and Locomotion Systems. *Int. J. Adv. Robotic Syst.* **2016,** *13* (1), 7.
16. Akib, A.; Tasnim, F.; Biswas, D.; Hashem, M. B.; Rahman, K.; Bhattacharjee, A.; Fattah, S. A. In *Unmanned Floating Waste Collecting Robot.* Tencon 2019–2019 IEEE Region 10 Conference (TENCON) 2019. Doi:10.1109/Tencon.2019.8929537
17. Hachicha, S.; Zaoui, C.; Dallagi, H.; Nejim, S.; Maalej, A. Innovative Design of an Underwater Cleaning Robot with a Two Arm Manipulator for Hull Cleaning. *Ocean Eng.* **2019,** *181*, 303–313.
18. Robotics Innovation Center. Project: Wasteshark—An Autonomous Catamaran to Remove Floating Plastic Debris in Ports And Harbours. (N.D.) [Online]. March 4, 2021. https://robotik.dfki-bremen.de/en/research/projects/wasteshark.html
19. THE OCEAN CLEANUP. Oceans, [Online]. March 04, 2021, https://theoceancleanup.com/oceans/
20. THE OCEAN CLEANUP, [Online]. Tackling Trash in Rivers, March 4, 2021.https://theoceancleanup.com/rivers/
21. Rahmawati, E.; Sucahyo, I.; Asnawi, A.; Faris, M.; Taqwim, M. A.; Mahendra, D.; A Water Surface Cleaning Robot. *J. Phys.: Conf. Series* **2019,** *1417*, 012006.

22. Wang, F.; Lei, S.; Li, C.; Ou, J.; Xue, M.; Li, W. Superhydrophobic Cu Mesh Combined with a Superoleophilic Polyurethane Sponge for Oil Spill Adsorption and Collection. *Indus. Eng. Chem. Res.* **2014,** *53* (17), 7141–7148.

23. Schmickl, T.; Thenius, R.; Moslinger, C.; Timmis, J.; Tyrrell, A.; Read, M.; … Sutantyo, D. In *Cocoro—the Self-Aware Underwater Swarm*. 2011 Fifth IEEE Conference On Self-Adaptive And Self-Organizing Systems Workshops, 2011. doi:10.1109/sasow.2011.11

24. Molchanov, P. A.; Asmolova, O.; Sense and Avoid Radar for Micro/Nano Robots. Unmanned/Unattended Sensors and Sensor Networks X, **2014.** doi:10.1117/12.2071366

25. Heidarsson, H. K.; Sukhatme, G. S. In *Obstacle Detection and Avoidance for an Autonomous Surface Vehicle Using A Profiling Sonar*, 2011 IEEE International Conference on Robotics and Automation, 2011. doi:10.1109/Icra.2011.5980509

26. Velez, F. J.; Nadziejko, A.; Christensen, A. L.; Oliveira, S.; Rodrigues, T.; Costa, V.; … Gomes, J. In *Wireless Sensor and Networking Technologies for Swarms of Aquatic Surface Drones*, 2015 IEEE 82nd Vehicular Technology Conference (VTC2015-Fall), **2015.** doi:10.1109/Vtcfall.2015.7391193

27. Ozcan, O.; Wang, H.; Taylor, J. D.; Sitti, M. In *Surface Tension Driven Water Strider Robot Using Circular Footpads*, 2010 IEEE International Conference on Robotics and Automation, 2010. doi:10.1109/Robot.2010.5509843

28. Henriksen, E. H.; Schjolberg, I.; Gjersvik, T. B. In *UW MORSE: The Underwater Modular Open Robot Simulation Engine*, 2016 IEEE/OES Autonomous Underwater Vehicles (AUV), 2016. doi:10.1109/Auv.2016.7778681

29. Royer, S.; Deheyn, D. D. The Technological Challenges of Dealing With Plastics in the Environment. *Marine Technol. Soci. J.* **2019,** *53* (5), 13–20.

30. Tan, Y.; Zheng, Z. Research Advance in Swarm Robotics. *Def. Technol.* **2013,** *9* (1), 18–39.

CHAPTER 4

An Analysis of City Command Centers of Indian Smart Cities

AMARA ADITYA[1], ROHIT TANWAR[2], and MRINAL GOSWAMI[2]

[1]University of Petroleum & Energy Studies (UPES), Bidholi, Dehradun, India

[2]Department of Systemics, University of Petroleum & Energy Studies, Bidholi, Dehradun, India

ABSTRACT

The idea of a smart city is to enhance the lifestyle of the people who are living in urban areas. Smart City Mission of the Indian Government is to target these urban areas to transform them into a smart city. Through amalgamation and orchestrated rollout aided by greater endorsement of the previous cash economy, these smart cities are probably expected to bring a countrywide rising tide that promises to generate jobs and leftovers to sustain the government's new bold initiatives to take India on a high accelerated economic growth which alone can bring inclusive expansion. This paper on city command centers (CCC) in Indian smart cities highlights the features of smart city where its applications are in banking & finance, conventional & renewable energy, housing, healthcare, water & waste management, transport, including the need for a CCC in a smart city. Various CCCs that are already implemented in Indian cities have been listed.

Computational Intelligence in Analytics and Information Systems, Volume 2: Advances in Digital Transformation, Selected Papers from CIAIS-2021. Parneeta Dhaliwal, PhD, Manpreet Kaur, PhD, Hardeo Kumar Thakur, PhD, Rajeev Kumar Arya, and Joan Lu (Eds.)

4.1   INTRODUCTION

The definition of smart cities varies from person to person and place to place, and it is totally depending upon the people's participation in the model of the development implemented with the resources available. Because the situation of the Indian cities is different compared to the cities in the UK, Far Asia, etc. Within India also the scenario of development of each city differs and thus a globally accepted definition is not available for a smart city. Thus, a smart city can be defined as the creation of a certain lifestyle to the people living in a city. However, certain boundaries do exist in transforming a city into a smart city. In India, the picture of a smart city has a wish list of infrastructure facilities and services that describe a high level of aspiration.

India's Prime minister, Mr. Narendra Modi, introduced Smart Cities Mission (SCM) on June 25, 2015, and defined it as "one which is one or two steps ahead of the aspirations of people." Institutional, social, economic, and physical infrastructures are considered as the pillars of the model of development. To renovate the nation, cities can work toward inclusive infrastructure which dynamically adds on layer of "smartness." Comprehensive development of a replica model will act like a lighthouse to upcoming smart cities. The aim of the SCM is to drive monetary growth and to progress the quality of life to the citizens by empowering local area development through technology. The smart city mission motto is to bring the change in the lifestyles of the citizens. A large increase in migration of people from rural to urban centers was observed, which strictly impacted the services offered to people.[1] Consequently, cities do not only grow but the people can also enjoy a smart lifestyle in a smart city and smart nation. The concept smart city is a process of solving the general problems of the city. Thus, the requirements in a smart city are as follows[2–5].

4.1.1   *SUSTAINABLE ECONOMY*

To provide a high infrastructure and quality lifestyle, transformation of many aspects of the city is subjected to the smart city development. It is important to have a sustainable economy for looking over all the major and minor aspects of a city.

4.1.2   SMART MOBILITY

Smart transport system, global positioning system, effective traffic management, smart parking, smart shopping, etc., services are to be implemented for ecofriendly environment within the city.

4.1.3   QUALITY LIFESTYLE

The model of a smart city plays an important role in fulfilling the changing needs of the people. People from various social and economic backgrounds must be provided an ease of living needs in the city. This not only helps the population growth of the city but also increases the tourism in the city.

4.1.4   INFORMATION AND TECHNOLOGY

Effective technology will not only reduce the work load on the citizens but also makes the citizens as "smart citizens." Proper administration in the information and technology cluster must be monitored from time to time in order to have an effective mechanism of the technology.

4.1.5   AWARENESS AMONG PEOPLE

Without rules and regulations, smart city concept alone cannot be implemented by the government. People must be aware of what to do, and what to follow in a smart city. They must be aware of the facilities in-order to a have transparency between the government and the citizens.

4.1.6   SMART AGENTS

The people in the city should be guided and monitored by these agents. These agents can work as the safety agents for the citizens, Sensex ratio, and relative migration can also be calculated by these people. This aspect of having smart agents will raise new employment within the city.

4.1.7 SMART GOVERNANCE

This is the crucial requirement in a smart city. Smart governance acts as the bridge between the citizens and the government. The government policies, working, budget distribution, schemes for the citizens, etc., must be updated from time to time and it must be accessible for every citizen to verify and question the government. This increases the responsibility of the government but it brings a healthy governance in a smart city.

4.1.8 EFFECTIVE WASTE MANAGEMENT

The major part of the city would be clean and the number of dumping sites will be reduced by implementing effective waste management. Having a track of garbage right from a household to the dump yard would help us to monitor the waste and send it to the nearest places for recycling the waste. Plastic and nonplastic management, sewage management must be given more priority and the government should take an initiative for helping farmers by making compost pits with the collected biodegradable waste. Many implementations can be made regarding the waste management in a smart city.

4.1.9 SMART HEALTHCARE

Facilities in public and private hospitals must be monitored from time to time. A special budget for hospital and first-aid centers must be allotted. Proper health measures from season to season, health camps, fatal issues, diseases and their remedies, etc., are the important aspects of healthcare to be administrated.

4.1.10 INNOVATION AND IMPLEMENTATION

New services are to be provided from time to time to the citizens. This ensures proper usage of the services by the citizens. We need to calibrate new innovative ideas from time to time by comparing to the facilities in different countries.

Internet of Things (IoT) smart sensors have been installed and connected over the network and helped us to maintain the smart device connectivity in the smart cities. IoT is now changing to block chain technology incorporated with IoT (BIoT) which ensures more security toward the data and tends to provide more digital services.[6] Estonia government already introduced block chain to their citizens for giving their privacy to their individual data. Dubai is the initial smart city that collaborated with IBM for testing the block chain projects. Firstly, they have introduced a real-time tracking of the shipment data of the imports and exports. These data are furtherly used for the development of the city services. In India, this block chain with IoT is still in the planning stage but has a great impact on the monetary development of the country.

4.2 CITY COMMAND CENTER (CCC)

IoT is an emerging technology across the globe. When we are conscious about the overseas nations that have already implemented a smart ecosystem, they are far upgraded from us and are updating their infrastructure day on day. This section explains how city command center (CCC) runs on IoT technology with the help of a human body as an emblem.

Brain of a human (Fig. 4.1) acts as a middle point that plays a crucial role in all the decisions to be done by all the different parts of human body with help of the feedback given to it. When the body senses any hot object, the receptors send information to the brain and the brain sends a signal and we would perform the required action. This is a simple example where the brain reacts to the changes that are passed off in the human body. CCC of a smart city acts as the brain. The major decisions and changes to be implemented are taken by the CCC. The CCC gives the instructions to the devices in the smart city cluster so that they can take an action as according to the difficulty came about.

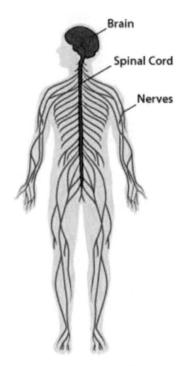

FIGURE 4.1   Human being central nervous system view.

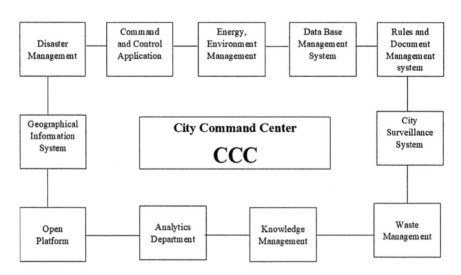

FIGURE 4.2   Block diagram of city command center.

CCC consists of a significant part which is the connecting medium to all the departments serving the smart city, such as police departments, waste management, hospitals, water management, traffic management, and many other devices connected inside a city. If at all there are emergencies that happened in any sector, an immediate notification is given to the CCC. For example, let us consider the waste management system of a smart city. There are several smart bins over the city and these bins are filled with sensors and IoT equipment so that when the bin is filled to its capacity, the GPS or GIS system is initialized and the information of its location is triggered to the CCC and this center will send a message or notification to the municipal department which are responsible for that area so that they can replace the bins. This CCC plays a major role for the decision-making or managing all the smart city services. In simple, the CCC consists of the above responsibilities (Fig. 4.2) in a smart city. CCC is a crucial part of a smart city. All the micro- and macro-level actions are taken from the command control center. Hardware may change from application to application, time to time but the control center must be compatible with each and every application in the smart city. It has the all-city monitoring and city administration system. In India, the command centers are allocated via bidding.[1] The companies establish a smart city monitoring report along with CCC in the bidding document. Some of the companies are in partnership with the foreign companies in establishing fully developed CCCs. Let us discuss the existing CCCs which are available in India.

4.2.1 *IBM INTELLIGENT OPERATIONS CENTER FOR SMARTER CITIES*

IBM intelligent operations center for smart cities combines data visualization, deep analysis, and real-time collaborations that can help the people in CCCs to manage and coordinate when there is a problem with a service. This also helps to continuously monitor the efficiency of the city services so that they can predict the problems and can compete with complex operations. They provide emergency response operating procedures when there is an unexpected disaster or extreme change in the weather. Executive dashboards are provided to view the operations, resources so that they can have a unified view of all in their dashboard which helps them to take a decision or have a summary for further improvement.[7]

4.2.2 *TRINITY ICCC (INTEGRATED COMMAND AND CONTROL CENTER)*

Trinity ICCC acts as a common platform for all the city operations which provides features like GIS-based map and video visualization. It has mobile support so that full visibility to the field responder can take an immediate action when he is out for any Incident. There is smart alarm management which is based on the data aggregation of the sensors connected over the city. It differs from application to application but has a rule engine based on sensor data correlation. There are different dashboards such as CEO, control room, and operational dashboards which give a clear understanding of particular operations to the particular individual. The map-based situational awareness of resources, events, and assets is on a single pane, and the total view of the building, parking space, etc., is viewed in a layout so that the building overall view of moving resources is clearly visible.[8]

4.2.3 *FLUENTGRID ACTILLIGENCE (ICCC)*

Fluentgrid Actilligence is a multipurpose integrated command control and communication center. In a disaster situation, the information and communication are done over the city scale to carry out emergency operations. They are having coordination among various agencies at disaster and a faster restoration of operations or city services postdisaster. In emergency situations, the communication is made over an area scale. The motto is to provide a common emergency operational services over the departments with clear action or points for a joint action. In normal situations, the scale is meant to be person-to-person or person-to-department. This helps us to know the citizens' complaints more interactively that leads to their satisfaction. Providing various online tools even to the citizens so that they can use the resources at their end easily without the intervention of any administration. Visualizations, security operations procedures (SOPs), and various work-force management are also provided by Fluentgrid Actilligence.[9]

4.2.4 *CISCO SMART + CONNECTED CITY OPERATIONS CENTER*

Cisco CCC has a single screen layout tool (software) that allows the map, camera, data, alarm contents to integrate, and display their contents in a single pane in which it meets the operator's needs and this process is done using the drag-and-drop layout. The software allows different inputs beyond cameras, such as PC, web pages, and other external devices. Collects the major information in XML format and also uses dynamic channel coverage functions for efficient bandwidth usage. N3N collaborated with Cisco, one of the leads in IT, delivers a preintegrated Cisco city operation center solution maintained by professional services to manage smart cities services so that the operations are more responsive and interactive to citizen needs. Major innovations like data fusion to decrease fake alarms and the integration of different applications into an inclusive solution, make it the solution of choice for today's challenging law execution departments and smart city planners.[10]

4.3 COMPARATIVE ANALYSIS AND FINDINGS

Few other CCCs developed by companies were implemented but not in a large scale. Every company is trying to bring the best architecture for the management of a smart city. Command centers in the city must be mainly focused on the below five elements.

4.3.1 DIRECTNESS OF THE SYSTEM

Directness is based on the environment where the system is implemented. The environment depicts the IT updates. The more the technology is embedded, the effective system is developed and it results in a great outcome as per as the requirements in the city. Based on the requirements and new technology updates, we must be updating the system so that it gets iterated and produces precise outcomes (Fig. 4.3).

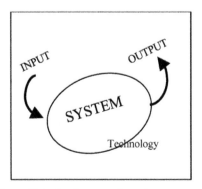

FIGURE 4.3   System view with technology as a boundary.

4.3.2   CAPABLE OF INTEROPERATIONS

FIGURE 4.4   Interoperability aspects of the system.

The system or the software must be capable of exchanging the information or making use of it. In a smart city, there are different types of data collected and different people interacting. The system must have the ability to transfer the information between different hardware or a different department. Moreover, the data must be private and should not be accessed by anyone. If a citizen of a smart city wants to change his place or needs his information at the hospital, then his information must be transferred and exchanged (Fig. 4.4).

4.3.3   ROBUST

Robustness is one of the main aspects of a system. Robustness defines that a system must functionally work correctly when there are invalid inputs or extreme weather conditions. A system must be designed by considering the worst cases and such measures are also called as SOPs.

4.3.4 SCALABLE

A system is said to be scalable if the system is capable of handling an increased amount of work. Typically, hardware can be considered as system scalability. It is not a property of a system but if the hardware is enlarged enough to accommodate the output even for large inputs then the system is said to be scalable.

4.3.5 SERVICE ARCHITECTURE

The system architecture is a service-oriented architecture for distribution among various application components that include access control, data security, visualization, mapping, etc., features. The architectural model is used to write the approaches which help to meet the goals. It also shows the requirement specifications that are usually linked in the development of the system.

Based on the above considerations, every models advantage and disadvantages toward the development of smart city are discussed in Table 4.1.

TABLE 4.1 Advantages and Disadvantages of Discussed CCCs.

CCC	Remarks	
IBM[7]	**Advantages**	**Disadvantages**
	1. They are having a robust system and dedicated system with IoT	1. There is drop in the brand Value due to litigations
	2. They are good in updating their systems and the software are useful for data analytics and cloud based solutions	
TRINITY[8]	**Advantages**	**Disadvantage**
	1. Emerged with IoT models with alarm management and situational awareness	1. Integration of systems are limited a few devices
	2. Integrated with the mobile application so that any field responder can respond	
	3. With a preintegrated social analytics manner	

TABLE 4.1   *(Continued)*

CCC	Remarks	
CISCO[9]	**Advantages**	**Disadvantages**
	1. Automation of incident detection and early response	1. A single pane-of view for operations centers
	2. Less bandwidth and simplified integration of third party systems	
	3. Drag-and-drop tool for customizing the dashboard	
FLUEN-TGRID[10]	**Advantages:**	**Disadvantages:**
	1. Configuration can be changed as per as the need	1. High pricing model
	2. Highly flexible for connecting a greater number of devices	
	3. Multipurpose integrated command and control center	
	4. High configuration than IBM models	

As we compared the above models, there is a understanding that every model is having a few unique features, and rest of the services are given in every model. In the view of smart CCC, models are trying to give edge-to-edge connections between devices and have a sustainable communication between the command center and the city services. The best model only depends upon the geographical location and some of the sources available in a city. If the city is having multiple departments where complex operational costs must happen, then Fluentgrid model can help us to have the multipurpose ICCC. If the smart city is really having simple operations with no complex operations, CISCO model would help the city operations to run on a decent level of communications. If you need to connect more no of devices, you can opt either trinity or fluent-grid model city centers. There is the huge scope of data visualizations and data manipulation services in IBM services. Compared to all, trinity is a new emerging company which is initializing its models to provide more services over a low economic value. Authors would recommend to explore all the company model features and select accordingly using their geographical location and select a CCC model for a city.

4.4 CONCLUSION AND FUTURE SCOPE

Implementation of CCC with high infrastructure is a long-run trail. There is a large scope that Indian Command Centers would become automated for smart city maintenance. It is really a big concept of developing IoT infrastructure considering a whole city operation from bin collection to the government transactions. These models are further trained at the priority needs of the particular city. It will not only bring the advancement in the technological aspect but also the lifestyle would be improved and new way of living will be standardized in urban areas.

Further research on CCC models can be extended as to comparing our Indian models with other countries CCC models. The concept will keep on expanding along with the smart city development and in India, many other things should be considered for the development of a CCC. The further research can be on proposing a new type of CCC and apply the SWOT analysis which would get ready for a sprint and kick start in smart city development.

KEYWORDS

- **city command centers, CCC**
- **smart cities**
- **city command center**
- **IoT**
- **automation**
- **smart city mission**

REFERENCES

1. Smart Cities Mission. Ministry of Housing and Urban Affairs, Government of India [Online], http://smartcities.gov.in/content/innerpage/what-is-smart-city.php (accessed Jan 23, 2021).
2. Arasteh, H.; et al. In *Iot-Based Smart Cities: A Survey*, 2016 IEEE 16th International Conference on Environment and Electrical Engineering (EEEIC), Florence, 2016, pp. 1–6. doi: 10.1109/EEEIC.2016.7555867
3. Gharaibeh, A.; et al. Smart Cities: A Survey on Data Management, Security, and Enabling Technologies. *IEEE Commun. Surv. Tutor.* **2017,** *19* (4), 2456–2501.

4. Su, K.; Li, J.; Fu, H. In *Smart city and the applications*, 2011 International Conference on Electronics, Communications and Control (ICECC), Ningbo, 2011, pp. 1028–1031. doi: 10.1109/ICECC.2011.6066743.

5. Jin, J.; Gubbi, J.; Marusic, S.; Palaniswami, M. An Information Framework for Creating a Smart City Through Internet of Things. *IEEE Internet Things J.* **2014,** *1* (2), 112–121.

6. Novo, O. Blockchain Meets IoT: An Architecture for Scalable Access Management in IoT. *IEEE Internet Things J.* **2018,** *5* (2), 1184–1195.

7. Software Group. Industry Solutions Division. *IBM Intelligent Operations Center for Smarter Cities* [Online]. https://www.ibm.com/downloads/cas/EMJY7VY4 (accessed Jan 23, 2021).

8. Trinity ICCC (Integrated Command & Control Center). Smart City Digital Platform [Online], https://www.trinitymobility.com/files/trinityICCC-Brochure.pdf (accessed Jan 23, 2021).

9. Smart Solutions for Sustainable Smart Cities. Fluentgrid Actilligence [Online], https://fluentgrid.com/wp-content/uploads/2020/10/Fluentgrid-Actilligence-Datasheet.pdf (accessed Jan 23, 2021).

10. Cisco Smart + Connected City Operations Center. Unified Management for City Infrastructure [Online], https://www.cisco.com/c/dam/en_us/solutions/industries/docs/scc/scc-city-operations-center-aag.pdf (accessed Jan 23, 2021).

CHAPTER 5

Design of a Vehicle Pollution Detection System Using IoT

AKSHI GOSWAMI, PARUL TOMAR, and SAPNA GAMBHIR

Department of Computer Engineering, J.C. Bose University of Science & Technology, YMCA, Faridabad, India

ABSTRACT

In this modernized world, where there is unstoppable development going on at a fast pace, the onset of various problems started as well. One of such problems is pollution that is acting as a slow poison to every living or nonliving things in the ecosystem. There are many reasons for the air pollution and one of the reasons for pollution is from the emissions of the vehicles. The main aim of the work is to establish a system that would help to put the situation under control with minimum chances of any fraud or any other issue with the help of Internet of Things and other underlying technologies.

5.1 INTRODUCTION

Everything which is surrounding us is called as our environment. Environment constitutes of everything around including air, the water, the ecosystem which supports life. Not only environment but environment which is clean in quality is required or necessary for a prosperous and healthy life or society. Each and every species depends on environment for survival and hence gets

---

Computational Intelligence in Analytics and Information Systems, Volume 2: Advances in Digital Transformation, Selected Papers from CIAIS-2021. Parneeta Dhaliwal, PhD, Manpreet Kaur, PhD, Hardeo Kumar Thakur, PhD, Rajeev Kumar Arya, and Joan Lu (Eds.)

affected by the quality or condition of the environment deeply. The clean environment decides whether an ecosystem is healthy or not. The pollution of environment is contamination by pollutants that may directly or indirectly be produced by humans and that degrades the quality of environment and thus affects the ecosystem.

Air pollution caused by automobiles is one of the hazardous challenges that continue to provide harm to the environment. Automobiles are one of the greatest inventions which have helped to make the life easier but excess use of anything is not good. The vehicular pollution may result either from evaporative emissions, refueling losses, or exhaust emissions. The fumes resulting from exhaust emissions are one of the key constituents. The composition is a mixture of gasses like carbon dioxide, carbon monoxide, and oxides of nitrogen. The government of our country has taken many actions to take the situation in control. There is a certificate called Pollution Under Control (PUC) certificate in India which is mandatory for every vehicle and that indicates the vehicle is producing the emission which is under the safe zone and thus the vehicle is allowed to be used.

Although the government has made many rules and regulations for controlling the vehicular pollution but still there are some loopholes. There are many problems associated with the PUC certificate. For example, lack of continuous monitoring at self and centralized levels.

This paper is presenting a solution to the above-said problem by making an IoT-based solution for continuous monitoring of vehicular pollution.

5.2   LITERATURE REVIEW

5.2.1   INTERNET OF THINGS (IOT) FOR ENVIRONMENT

The Internet of Things (IoT) is a recent communication paradigm that shows the near future, in this, the objects of daily life will be equipped with micro-controllers, mobile communication transmitters, and suitable protocols that will make possible the interconnection with other devices and with users will undoubtedly become an important part of the new age of the Internet. What practically imagine with the IoT is to make the internet more penetrating in terms of its use with objects not currently related to the network. In the current cities and their environment today, the existence of many deficiencies (pollution, fire accidents, industrial accidents) can be seen, which can be reduced with the use of technology, in this case with the implementation of this paradigm, that of IoT, it is possible to make spaces of the city to become aware, to integrate these spaces in the way their citizens relate to it. A safe city is characterized by the use of information and communication technology infrastructure (ICT),[7] human resources, social capital, and industrial resources for economic development, social or environmental sustainability, and high quality of human life. From this point of view, the flow of information to keep the population updated would be the ideal of an organized society. The development brings with it some drawbacks, which if not properly managed can make life in cities unsustainable.

IoT is one of the technology[6] that has results which are inevitable result in nature in the area of development of computer science and the underlying technology. It aims in serving humanity in various forms, such as virtual reality equipment, environmental monitoring equipment, and so on. IoT helps in achieving the complete functionality of a service or a product with minimum or no human intervention or interference.

5.2.2 AIR POLLUTION

Air pollution is also one of the major environmental issues which has been ignored but should be dealt carefully so that there is a permanent solution for it. It has not only harmful effects for the humans but also for the economy of a country. There are many reasons that have contribution in the rise of air pollution, such as urbanization, vehicular emissions, or industrial emissions and a conclusion can be made that the careless utilization of resources of nature is the main source of air pollution.

According to a study, Ghaziabad (India), Hotan (China), and Gujranwal (Pakistan) are the three most polluted cities in the world. On the basis of PM2.5 readings that refer to particulate substances having a diameter less than 2.5 micrometers, it is can be observed that six out of them are the cities which are in India. Therefore, the picture of India in terms of pollution is not very good and creates an alarming situation.

The automobile sector is one of the sectors that have a prominent role in the development of India and its economy. But, it is also one of the reasons that have polluted the air. Taking reference from the past, with the increase in number of vehicles, there is a tremendous decrease in the quality of air.[8,9] Government has taken many actions in order to control the situation but considering the situation in India which represents the cities that are most polluted worldwide in 2019, an observation can be made that all steps that have been taken for solving the problem of air pollution are not sufficient enough.

5.2.2.1   VEHICULAR POLLUTANTS

Various emissions such as carbon monoxide, hydrocarbons, and oxides of nitrogen are the pollutants that are released by vehicles which form the area of concern. Tables 5.1–5.3 show summarized effects of these pollutants on nature and humans. This means that the pollutants affect not only the environment but also living organisms directly or indirectly in one or some other way.

TABLE 5.1   Health Effects from Pollutants.[10]

Pollutants	Health Effects	
	Direct	**Indirect**
CO	Yes	No
HC	Yes	Yes
NOx	Yes	Yes
PM	Yes	No
SOx	Yes	No

TABLE 5.2   Environmental Effects from Pollutants.[11]

Pollutants	Environmental Effects		
	Acid Rain	**Eutrophication**	**Visibility**
CO	Yes	No	No
HC	Yes	Yes	No
NOx	Yes	Yes	Yes
PM	Yes	No	Yes
SOx	Yes	No	Yes

TABLE 5.3   Climatic Effects from Pollutants.

Pollutants	Climate change	
	Direct	**Indirect**
CO	No	Yes
HC	No	Yes
NOx	Yes	No
PM	Yes	No
SOx	No	Yes

Automobiles or vehicles can also be referred to as polluters that are mobile in nature. Among all the vehicles, vehicles for which petrol is used as fuel are the most polluting. The amount of rate of emissions is highest during idling of motor, and lowering of speeds (Table 5.4) which generally occur at the intersection of roads, for instance at the traffic light and at turns that are sharp in cities tends to slow down the speed and traffic and put an increase in the pollution rates. These actions tend to bring an increase in the emission of gasses hydrocarbons and carbon monoxide.

TABLE 5.4   Contribution of Car Actions to Pollution.

S. No.	Operating Mode	Hydrocarbons	NO	CO
1	Idling	High	Low	Very High
2	Uniform Speed	Minimum	Minimum	Minimum
3	Deceleration	High	Very Low	Very High
4	High speed	Very low	Very High	Very low
5	Acceleration	Low	High	Low
6	Low speed	Moderate	Low	Moderate

Air pollution is one of the issues which cannot be ignored and still it is not too late to take action for solving the situation. In order to control the vehicular air pollution, various steps have been taken which are to be followed by every vehicle owner in India. These steps involve embarkation of money to increase strictness in order to reduce chances of negligence. Their main aim is to improve the situation of air pollution by vehicles or automobiles. These steps are as follows:

- In India, there is a rule which states that no vehicle is allowed to be used if it is being used for more than 15 years. Since, the older a vehicle gets, the more chances are there for an increase in harmful gases.
- System of public transport has been augmented.
- Increase in strictness that affects supply of vehicles.
- Strictness is traffic management and policies
- Increase in the taxes regarding automobile and fuels.
- Increase in strictness of usage of quality of fuel.
- Spreading awareness about the usage of alternative fuels which produce less emission.
- Adulteration of fuel is curbed
- Increase in inspection of vehicles that is random in nature.

- Strengthening the monitoring of pollutants.
- Use of technology to improve the methods of controlling and monitoring.
- Spreading of awareness regarding air pollution
- Formulation of air monitoring strategy
- Usage of modern and economic equipment for checking the emission from vehicles.
- Segregation of lane for emergency vehicles and cycles
- To increase the usage of pollution-free vehicles.

5.2.2.2   PUC LAW

PUC certificate is the short form of Pollution Under Control certificate. This is a legal certificate that is issued to a vehicle only after getting and clearing a test. The certificate indicates that a vehicle is allowed to be used on the roads in India. It has readings about the emissions from the vehicles. It also suggests that a vehicle after clearing PUC procedures has emissions in alignment with the standard set by pollution Monitoring units. It is valid for only 1 year when the vehicle is new and after that, the certificate has to be renewed.

TABLE 5.5   Thresholds.

S. No.	Vehicle Type	CO (in percentage)	Hydrocarbon (in ppm)
1	2 and 3 wheelers (e stroke) that are manufactured on and before 31st March 2000	4.5	9000
2	2 and 3 wheelers (2 stroke) that are manufactured on and after 31st March 2000	3.5	6000
3	2 nad 3 wheelers (4-stroke) that are manufactured on and after 31st March 2000	3.5	4500
4	4 wheelers before BS II norms	3	1500
5	4 wheelers before subsequent norms	0.5	750

Table 5.5[12] shows the allowed value of emissions from different vehicles. The PUC certificate gives information about the following details:

Serial number of certificate.
License plate number of vehicle.

Date in which test has been conducted.

Date after which the certificate will become invalid.

Readings of the emissions from vehicles

The test for PUC certificate is conducted on petrol pumps and by testing centers that are independent in nature. This certificate needs to be present with the driver of vehicle whenever the vehicle is on the roads. This will be asked by policemen whose inspection is random in nature, and during this time, the driver has to provide the certificate otherwise strict actions will be imposed on driver. The PUC certificated must be renewed that depends on the expiry date of the certificate otherwise the penalty will be imposed on the driver. The expiry of certificate varies from state to state in India. Some states have validity up to 6 months and some validity of 3 months.

The PUC certificate aims to provide a legal document that would be able to justify the alignment of the levels of pollutants from the vehicles with the thresholds set by the government. But, this system has got some issues that need to be improvised. These are as follows:

- **Pollution Under Control (PUC) Certificate**

All vehicles in India are mandated to have a valid PUC certification which indicates that the vehicle's emissions are in alignment with standard pollution norms and are not harmful to the environment. They must be shown when asked by authorized officer, and if in case there is some issue then they are subjected to legal actions. But, there are certain issues related to PUC. By the usage of the present application of PUC, self-monitoring cannot be done. There are higher chances of fraud with the present system. They are only valid for a certain period of time and after that, one has to go to the authorized place to get the certificate. Factors such as time consuming and paper wastage are also there.

- **Centralized Monitoring**

Taking the present scenario into consideration, there is no way of centralized monitoring of emission of gases of the vehicles. The PUC certificate is checked by traffic polices officers randomly and chances of fraud are there. This is the demand of time because it helps in keeping an eye on the industries and helps in knowing the location of the industry which may not be working properly.

- **Use of Green Technology**

In this modern era, development is happening in almost every field. A technology forms the base of development. Almost every day, some technologies become old and are not effective for usage and some new technologies come into the play with exciting features which try to aim for certain optimization in certain field. But, taking into the consideration of present scenario of the environment, this modernization hinders the future of whole ecosystem as development in any field demands for resources and which in turn come from environment in one or another form. Development is good for a society only when it is sustainable in nature, that is, it is able to make changes to society by fulfilling all the promises but in such a way that it does not produce negative impact to the environment and helps in saving the environment for future. So, we need greener technology for the society. Greener means, it itself does not degrade the quality of environment and also helps in improving the condition of ecosystem by providing certain methods of controlling or monitoring or both.

5.3   PROPOSED WORK

The careful study of the environment and problems that have happened to due to air pollution from vehicles helps in stating a point that a solution with strict implementation is the need of the hour. Any technology that is green in nature can be used for improving the scenario and IoT is one such technology as it does not further produce pollution.

The problems related to the existing methods that aim to provide control and monitoring of the pollution from the vehicles help to build a path for providing solutions for the same with the help of IoT. The proposed work focuses on:

- To reduce the chances of fraud that may arise with the usage of PUC system.
- To implement centralized monitoring which helps in proper management.
- To implement and build and IoT environment which aims at controlling and self-monitoring of the emission of gasses by different industries.

5.3.1 PHASES OF THE PROPOSED SYSTEM

The model of the proposed system consists of various phases that help to study the working. The working of proposed starts by setting up of the system or devices in the vehicle. After the device is set up with the availability of WiFi, thresholds for different emissions are set up in accordance with the governmental rules. When the vehicle starts, the phase of sensing of emission, that is, data sensing starts. After monitoring, data analysis is carried on which helps to determine the actions. Figure 5.1 shows the phases involved in the proposed system.

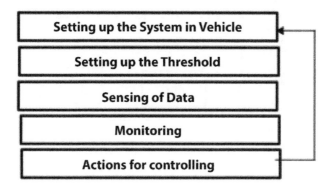

FIGURE 5.1 Model of proposed system.

5.3.2 BLOCK DIAGRAM AND WORKING OF PROPOSED SYSTEM

The flow or working of the system can be seen as shown in Figure 5.2 when the set-up of the system is done on a vehicle, the sensors would sense the data and collect them for further phase as soon as the vehicle starts moving. The values that are resulted from the sensors may be of analog in nature and needs to be converted to the digital one because raspberry Pi requires digital signal, and for the purpose analog to digital converter would be used. The value needs to converted to one of the SI units and in the proposed work the value is being converted to parts per million. All the data need not be sent to the centralized authority for analysis as there might be the condition where the vehicle might not be producing emissions beyond the thresholds and thus the average of a day needs to be calculated. The average of the data from every sensor is taken and has to be transferred for further monitoring. At the central level, during the monitoring phase if the data are reflecting that there is some problem with the vehicle or the emissions are crossing the threshold for a fixed interval of time, then the vehicle is the defaulter and subjected to strict actions, otherwise the vehicle is not a defaulter and then the movement of the vehicle is checked, if the vehicle is still moving, the whole process has to be started again as there is a continuous monitoring, but if the vehicle has stopped then the process is stopped.

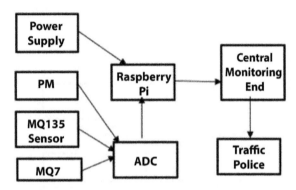

FIGURE 5.2   Block diagram.

5.4   CONCLUSION

Development in any society in any form is welcome and is necessary because it is good to move with an intension to make the life easier and better in terms of quality of living. But, development at the cost of environment is not needed or it can be stated the development should be sustainable in nature, that is, to make development in such a way that the operations involved in the procedure should not harm the quality of environment in any way at present and future. The condition of India at present is not good in terms of healthy living. Many statistics are there which suggest that pollution levels in India are very high.

The design of vehicle pollution detection system using IoT intends to work with the same intention of improving the condition of the environment and to put build a mechanism that will put a control and will monitor the levels of emissions from the vehicles. Different technologies have been used to build a POC for the same. The system works by taking the values of emissions from the vehicles and comparing it with the standard set by the government and passing the information to the traffic police if the levels are continuously reaming the same for a fixed interval of time. Therefore, this system is used to carry out the controlling and monitoring operations.

KEYWORDS

- **IoT**
- **air pollution**
- **sensors**
- **pollution control**
- **pollution monitoring system**

REFERENCES

1. Gubbi, J.; Buyya, R.; Marusic, S.; Palaniswami, M. Internet of Things (Iot): A Vision, Architectural Elements, and Future Directions. *Future Generation Comp. Syst.* **2013,** *29* (7), 1645–1660.
2. Xu L. D.; He W.; Li S. Internet of Things in Industries: A Survey. *IEEE Trans. Industr. Inform.* 2014, *10* (4), 2233–2243.
3. Balamurugan, S; Saravanakamalam, D. In *Energy Monitoring and Management Using Internet of Things*, Proceedings of the International Conference on Power and Embedded Drive Control (ICPEDC), Chennai, 2017; pp. 208–212.
4. Mohod, S. W.; Deshmukh, R. S. Internet of Things for Industrial Monitoring and Control Applications. *Int. J. Sci. Eng. Res.* **2016,** *7* (2).
5. Ahluwalia, I. J. *Industrial Growth in India: Stagnation since the Mid-Sixties*; Oxford University Press, 1985.
6. Zanella, A.; Bui, N.; Castellani, A.; Vangelista, L.; Zorzi, M. Internet of Things for Smart Cities. *IEEE Internet Things J.* **2014,** *1* (1), 22–32.
7. Monzon, A. In *Smart Cities Concept and Challenges: Bases for the Assessment of Smart City Projects*, International Conference on Smart Cities and Green ICT Systems (SMARTGREENS), 2015; pp. 1–11, May 2015.
8. Bhatnagar, A.; Sharma, V.; Raj, J. In *Iot based Car Pollution Detection Using AWS*, 2018 International Conference on Advances in Computing and Communication Engineering (ICACCE-2018) Paris, France, 22–23 June 2018.
9. Jenifer; Aravindhar, D. J. In *IoT Based Air Pollution Monitoring System Using ESP8266-12 With Google Firebase*, International Conference on Physics and Photonics Processes in Nano Sciences, Journal of Physics: Conference Series, 1362, 2019, 012072.
10. https://www.niehs.nih.gov/health/topics/agents/air-pollution/index.cfm
11. Manisalidis, I.; Stavropoulou, E.; Stavropoulos, A.; Bezirtzoglou, E. Environmental and Health Impacts of Air Pollution: A Review. https://www.ncbi.nlm.nih.gov/pmc/articles/PMC7044178/
12. https://www.coverfox.com/car-insurance/articles/puc-certificate-law-in-india/

CHAPTER 6

Fog Computing: The Next Generation Computing Paradigm

SAPNA GAMBHIR, PARUL TOMAR, and PARKHI JAIN

Department of Computer Engineering, J.C. Bose University of Science & Technology, YMCA, Faridabad, India

ABSTRACT

In the coming years, so much data will be produced by IoT devices as usage of IoT devices is increasing. So, it becomes very difficult for the cloud to handle that amount of data day by day produced from edge devices and it faces problems of bandwidth, storage, processing due to which there will be latency in the response. To deal with these problems, a new computing paradigm is introduced by CISCO, that is, fog computing helps to make a bridge between cloud and the IoT devices. The objective is to find out solutions of those problems that are faced by cloud during IoT data processing. Fog just complements cloud as we need both cloud and fog to handle the data that arises from IoT devices. So, in this paper, comparison analysis of cloud and fog computing is done along with details of each concept.

6.1 INTRODUCTION

Nowadays everyone is becoming dependent on digital devices such as computers, mobile phones, all smart devices, etc., in order to make their

Computational Intelligence in Analytics and Information Systems, Volume 2: Advances in Digital Transformation, Selected Papers from CIAIS-2021. Parneeta Dhaliwal, PhD, Manpreet Kaur, PhD, Hardeo Kumar Thakur, PhD, Rajeev Kumar Arya, and Joan Lu (Eds.)

life more comfortable. The data from these devices generate a huge amount of data on regularly that is produced by sensors and different applications.[1] These data that are generated from IoT devices have increased exceedingly. To handle these data, organizations wish to have a dynamic IT platform because of the change in cloud computing due to its accessibility, scalability, and pay-per-use features. The common services that are provided by the cloud are software as a service (SaaS), platform as a service (PaaS), and infrastructure as a service (IaaS), all of which are heading toward anything as a service (XaaS).[2] However, this big data (data generated from billions of sensors), at one stage cannot be transmitted and refined at the cloud layer. Also, some of the data need to be processed faster as compared to cloud's current potential as this type of data requires an instant response. To get a solution to this problem, fog computing is introduced, through which the processing power of devices located closer to client is tackled to guide processing, correct utilization of space for storage, and networking at the edge.[3] The flow of this paper is organized as follows: Section 6.2 describes the introductory part of cloud computing along with detailed explanation cloud service models and cloud deployment models. Section 6.3 discusses the definition of fog computing, discusses the characteristics, working of fog, and the application areas which motivate to do research on fog computing. Section 6.4 basically presents a comparison table between cloud computing and the fog computing environment. Section 6.5 presents the open challenges that are faced by fog and are not present in the cloud computing paradigm. Section 6.6 concludes the overall paper.

6.2   OVERVIEW OF CLOUD COMPUTING

Cloud computing[4] is an arising technology in the IT world where information and resources both hardware and software[5] are provided on demand. It is internet computing where resources are maintained using network and remote servers. Cloud computing is a new software technology, which allows resource provisioning dynamically, on various resources using different techniques like parallel computation,[6] distributed computing,[7] and the virtualization.[8] Cloud computing is more popular among business and research areas due it advantageous properties of easy software deployment and elasticity[9] to generate more resources using virtualization. The flexibility of cloud computing compels the businesses of all types to migrate on cloud. As the demand of the cloud is increasing exponentially, the service providers[10] are also increasing and provide services at reasonable costs. Cloud computing wants to provide the computational services[4] the world from personal computers, laptops to the internet, that is, movable computation. Cloud provides its users the secure services over the internet which is not even accessed by service providers. Cloud computing model is referred as "pay-per-use model[11]" because users have to pay only for resources that they use. Implementation of virtualization in cloud computing where a single physical system can be divided into defined number of virtual systems which are software implementation. When a request is received by user, load balancer helps in taking decision of which user will use which virtual machine (VM) and which VMs will wait. Virtualization technology helps in dynamically balancing the load where VMs and hardware resources are generated according to the user's requirements and load change. Virtualization technology is most commonly implemented in cloud computing and it gave pace to cloud computing. There are many roadblocks that needs to be handled like scalability, throughput, availability, relocation of VMs,[12] fault tolerance,[13] among all these challenges load balancing raised as the main challenge. It is the process of balancing (distributing) the load among various VMs in a centralized or distributed data centers to minimize overhead and resource utilization ratio[14] and also to avoid the problem of overload and underload, that is, no VM is idle or overutilized.

6.2.1 CLOUD SERVICE MODELS

Reference models on which cloud computing is based:

- Infrastructure as a service (IaaS): It is the delivery of infrastructure as an on demand scalable service. It provides access of fundamental resources such as physical machine, VM, virtual storage, etc. Examples of IaaS are Amazon Web Services, Cisco Metapod, Microsoft Azure, Google Compute Engine.[7]
- Platform as a service (PaaS): This model is mostly used by developers as it provides runtime environment for applications, development and deployment tools, etc. It provides all the facilities required to assist user throughout the life cycle of applications/services development entirely on the internet. In this model, application and data are managed by the consumer, and everything else (O.S., storage virtualization, etc.) is managed by the cloud provider. Some examples of PaaS are Heroku, Google App Engine, and Red Hat's OpenShift.

- Software as a service (SaaS): This model provides consumers with applications and software he/she willing to use. Consumer is only concerned with the application/software he/she willing to use (and nothing else like O.S., infrastructure, etc.) and use them over the internet instead of buying it. Examples of SaaS can be Google Apps, Dropbox, Salesforce, Cisco WebEx, Concur, and GoToMeeting.

6.2.2   CLOUD DEPLOYMENT MODELS

There are three types of deployment models in the cloud environment, which are as follows:

- Public cloud: In this deployment model, cloud services are openly available to anyone. It allows systems and services to be easily accessible to the general public. Due to its openness, this deployment model is less secure (compared to other deployment models), for example, e-mail. Vendors that provide public cloud services offer many benefits to the cloud users, such as, no initial investment on basic infrastructure, transferring the risk of failure of infrastructure from user to provider. Public cloud users have less control on the data, security settings, network, etc.
- Private cloud: The private cloud refers to internal data centers for a business or any organization and is not made available to the common public. It allows systems and services to be accessible within an organization only. It has increased security due to its private nature. Although a public cloud gives the benefit of decreased capital investment and good speed of deployment, private clouds are more popular at enterprises level. A survey in IDG exposed that cloud providers give preimplemented infrastructure of private cloud to vendors, which results in less total expenditure. Loads are more predictable and controlled in a private cloud, if compared with public cloud.
- Community cloud: This deployment model is similar to private cloud model. Only difference is that it allows access of system and services to multiple organizations or a group of organizations. This kind of cloud infrastructure is used by community of users from organizations that have similar goals.[15]
- Hybrid cloud: A hybrid cloud is a mix of private and public cloud that attempts to address the drawbacks of each technique. The important operations are handled by the private cloud while the noncritical tasks

are handled by the public cloud. Part of the service infrastructure runs in a private cloud while the rest runs on public clouds. Hybrid cloud gives more flexibility than other cloud models. These provide more control and security on applications data compared to the public clouds while facilitating service which is on-demand expandable and contracted.[16]

6.3   OVERVIEW OF FOG COMPUTING

Fog computing is normally combined with cloud computing and is a newest decentralized computing paradigm.[17,18] Fog computing is defined as a distributed computing infrastructure that extends cloud computing's computational functions to the network's edge. It[19] is introduced by CISCO which represents a new model of computing that can transform a network edge into a distributed computing infrastructure capable of implementing IoT applications. It mainly focuses on the extension of cloud services nearer to IoT devices that produce and consume high amount of data daily, aim to fasten the processing speed, and which in turn, make storage resources closer to users. Main problem that we are facing in cloud computing is the problem of latency, storage, and processing as by the time passes all the edge devices send their data to cloud so it is very obvious that we will face these problems for sure. So, we have to find something better than cloud which is fog. The fog layer serves as a bridge between the cloud and the gadgets. The general architecture of fog computing is shown in Figure 6.1.

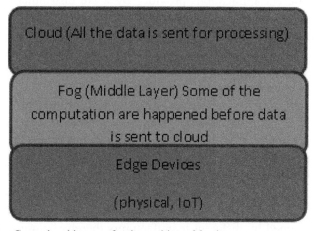

FIGURE 6.1   General architecture for the position of fog layer.

Rather to push all the data to cloud for processing, fog computing aims to handle some of the workloads produced by devices that are close to users, which are known as fog servers or fog nodes. Each fog node has its own aggregated fog node and can be deployed anywhere inside the network that has network connectivity (ability to connect directly with IoT devices, via other fog nodes, and via cloud). Fog nodes have computing, storage, and networking capabilities: controllers, switches, routers, embedded servers, surveillance cameras, etc. By placing resources closer to the edge of the network, the time becomes negligible for the data to reach the processing station.

6.3.1   *CHARACTERISTICS OF FOG COMPUTING*

However, fog computing is an expanded paradigm of cloud computing but closer to IoT devices. As shown in Figure 6.1, fog computing serves as a bridge between the cloud and IoT devices, bringing processing, storage, and networking functions closer to fog nodes. These fog nodes can be found across a network. Fog nodes can be industrial controls, switches, routers, embedded servers, and video surveillance cameras since they include computation, storage, and network connection.[20,21] The characteristics of fog computing are as follows:

- Location awareness and low latency: As fog nodes are deployed anywhere in the network at different locations, fog computing supports location awareness. Also, it has the capability to solve latency problem by bringing fog closer to IoT devices.
- Geographical distribution: As in fog computing, all the services and different applications provided by it are distributed and can be deployed anywhere, it supports geographical distribution which is in contrast to cloud computing.
- Scalability: Fog computing provides distributed computing as there are various large-scale sensor networks. So, fog computing provides storage resources to those large-scale end devices.
- Mobility support: One of the most significant features of fog applications is the ability to connect directly to mobile devices and therefore enable mobility techniques, which necessitate the use of a distributed directory system.
- Real-time interactions: Rather than batch processing in the cloud, fog computing applications enable real-time interactions between fog nodes.
- Heterogeneity: There are so many fog nodes and IoT devices that are designed by different manufacturers thereby coming in different

forms and need to be deployed accordingly. Thus, fog computing has the ability to work properly in different platforms.

- Interoperability: Fog components may communicate with one other and work across domains and service providers.
- Support for online analytics and cloud integration: The fog is positioned between the cloud and the end devices to aid in the absorption and processing of data near to the devices.
- Save storage space: Fog computing is a fantastic way to keep unsuitable or irrelevant data from reaching the general network, which saves space and decreases latency

6.3.2 WORKING OF FOG

As there are three types of data depicted in Figure 6.2, that is, firstly, very time-sensitive data (data that should be analyzed within fractions of second). It is analyzed at nearest node itself and sends the response to devices means it has capability to response faster. Secondly, we have less time-sensitive data (data that can be analyzed after seconds or minutes). It is analyzed and sent to aggregated nodes. After analyses, aggregated nodes send response to devices through the nearest node. Thirdly, we have not time-sensitive data (data that can be wait for hours, days, or weeks). It is sent to the cloud for storage and future analysis. So, fog nodes work according to the type of data they receive. Therefore, an IoT application should be installed to each fog node to handle these types of data.

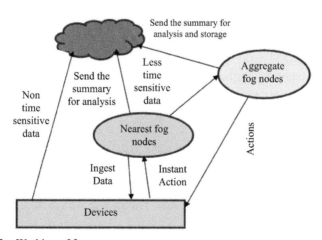

FIGURE 6.2   Working of fog.

Fog computing offers advantages such as security, low operational cost reduces unwanted accidents, better privacy, supports mobility, better data handling, deployable in remote places, etc., and also has some of the drawbacks such as power consumption, data security, reliability, fault tolerance, and programming architecture.

6.3.3   APPLICATION AREAS OF FOG COMPUTING

There are various application areas of fog computing environment discussed below:

- Smart traffic lights: When an ambulance passes through, video camera presents automatically change street lights after seeing ambulance flashing lights. The main idea behind smart aggregate fog nodes nearest fog nodes devices traffic lights is that these lights interact with sensor locally and detect the presence of bikers, motor cars, and the pedestrians, also measures the distance and speed of the vehicle passes by. WiFi, 3G, road-side units, and smart traffic lights are deployed along the roads.
- Connected car: Connected cars are the latest trend that is approaching day by day. Connected car means which as inbuilt software that has automatic steering and does hands-free operations.
- Smart grids: Smart grid is another well-known fog computing application. These smart gadgets may switch to alternative energies such as solar and wind based on energy need, ability, and cheap cost. The fog collection data are processed at the edge, and control commands are sent to the actuators.
- The filtered data are consumed locally, with the remaining data being sent to higher tiers for visualization, real-time reporting, and transactional analytics. At the highest layer, fog enables semi-permanent storage while at the lowest rung, it supports temporary storage.
- Self-maintaining train: Another use of fog computing is self-maintenance trains. Trains that are self-maintaining include temperature sensors that immediately warn the train operator if a problem arises. As a result, calamities and accidents may be prevented with ease.

6.4 COMPARISON ANALYSIS BETWEEN CLOUD AND FOG COMPUTING

If we compare fog computing with cloud computing, as shown in Table 6.1, then fog computing consists of fog clusters where there are multiple fog devices that participate actively and helps in fast processing. Whereas in cloud computing data center plays a vital role. Due to which in cloud computing, operational cost and energy consumption are high as compared to fog computing. Fog computing architecture illustrates that fog is nearer to IoT devices or end-users so the distance between them could be one or a few hops, which is also agreed by Hu et al.[22] But in cloud, distance between users and cloud is very high that is of multiple hops. Due to this distance, communication latency is proved to be high in the cloud as compared to fog. Cloud computing is centralized whereas fog is distributed.[23]

Due to high latency in cloud, real-time interaction is not possible that can be solved by fog very easily. On the other hand, the rate of failure in the fog is high because of wireless connectivity, decentralized management, and power failure.[23–26] Most of the devices in fog are connected wirelessly thinking of future.[27] Due to device failure in fog, users are not aware of malicious software. Comparison table shows that some of the parameters of cloud and fog are the same,[28–30] whereas other parameters show that fog computing gives better and advance benefits than cloud computing.[31–33]

TABLE 6.1 Comparison between Cloud and Fog Computing.

Parameters	Cloud computing	Fog computing
Goal	Give a request of greatness change in the practical, powerful provisioning of IT administrations	Enhance proficiency and execution of process that should be transported to the cloud for handling, investigation, and storage
Abstraction level	High	High
Bandwidth	Preserves less bandwidth	High bandwidth
Client and server distance	Multiple hops	Single hop
Computational cost	High	Low
Future	Fog Computing	Next generation of Internet and computing
Latency	High	Low
Location awareness	No	Yes

TABLE 6.1   *(Continued)*

Parameters	Cloud computing	Fog computing
Management	Centralized and contains large amount of data around globe	Scattered and contain several small nodes and bring closer to end devices
Nature of failure	Predictable	Highly diverse
Node mobility	Very low	High
Ownership	Single	Multiple
Power consumption	High	Low
Response time	Low	Fast
Resource	Unlimited	Limited
Security	Less secure, undefined	More secure and can be defined
Security measures	Defined	Hard to define
Server nodes location	Within network	At the edge of local network
Storage capacity	High	Low
Transmission	Device to cloud	Device to device

6.5   CHALLENGES OF FOG DIFFERENT THAN THAT OF CLOUD

There are various challenges that fog computing environment other than cloud computing environment, as discussed below:

- Authentication and trust issues: Because fog computing services are provided on a wide scale, authentication is one of the most prominent challenges. Different parties, such as cloud service providers, internet service providers, and end-users, who are essentially fog service providers may be involved. This further complicates the fogs overall structure and trust issue.
- Privacy: As fog computing consists of several fog nodes that are deployed anywhere in the network. So, when there are many networks involved in a system, there will always a privacy issue.
- Security: Fog computing for security because there are so many devices connected to fog nodes and at different gateways security issues arise. Each device has a unique IP address, and any hacker may impersonate your IP address in order to obtain access to your personal data contained in that fog node.

- Fog servers: It is critical to put fog servers in the appropriate places so that you can evaluate demand and work done by fog nodes and save money on maintenance.
- Energy consumption: Fog architecture has several fog nodes present in it. As these fog nodes consume huge amount of energy, so there is a need to consume energy in fog computing to make it more energy-efficient and save cost.

6.6 CONCLUSION

Based on the findings, we can infer that fog computing is a cloud extension with certain additional capabilities for service providers and end-users. In this chapter, we discuss the cloud computing concept and its limits, as well as the possible reasons for the emergence of fog computing. Fog computing outperforms cloud computing in the current environment of massive data and IoT. Fog computing has so far served as a support mechanism for existing cloud computing platforms. Fog computing will improve the quality of service for smart grid and connected car applications, as well as enable new service models in the future. At last, we made a comparison between both cloud and fog which conclude that fog computing can reduce problems that are in cloud computing and are a next-generation computing paradigm.

KEYWORDS

- **cloud computing**
- **fog computing**
- **intermediate**
- **overhead**
- **virtual machine**

REFERENCES

1. Assunção, M. D.; Calheiros, R. N.; Bianchi, S.; Netto, M. A.; Buyya, R. Big Data Computing and Clouds: Trends and Future Directions. *J. Parallel Distri. Comput.* **2015,** *79*, 3–15.
2. Alhaddadin, F.; Liu, W.; Gutiérrez, J. A. In *A User Profile-Aware Policy based Management Framework for Greening the Cloud*, Proceeding of the IEEE Fourth

International Conference on Big Data and Cloud Computing (Bdcloud), IEEE, pp. 682–687, 2014.

3. Dastjerdi, A. V.; Gupta, H.; Calheiros, R. N.; Ghosh, S. K.; Buyya, R. Fog Computing: Principles, Architectures, and Applications. In *Internet of Things: Principle & Paradigms*; Kaufmann, M., Ed.; USA, 2016.

4. https://en.wikipedia.org/wiki/cloud_computing

5. https://en.wikipedia.org/wiki/hardware_virtuali zation

6. Hu, J.; Gu, J.; Sun, G.; Tianhai Z. In *A Scheduling Strategy on Load Balancing of Virtual Machine Resources in Cloud Computing Environment*, Third International Symposium on Parallel Architectures, Algorithms and Programming (PAAP), 2010, IEEE, pp. 89–96, 2010.

7. https://www.sciencedirect.com/science/article/pi i/s1319157817303361

8. Tsygankov, M.; Chen, C. In *Network Aware VM Load Balancing in Cloud Data Centers Using SDN*, IEEE International Symposium on Local and Metropolitan Area Networks (LANMAN), 2017, IEEE, pp. 1–6, 2017.

9. Kumar, M.; Dubey, K.; Sharma, S. C. Elastic and Flexible Deadline Constraint Load Balancing Algorithm for Cloud Computing. *Procedia Comput. Sci.* **2018**, *125*, 717–724.

10. https://searchdatacenter.techtarget.com/definition/data-center

11. Chhabra, S.; Singh, A. K. A Probabilistic Model for Finding an Optimal Host Framework and Load Distribution in Cloud Environment. *Procedia Comput. Sci.* **2018**, *125*, 683–690.

12. Hu, J.; Gu, J.; Sun, G.; Zhao, T. In *A Scheduling Strategy on Load Balancing of Virtual Machine Resources in Cloud Computing Environment*, Third International Symposium on Parallel Architectures, Algorithms and Programming (PAAP), 2010, IEEE, pp. 89–96, 2010.

13. Kumar, M.; Dubey, K.; Sharma, S. C. In *Job Scheduling Algorithm in Cloud Environment Considering the Priority and Cost of Job*, Proceedings of Sixth International Conference on Soft Computing for Problem Solving. Springer: Singapore, 2017.

14. Kumar, M.; Sharma, S. C. Dynamic Load Balancing Algorithm to Minimize the Makespan Time and Utilize the Resources Effectively in Cloud Environment. *Int. J. Comput. Appl.* 2017, 1–10.

15. Lagwal, M.; Bhardwaj, N. In *Load Balancing in Cloud Computing using Genetic Algorithm.* International Conference on Intelligent Computing and Control Systems (ICICCS), 2017, IEEE, pp. 560–565, 2017.

16. Peng, J.; Tang, M.; Li, M.; Zha, Z. A Load Balancing Method for Massive Data Processing Under Cloud Computing Environment. *Intell. Autom. Soft. Comput.* **2017**, *23* (4), 547–553.

17. Mahmud, R.; Buyya, R. Fog Computing: A Taxonomy, Survey and Future Directions. In *Internet of Everything*; Springer, 2017.

18. Gao, L.; Luan, T. H.; Yu, S.; Zhou, W.; Liu, B. Fogroute: Dtn-Based Data Dissemination Model in Fog Computing. *IEEE Internet Things J.* **2017**, *4* (1), 225–235.

19. CISCO. *Fog Computing and the Internet of Things: Extend the Cloud to Where the Things are* [Online], Cisco White Paper; 2015. https://www.cisco.com/c/dam/en_us/solutions/trends/iot/docs/computing-overview.pdf (accessed Nov 25, 2018).

20. Verma, M.; Bhardwaj, N.; Yadav, A. K. Real Time Efficient Scheduling Algorithm for Load Balancing in Fog Computing Environment. *Int. J. Inf. Technol. Comput. Sci.* **2016**, *8*, 1–10.

21. CISCO. *Fog Computing and the Internet of Things: Extend the Cloud to Where the Things are*; White Paper; 2016. http://www.cisco.com/c/dam/en_us/solutions/trends/iot/docs/computing-overview.pdf (accessed April 8, 2018).

22. Hu, P.; Dhelim, S.; Ning, H.; Qiu, T. Survey on Fog Computing: Architecture, Key Technologies, Applications and Open Issues. *J. Network Comput. Appl.* **2017,** *98* (15), 27–42.

23. Mahmud, R.; Koch, F. L.; Buyya, R. In *Cloudfog Interoperability in Iot Enabled Health Care Solutions*, Proceedings of the 19th International Conference on Distributed Computing and Networking, Ser, ICDCN '18: New York, NY, USA: ACM, pp. 32:1–32:10, 2018.

24. Wang, Y.; Uehara, T.; Sasaki, R. In *Fog Computing: Issues and Challenges in Security and Forensics*, IEEE 39th Annual Computer Software and Applications Conference (COMPSAC), 2015, Vol. 3. IEEE, pp. 53–59, 2015.

25. Syed, M. H.; Fernandez, E. B.; Ilyas, M. In *A Pattern for Fog Computing*, Proceedings of the 10th Travelling Conference on Pattern Languages of Programs. ACM, p. 13, 2016.

26. Yi, S.; Hao, Z.; Qin, Z.; Li, Q. In *Fog Computing: Platform and Applications*, Third IEEE Workshop on Hot Topics in Web Systems and Technologies (Hotweb), 2015, IEEE, pp. 73–78, 2015.

27. Chiang, M.; Zhang, T. Fog and Iot: An Overview of Research Opportunities. *IEEE Internet Things J.* **2016,** 3 (6), 854–864,

28. Dijiang, H.; Wu, H. Mobile Cloud Computing: Foundations and Service Models. Morgan Kaufmann, 2017.

29. Mao, Y.; You, C.; Zhang, J.; Huang, K.; Letaief, K. B. A Survey on Mobile Edge Computing: The Communication Perspective. *IEEE Commun. Surv. Tutorials* **2017,** *19* (4), 2322–2358.

30. Laghari, A. A., He, H.; Karim, S.; Shah, H. A.; Karn, N. Kumar. Quality of Experience Assessment of Video Quality in Social Clouds. *Wirel. Commun. Mob. Comput.* **2017,** *2017*, 1–10.

31. Bonomi, F.; Milito, R.; Natarajan, P.; Zhu, J. Fog Computing: A Platform for Internet of Things and Analytics. In *Big Data and Internet of Things: A Roadmap for Smart Environments*; Springer: Cham, 2014; pp. 169–186.

32. Aazam, M.; Huh, E.-N. In *Fog Computing and Smart Gateway based Communication for Cloud of Things*, International Conference on In Future Internet of Things and Cloud (Ficloud), 2014, IEEE, pp. 464–470, 2014.

33. Aazam, M., Huh, E.-N. In *Fog Computing Micro Datacenter based Dynamic Resource Estimation and Pricing Model for Iot*, IEEE 29th International Conference on Advanced Information Networking and Applications (AINA), 2015, IEEE, IEEE, pp. 687–694, 2015.

CHAPTER 7

Logical Study of Predictions and Gathering Methodologies to Enhance Co-Clustering Formulation from a Period of Change Information in Machine Learning

GANESH GUPTA[1], VIVEK SHARMA[1], and TANUJ JOSHI[2]

[1]*Department of Computer Science and Engineering, G L Bajaj Institute of Technology and Management, Greater Noida, India*

[2]*Department of Mechanical Engineering, Amity University, Gurugram, India*

ABSTRACT

These days, AI is assuming an imperative function to remove and distinguish the helpful highlights that best speak to information in different fields, containing natural information examination, content mining, and social examinations. Customary bunching and highlighted choice approaches consider the data cross-section as static. Nonetheless, the data cross-sections advance effectively after some time in various applications. The unaided example mining, existing co-clustering methods consistently envision that the data cross-sections are static; that is, they do not create after some time. Nonetheless, in various genuine areas, the methodology that created the data are time creating. The scientific investigation centers around a transformative co-grouping definition for perceiving co-clusters from time-changing data that utilizes sparsity-inciting regularization to perceive block structures from

Computational Intelligence in Analytics and Information Systems, Volume 2: Advances in Digital Transformation, Selected Papers from CIAIS-2021. Parneeta Dhaliwal, PhD, Manpreet Kaur, PhD, Hardeo Kumar Thakur, PhD, Rajeev Kumar Arya, and Joan Lu (Eds.)

the time-changing data cross-sections in the article. The scientific investigation audits and studies the different forecasts and clustering procedures of AI with highlights and constraints to plan an effective and hearty method to settle ongoing issues.

7.1 INTRODUCTION

Machine learning is a platform, which brings statistics and computer science together to bind that predictive power. It has extraordinary expertise for all aspiring data analysts and scientists. Machine learning extracts and identifies useful landscapes that best signify your data, that is, machine learning algorithms. Co-clustering investigates applications in numerous zones, containing biological data analysis, content mining, and social investigations. Co-clustering objectives identify block structures of information lattices by clustering the columns and rows concurrently into co-clusters. The essential information can be more precisely depicted by a "checkerboard" edifice in which a subset of rows and columns structure a block.

Bunching or grouping means to find fundamental designs in information or records and mastermind them into indispensable subgroups for additional investigation and examination. Existing strategies covetously select the accompanying regular thing set that delineates the accompanying gathering to oblige the covering among the reports or information that involve both the thing set and some excess thing sets. As it were, the grouping or clustering outcome depends on the demand of grabbing the item sets, which in turn based on the avaricious heuristic. The technique does not take after a subsequent request of selecting groups or clusters.

Conventional clustering and selection of feature techniques consider information lattice as static. However, the information lattices advance easily after some time in numerous applications. An easy method to learn from information frameworks is to investigate them independently. The existing co-clustering techniques always imagine that the information lattices are static, that is, it does not develop after some time. However, in numerous real-world domains, the procedures that produced the information are time developing. However, in many realistic domains, the data-generating process involves lots of time. Hence, the observed data are frequently in a dynamic form.

The analytical study focuses on an evolutionary co-clustering formulation for recognizing co-clusters from dynamic information which pays sparsity-inducing regularization to distinguish block structures from dynamic information lattices. It also plans to develop temporal smoothness over the block structures recognized from measurements of the information lattices. The analytical study reviews and studies the various predictions and clustering methodologies of machine learning with features and limitations to design an efficient and robust technique to solve recent issues. The proposed study supports smooth changes in the row and column section designs over the long run, accordingly catching the time-developing nature of the hidden process reliably. The structure is entirely adaptable and can be applied to applications in which just one dimension of data metrics evolves. In numerous application areas, the information lattices advance over the long run, and consequently the data metrics at various time focuses are related to one another.

7.2 LITERATURE SURVEY

The author in[1] described the people by distinguishing their physical behavior. The feature gets extracted from the video samples by using histogram of gradient transform and then applies machine learning approach for classification and regression. The author in[2] used the face detection system to extract the images using the skin color model and then calculated eye direction using the subtraction method to control the application. The author in[3] proposed a novel generative co-clustering model that uses VMF distribution, by which the performance of the proposed model gets increased. The author in[22] proposed a Bayesian formulation of the VMF mixture for text data clustering. The author in[4] used the graph clustering method to learn multiple kernals. The low kernel and near to combined kernel improve the performance of the proposed model. To solve the data mining heterogeneous attribute the author in[5] proposed a cluster-based approach that considers a relationship to execute either dependent clustering or disparate clustering constraints. As per communication brought together the information-driven system is dependent on a reverse ideal vehicle that can learn versatile, nonlinear cooperation cost work from a loud and fragmented observational coordinating grid in different coordinating settings. The technique underscores that the discrete ideal vehicle assumes the part of a variety rule which offers ascend to an improvement-based system for displaying the noticed observational coordinating information. In[15] the author surveyed profound learning-based methodologies for the multi-modular clinical picture division task. First, it presented the overall guideline of profound learning and multi-modular clinical picture division.

In[6] the author explained the phantom grouping calculation dependent on a complex-esteemed lattice portrayal of digraphs. In[7] the author explained the equal projection strategy for metric-obliged improvement that permits them to accelerate the intermingling rate practically speaking. The way to approach is another equal execution plan that considers performing projections at different metric imperatives all the while with no contentions of factors. In[8] the author communicated double-coupling support vector machines (DC-SVM), for grouping them at the same time. DC-SVM considers the outside connections between different information transfers, while taking care of the inside relationship inside the individual information stream. In Ref. 9, the author learned about points (1) vigorous information recuperation, (2) powerful information moves, and (3) hearty information combination, jogged on a few significant applications. The framework examines about strong information move and combination given numerous datasets with various information streams. In[10] the author addressed a spatially compelled phantom bunching system for district depiction that joins the exchange between locale homogeneity and spatial contiguity. The system utilizes an adaptable, shortened dramatic part to address the spatial contiguity limitations, which is coordinated with the scene including likeness framework for area depiction.

In Refs. [12–16] versatile DPC calculation with Fisher straight separate for the grouping of complex datasets, called ADPC-FLD. The portion thickness assessment work is acquainted with figure the nearby thickness of the example focuses. In Refs. [17, 18] the authors portrayed the technique for separating essentialness territories and coordinating spatiotemporal highlights bunching. The spatial and fleeting dissemination examples of the metropolitan essentialness regions are found, and the driving variables of different imperativeness designs are examined by consolidating focal points (Pointing of Interest)-based land qualities. In[16,18-20] the authors communicated the dropout system into NMF and addressed a dropout NMF calculation. In particular, it plans a straightforward dropout technique that melds a dropout veil in the NMF structure to forestall/include co-transformation. In[21-25] the authors clarified an inadequate tensor calculation benchmark suite for single- and multi-center CPUs. It focuses on: (1) encouraging application clients to assess diverse PC frameworks utilizing its delegate computational outstanding burdens; (2) giving bits of knowledge to all the more likely use existing PC engineering. In Ref. [26, 27] the authors exploited for the old-style network stream detailing of MOT to characterize a completely differentiable structure dependent on Message Passing Networks (MPNs). By working straightforwardly on the diagram space, the strategy can reason all around the world over a whole arrangement of location and anticipate arrangements.

7.3   CURRENT APPROACHES

The section reviews and studies the various predictions and clustering methodologies of machine learning with features and limitations to design an efficient and robust technique to solve recent issues. There are various prediction methodologies that are discussed to extract and identify the useful features that best represent data from various biological data analysis, content mining, and social investigations where data clustering mechanisms can be hierarchical. Hierarchical methodologies discover progressive groups utilizing previously created clusters. Agglomerative algorithms start with every component as a different group and combine them into progressively bigger clusters. Disruptive methods start with the entire set and continue to split it into progressively smaller groups. Partitioned methodologies commonly discover all groups without a moment's delay. The co-grouping or bi-clustering are clustering techniques where the entities are grouped or clustered with the attributes of the entities.

7.3.1   KNN (K-NEAREST-NEIGHBOR) CLASSIFICATION

The website trained K-Nearest-Neighbor classification that recognized web clients/visitors click stream information, matching the web client to a specific web client group. It recommended a tailored browsing option that satisfied the requirement of the particular web document at the time of browsing.

7.3.2   DECISION TREE CLASSIFIER

Decision tree discussed issues in building a classifier and presented a new classifier called SLIQ (Supervised Learning in Quest). Decision trees are popular where it can be straightforwardly understood by humans and are efficient to build. Numerous decision tree algorithms contain in phases, that is, building phase followed by the pruning phase. The method is found in similarity to decision tree classifier that handles both the categorical and numeric attributes. The SLIQ integrated sorting procedure with a breadth-first tree of a growth strategy that enabled classification to disk-resident datasets. The combined techniques enabled SLIQ that scaled for large data sets and classified data sets irrespective of attributes classed and records that made it an attractive tool for data mining.

7.3.3   *HIERARCHICAL CLASSIFICATION*

Hierarchical classification is the method that assigns a few or several appropriate classes from a hierarchical category. The hierarchy of categories can be applied in all stages of automated document classification, namely, learning, classification, and feature extraction. It is a top to the down level-based arrangement that classified documents into both internal and leaf categories.

7.3.4   *SUPPORT VECTOR MACHINE CLASSIFIER*

Support Vector Machine Classifier Classification has a popular problem with several applications in a variety of areas, such as computer vision, bioinformatics, speech recognition, robotic control, marketing, drug discovery, and medical diagnosis. The Support Vector Machine (SVM) classifier such as two-class and one-class is discussed. The kernel method for the classification is a freshly established technique in the field of machine learning. The main theme is to separate the data just by drawing a separator among them and dividing them into two classes.

7.3.5   *PARTITIONED CLUSTERING*

A partitioned clustering methodology gets a single partition of the information. Partitioned approaches have benefits in an application, that is, high-volume data. An issue going with the utilization of a partitioned method is the decision of the number of necessary output groups or clusters.

7.3.6   *MIXTURE RESOLVING AND SEEKING METHOD*

The basic hypothesis that the patterns are grouped or clustered is drawn from one of a few allocations, and the objective is to recognize the constraints of each and their number. The Expectation-Maximization (EM) methodology is the recently utilized one.

7.3.7   K-MEANS CLUSTERING

The K-means algorithm allows every point to the group or cluster whose middle (centroid) is closest. The midpoint is the average of all considerable numbers of points in the group or cluster; that is, its directions are the arithmetic mean for every measurement independently over all the points in the group or cluster. The K-means algorithm weakness is that it does not yield a similar outcome with every run because of the subsequent groups or clusters based on the initial arbitrary tasks. The K-means algorithm reduces intra-group variation; however, it does not guarantee that the outcome has a worldwide minimum of variation.

7.3.8   QUALITY THRESHOLD (QT) CLUSTERING ALGORITHM

Quality Threshold (QT) clustering or grouping is a substitute technique for partitioning information, developed for quality grouping or clustering. The QT clustering algorithm necessitates more calculating power than k-means; however, it does not need indicating the number of groups from the earlier, and always restores a similar outcome when running a few times. The client selects a maximum distance for groups or clusters.

7.3.9   ARTIFICIAL NEURAL NETWORK (ANN)

The collected data are divided into training, testing, and validation subsets, which are highly useful for the Artificial Neural Network (ANN). The ANN introduced two methodologies for dividing the collected data into representative subsets called Self-Organizing Map (SOM) and genetic algorithm (GA). SOM and GA were utilized to forecast salinity in the river. The SOM performed poorly with the ANN model by the fact given with poor performance being related to the data themselves but not the choice of ANN's parameters or architecture.

7.3.10   GROWING NEURAL GAS (GNG) ALGORITHM

Growing Neural Gas (GNG) algorithm examined the neural gas networks to create a specific biological plausible hybrid version. The neural gas networks developed a hybrid algorithm that retained most of the advantages in the GNG algorithm, while it adapted a reduced parameter and several biologically plausible designs. The method developed a prototype based on a supervised clustering algorithm named Supervised Growing Neural Gas Algorithm (SGNG) that incorporated unsupervised GNG algorithms like cluster repulsion mechanisms and adaptive learning rates of Robust Growing Neural Gas algorithm.

7.3.11   NEURO-FUZZY MODEL

The neuro-fuzzy model is critical to determine effective market strategies from raw data or hidden data. It discovered hidden and meaningful information on web user's usage that helped in achieving future growth. The raw data or hidden data developed a concurrent neuro-fuzzy model that discovered and analyzed useful knowledge from the weblog data.

7.3.12   HYPERTEXT PROBABILISTIC GRAMMAR (HPG)

A specific web usage mining technique for the knowledge discovery process from the web log clicks named as click-stream. A hybrid approach is presented for analyzing click sequences. The approach combined the existing approaches with Hypertext Probabilistic Grammar (HPG).

In addition, the comparative study of different machine leering techniques are shown in Table 7.1. In addition, Figure 7.1 shows the comparative results of different machine learning technique.

TABLE 7.1   Comparative Analysis of Machine Learning Technique.

Techniques	k-Mean	GNG	HPG	QT	SLIP
CN2 inducer	1.000	0.990	0.990	0.990	0.990
Random forest	0.955	0.867	0.868	0.869	0.867
Naïve bayes	0.979	0.965	0.965	0.965	0.965
Tree	0.988	0.981	0.980	0.981	0.981
SVM	0.998	0.956	0.956	0.958	0.956

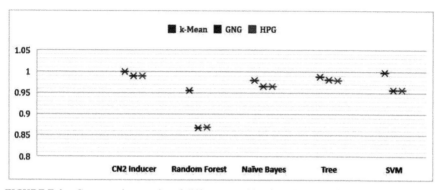

FIGURE 7.1   Comparative results of different machine learning techniques.

7.4   CONCLUSION

The study studies the various predictions and clustering methodologies of machine learning with features and limitations to design an efficient and robust technique to solve recent issues in the machine learning domain. The system studied about the feature selection problem in clustering on dynamic data. The study is planning for combining the fused Lasso regularization in the proposed technique of sparse feature selection, an evolutionary feature selection formulation to identify clusters and shared features in time-varying data simultaneously.

In future proposed work, the paper can be extended to develop an evolutionary co-clustering formulation mechanism for recognizing co-clusters from time-changing information that employs sparsity inducing regularization to recognize block structures from the time-changing information lattices. It also plans to develop temporal smoothness over the block structures recognized from the measurements of the information lattices. The method can be also brought to solve the optimization issues of feature selection in clustering.

KEYWORDS

- **co-clustering construction**
- **guesses**
- **clustering procedures**
- **period of change information**
- **machine learning**

REFERENCES

1. Monisha, S. J.; Sheeba, G. M. In *Gait Based Authentication with Hog Feature Extraction*, Second International Conference on Inventive Communication and Computational Technologies (ICICCT), 1478–1483, 2018.
2. Sheeba, G. M.; Memala, A. In *Detection of Gaze Direction for Human–Computer Interaction*. International Conference on ISMAC in Computational Vision and BioEngineering, 1793–1803, 2018.
3. Salah, A.; Mohamed, N. Directional Co-Clustering. *Adv. Data Anal. Class.* **2019**, *19*, 591–620.
4. Kang, Z.; Liangjian, W.; Wenyu, C.; Zenglin, X. Low-Rank Kernel Learning for Graph-Based Clustering. *Knowledge-Based Syst.* **2019**, *163*, 510–517.
5. Easterling, D. R.; Layne, T.; Watson, N. R.; Richard, F. H.; Satish T.; Hossain M. S. Unified Approach to Dependent and Disparate Clustering of Non-homogenous Data. *Int. J. Appl. Math.* **2019**, *32*, 391–422.
6. Li, R.; Xiaojing Y.; Haomin Z.; Hongyuan Z.; Learning to Match via Inverse Optimal Transport. *J. Mach. Learn. Res.* **2019**, *20*, 1–37.
7. Zhou, T.; Su R.; Stéphane C. A Review: Deep Learning for Medical Image Segmentation using Multi-Modality Fusion. *Array* **2019**, *3–4*, 100004.
8. Cucuringu, M.; Huan, L.; He S.; Luca, Z. Hermitian Matrices for Clustering Directed Graphs: Insights and Applications. 2019, arXiv:1908:02096.
9. Ruggles, C.; Nate, V.; David, F. G.; A Parallel Projection Method for Metric Constrained Optimization. 2019, arXiv:1901.10084.
10. Shi, Y.; Zhaohong, D.; Haoran, C.; Kup-Sze, C.; Shitong, W. Double Coupling Learning for Multi-Task Data Stream Classification. 2019, arXiv:1908.06021.
11. Ding, Z.; Ming, S. Robust Knowledge Discovery via Low-rank Modeling, 2019. arXiv:1909.13123.
12. Yuan, S.; Pang-Ning, T.; Kendra, S. C.; Sarah, M. C.; Patricia, A. S. Spatially Constrained Spectral Clustering Algorithms for Region Delineation. 2019, arXiv:1905.08451.
13. Sun, L.; Ruonan, L.; Jiucheng, X.; Shiguang, Z. An Adaptive Density Peaks Clustering Method with Fisher Linear Discriminant. *IEEE Access* **2019**, *7*, 72936–72955.
14. Liu, S.; Ling, Z.; Yi, L. Urban Vitality Area Identification and Pattern Analysis from the Perspective of Time and Space Fusion. *Sustainability* **2019**; *11*, 4032.
15. He, Z.; Jie, L.; Caihua, L.; Yuan, W.; Airu, Y.; Yalou, H. Dropout Nonnegative Matrix Factorization. *Knowl. Inf. Syst.* **2019**, *60*, 781–806.
16. Xie, X.; Sun, S. Multi-View Support Vector Machines with the Consensus and Complementarity Information. *IEEE Trans. Knowl. Data Eng.* **2020**, *32* (12), 2401–2413.
17. Brasó, G.; Laura, L. Learning a Neural Solver for Multiple Object Tracking. 2019, *arXiv*:1912.07515.
18. Yan, X.; Yangdong, Y.; Yiqiao, M.; Hui, Y. Shared-Private Information Bottleneck Method for Cross-Modal Clustering. *IEEE Access* **2019**, *7*, 36045–36056.
19. Alostad, J. M. Improving the Shilling Attack Detection in Recommender Systems Using an SVM Gaussian Mixture Model. *J. Inform. Knowl. Manag.* **2019**, *18*, 1950011.
20. Gong, X.; Linpeng, H.; Tiancheng, L.; Zhiyi, M. Semantic Weighted Multi View Clustering for Web Content. *IEEE Access* **2019**, *7*, 128097–128113.
21. Gopal, S.; Yang, Y. In *Von Mises–Fisher Clustering Models*, Proceedings of the 31st International Conference on Machine Learning, PMLR, pp. 154–162, 2014.

22. Joshi, T.; Sharma, R.; Mittal, V. K.; Gupta, V. Fabrication of Hybrid Bicycle for Minimizing Pollutant Emissions. *J. Phys. Conf. Ser.* **2020,** *1478,* 1.
23. Joshi, T.; Ganesh, G. Effect of Dynamic Loading on Hip Implant using Finite Element Method. *Mater. Today Proc.* **2021,** 46, 10211–10216.
24. Joshi, T.; Sharma, R.; Mittal, V. K.; Gupta, V. Comparative Investigation and Analysis of Hip Prosthesis for Different Bio-Compatible Alloys. *Mater. Today Proc.* **2021,** *43,* 105–111.
25. Josh, T. Automated Double Hacksaw Cutter. *Int. J. Eng. Res. Technol.* **2018,** *7,* 49–56.
26. Joshi, T.; Kant S. A Review on Finite Element Analysis of Leaf Spring for Composite Material. *Int. J. Innovat. Sci. Res. Technol.* **2018,** *3,* 399–409.
27. Gupta, G.; Jaglan, V.; Raghav, A. K. In *Adaptive Backup Power Management in Ad Hoc Wireless Network*, International Conference on Intelligent Computing and Smart Communication. Algorithms for Intelligent Systems; Singh Tomar, G., Chaudhari, N. S., Barbosa, J. L. V., Aghwariya, M. K., Eds.; Springer: Singapore, 2019.

CHAPTER 8

A Review on Machine Learning Techniques for Recognition of Human Actions

DIANA NAGPAL and RAJIV KUMAR

Department of Computer Science and Engineering, Chandigarh University, Gharuan, Punjab, India

ABSTRACT

The recognition of human activities is a remarkable research bearing in the field of computer vision. Automatic recognition of human exercises for example HAR has now developed as a cutting edge zone in human–computer relationship, mobile computing, and many more. Human activity recognition provides data on a client's conduct that permits computing frameworks to proactively help clients with their undertakings. Currently, we are using smartphone sensors to detect the human activities such as accelerometer, gyroscope, barometer. In this paper, a brief understanding of human action recognition (HAR) has been provided, that is, sensor-based and vision-based HAR. The best in time techniques of machine learning such as decision trees, K-nearest neighbor have been reviewed for HAR. The results got by every technique and the sort of dataset they have utilized are being introduced. Also, deep learning neural network strategies

Computational Intelligence in Analytics and Information Systems, Volume 2: Advances in Digital Transformation, Selected Papers from CIAIS-2021. Parneeta Dhaliwal, PhD, Manpreet Kaur, PhD, Hardeo Kumar Thakur, PhD, Rajeev Kumar Arya, and Joan Lu (Eds.)

have been depicted, for example, artificial neural network, recurrent neural network, and convolutional neural network and the results got by these methods have also been introduced.

8.1 INTRODUCTION

Understanding human behavior has become one of the most dynamic study themes in computer vision. Human activity recognition is a difficult assignment that includes foreseeing the development of an individual dependent on sensor information. Recently, profound learning techniques, for example, convolutional neural networks, recurrent neural networks have demonstrated best in class results via naturally learning features from the raw sensor information.

There are four classes of human activities relying on the body parts that are associated with activity:

- Gesture: Gesture is a body activity that represents a particular message. It is a development done with different body parts rather than verbal communication, for example, okay gesture and thumbs-up gesture.
- Action: Action is a collection of physical movements such as standing, sitting, walking, and running.
- Interaction: These are the arrangement of activities that are executed by all things considered at most two actors out of which, one subject must be an individual and other subject might be an individual or an item, for example, shaking hands, talking, and so forth.

Group Activities: These exercises are the blend of gestures, activities, and interactions. The quantity of subjects is at any rate more than two, for example, hurdle racing, playing football etc.[19]

Human activity recognition has increased significantly nowadays on account of its applications in different fields, for example, amusement, security and observation, wellbeing, and intelligent situations. A great deal of work has already been accomplished on human activity recognition and specialists have even utilized a wide range of approaches. An examination proposed another scientific classification for sorting the exploration work led in this area of activity recognition and separating current writing into three subterritories: activity based, movement based, and cooperation based.[1]

8.2   LITERATURE SURVEY

8.2.1   *SENSOR-BASED HUMAN ACTION RECOGNITION*

Because of the low expense and progression in sensor technology, the vast majority of the exploration in this area has moved toward a sensor-based methodology. Various sensors are utilized to check the behavior of a human being when they were performing daily life exercises in this technology.[2] In wearable approach, notable measure of work has already been accomplished in this area utilizing wearable approach; however, the major problem with wearable sensor is that tag is not comfortable all the time.

From the previous years, scientists are concentrating on device-free methodology. In this technique, users are not asked to bring tag or any kind of device with them. Primary thought is to install sensors in the environment. For example, the sensors are installed at such places where the activities are carried out. Whenever any individual plays out any activity, the information will be caught through those sensors, which would then be able to be utilized for the recognition of various activities. This method is more efficient than the other two methodologies since it does not ask the person to bring any device when they are doing any activity. In any case, there are some challenges in this methodology as well. The major challenge is, for example, obstruction from nature. In the past few years, the sensors are getting faster, cheaper, and smaller that have multiple technologies in it. A study presents active and assistive learning (AAL) highlights of the recent technologies and trends in AAL.[3]

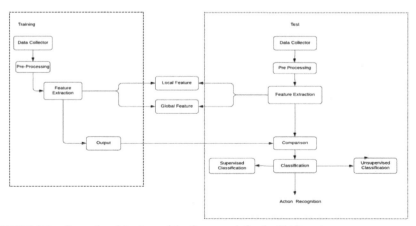

FIGURE 8.1   General architecture of the framework for the HAR system.

Figure 8.1 depicts the general architecture of any Human Activity Recognition system. An instrument of feature extraction figures any symbolic data extracted from some pictures or any kind of video outlines. At that point, labels are accordingly influenced to these removed highlights by a classifier. The procedure comprises numerous methods that guarantee the productive portrayal of activities.[19]

8.2.2   VISION-BASED HUMAN ACTION RECOGNITION

An optimal scheme of recognition of human action system was suggested.[4] This hypothesis did a thorough investigation of best in class strategies for human activity recognition and proposed a progressive scientific categorization for classifying these techniques. They reviewed various methodologies for example unimodal and multimodal and as per the source channel every one of these methodologies employs to perceive human activities.

Vision-based action recognition of human has pulled in numerous researchers because of its difficulties and a heaps of assortment of uses. For instance, the applications may start from straightforward gesture recognition to convoluted behavior understanding in surveillance framework. This prompts significant improvement in the methods identified with human movement representation and recognition. Another hypothesis underlines human movement representation. Also, it represents some recognition techniques alongside the preferences and drawbacks of these techniques.[5]

Deep, convolutional, and recurrent approaches have been used that beat the cutting edge strategies.[6] They have also provided guidelines for the researchers who want to apply deep learning in their problem solving. An investigation features the advances of a best-in-class activity recognition approach, essentially for the activity representation and classification techniques. This examination means to give a review of representation and classification strategies and look at them.[7]

A study provides high-quality and learning-based procedures for human activity recognition,[8,9] However, it concludes that studies based on high-quality techniques are not suitable for complex circumstances. Then again, learning-based procedures are more suitable. Preparing a robot that can estimate human pose and trajectory in the near future is another study[10] with the help of dynamic classifier selection architecture. A vision-based gait analysis approach was proposed which can be performed on a smartphone using cloud computing assistance.[11] They planned and actualized a lot of shrewd video surveillance framework in parking environment.[12,13] This audit expects to present the key cutting edge in marker less movement capture investigated from PC vision that has probably a future effect in biomechanics, while considering the difficulties with precision, strength.[14] The framework was used for strange behaviors recognition and alarm. The technologies introduced are foreground detection, feature extraction, movement behavioral categorization, and recognition. Practically, the system worked well and the identification result of strange behaviors was palatable. An algorithm in the field of deep machine learning, that is, YOLO (you only look once) was developed to reduce the burden of inspectors by automatically detecting crime scenes in a video surveillance.[15]

Human activity recognition stays to be a significant issue in computer vision. This is the reason for some applications, for example, video observation, medicinal services, and human–computer cooperation. In any case, challenges despite everything exist while confronting sensible views. The hypothesis proposes a reliable technique for activity location and recognition of certifiable observation video datasets.[16] Recently, deep CNNs are used to perceive the activity of human along with an arrangement of pictures. This theory proposed a capsule neural network to achieve this.[17] To detect and recognize human walking and running motion even in darker surroundings in video streams, a line skeleton scalable model was developed.[18]

Another theory presented a detailed correlation of all the current datasets in this area.[19] A study explores machine learning techniques for the authentication of user by recording different activities, for example, walking, running, sitting, and standing.[20] They proposed a human recognition system by implementing 10 different machine learning algorithms on the HugaDB database. The samples were collected from 18 participants and the system gives 99% accuracy.

A study approves a two-camera open pose-based marker framework for gait investigation by thinking about three variables for exactness: video resolution, relative distance of the camera, and the direction of gait. The study infers that the expansion of camera distance and resolution of video assists with accomplishing the best performances.[21] Another theory assesses the machine learning methods dependent on recurrent neural networks to check fatigue dependent on various repetitive activities.[22]

8.2.3   LEARNING METHODS FOR HUMAN ACTION RECOGNITION

HAR is an area of study that has increased noteworthy consideration lately because of the inescapability of sensors, which are presently accessible in smartphones and wearable gadgets.

Activity recognition can be perceived as a classification issue, a typical sort of issue found in supervised learning.[23]

In an investigation, the activity recognition chain (ARC) was proposed[24] in which an arrangement of steps is followed so as to fabricate HAR frameworks as appeared in Figure 8.2. It shows the various advances associated with the ARC.

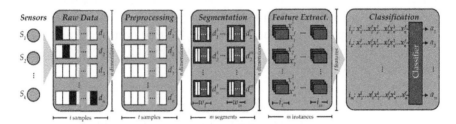

FIGURE 8.2   Steps followed so as to fabricate HAR frameworks.

(a) According to the execution mode, the framework can be disconnected or on the web. On account of online framework, the framework can perform activity recognition progressively.

(b) According to its speculation capacity, the framework can be client autonomous or client explicit. In the client-free case, the framework ought to have the option to perceive the activity in any event. It is helpful for the kind of clients who are utilizing the framework just for the first time.

(c) In accordance with the sort of recognition, this framework can process nonstop floods of information or confined information. In that case, the counterbalance of every activity is recently known.

(d) In accordance with the sort of exercises, the exercises could be occasional, irregular, or static.

(e) In accordance with the framework model, it tends to be stateless or stateful. On account of stateful, the framework not exclusively knows about the sensors information yet additionally considers a model of environment.[27]

8.3   MACHINE LEARNING TECHNIQUES

8.3.1   *CLASSIC MACHINE LEARNING TECHNIQUES*

A survey was conducted on the machine learning techniques first for the best-in-time techniques.[26] As shown in Table 8.1, an outline of decision trees and KNN is presented after conducting the survey.

TABLE 8.1 Outline of Decision Tree and KNN.

Method	Dataset	Model/variation	Accuracy
Iterative dichotomise 3 decision tree (ID3 DT)[26,29]	Using smartphones (accelerometers)	Vector (POS, action)	73.72
		POS (decision tree for the classification of smartphone position)	79.56
		Action (classify activity-position independent)	88.32
KNearest neighbor (KNN)[30]	Online activity recognition framework working at Android	KNN algorithm	–
	stages	K-nearest neighbor (clustered)	92

8.3.2 NEURAL NETWORK METHODS

8.3.2.1 ARTIFICIAL NEURAL NETWORKS

In another theory, an information-securing module model has been created.[29] It collects the statistics of the affected person and perceives abnormal repute of the affected person's wellbeing with the aim that early remedy might be accessible.

For arm pose recognition,

Information gadget: Accelerometer installed in smart watch.

Preprocessing: Filtering, standardization, feature extraction.

Another dataset with various arrangements of accelerometer information and information from pulse sensor was utilized to recognize different exercises.

8.3.2.2 CONVOLUTIONAL NEURAL NETWORKS

In another hypothesis, Convolutional Neural Networks (CNNs) are being suggested to group human exercises.[31] These models utilize crude data got from a great deal of inertial sensors.

They utilized a few blends of exercises, for example, walk, strolling balance, standing parity, and quality. They have likewise investigated sensors to demonstrate how movement signs can be adjusted to be taken care of into CNNs by utilizing diverse system models. Table 8.2 summarizes the ANN, CNN, and RNN techniques. Information gadget utilized is inertial development unit sensors and triaxial sensors.[28]

TABLE 8.2   Summaries of ANN, CNN, and RNN.

Dataset used	Classification of activities	Implementation method	Accuracy
Self-made dataset[31]	Arm movement (forward, upwards, backwards, horizontal)	ANN	100%
Self-made dataset[31]	Sitting left and right lateral recumbent	ANN	99.96%
Different dataset[26,31]	Standing Walking (Forward, Backward) Running (Forward, Backward)	ANN	99.08%
Otago exercise dataset[32]	Walk Walking balance Standing balance Strength	CNN	Mix of a few sensors produces better outcomes.

8.3.2.3   RECURRENT NEURAL NETWORKS

The theory presented a profound learning model that figures out how to group human exercises without utilizing any earlier information. The examination proposes a long short term memory (LSTM) RNN that is equipped for remembering things. LSTM was applied to three genuine keen home datasets. The proposed approach outflanks the current ones as far as exactness and execution.[33]

The information gadgets utilized are sensors that are empowered at different areas of the house.

8.4   CONCLUSION

To automatically comprehend and analyze the activities of any human is a fascinating, still complicated, task. Also, real-life applications in uncontrolled condition make it more demanding and fascinating. In this paper, an intensive investigation of different procedures has been completed, for example, the strategies that could be utilized in the field of human activity recognition. It incorporated various machine learning algorithms and also various neural network techniques. Various procedures had been applied on various datasets and most of them had changing perceptions that rely on the environmental conditions, kind of information utilized, for example, accelerometer information or online activity recognition framework or any other sensor information, sensor placement, and techniques for execution. It tends to be concluded from this examination that there is no single strategy that is suitable to perceive any activity. Different environmental conditions, position of sensors, and sort of information collected should be considered so as to select a specific method for a particular application. For instance, if information is being gathered by sensors and various sensors should be put on by the individual then the placement of the sensors is another problem. If classification methods are being used, for example, decision trees and the neural networks, over estimation can occur and in case of SVM, under estimation can occur if the data that is available is less trained. In this way, despite having various techniques, certain difficulties stay open and should be resolved.

KEYWORDS

- **human action recognition**
- **machine learning**
- **neural networks**
- **human action recognition (HAR)**
- **K-nearest neighbor**

REFERENCES

1. Hussain, Z.; Sheng, M.; Zhang, W. E. Different Approaches for Human Activity Recognition: A Survey. 2019, Arxiv:1906.05074.
2. Wang, S.; Zhou, G. A Review on Radio Based Activity Recognition. *Digit. Commun. Net.* **2015,** (1), 20–29.
3. Manoj, T.; Thyagaraju, G. S. Active and Assisted Living: A Comprehensive Review of Enabling Technologies and Scenarios. *Int. J. Adv. Res. Comp. Sci.* **2018,** *9* (1).
4. Vrigkas, M.; Nikou, C.; Kakadiaris, I. A. A Review of Human Activity Recognition Methods. *Front. Robot. AI* **2015,** *2,* 28.
5. Kale, G. V.; Patil, V. H. A Study of Vision Based Human Motion Recognition and Analysis. *Int. J. Ambient Comp. Intell.* **2016,** *7* (2), 75–92.
6. Hammerla, N. Y.; Halloran, S.; Plötz, T. Deep, Convolutional, and Recurrent Models for Human Activity Recognition Using Wearables. arXiv preprint arXiv:1604.08880.
7. Zhang, S.; Wei, Z.; Nie, J.; Huang, L.; Wang, S.; Li, Z. A Review on Human Activity Recognition using Vision-Based Method. *J. Healthc. Eng.* **2017,** *2017.*

8. Sargano, A. B.; Angelov, P.; Habib, Z. A Comprehensive Review on Handcrafted and Learning-Based Action Representation Approaches for Human Activity Recognition. *Appl. Sci.* **2017,** *7* (1), 110.

9. Jiang, W.; Yin, Z. In *Human Activity Recognition using Wearable Sensors by Deep Convolutional Neural Networks.* Proceedings of the 23rd ACM International Conference on Multimedia; pp. 1307–1310, October, 2015.

10. Perera, A. G.; Law, Y. W.; Al-Naji, A.; Chahl, J. Human Motion Analysis from UAV Video. *Int. J. Intell. Unmanned Syst.* **2018.**

11. Nieto-Hidalgo, M.; Ferrández-Pastor, F. J.; Valdivieso-Sarabia, R. J.; Mora-Pascual, J.; García-Chamizo, J. M. Gait Analysis using Computer Vision Based on Cloud Platform and Mobile Device. *Mobile Inform. Syst.* **2018,** *2018,* 1–10.

12. Xu, H.; Li, L.; Fang, M.; Zhang, F. Movement Human Actions Recognition based on Machine Learning. *Int. J. Online Biomed. Eng.* **2018,** *14* (4), 193–210.

13. Khan, A.; Janwe, M. N. Review on Moving Object Detection in Video Surveillance. *Int. J. Adv. Res. Comp. Commun. Engg.* **2017,** *6,* 664–670.

14. Colyer, S. L.; Evans, M.; Cosker, D. P.; Salo, A. I. A Review of the Evolution of Vision-Based Motion Analysis and the Integration of Advanced Computer Vision Methods Towards Developing A Markerless System. *Sports Med. Open.* **2018,** *4* (l), 24.

15. Cui, Y. *Using Deep Machine Learning to Conduct Object-based Identification and Motion Detection on Safeguards Video Surveillance (No.BNL-207942-2018-COPA);* Brookhaven National Laboratory (BNL): Upton, NY, US, 2018.

16. Kumaran, N.; Reddy, U. S.; Kumar, S. S. Multiple Action Recognition for Human Object with Motion Video Sequence using the Properties of HSV Color Space Applying with Region of Interest, 2019.

17. Basu, A.; Petropoulakis, L.; Di Caterina, G.; Soraghan, J. Indoor Home Scene Recognition Using Capsule Neural Networks. *Procedia Comp. Sci.* **2019,** *167,* 440–448.

18. Yong, C. Y.; Chew, K. M.; Sudirman, R. Human Motion Analysis in Dark Surrounding using Line Skeleton Scalable Model and Vector Angle Technique. *Mater. Today Proc.* **2019,** *16,* 1732–1741.

19. Jegham, I.; Khalifa, A. B.; Alouani, I.; Mahjoub, M. A. Vision-Based Human Action Recognition: An Overview and Real World Challenges. *Foren. Sci. Int. Digit. Invest.* **2020,** *32,* 200901

20. Kececi, A.; Yildirak, A.; Ozyazici, K.; Ayluctarhan, G.; Agbulut, O.; Zincir, I. Implementation of Machine Learning Algorithms for Gait Recognition. *Eng. Sci. Technol. Int. J.* **2020.**

21. Zago, M.; Luzzago, M.; Marangoni, T.; De Cecco, M.; Tarabini, M.; & Galli, M. 3D Tracking of Human Motion using Visual Skeletonization and Stereoscopic Vision. *Front. Bioeng. Biotechnol.* **2020,** *8,* 181.

22. Hernandez, G.; Valles, D.; Wierschem, D. C.; Koldenhoven, R. M.; Koutitas, G.; Mendez, F. A.; … Jimenez, J. In *Machine Learning Techniques for Motion Analysis of Fatigue from Manual Material Handling Operations using 3D Motion Capture Data.* 2020 10th Annual Computing And Communication Workshop And Conference (CCWC), IEEE, pp. 0300–0305, January, 2020.

23. Baldominos, A.; Cervantes, A.; Saez, Y.; Isasi, P. A Comparison of Machine Learning and Deep Learning Techniques for Activity Recognition using Mobile Devices. *Sensors* **2019,** *19* (3), 521.

24. Bulling, A.; Blanke, U.; Schiele, B. A Tutorial on Human Activity Recognition using Body-Worn Inertial Sensors. *ACM Comput. Surv. (CSUR)* **2014,** *46* (3), 1–33.

25. Saez, Y.; Baldominos, A.; Isasi, P. A Comparison Study of Classifier Algorithms for Cross-Person Physical Activity Recognition. *Sensors* **2017,** *17* (1), 66.

26. Jobanputra, C.; Bavishi, J.; Doshi, N. Human Activity Recognition: A Survey. *Procedia Comp. Sci.* **2019,** *155*, 698–703.

27. Hara, K.; Kataoka, H.; Satoh, Y. In *Can Spatiotemporal 3rd Cnns Retrace the History of 2nd Cnns and Imagenet? Proceedings of The IEEE Conference on Computer Vision And Pattern Recognition.* pp. 6546–6555, 2018.

28. Cho, H.; Yoon, S. M. Divide and Conquer-Based 1D CNN Human Activity Recognition using Test Data Sharpening. *Sen,* **2018,** *18* (4), 1055.

29. Fan, L.; Wang, Z.; Wang, H. In *Human Activity Recognition Model based on Decision Tree.* 2013 International Conference on Advanced Cloud and Big Data, IEEE; pp. 64–68, December, 203.

30. Paul, P.; George, T. *An Effective Approach for Human Activity Recognition on Smartphone, 2015 IEEE International Conference on Engineering and Technology (ICETECH)*; IEEE, pp. 1–3, March, 205.

31. Oniga, S.; Sütő, J. In *Human Activity Recognition using Neural Networks*, Proceedings of the 2014 15th International Carpathian Control Conference (ICCC); IEEE, pp. 403–406, May, 2014.

32. Bevilacqua, A.; Macdonald, K.; Rangarej, A.; Widjaya, V.; Caulfield, B.; Kechadi, T. In *Human Activity Recognition with Convolutional Neural Networks*, Joint European Conference on Machine Learning and Knowledge Discovery in Databases; Springer: Cham, pp. 541–552, September, 2018.

33. Singh, D.; Merdivan, E.; Psychoula, I.; Kropf, J.; Hanke, S.; Geist, M.; Holzinger, A. In *Human Activity Recognition Using Recurrent Neural Networks*, International Cross-Domain Conference for Machine Learning and Knowledge Extraction; Springer: Cham, pp. 267–274, August, 2017.

CHAPTER 9

Proposed Intelligent Vehicular Accident Detection and Alerting Based on Internet of Things

DEEPSHIKHA AGARWAL

Computer Science & Engg & Information Tech, Amity University Lucknow Campus, Lucknow, India

ABSTRACT

Internet of things (IoT) is a system consisting of interrelated devices that are continuously connected to each other using Internet. This eliminates the requirement of human-to-human or human-to-computer communication. This paper discusses about an application of Iot in transportation for making it intelligent in autonomous detection of accident happening between vehicles on the road. This system has been proposed due to the underlying poor working of accident management system particularly in India. When an accident happens, human help is not offered due to police enquiries and long procedures involved in it. Medical help is available only after the police is informed by phone calls. In case of large delay, injured people may often lose their lives. To deal with this situation, our intelligent transportation method uses IoT to eradicate the human intervention and directly informs the suitable authority without any delay.

Computational Intelligence in Analytics and Information Systems, Volume 2: Advances in Digital Transformation, Selected Papers from CIAIS-2021. Parneeta Dhaliwal, PhD, Manpreet Kaur, PhD, Hardeo Kumar Thakur, PhD, Rajeev Kumar Arya, and Joan Lu (Eds.)

9.1   INTRODUCTION

Internet of Things, also referred to as IoT,[1] is a relatively new technology and in recent years it has been very actively worked upon by developers. It can offer several services to humans[2-4] like an alarm clock that can also send notifications to the person regarding meetings, scheduled events, etc. apart from giving morning alarms. It can also instruct various machines at your house, for example, coffee machine to start brewing coffee, smart home system to open the curtains in your bedroom, smart TV to turn on your favorite music on TV. Similarly, it can be very useful in medical profession; for example, it can track the data of your heart and then send this data to your doctor so that he can analyze this data and predict the possibility of diseases or any other deviations from the normal form.

It is no more a secret that the IoT market is now actively evolving day by day and growing with great speed; also, many new start-ups are appearing every day.[5,6]

9.2   COMPONENTS OF IOT

The major components[7-9] of IoT are namely:

1.   Smart device (thing)
2.   Gateway
3.   Cloud
4.   Analytics user interface

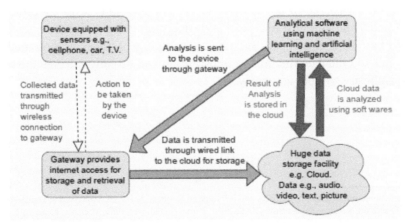

FIGURE 9.1   Components of IoT.

As shown in Figure 9.1, smart devices are equipped with sensors that can sense a parameter and can communicate with other devices. These are small transducer devices capable of sensing a parameter. Wireless sensors can also communicate this parameter to a nearby device through wireless communication by taking multihops. These sensors can sense parameters such as pressure, humidity, temperature, heat, velocity, strain, salinity, light as physical values that are converted into electrical signals for transmission purposes. Gateway is the router or terminal that allows the information generated by the device to be conveyed outside the local domain. It works at the application layer. The cloud offers a platform for managing the huge amount of data generated by the Iot system. Cloud is the place that provides storage of the data on the fly. There are also several software and other applications available which can be accessed using the cloud by the ubiquitous device to process the data and produce analytical results. Cloud can allow fast access and retrieval of stored data which is a necessary requirement of any IoT network. Analytics helps engineers to find out irregularities in the collected data and act fast to prevent an undesired scenario. The user interface allows the user to easily use the system for his advantage.[10,11] This interface provides the actual man to machine communication. It hides all the complex details of the undying protocols and the working procedure of the network and makes it handy for any user to work in the IoT application. Interface can be realized in the form of a software or hardware.

IoT finds its applications in smart cities[12] where monitoring can be done using smart interconnected communicating devices. Few papers[13] have discussed the hardware design for antennas and provided an understanding of the framework for making communications in WAN.[14]

9.3   LITERATURE REVIEW

In India, everyday nearly 400 people die due to negligence in road accidents. There is no proper mechanism to detect an accident on time and take suitable actions. If there is a proper mechanism, the number of such causalities can be reduced to a large extent. Normally, a person who has met with an accident needs proper medical attention within the first 15 minutes. If he gets the help within this time, the chances of survival increase to a large extent. The paragraph below presents some major review on accidents that occur in India and abroad and fatality rates.

The author[15] has shown that due to increase in vehicles, rate of accidents occurring in India is growing fast. In 2016, nearly 1.5 lakh people died due to road accidents and delay in getting medical assistance. This paper[16] has classified accidents into three categories, namely, environmental, physical, and mental. It also proposes a fuzzy system for the road accident prevention system, but it is limited to a short range. Furthermore,[17] the author presents a survey on the accidents that had occurred in the past in Thailand. According to the author, there are several factors involved in the happening of road accidents. As stated in,[18] data mining techniques can be used to understand the situation of accidents happening on the road. In,[19] the authors have tried to elaborate on the factors due to which accidents occur on highways in India. Furthermore, some researchers have tried to build a predictive model for understanding the severity of an accident. But, it does not incorporate measures that can be taken to rescue the injurious people. This system is only a classification system and lacks complete implementation details.

9.4 PROPOSED ACCIDENT DETECTION SYSTEM

The proposed system is shown in Figure 9.2 which is drawn using smart-draw software. As shown in the figure, all vehicles are equipped with mobile devices and wireless sensors. The sensors on the vehicles can sense blood, strain, and sound of impact which is of high decibels. The people on-board also have wearable sensors attached to them which continuously monitor their heartrate, temperature, blood pressure, and breathing rate. There is a 2-tier sensor network in every vehicle where the first tier is the wearable sensors and the second tier is the vehicle-attached sensors. The vehicle-attached sensors are more powerful because they act as sink nodes that collect all the sensed information and relay it to the IoT device that is the mobile device. If two or more vehicles collide, several effects happen which are captured by the sensor devices. For example, the vehicle-attached sensors are able to sense the impact of damage due to collision and the wearable sensors detect the parameters related to people who were on-board. Every parameter that is sensed has a threshold. If the sensed value of a parameter is above the threshold limit, this means that some casualty has happened. In such a case, all the sensed parameters from the wearable device are wireless communicated or sensed by the sensors that are connected to the vehicle. A packet is created by the vehicle-attached sensor node which acts as a sink and is relayed to the mobile device situated at a secure place in the vehicle. The packet sent by the sink node contains several fields including the vehicle number, values of the sensed parameters, and the timestamps. Timestamp is an important field because the time duration after the accident can be estimated. When the mobile node will receive the data packet, it will immediately broadcast it to all nearby vehicles. The vehicle moving in the vicinity of this vehicle can relay this information to the nearest toll booth and send an alert to the nearby police station. The police station can immediately send ambulance to the spot of accident to rescue the injured people and suitable medical assistance can be provided without delay. This system will reduce the delay time of detection and increase life expectancy of the injured persons.

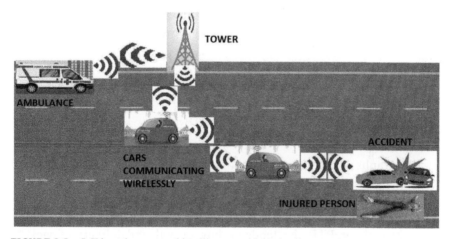

FIGURE 9.2   IoT-based automated intelligent accident alerting system.

However, some issues can be forecasted in the complete implementation of this system. First, the mobile devices have to be continuously connected to the Internet for immediate dissipation of information. If the accident happens in an area which does not have mobile towers, the connection might be lost. Second, the sensors attached to the body of the vehicle should be well protected and encased so that the impact of the accident does not damage the sensor nodes. Third, there should be a decision on how many packets should be relayed at a time to avoid congestion in the network. If these problems can be tackled with, this system can become an ideal one.

9.5 SIMULATION AND RESULTS

The simulation has been done on Cooja simulator.0 to present the packet loss, delay, and network lifetime. Table 9.1 shows the parameters. We present a comparison between the two metrics for RPL (Routing protocol for Low power and Lossy network) protocol–ETX (expected number of transmissions) and PTR (Packet transmission Rate). Both these metrics are used for IoT implementation. The comparison will be helpful in analyzing which metric is better suited for our proposed system.

TABLE 9.1 Simulation Parameters.

Parameters	Values
Number of nodes	1–20
Metrics	ETX, PTR
Area	200 m × 200 m
Tx and Rx ratio	TX = 80%, RX = 80%
Initial battery charge	15 Joules
UDP data	20 Bytes

The graphs show comparison of two metrics—PTR and ETX for efficient RPL routing protocol. Figure 9.3 shows the total number of packets delivered. It can be observed that PTR shows a steady rise in the number of packets delivered, whereas in the case of ETX it remains stable throughout. PTR also tends to show growth and delivery of packets seems to increase later on. Figure 9.4 shows end-to-end delay in packet transmission. As can be seen from the graph, PTR has a decrease in the delay involved for packet transmission as the number of nodes increases. Also, in ETX we can say that it remains stable and does not depend on the number of nodes.

Figure 9.5 shows the total network lifetime. Again, we can observe that PTR metric slowly rises the lifetime with the number of nodes but, ETX remains stable. This is a turning point as ETX seems to have the same lifetime even with fewer nodes.

So, based on the above discussion, we can say that the PTR is better as more number of IoT nodes are involved for rapid communication. But if an application requires use of very few nodes, ETX is a better choice.

9.6 CONCLUSION AND FUTURE SCOPE

This paper presents a brief discussion of the technology called Internet-of-Things. It is a new technology that aims at making every device known to human beings, capable of sending and receiving information. This breakthrough technology can change the future of communication system. Human beings will be connected remotely throughout the day and intelligent devices will provide the convenience and quick monitoring of events. Based on the monitored parameters, these devices can also take actions for example, closing the relay, switching on/off lights of the room, automatic locking of house etc. This paper presents an idea by which accident occurring on the road can be automatically detected using IoT and information can be floated to the hospital and police without any delay. If this system is implemented, the number of casualties occurring everyday can be reduced to a large extent due to real-time detection and communication. This paper has tried to show which metric in RPL will be best suited for implementing the proposed accident detection system. However, a better performance can be achieved if some more metrics can be used which will be specific to the application. Also, currently, this method is suitable for urban cities only.

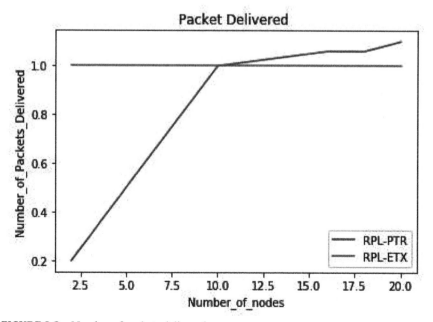

FIGURE 9.3 Number of packets delivered.

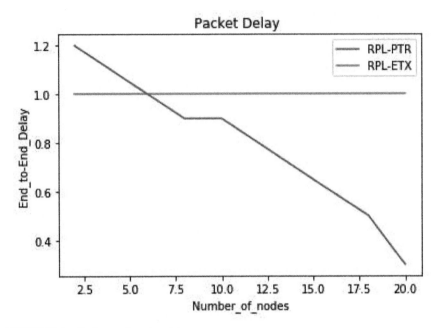

FIGURE 9.4   End-to-end packet delay.

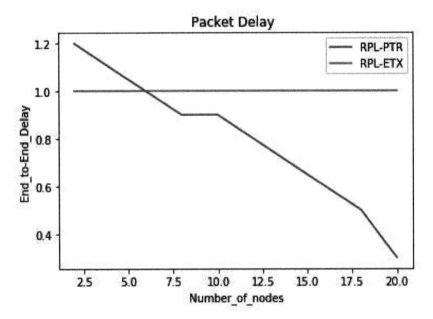

FIGURE 9.5   Network lifetime.

Some modifications can be done to make it suitable for rural areas as well. Legal issues from the government regarding interoperability of the devices and communication system are also to be looked upon. Proper measures have to be deployed to safeguard the miniature sensor nodes and IoT devices also so that they may not get damaged due to wear and tear.

KEYWORDS

- **accident**
- **alerting**
- **detection**
- **IoT**
- **intelligent**
- **sensor**
- **wireless**

REFERENCES

1. Zanella, A.; Angelo, C. Internet of Things for Smart Cities. *Int. J. Internet Things* **2014,** *1*, 22–32.
2. Chen, S.; Xui, H. A Vision of Iot. *Int. J. Internet Things* **2014,** *1*, 349–359.
3. Liu, T. The Application and Development of IoT. *Proc. Int. Symp. Inf. Technol. Med. Educ.* **2012,** *2*, 991–994.
4. Husam, R. In *IoT based Smart Cities*, 2018 International Symposium on Networks, Computers and Communications (ISNCC), Rome, Italy;, vol. 1, 2018, pp. 1–4.
5. Yang, J. Broadcasting with Prediction and Selective Forwarding in Vehicular Networks. *Int. J. Distrib. Sensor Networks* **2019,** 1–9.
6. Dachyar, M. Knowledge Growth and Development: Iot Research. *Sci. Direct Heliyon* **2019,** *5*, 1–14.
7. Widyantara, M. O. Iot for Intelligent Traffic Monitoring System. *Int. J. Comput. Ttrends Technol.* **2013,** *30*, 169–173.
8. Hammi, B. Iot Technologies for Smart Cities. *IET J.* **2014,** 1–14.
9. Margeret, V.; A Survey on Transport System Using Internet of Things. *IOSR J. Comput. Eng.* **2018,** *20*, 1–3.
10. Sharma, B. Comparative Analysis of IoT Based Products, Technology and Integration of IoT with Cloud Computing. *IET Networks* **2012,** 1–14.
11. Bekasiewicz, A. Compact UWB Monopole Antenna for Internet of Things Applications. *IET Electron. Lett.* **2016,** *52*, 492–494.
12. Kim, M. Performance Enhancement of Dual-Band Antenna for Internet of Things Applications using Closed Loops. *IET Electron. Lett.* **2019,** *55*, 1324–1326.

13. Agbinya, J. I. Framework for Wide Area Networking of Inductive Internet of Things. *Electron. Lett.* **2011,** *47,* 1199–1201.

14. Koley, S.; Srivastava, S.; Ghosal, P. In *Correlating Fatality Rate to Road Accidents in India: A Case Study Using Big Data,* IEEE International Symposium on Smart Electronic Systems (iSES) (Formerly iNiS), 2018, pp. 171–176.

15. Razzaq, S.; Riaz, F.; Mehmood, T.; Ratyal, N. I. In *Multi-Factors Based Road Accident Prevention System,* International Conference on Computing, Electronic and Electrical Engineering (ICE Cube) 2016, pp. 190–195.

16. Ditcharoen, A.; Chhour, B.; Traikunwaranon, T.; Aphivongpanya, N.; Maneerat, K.; Ammarapala, V. In *Road Traffic Accidents Severity Factors: A Review Paper,* 5th International Conference on Business and Industrial Research (ICBIR); 2018, pp. 339–343.

17. Sonal, S.; Suman, S. In *A Framework for Analysis of Road Accidents,* International Conference on Emerging Trends and Innovations In Engineering And Technological Research (ICETIETR), 2018, pp. 1–5.

18. Naqvi, H. M.; Tiwari, G. Factors Contributing to Motorcycle Fatal Crashes on National Highways in India. *Transport. Res. Procedia* **2017,** 2089–2102.

19. Cuenca, L. G.; Puertas, E.; Aliane, N.; Andres, J. F. In *Traffic Accidents Classification and Injury Severity Prediction,* IEEE International Conference on Intelligent Transportation Engineering (ICITE) 2018, pp. 52–57.

20. Babu, B. S.; and Padmaja, P. L. Role of COOJA Simulator in IoT. *Int. J. Emerg. Trends Technolo. Comput. Sci.* **2017,** *6,* 139–143.

CHAPTER 10

Intelligent Spectacles for Accident Prevention

SRIKANT SONEKAR, GAURAV HABAD, KRUTI SONTAKKE, GAURAV KSHIRSAGAR, HARSHAL BHOYAR, and ABHISHEK BARVE

JD College of Engineering and Technology, Nagpur, India

ABSTRACT

As development in this era is increasing rapidly, technological advancements are becoming an integral part of humans. Road accidents are increasing every day. It can be reduced to some extent with Intelligent Spectacles. The intelligent spectacles are designed that use the deep learning approach to enhance the captured images and process only necessary information. This paper presents a brief overview of how such intelligent spectacles can be implemented with the technologies available today. Machine learning applications such as Object Detection, Speech Recognition, or Web Automation can be used to build a multifunctional Intelligent Spectacle with only Accident Prevention in mind. These Spectacles are wearable devices that can interact with the user via voice, detect objects in front, keep the user updated with the latest weather or traffic updates, and help in navigation. It can reduce the accident rates and overcome the difficulty incurred in previous glasses. We are proposing a potential direction of creating a product by combining various inputs.

Computational Intelligence in Analytics and Information Systems, Volume 2: Advances in Digital Transformation, Selected Papers from CIAIS-2021. Parneeta Dhaliwal, PhD, Manpreet Kaur, PhD, Hardeo Kumar Thakur, PhD, Rajeev Kumar Arya, and Joan Lu (Eds.)

10.1 INTRODUCTION

Road accidents do affect not only people but also the country and the effect is very worse; thus, it is a need to reduce road accidents. There are several reasons for road accidents; some of them are very uncertain but few of them are avoidable with certain measures. In this era, technology is spreading rapidly in every aspect of life. It is because it not only makes the execution process swift but also provides efficiency and precision for coming with the solution. In contrast to popular myths, new technologies are easily adaptable. Not because they are easy, but they are convenient and resolve certain problems.

Enlisted actions sometimes cause life-threatening road accidents. Most of them can be avoided if taken into consideration:

1. Crossing speed limit
2. Not following rules and regulations on the road
3. Distraction (mobile)
4. Road accidents caused due to animals
5. Condition of road
6. Low light during night-time
7. High-intensity light affects the eye at night-time.

All the above reasons can cause road accidents, so if something that can overcome such problems and help the driver while driving can be made available, it may reduce the accidents significantly. Various steps are taken to control such life-threatening incidents such as speed breakers, traffic signals, road monitoring, but at the end of the day, the driver needs to take an initiative and make a significant difference for this accident prevention. If technology can make an impact here, then it will bring precision, efficiency, as well as comfortable and easier execution.

A user can be assisted while driving by the assistant to observe and monitor the road throughout the path traveled. It will limit the processing of information to the required one only. The assistant can warn the driver while crossing the speed limit, remind all the rules and regulation for the driver, observe and monitor the road for all types of activities, keep track of new mobile notifications and incoming calls, reduce the glare and improve the vision at night-time, take care of sudden activities such as animal crossing and potholes detection, respond to the user with the result, inform close contacts and a nearby hospital in case of emergency. All these activities can reduce the occurrence of road accidents.

Similar spectacles can be seen, like Google Glass. But these smart glasses are too generalized and are very costly. In contrast, if glasses can be built with only specific problems in mind, it can reduce the cost as well as limit the heavy processing, hence making it effective,[11,12] but they are the only functions for the specific feature and are also costly. The smart helmet is designed for observing roads and obeying the traffic rules, but this is not enough; just like the smart helmet there are other products in the market with some limitations. While driving we need a lightweight and smart system that can be helpful to the driver in all the aspects mentioned.[6,13]

It is observed that spectacles are the most usable and convenient object while driving and can be used to implement all these features effectively. A spectacle can be developed to act as a small but smart assistant for the driver who always assists and makes the journey safe. This assistant can take care of traffic rules, inappropriate actions such as over speeding, road signs, which can also monitor road and assist with animal crossing, heavy traffic routes, bad road situation, etc. Before going to any destination the assistant can inform the user about some prerequisites such as weather, route, time; it can keep monitoring mobile and its notifications, help in the night to detect objects in front and assist the driver at night-time.

10.2 METHODS AND TOOLS

10.2.1 OBJECT DETECTION

Object detection is one of the important modules of a project. Object detection is done with the help of an infrared/night vision camera and python package to detect the object of similar classes. There are various algorithms in existence such as Resnet, You Only Look Once (YOLO), Faster Convolutional Neural Network (CNN), used for object detection. Moreover, python's package Open-Source Computer Vision (OpenCV) makes it easier to work with machine learning, image processing, and object detection. OpenCV is a machine learning software library. OpenCV processes images and videos to identify objects, faces, human actions, and track moving objects and the handwriting of a human being. It all can be done with the help of 2500+ optimized algorithms that include classic and state-of-the-art computer vision and machine learning algorithms integrated with it. It can also extract a 3D model of the object and produce 3D point clouds from a stereo camera and then stitch images together to produce a high-resolution image of an entire scene, find similar images from an image database, recognize scenery and overlay it with augmented reality. With the help of the OpenCV package, we can read, write, capture, store, filter, transform, and process images. It also performs a feature of light detection like detecting specific objects such as faces, eyes, cars, trucks, in the videos and images. Subtract the background data of an image and video, and also track objects in it.[1,10]

10.2.2   WEATHER UPDATES

Weather update is done by using the web-scraping tool and python package Selenium to fetch the weather update from trustworthy webpages as per user request. Beautiful Soup, request, lxml, url lib, etc are more tools in existence that can also be used. Selenium, a web-scraping tool, makes it easier to work with Web Automation. Web scraping is an autonomous process where an application processes the HTML and web pages to extract essential data as per user requirement. Selenium provides features such as data mining, weather data monitoring more accurately than other web-scraping tools. The script of selenium uses a weather forecast to fetch the forecast from genuine sources. It requires the city name to get the forecast and request for the same. The city name will be passed automatically via URL after detecting the current Geo Location of the user. Then the URL generated can access the HTML (dev) containing the content of the forecast and fetch it through the class name. Since there are more elements associated with the same class an array of elements is returned. The forecast for the required days is at the index.

10.2.3   NIGHT VISION

An infrared (IR) camera is used to detect objects due to its high accuracy ratings in dark. IR cameras can detect infrared energy (heat) without being in close contact with the object.[2] Digital infrared cameras are conveniently built with a sensor that is sensitive to the IR radiation, but they are being able to detect inside energy and do not produce inside images due to infinite cut of filters that block IR light from reading the sensors and producing wired colors because of mixed IR and visible light.[16] Digital infrared camera will convert detected infrared energy into electronic signals and process these heat signals to produce a corresponding and precise thermal image. The infrared camera needs long exposures even in broad daylight to allow enough time for reflected IR light to pass through. These images will be processed with the object detection module to detect objects in them.

10.3 OBJECTIVES

Spectacles are developed as it is the most convenient device to wear at the time of driving. To make these spectacles intelligent some features are included and explained here. The main objectives of the paper are to explain:

1. Reducing the road accident rates, occurred due to the disturbance of intensified headlights or reckless driving.
2. Providing the navigation that will help the user to reach their destination by using voice assistance.
3. Providing information regarding potholes, pedestrian detection, animal crossing, and speed breakers.
4. Providing information regarding the weather and traffic updates.

10.4 PROCESS DESCRIPTION

Detecting only necessary objects can limit the data to be processed by the user and decrease distraction. For object detection, the HAAR cascade classifier is used in OpenCV. The classifier sorts the data into labeled data with the help of the dataset that it is trained on, like supervised learning. Haarlike features are the digital image features used for object detection in any image.[1] OpenCV uses edge, line, and center-surrounded haar-like features for object detection [referred from OpenCV Documentation]. Voice assistant is built to operate the entire device using voice commands. The major features for the aid of the user include detecting necessary objects and giving an immediate response, keeping updated with the latest news such as weather and traffic information, helping with navigation, and others. Voice assistant is built using Google Text-To-Speech (TTS) and speech recognition, the python package. The main advantage of these libraries is that it gives access to various pretrained speech recognition modules such as Google-cloud-api, watson-developer-cloud, wit et al. Most of these speech recognition modules work on Hidden Markov Model (HMM).[5,7] HMM is used to handle data, which can be represented in a series or sequence across time. It keeps track of enough past data to predict the upcoming one is in a series. Voice assistant is programmed to respond to some common queries and action related to the device and to make generalized communication with a user as other assistants do such as Siri or Alexa. If a mic catches the common set of keywords in a user's voice command like "Object Detection" or "Check Weather," it will trigger the corresponding module to work and respond via the assistant's voice itself. In the case of weather or traffic updates, Selenium, a web-scraping tool, is used. Selenium makes it easier to automate most web browser actions. It will fetch the data related to weather and traffic around the user's location from trustworthy web sources and will give the most recurring information. Then it will respond to a user via voice. As all these modules must be deployed on hardware, raspberry Pi is used to build a working prototype. Raspberry Pi might be less effective in this scenario, as all these modules are to be stored and run consecutively as per the user's demand. All these modules are deployed over the cloud and are accessed via Application Program Interface (API) Calls. These API Calls are integrated with the recursive conditional loop so that the voice command will trigger its respective API Call and in turn, the respective module will be triggered. After the execution of the called module, it will send the response to the source and the assistant will dictate using Google-TTS the user response.

10.5 ALGORITHM

10.5.1 TRAINING/DEVELOPMENT PHASE

1. Select necessary and efficient models.
2. Train the models on high GPU environment.
3. Deploy the trained models on the embedded system directly OR deploy the trained models on server and access via REST API on embedded system.

10.5.2 AFTER TRAINING/DEPLOYMENT OF MODELS PHASE

1. Listen to user command using microphone.
2. Convert it into text using speech recognition.
3. Send the text to the API-calling function.
4. Find the best match of the text in the predefined set of keywords and call its corresponding Module's API Call.
5. API Call runs the module and returns the text.

6. The text gets converted into speech using Google-TTS.
7. Dictate the output in the predefined format using microphone.

The entire process is divided into two phases. The training phase will include data collection, its analysis, model implementation, training, and deployment. The later phase is the part of the deployment process that presents how the user will access the trained models based on various inputs and commands. The product will work on various models based on the features required. Initially, the user will give the command by voice. This voice command will be processed using Google Cloud Text-To-Speech API and then will trigger one of the models based on voice command. If the user's voice command matches the keyword set for Object Detection, the product will start the object detection model. Similarly, models such as Night Vision or navigation will work. After all the processing of the model, the processed output will be dictated to the user.

10.6 OBSERVATION AND MATHEMATICAL MODEL

The Object Detection Model is tested for precision against the manually built 1000 set of labeled images to calculate the precision of the model. It is observed that the model gives a more all-rounder result at the threshold percentage of approximately 45%. At this value, the model detects most of the classes on which this model is trained.

$$Precision\ Value = TP/(TP + FP) \tag{1}$$

where
TP: true positive
When the model predicts the positive class correctly in an image/frame
FP: false positive
When the model predicts the positive class but is incorrect
calculation is based on a set of 1000 images of different objects.

TABLE 10.1 Precision Observations.

Threshold value		Precision value
	In percentage	In percentage
	95	0
	90	64.56
	85	58.23

TABLE 10.1   *(Continued)*

Threshold value		Precision value
	In percentage	**In percentage**
	80	21.93
	75	36.12
	70	48.38
	65	55.48
	60	60.64
	55	62.58
	50	63.22
	45	78.89
	40	69.51
	35	66.45
	30	67.74
	25	68.38

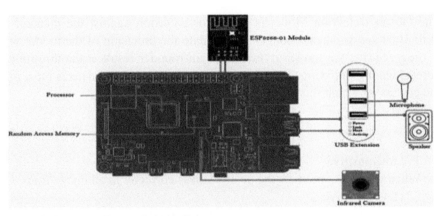

FIGURE 10.1   Raspberry Pi circuit diagram.

10.7   WORKING MODEL

Figure 10.1 shows the circuit diagram of the prototype built on raspberry pi and the components used. Microphone and speaker were used for input and output functionalities. An infrared camera for object detection is used. The working model as shown in Figure 10.2 presents the overall flow of the product. The user will give a voice command that will be processed using the

GMM/HMM model. Then one of the pretrained models will be triggered and the inputs will be taken from the environment for processing by the camera for object detection or night vision. The final output will again be processed using the GMM/HMM model and will be dictated to the user. In figure I, OD represents the object detection model and NV represents night vision. The voice command will be processed to identify preset keywords for selected models using speech recognition. The first model is for providing navigation instructions to the user, whereas the second model is for the object detection model which will help in the detection of potholes, pedestrians, breakers, and vehicles. Model 3 will be trained for night vision and Model 4 for fetching notifications from user mobile. Model 5 will get triggered if the user exceeds the speed limit and the last one will warn before breaking any traffic rules.

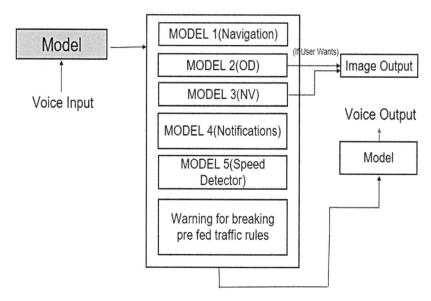

FIGURE 10.2 Overall working design.

10.8 CONCLUSION AND FUTURE SCOPE

Development in smart glasses is not a new one; however, in the last few years, it has seen extensive growth. According to the technical perspective, many of the advanced technologies are included in such glasses. The development of spectacles can reduce the rate of accidents. It will be helpful for people who drive daily. The technology adopted by the spectacles such as object detection, image manipulation, speech recognition, will provide the necessary information to the user. Most road accidents were happened because of reckless driving and various distracting environmental factors. The spectacles can help in avoiding the road accident rates by warning about forthcoming obstacles and avoiding distractions by providing only the required information. The problems of battery consumption, high processing can be resolved with the development of upcoming technologies. Many algorithms are still being improved to increase efficiency, which can greatly help in forming an ideal product.

KEYWORDS

- **machine learning**
- **object detection**
- **speech recognition**
- **web automation**
- **intelligent spectacles**

REFERENCES

1. Lin, T.; Goyal, P.; Girshick, R.; He, K.; Dollár, P. P. In *Focal Loss for Dense Object Detection*, IEEE Transactions on Pattern Analysis and Machine Intelligence, Feb 1, 2020; vol. 42, no. 2, p. 318327, 2020.
2. Raghatate, R.; Rajurkar, S.; Waghmare, M.; Ambatkar, P. Night Vision Techniques and Their Applications, 2013. *IJMER* **2013**, *3* (2), 816–820.
3. Capece, N.; Erra, U.; Scolamiero, R. In *Converting Night-Time Images to Day-Time Images through a Deep Learning Approach*, 2017 21st International Conference Information Visualisation (IV), London, 2017, pp. 324–331.
4. Sonekar, S. V.; Kshirsagar, M. In *Mitigating Packet Dropping Problem and Malicious Node Detection Mechanism in Ad Hoc Wireless Networks*, Proceeding of the 4th International Conference on Frontiers in Intelligent Computing: Theory and Applications, 2015, pp. 317328.
5. Abdel-Hamid, O.; Mohamed, A.; Jiang, H.; Deng, L.; Penn, G.; Yu, D. Convolutional Neural Networks for Speech Recognition. *IEEE/ACM Trans. Audio Speech Lang. Process.* **2014**, *22* (10), 1533–1545.
6. Ok, A. E.; Basoglu, N. A.; Daim, T. In *Exploring the Design Factors of Smart Glasses*, 2015 Portland International Conference on Management of Engineering and Technology (PICMET), Portland, OR, 2015, pp. 1657–1664.

7. Kłosowski, P.; Dustor, A.; Izydorczyk, J.; Kotas, J.; Ślimok, J. In *Computer Networks, CN 2014. vol 431 of Communications in Computer and Information Science*, Speech Recognition based on Open Source Speech Processing Software. 21st International Science Conference on Computer Networks (CN), Brunow, Poland, Jun 23–27, 2014; Kwiecień, A., Gaj, P., Stera P., Eds.; Springer: Cham, 2014.

8. Meile, L.; Ulrich, A.; Magno, M. In *Wireless Power Transmission Powering Miniaturized Low Power IoT devices: A Revie*, 2019 IEEE 8th International Workshop on Advances in Sensors and Interfaces (IWASI), Otranto, Italy; 2019, pp. 312–317.

9. Sonekar, S. V.; Kshirsagar, M. In *A Loom for Revealing Selfish and Malicious Node in Cluster based Adhoc Wireless Networks*, Proceeding of the 2nd IEEE International Conference on Computing for Sustainable Global Development (INDIACom), March 2015; New Delhi, India, 2015, pp. 370–375.

10. Lin, T.; Dollár, P.; Girshick, R.; He, K.; Hariharan, B.; Belongie, S. In *Feature Pyramid Networks for Object Detection*, 2017 IEEE Conference on Computer Vision and Pattern Recognition, Honolulu, HI, July 21–26, 2017, pp. 936–944.

11. Harsha, S.; Bhavya G. Google Glass. *IJARIIT*, www.ijariit.com.

12. Boksha, J.; Nath, A. Scope and Challenges in Smart Glasses: A Comprehensive Study on Present Scenario. *Int. J. Comput. Sci. Eng.* **2020**, *7* (1), 619–626.

13. Rehman, U.; Cao, S. Augmented-Reality-Based Indoor Navigation: A Comparative Analysis of Handheld Devices Versus Google Glass. *IEEE Trans. Hum. Mach. Syst.* **2017**, *47* (1), 140–151.

14. Sonekar, S. V.; Kshirsagar, M. M.; Malik, L. Cluster Head Selection and Malicious Node Detection in Wireless Ad Hoc Networks. *Next-Generation Networks* pp. 547–554, 2018.

15. Rinna J., 2015, Google Glass. *IJERT* **2015**, *3*, (28).

16. Neumann, L.; Karg, M.; Zhang, S.; Scharfenberger, C.; et al. In *Night Owls: A Pedestrians at Night Dataset*, Asian Conference on Computer Vision, 2018.

17. Mannor, S.; Peleg, D.; Rubinstein, R. The Cross-Entropy method for Classification Machine Learning, Association for Computing Machinery, pp. 561–568, 2005.

CHAPTER 11

Impact of Co-doping on Armchair Silicene Nanoribbon using Al and P: A Potential Material for Efficient Computing

SAURABH KHARWAR and SANGEETA SINGH

Microelectronics and VLSI Lab, Electronics and Communications Engineering, National Institute of Technology Patna, Patna, India

ABSTRACT

In the work, the structural, electronic, and quantum transport properties of one atom thick Al and P substitutionally codoped armchair silicene nanoribbon (ASiNR) have been investigated using density functional theory based on the first principles method. The study of formation energy (E_{form}), bond length, band structure, and density of states demonstrated that Al and P codoped ASiNR structures have stronger structural stability. It has been observed that the quantum transport properties at the atomic level are strongly doping position-dependent. The doped ASiNR exhibits p-type behavior due to the downward shifting of the Fermi level (E_F). Moreover, the reverse rectification ratio and negative differential resistance behavior have been found for codoped ASiNR, which has potential applications in high-speed switches, highly efficient computing circuits, tunnel diode, and ultra-thin nanodevices, respectively.

Computational Intelligence in Analytics and Information Systems, Volume 2: Advances in Digital Transformation, Selected Papers from CIAIS-2021. Parneeta Dhaliwal, PhD, Manpreet Kaur, PhD, Hardeo Kumar Thakur, PhD, Rajeev Kumar Arya, and Joan Lu (Eds.)

11.1   INTRODUCTION

In 2004, the synthesis of the first two-dimensional graphene nanosheets has been reported by Novoselov and his coworkers[1] using a micromechanical exfoliation method. Graphene nanosheet is a one-atom thin hexagonally arrangement of carbon atoms, which has attractive structural, electronic, and transport properties.[2-4] These fascinating properties of graphene nanosheets increase the investigation of other alternative two-dimensional materials. Graphene has various advantages still it is not suitable for current silicon-based electronic industries due to some challenges like dimensional controlled structural growth and incompatibility with nanoelectronic technology. Silicene is the silicon analog of graphene, which has also gained significant importance due to its graphene-like behavior. Interestingly, silicene is compatible with current silicon-based nanoelectronic devices. Recently, the experimental synthesis of high-quality silicene has been reported on Ag, Ir, and ZrBr substrate.[5-9] Moreover, the quasi-one-dimensional form of silicene, that is, silicene nanoribbon has been experimentally synthesized using the suitable catalyst. Based upon edge structural configuration, silicene nanoribbon has been categorized as zigzag silicene nanoribbon (ZSiNR) and armchair silicene nanoribbon (ASiNR).[10,11] In contrast to planar graphene, SiNR exhibits a stable buckled structure perpendicular with a buckling height of 0.44 Å due to its larger Si–Si bond length.[12] Furthermore, various structural modification has been experimentally and theoretically reported, which tailored the stability, bandgap, and Fermi level of SiNRs. The study of the substitutionally co-doping effect on structural, electronic, and quantum transport properties of SiNRs at the atomic level is still an area of research. Pristine ZSiNR exhibits metallic properties, whereas ASiNR exhibits width-dependent semiconducting properties. Sukhbir Singh et al.[13] studied the effect of p-type and n-type doping on ASiNR and observed negative differential effects and rectification properties. It has been observed that the bandgap of ASiNR can be tailored by structural modification, which has potential application in future nanoelectronic devices. In this study, the effects of co-doping on structural and electronic and quantum transport properties of ASiNRs have been studied using the density functional theory (DFT) computational method. Discusses the structural stability and the electronic behavior of each considered structures by calculating formation energy, electronic band structures, and the density of states (DOS) have been made. Further, the quantum transport properties of codoped ASiNR based on two-terminal devices have been studied.

The rest of this paper is summarized as: the computational framework and structure of ASiNRs are presented in the computational method section. The structural, electronic, and quantum transport properties of ASiNRs substitutionally codoped with Al and P atom are discussed in the result and discussion section. Finally, the conclusion section discussed the concluding remarks of this work.

11.2   COMPUTATIONAL METHOD

The structural and electronic properties of Al and P substitutionally codoped ASiNRs have been studied and compared with pristine ASiNRs nanostructure. Hydrogen passivated ASiNRs structures are used with N_a dimmer lines, where N_a represents the width of the structure. In the present study, N_a is considered as 7 for considered five structures, that is, pristine ASiNR (A), Al and P codoped at the left side (B), Al and P codoped at the upper corner edge (C), Al and P codoped at the diagonal corner (D), and Al and P codoped at the center of left and right sides (E), respectively, as shown in Figure 11.1. The calculation used the DFT computational method with a local density approximation exchange-correlation function. DFT modeling combined with a double-zeta polarized basis set is applied for electron density expedition with 150 Ry mesh cutoff. The $1 \times 1 \times 50$ k-point is used for Brillouin zone sampling with 10 Å vacuum padding. The formation energy (E_{form}) is calculated using eq 11.1:[15]

$$E_{form} = \frac{E_T - \left(n_{Si}E_{Si} + n_{Al}E_{Al} + n_P E_P + n_H E_H\right)}{N} \qquad (11.1)$$

where E_T, E_{Si}, E_{Al}, E_P, E_H, n_{Si}, n_{Al}, n_P, n_H, and N represent total energy, isolated energy of silicon, aluminum, phosphorus, hydrogen, and the total number of atoms, respectively. Two-probe device structures are used to calculate transport properties. The current–voltage characteristics have been calculated by eqs 11.2 and 11.3:[16]

$$T(E,V) = T_r \left[{}_L G^R(E,V) {}_R G^A(E,V) \right] \qquad (11.2)$$

$$I(V) = \frac{2e^2}{h} \int T(E,V) \left\{ f(E - {}_L) - f(E - {}_R) \right\} dE \qquad (11.3)$$

where $\varepsilon_L / \varepsilon_R$ is the electrochemical potential of left/right electrode, respectively. G^R, G^A, and $T(E, V)$ represent retarded, advanced Green's function and transmission spectrum at vias voltage.

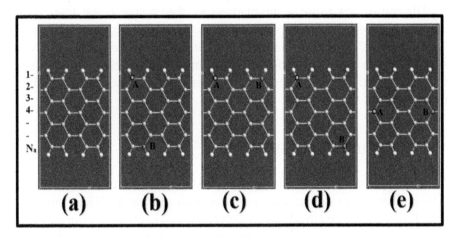

FIGURE 11.1   Atomic structures of (a) A, (b) B, (c) C, (d) D, and (e) E, respectively. Gray spheres and white spheres represent silicene and hydrogen atoms, respectively. Solid circle with position A and dotted circle with position B indicate doping site of Al and P, respectively.

TABLE 11.1   Calculated Fermi Energy (eV), Bandgap (eV), and Formation Energy (E_{form}) of (a) A, (b) B, (c) C, (d) D, and (e) E, Respectively.

Structure	E_F	E_g	E_{form}
A	−4.08	0.45	−5.18
B	−4.11	0.21	−5.14
C	−4.10	0.23	−5.14
D	−4.12	0.36	−5.14
E	−4.09	0.59	−5.16

11.3   RESULT AND DISCUSSION

11.3.1   STRUCTURAL PROPERTIES

The structural properties of pristine and codoped ASiNR structures have been analyzed by calculating bond lengths, E_{form}, and compare with pristine ASiNR structure. After the structural optimization, all the considered structures exhibit buckled structures with a buckling height of 0.44 Å, which is also observed in previous studies.[13] The calculated bond length of Si–Si,

Si–Al, Si–P, and Si–H are found to be 2.28 Å, 2.38 Å, 2.20 Å, and 1.10 Å, respectively. The observed bond length of Si–Si and Si–H is consistent with previous literature.[13] The geometrical stability of codoped ASiNR structures has been investigated and compared with pristine structure. E_{form} calculation has been performed using eq 11.1 to calculate the stability of all considered structures and is listed in Table 11.1. The calculated E_{form} of all the structures shows negative energy which advocates that all the considered structures are stable. In all the considered codoped ASiNR structures, the E_{form} of structures E is found to be more negative, which indicates its highest stability.

11.3.2 ELECTRONIC PROPERTIES

In this section, the electronic properties of Al and P codoped ASiNR structures are investigated using band structures and DOS and compared with pristine ASiNR structure A. The computed band structures of 7-ASiNR are shown in Figure 11.2. All the considered structures show semiconducting properties irrespective of their doping positions. The calculated bandgap values of all the considered structures are listed in Table 11.1. The relative order of bandgap values of all the considered structures are found to be $E > A > B > C > D$. In contrast to pristine ASiNR, the additional electronic bands are observed near the Fermi level. The additional electronic bands are generated due to the edge energy state and are induced due to dopant which results in lower bandgap values. The bandgap value of structure E is found to be maximum as Al and P are at the center; therefore, edge states are occupied and hence bandgap value is found to the maximum. Furthermore, to clarify the effect of co-doping on ASiNR with Al and P atoms, the DOS of all the considered structures has been studied and depicted in Figure 11.3. The inspection of the DOS profiles shows the zero-dimensional (0D) and one-dimensional (1D) nature of electron peaks. In contrast to pristine ASiNR, the additional electronic states are found around the Fermi level (E_F) due to delocalized p-orbital electrons. Furthermore, the calculated E_F of each considered structure is listed in Table 11.1, which shows the downward shifting of E_F. The downward shifting of E_F advocates p-type behavior for Al and P codoped ASiNR structures. A similar type of downward shifting of E_F is also reported in the previous literature.[13]

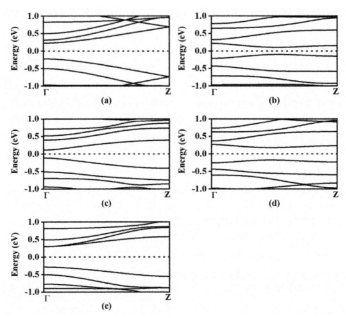

FIGURE 11.2   Calculated band structures of (a) A, (b) B, (c) C, (d) D, and (e) E, respectively. The Fermi level is represented by the dotted line.

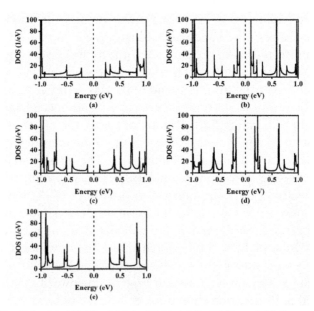

FIGURE 11.3   Calculated DOS of (a) A, (b) B, (c) C, (d) D, and (e) E, respectively. The Fermi level is represented by the dotted line.

11.3.3 TRANSPORT PROPERTIES

In this section, the transport properties of two-terminal-based Al and P codoped ASiNR devices in the biasing range from −1 V to 1 V are studied and compared with the pristine ASiNR device. The two-terminal device of the pristine ASiNR device is depicted in Figure 11.4. The current–voltage curves of all the considered structures are shown in Figure 11.5. The current–voltage curve of pristine ASiNR device exhibits symmetric behavior in both positive and negative biasing, which is similar with pristine graphene-based device. The current for devices A and C starts rising from 0.4 V in both negative and positive biasing while for devices B, D, and E gradually increases concerning bias voltage. The current–voltage characteristics of substitutionally codoped ASiNR devices exhibit asymmetricity in opposite biasing, which predicts the possibility of rectification behavior. The rectification ratio

(RR) is calculated by $RR = \dfrac{|I(V)|}{|I(-V)|}$ and reverse rectification ratio (RRR) is

calculated by $RRR = \dfrac{|I(-V)|}{|I(V)|}$.[17] The calculated values of RR are found to be

less than 1 for all the considered devices. The calculated values of RRR are listed in Table 11.2.

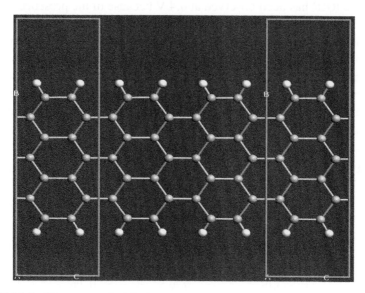

FIGURE 11.4 The two-terminal device structure of pristine ASiNR.

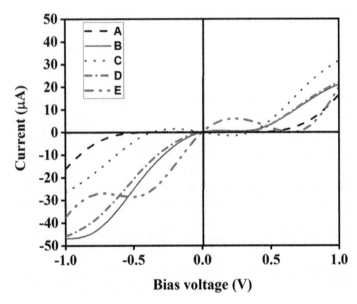

FIGURE 11.5   Calculated current–voltage characteristics of device (a) A, (b) B, (c) C, (d) D, and (e) E, respectively.

The perusal of Table 11.2 reveals that device D exhibits maximum RRR at 0.4 V. The RRR has been observed at 0.4 V because of the presence/absence of transmission spectra at −0.4 V/0.4 V in the bias window of left and right electrodes. Interestingly, negative differential resistance (NDR) behavior has been observed for device E as the current value of device E increases till 0.3 V and beyond 0.3 V current starts decreases till 0.6 V. The NDR behavior is observed because of the presence of a larger transmission region at 0.3 V and after that, it decreases till 0.6 V which results in lower current at 0.6 V, which has potential application for switching and tunnel diode.

TABLE 11.2   Calculated RRR of Device B, C, D, and E Respectively.

Voltage	Device			
	B	**C**	**D**	**E**
0.4	14.83	0.72	4.50E-06	6.57
0.8	3.01	0.82	9.88E-06	8.01
1.2	2.05	0.81	9.79E-06	1.47
1.6	3.19	0.70	5.23E-06	2.282
2	2.42	0.96	4.292E-06	2.56

11.4 CONCLUSION

The effect of substitutionally codoped with Al and P on ASiNR has been investigated using first-principles DFT. The investigation of structural properties reveals that Al and P codoped at the center of both sides are structurally more stable. It has been observed that the structural and electronic properties of ASiNR can be tailored by doping position. Interestingly, the Al and P codoped ASiNR-based device exhibits reverse rectification and negative differential behavior.

These results indicate that codoped ASiNR with Al and P significantly enhanced the structural, electronic, and quantum transport properties, which has potential application for future high-speed nanorectifiers and highly efficient computing circuits.

ACKNOWLEDGMENT

Computational resources were provided by the Indian Institute of Information Technology, Allahabad, India.

KEYWORDS

- **armchair silicene nanoribbon (ASiNR)**
- **electronic properties**
- **co-doping effect**
- **rectifier**

REFERENCES

1. Novoselov, K. S.; Geim, A. K.; Morozov, S. V.; Jiang, D.; Zhang, Y.; Dubonos, S. V.; ... Firsov, A. A. Electric Field Effect in Atomically Thin Carbon Films. *Science* **2004,** *306* (5696), 666–669.
2. Bolotin, K. I.; Sikes, K. J.; Jiang, Z.; Klima, M.; Fudenberg, G.; Hone, J. E.; ... Stormer, H. L. Ultrahigh Electron Mobility in Suspended Graphene. *Solid State Commun.* **2008,** *146* (9–10), 351–355.
3. Zhang, Y.; Tan, Y. W.; Stormer, H. L.; Kim, P. Experimental Observation of the Quantum Hall Effect and Berry's Phase in Graphene. *Nature* **2005,** 438 (7065), 201–204.
4. Bostwick, A.; Ohta, T.; Seyller, T.; Horn, K.; Rotenberg, E. Quasiparticle Dynamics in Graphene. *Nat. Phys.* **2007,** *3* (1), 36–40.

5. Vogt, P.; De Padova, P.; Quaresima, C.; Avila, J.; Frantzeskakis, E.; Asensio, M. C.; ... Le Lay, G. Silicene: Compelling Experimental Evidence for Graphenelike Two-Dimensional Silicon. *Phys. Rev. Lett.* **2012**, *108* (15), 155501.

6. Feng, B.; Ding, Z.; Meng, S.; Yao, Y.; He, X.; Cheng, P.; ... Wu, K. Evidence of Silicene in Honeycomb Structures of Silicon on Ag (111). *Nano Lett.* **2012**, *12* (7), 3507–3511.

7. Mannix, A. J.; Kiraly, B.; Fisher, B. L.; Hersam, M. C.; Guisinger, N. P. Silicon Growth at the Two-Dimensional Limit on Ag (111). *ACS Nano* **2014**, *8* (7), 7538–7547.

8. Meng, L.; Wang, Y.; Zhang, L.; Du, S.; Wu, R.; Li, L., ... Gao, H. J. Buckled Silicene Formation on Ir (111). *Nano Lett.* **2013**, *13* (2), 685–690.

9. Fleurence, A.; Friedlein, R.; Ozaki, T.; Kawai, H.; Wang, Y.; Yamada-Takamura, Y. Experimental Evidence for Epitaxial Silicene on Diboride Thin Films. *Phys. Rev. Lett.* **2012**, *108* (24), 245501.

10. Cahangirov, S.; Topsakal, M.; Aktürk, E.; Şahin, H.; Ciraci, S. Two-and One-Dimensional Honeycomb Structures of Silicon and Germanium. *Phys. Rev. Lett.* **2009**, *102* (23), 236804.

11. Le Lay, G.; Aufray, B.; Léandri, C.; Oughaddou, H.; Biberian, J. P.; De Padova, P.; ... Kara, A. Physics and Chemistry of Silicene Nano-Ribbons. *Appl. Surf. Sci.* **2009**, *256* (2), 524–529.

12. Guzmán-Verri, G. G.; Voon, L. L. Y. Electronic Structure of Silicon-Based Nanostructures. *Phys. Rev. B* **2007**, *76* (7), 075131.

13. Singh, S.; De Sarkar, A.; Singh, B.; Kaur, I. Electronic and Transport Behavior of Doped Armchair Silicene Nanoribbons Exhibiting Negative Differential Resistance and its FET Performance. *RSC Adv. 7* (21), 12783–12792.

14. Jaiswal, N. K.; Srivastava, P. First Principles Calculations of Cobalt Doped Zigzag Graphene Nanoribbons. *Solid State Commun. 152* (15), 1489–1492.

15. Kharwar, S.; Singh, S.; Jaiswal, N. K. First-Principles Investigation of Pd-Doped Armchair Graphene Nanoribbons as a Potential Rectifier. *J. Electron. Mater.* **2021**, *50,* 1196–1206.

16. Jha, K. K.; Jaiswal, N. K.; Pattanaik, M.; Srivastava, P. First-Principle Investigations for Electronic Transport in Nitrogen-Doped Disconnected Zigzag Graphene Nanoribbons. *Microelectron. Eng.* **2018**, *199*, 96–100.

17. Joshi, A.; Ramachandran, C. N. High-bias Negative Differential Resistance Effect in Pure, Doped and Co-Doped Carbon Nanotubes Connected to Boron Nitride Nanotubes. *Phys. E: Low-Dimens. Syst. Nanostructures* **2019**, *113*, 1–7.

CHAPTER 12

DOIFCM: An Outlier Efficient IFCM

SONIKA DAHIYA[1] and ANJANA GOSAIN[2]

[1]Department of Computer Science and Engineering, Delhi Technological University, Delhi, India

[2]University School of Information & Communication Technology, Guru Gobind Singh Indraprastha University, Delhi, India

ABSTRACT

Fuzzy-C-means (FCM) clustering algorithm is one of the most popular and widely used fuzzy clustering algorithms owing to its high efficiency and ease in implementation. However, FCM fails to provide accurate centroid computation in the presence of outliers which is generally the case for real-world data. This paper introduces a new clustering algorithm that merges intuitionistic fuzzy set theory to improve cluster computation with density-oriented outlier detection, resulting into a robust clustering algorithm— density-oriented intuitionistic fuzzy-C-means (DOIFCM). The performance of DOIFCM is compared with the performance of other clustering algorithms such as FCM, credibilistic FCM, possibilistic FCM (PFCM), intuitionistic FCM, and density-oriented FCM, and the experimental results prove that DOIFCM has high efficacy in the outlier contaminated data.

12.1 INTRODUCTION

With the exponential growth of digitalization across the world, tremendous amounts of data are generated every day. It is crucial to use effective

Computational Intelligence in Analytics and Information Systems, Volume 2: Advances in Digital Transformation, Selected Papers from CIAIS-2021. Parneeta Dhaliwal, PhD, Manpreet Kaur, PhD, Hardeo Kumar Thakur, PhD, Rajeev Kumar Arya, and Joan Lu (Eds.)

processing and analysis methods to maintain and analyze the collected data. It is also necessary to identify data points that deviate from the average data points by a substantial margin so that such data points are not considered while processing the data.

In statistics, an outlier is an observation that significantly differs from other observations, that is, an outlier deviates from the average data point by a substantial margin.[30] By removing or mitigating outliers' influence from a dataset, clustering results can be improved significantly. In addition, outlier detection itself plays a fundamental role in various applications such as fraud in financial data,[1] healthcare fraud,[2] intrusions in communication networks,[3] fault diagnosis,[4,5,20,29] distributed tracking systems,[6] forgery detection,[7] etc.

Cluster analysis is an unsupervised categorization method under data mining.[8,9] It is used to group similar data points in same group. Since the introduction of fuzzy sets, many fuzzy clustering algorithms have been proposed such as fuzzy-C-means (FCM),[13] possibilistic FCM (PFCM),[14] NC,[15,16] credibilistic FCM (CFCM),[17] FCM-σ,[18] intuitionistic FCM (IFCM),[12] IFCM-σ,[19] density-oriented FCM (DOFCM),[28] and many others.[24,26,29] Fuzzy-C-means and its variants have been used in various applications such as image resolution and pattern recognition.[10,11,27] FCM shows efficient performance on noiseless data; however, it is highly sensitive to outliers as it fails to differentiate outliers from normal data. Because of this constraint, centroids are often deviated from the cluster center in the presence of outliers. In 1998, CFCM[17] was introduced with a new parameter named credibility which helps in reducing the impact of an outlier in cluster computation but it still does not provide accurate centroid. Later on, PFCM[12] was introduced which combined possibilistic membership and fuzzy membership to compute cluster but it too fails in the presence of outlier, especially when clusters are of unequal size.

A new parameter, namely, Hesitation degree was introduced in IFCM and it was combined with the membership degree to further improve the accuracy of fuzzy clustering.[12] IFCM aims to improve centroid computation by diffusing the effect of outliers. Though a relatively robust algorithm, IFCM still has limitations in outlier contaminated data. All these algorithms diffuse the effect of outliers to improve the clustering process but DOFCM[28] proposed a complete new approach in which outlier identification is done as a preprocessing step and then clustering is performed using FCM.

This paper proposes a new clustering algorithm, namely, DOIFCM, which focuses on the identification of outliers and then performs clustering using intuitionistic fuzzy sets to improve cluster analysis and centroid computation. Results of above-discussed algorithms are compared on three standard datasets: D10, D12, and D15, and it is observed that DOIFCM outperforms in terms of clustering results.

In the following section, all relevant algorithms are briefly discussed. In Section 12.3, the proposed algorithm, DOIFCM, is explained and in the subsequent section, simulation results and their analysis are discussed. In the last section, the conclusion and future work have been discussed.

12.2 RELEVANT ALGORITHMS IN LITERATURE

This section briefly addresses various clustering algorithms such as FCM and its variants. In the following subsections, X denotes the dataset, where $X = \{x_1, x_2, ..., x_n\}$. v_k denotes the centroids of kth cluster, and d_{ik} denotes the Euclidean distance between the data point- "x_i" and cluster centroid- "v_k." "c" denotes the total number of clusters in the dataset.

12.2.1 FCM

FCM[13] is a clustering approach in which each data point can be a member of more than one cluster. It is based on the minimization of the objective function (J_{FCM}):

$$J_{FCM(U,V)} = \sum_{k=1}^{c}\sum_{i=1}^{n} u_{ki}^{m} d_{ki}^{2}$$ (12.1)

where u_{ki} is the membership of x_i in cluster "v_k" and $d_{ki} = \| x_i - v_k \|$. u_{ki} satisfies the relationship:

$$\sum_{k=1}^{c} u_{ki} = 1 \; i=1,2,...n$$ (12.2)

where m denotes the fuzziness index and the Euclidean approach is used to calculate d_{ki}.

Fuzzy partitioning is achieved by iteratively optimizing the function shown above (12.1), and modification of the membership u_{ki} and cluster centers v_k by:

$$u_{ki} = \frac{1}{\sum_{j=1}^{c}\left(\dfrac{d_{ki}}{d_{ji}}\right)^{\frac{2}{m-1}}} \forall \; i, k$$ (12.3)

where $1 \le i \le n$ and $1 \le k \le c$, and ,

$$v_k = \frac{\sum_{i=1}^{n}\left(u_{ki}^{m} x_i\right)}{\sum_{i=1}^{n}\left(u_{ki}^{m}\right)} \quad \forall\, i \tag{12.4}$$

12.2.2   IFCM

Intuitionistic FCM[12] introduces a new concept, namely, hesitation degree to improve cluster computation. The hesitation degree and membership degree together define intuitionistic fuzzy membership. The IFCM objective function includes two terms:

(i)   Intuitionistic fuzzy entropy.
(ii) An updated version of the objective function of FCM that includes hesitation degree.

IFCM objective function (J_{IFCM}) is:

$$J_{\text{IFCM}} = \sum_{k=1}^{c}\sum_{i=1}^{n} u_{ik}^{*m} d_{ik}^{2} + \sum_{i=1}^{n} n_i^{*} e^{1-n_i^{*}} \tag{12.5}$$

where m = 2, $u_{ik}^{*} = u_{ik} + n_{ik}$, where u_{ik}^{*} is "intuitionistic fuzzy membership" of x_i in v_k. n_{ik} represents the hesitation degree which is computed as follows:

$$n_{ik} = 1 - u_{ik} - \left(1 - u_{ik}^{\alpha}\right)^{\frac{1}{\alpha}}, \alpha > 0 \text{ and}$$

$$n_i^{*} = \frac{1}{N}\sum_{k=1}^{n} n_{ik}\,, \ k \in [1,\, N] \tag{12.6}$$

Membership updation equation and centroid updation equation are as follows:

$$u_{ki} = \frac{1}{\sum_{j=1}^{c}\left(\dfrac{d_{ki}}{d_{ji}}\right)^{\frac{2}{m-1}}} \forall\, i, k \tag{12.7}$$

$$v_k = \frac{\sum_{i=1}^{n}\left(u_{ki}^{*m} x_i\right)}{\sum_{i=1}^{n}\left(u_{ki}^{*m}\right)} \quad \forall\, i \tag{12.8}$$

The seeds are updated in every step of IFCM algorithm and each data point is assigned a membership degree respective to each cluster. When the algorithm ends, the given intuitionistic fuzzy sets are clustered according to the calculated degrees of membership.

12.2.3   CFCM

Crediblistic FCM,[17] proposed by Chintalapudi, introduced a new variable called credibility which measures the aptness of a vector for a dataset. An outlier is supposed to have a significantly low credibility value as compared to a nonoutlier. The credibility variable is defined as[21]:

$$\varphi_k = 1 - \frac{(1-\theta)\alpha_k}{max_{j=1..n}(\alpha_j)}, 0 \leq \theta \leq 1 \tag{12.9}$$

where $\alpha_i = \min(d_{ik})$ represents the distance of point x_i to its closest centroid "v_k." The noisiest point "x_i" gets its credibility value equal to ϕ and ϕ is the parameter that is responsible for controlling the minimum value of k. Objective function (J_{CFCM}) for CFCM is:

$$J_{CFCM(U,V)} = \sum_{k=1}^{c}\sum_{i=1}^{n} u_{ki}^{m} d_{ki}^{2} \tag{12.10}$$

subject to the constraint: $\sum_{i=1}^{c} u_{ik} = \varphi_k$.

CFCM limits the negative impact of noisy data on centroid computation. Therefore, it improves centroid computation but is unable to deliver precise centroids and loses its efficacy by assigning some outliers to clusters.[22]

12.2.4   PFCM

Possibilistic FCM[14,23] is a modification of the possibilistic approach in which Pal et al. merged the fuzzy and possibilistic approaches. As a result, PFCM has two forms of memberships—a fuzzy membership (u_{ki}) that calculates the extent to which a point belongs to different clusters and a possibilistic membership (t_{ki}) that determines the extent of "typicality" of any cluster's point.

PFCM minimizes the objective function (J_{PFCM}), as given below[21]:

$$J_{PFCM(U,V,T)} = \sum_{k=1}^{c}\sum_{i=1}^{n}\left(au_{ki}^{n} + bt_{ki}^{n}\right)d_{ki}^{2} + \sum_{k=1}^{c}\gamma_k\sum_{i=1}^{n}\left(1-t_{ki}\right)^{n} \tag{12.11}$$

$$\sum_{k=1}^{c} u_{ki} = 1 \forall i \tag{12.12}$$

where $0 \leq u_{ki}, t_{ki} < 1$. Membership updation equations are as follows:

$$u_{ki} = \frac{1}{\sum_{j=1}^{c}\left(\dfrac{d_{ki}}{d_{ji}}\right)^{\frac{2}{m-1}}} \tag{12.13}$$

and

$$t_{ki} = \cfrac{1}{1 + \left(\cfrac{b}{\gamma_k} d_{ki}^2\right)^{\frac{1}{n-1}}} \tag{12.14}$$

Centroid update equation is:

$$v_k = \frac{\sum_{i=1}^{n}\left(au_{ki}^m + bt_{ki}^n\right)n_i}{\sum_{i=1}^{n}\left(au_{ki}^m + bt_{ki}^n\right)} \tag{12.15}$$

PFCM's performance is comparatively better when compared to FCM and PCM individually. Nonetheless, it is unable to produce desirable results when presented with clusters that contain outliers and are fairly dissimilar.[20]

12.2.5 DOFCM

DOFCM[20] aims to diminish the noise sensitivity of FCM by pinpointing outliers present in the data prior to clustering, it constructs n clusters with $(n-1)$ clusters of data points to be processed and one cluster of outliers. In a dataset, r is computed as per Ester,[25] using r as radius and data point as the center, vicinity of that data point is defined. Each point is supposed to contain more than or equal to a minimum no. of different points in its vicinity. DOFCM describes a density factor which is termed as neighborhood membership which reflects an object's measured density relative to its neighborhood:

$$M_{neighborhood}^i = \frac{\eta_{neighborhood}^i}{\eta_{max}} \tag{12.16}$$

where $\eta_{neighborhood}^i$ represents the count of points present in the neighborhood of "x_i" and η_{max} is the maximum number of data points for any data point in the dataset. "q" satisfies the following equation if its present in i's neighborhood:

$$q \in X \,|\, dist(i,q) \le r \tag{12.17}$$

where r is neighborhood radius, and dist(i,q) denotes the distance between the points q and i. For a point "i" in a dataset[21]:

$$M^i_{neighborhood} < \alpha \ then \ i \ is \ an \ outlier \tag{12.18}$$

$$M^i_{neighborhood} \geq \alpha \ then \ i \ is \ not \ an \ outlier \tag{12.19}$$

DOFCM modifies FCM objective function as follows:

$$J_{(X, U, V)} = \sum_{i=1}^{c+1}\sum_{k=1}^{N}(u_{ik})^m (d_{ik})^2 \tag{12.20}$$

The membership function is updated as:

$$u_{ik} = \begin{cases} \dfrac{1}{\sum_{j=1}^{c}\left(\dfrac{d_{ik}}{d_{jk}}\right)^{\frac{2}{m-1}}} & if \ not \ an \ outlier \\ \\ 0 \ if \ outlier \end{cases} \tag{12.21}$$

Fuzzy membership constraint:

$$0 \ zz \sum_{i=1}^{c}\mu_{ik} \leq 1, k = 1, 2, ..., N \tag{12.22}$$

12.3 PROPOSED APPROACH

Among FCM, CFCM, PFCM, and IFCM, IFCM is most robust in dealing with noise.[24] This acted as motivation to propose DOIFCM. DOIFCM merges DOFCM[20] and IFCM[12] to improve the computation strength of IFCM by effectively dealing with outliers present in the dataset. It first identifies the outliers, excludes them from the dataset, and performs cluster analysis using intuitionistic fuzzy sets. DOFCM describes a density factor named as neighborhood membership which is relative density of an object with respect to its neighborhood. Outlier identification is based on the concept of neighborhood membership.[20] Neighborhood membership ($M_{neighbourhood}$) determines the density proportion respective to the most densely populated data point and ranges from 0 to 1. $M_{neighborhood}$ is formulated as follows:

$$M^i_{neighborhood} = \frac{\eta^i_{neighborhood}}{\eta_{max}} \tag{12.23}$$

where $i_{neighborhood}$ is the count of data points in neighborhood of i and η_{max} is the maximum count of data points in respective neighborhood of any point in the dataset.

12.3.1   ALGORITHM STEPS

Input: X (dataset), c (number of clusters), m (fuzziness index), maxIter, minImpr, thv (threshold value)

Output: U (membership matrix), OL (set of outliers), C (cluster centroids)
1. Determine neighborhood radius as per Ester[25]
2. Compute η_i for all $x_i \in X$ as per eq 12.6
3. Find η_{max}
4. Compute $M^i_{neighbourhood}$ for all $x_i \in X$
5. For all x_i, if $M^i_{neighbourhood} > $ thv, set $U(x_i)=0$, and OL $\leftarrow$ { OL } $\cup$ {x_i}
6. **Clustering steps:**
7. Randomly select initial U subject to condition specified in eq 12.2
8. Set $i=1$
9. Calculate C, *objective function* and new_U using eqs 12.8, 12.5, and 12.7 respectively
10. Increment i
11. Repeat step 9 and 10 until $((obj\_fun_i - obj\_fun_{i-1})$ or $(i <= maxIter)$
12. Return C, U, and OL.

12.4   SIMULATION AND RESULT ANALYSIS

FCM, CFCM, PFCM, IFCM, DOFCM, and DOIFCM are implemented using MATLAB R2017a on a system with 8 GB RAM and Mac operating system. The following setting is used for hyperparameters: $m = 2$, maxIter = 100, minImpr = 0.00001.

12.4.1   DATASET

For experimental analysis, comparison is drawn on D10, D12, D15. D10 is a noise and outlier-free dataset with two clusters. D12 is a minor corrupted form of D10 containing one noise data and one outlier. D15 is D10 with four outliers and one noise data. Notation for representing clustering results in Figures 12.1–12.3 is like centroids for each cluster are marked using star shape, each data point to one cluster is marked using triangle, each data point to another cluster is marked using the dot.

The ideal cluster centers for the dataset are:

Cluster 1 (cx : −3.34, cy : 0)
Cluster 2 (cx : 3.34, cy : 0)

12.4.2 *RESULT ANALYSIS*

12.4.2.1 *ANALYSIS FOR D10*

Clustering results on D10 dataset by FCM, IFCM, CFCM, PFCM, DOFCM, and DOIFCM are shown in Figure 12.1. Table 12.1 shows the average error in centroid computation using the algorithms—FCM, IFCM, CFCM, PFCM, DOFCM, and DOIFCM. From Figure 12.1 and Table 12.1, it is analyzed that for outlier free and noise free dataset, the performance of all these algorithms is similar and respectful as the average error is less than 0.08%. It is observed that FCM and DOFCM give exactly same results for noise-free data. Similar is the observation with IFCM and DOIFCM. In the case of noise and outlier-free dataset like D10, CFCM gives best result; however, one data point is equally assigned to both the cluster.

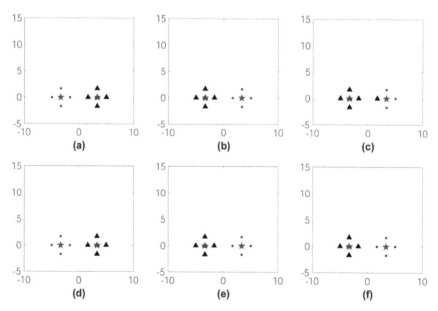

FIGURE 12.1 Clustering results on D10 dataset using (a) FCM, (b) IFCM, (c) CFCM, (d) PFCM, (e) DOFCM, (f) DOIFCM.

TABLE 12.1 Error on Centroid Computation on D10 Dataset.

D10	Cluster 1		Cluster 2		Error in cluster 1	Error in cluster 2	Average error
	cx^*	cy^*	cx^*	cy^*			cx^*
FCM	3.3590978	−0.0000010	−3.3590980	0.0000010	0.0003647	0.0003647	0.0003647
IFCM	3.3252261	0.0000000	−3.3252258	0.0000000	0.0002183	0.0002183	0.0002183
CFCM	3.3400559	0.0000000	−3.3400559	0.0000000	0.0000000	0.0000000	0.0000000
PFCM	3.3478502	0.0000000	−3.3478502	0.0000000	0.0000616	0.0000616	0.0000616
DOFCM	3.3591100	−0.0000014	−3.3591104	0.0000016	0.0003652	0.0003652	0.0003652
DOIFCM	3.3252260	0.0000000	−3.3252260	0.0000000	0.0002183	0.0002183	0.0002183

12.4.2.2   ANALYSIS FOR D12

Clustering results on D12 dataset by FCM, IFCM, CFCM, PFCM, DOFCM, and DOIFCM are shown in Figure 12.2. Table 12.2 shows that the average error in centroid computation using the algorithms—FCM, IFCM, CFCM, PFCM, DOFCM, and DOIFCM. On analyzing, Figure 12.2 and Table 12.2, it is observed that FCM and PFCM calculated centroids are deviated toward the outliers. Hence, FCM and PFCM are the algorithms that are most impacted by the presence of a single outliers. IFCM being more robust to noisy data is less affected and performs better. CFCM also shows better performance than FCM and PFCM, but relatively less effective than IFCM. DOFCM and DOIFCM successfully identify the outlier, this leads to more precise centroids.

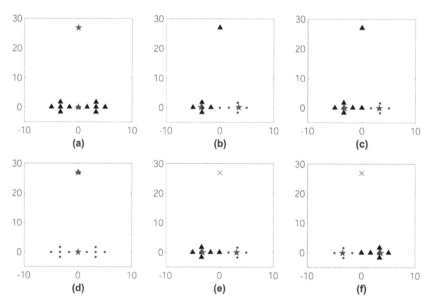

FIGURE 12.2   Clustering results on D12 dataset using (a) FCM, (b) IFCM, (c) CFCM, (d) PFCM, (e) DOFCM, (f) DOIFCM.

12.4.2.3   ANALYSIS FOR D15

Figure 12.3 shows clustering results on D15 dataset by FCM, IFCM, CFCM, PFCM, DOFCM, and DOIFCM. Table 12.3 shows the average error in centroid computation using the algorithms—FCM, IFCM, CFCM, PFCM,

DOFCM, and DOIFCM. It is observed that with the presence of such a good density of outliers, FCM, IFCM, and PFCM failed drastically as they formed one cluster of the four outliers and another cluster of the complete dataset. CFCM performs better with the help of the credibility variable. DOFCM and DOIFCM perform best as they identify all four outliers and then perform clustering, thus, resulting into the right clusters and most accurate centroids.

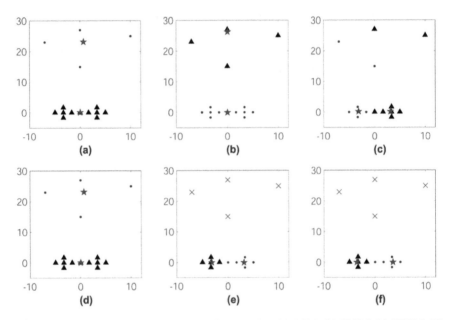

FIGURE 12.3 Clustering results on D15 dataset using (a) FCM, (b) IFCM, (c) CFCM, (d) PFCM, (e) DOFCM, (f) DOIFCM.

12.5 CONCLUSION AND FUTURE WORK

FCM is an effective clustering algorithm; however, FCM fails to perform in the presence of outliers as it treats each data point equally. Other variants of FCM such as CFCM, PFCM, IFCM, DOFCM improved the clustering performance to some extent; however, these algorithms too have the limitations. The proposed approach, DOIFCM, merges intuitionistic fuzzy set theory which offers improved cluster computation and density-oriented outlier detection to form an effective clustering algorithm. Based on experiments on D10, D12, and D15 datasets, it is observed that DOIFCM outperforms FCM and all major variants of the FCM algorithm.

In the future, one can explore to address the limitations of DOIFCM such as convergence to the threshold value, sensitivity to initialization problems, and time complexity.

KEYWORDS

- **fuzzy-C-means (FCM)**
- **intuitionistic fuzzy sets**
- **intuitionistic fuzzy-C-means (IFCM)**
- **possibilistic FCM (PFCM)**
- **credibilistic fuzzy c-means (CFCM)**
- **density-oriented intuitionistic fuzzy-C-means (DOIFCM)**

REFERENCES

1. Ngai, E. W.; Hu, Y.; Wong, Y. H.; Chen, Y.; Sun, X. The Application of Data Mining Techniques in Financial Fraud Detection: A Classification Framework and an Academic Review of Literature. *Decis. Support Syst.* **2011,** *50* (3), 559–69.
2. Van Capelleveen, G.; Poel, M.; Mueller, R. M.; Thornton, D.; Van Hillegersberg, J. Outlier Detection in Healthcare Fraud: A Case Study in the Medicaid Dental Domain. *Int. J. Account. Inform. Syst.* **2016,** *21,* 18–31.
3. Zhang, J.; Zulkernine, M. In *Anomaly Based Network Intrusion Detection with Unsupervised Outlier Detection,* 2006 IEEE International Conference On Communications, Jun 11, 2006; IEEE, 2006, Vol. 5, pp. 2388–2393.
4. Ramos, A. R.; Llanes-Santiago, O.; De Lázaro, J. B.; Corona, C. C.; Neto, A. S.; Galdeano, J. V. A Novel Fault Diagnosis Scheme Applying Fuzzy Clustering Algorithms. *Appl. Soft. Comput.* **2017,** *58,* 605–619.
5. Rodríguez-Ramos, A.; Da Silva Neto, A. J.; Llanes-Santiago, O. An Approach to Fault Diagnosis with Online Detection of Novel Faults using Fuzzy Clustering Tools. *Exp. Syst. Applicat.* **2018,** *113,* 200–212.
6. Nazari, M.; Pashazadeh, S.; Mohammad-Khanli, L. An Adaptive Density-Based Fuzzy Clustering Track Association for Distributed Tracking System. *IEEE Access* **2019,** *7,* 135972–135981.
7. Khan, M. J.; Yousaf, A.; Khurshid, K.; Abbas, A.; Shafait, F. In *Automated Forgery Detection in Multispectral Document Images using Fuzzy Clustering,* 2018 13th IAPR International Workshop on Document Analysis Systems (DAS), Apr 24, 2018; IEEE, 2018, pp. 393–398.
8. Han, J.; Kamber, M.; Pei, J. Data Mining Concepts and Techniques Third Edition. In *The Morgan Kaufmann Series in Data Management Systems*; Vol. 5 (4), 2011, pp. 83–124.

9. Kesavaraj, G.; Sukumaran, S. In *A Study on Classification Techniques in Data Mining*, 2013 Fourth International Conference on Computing, Communications and Networking Technologies (ICCCNT), Jul 4, 2013; IEEE, 2013, pp. 1–7.

10. Peizhuang, W. Pattern Recognition with Fuzzy Objective Function Algorithms (James C. Bezdek). *SIAM Rev.* **1983,** *25* (3), 442.

11. Law, M. H.; Figueiredo, M. A.; Jain, A. K. Simultaneous Feature Selection and Clustering using Mixture Models. *IEEE Trans. Patt. Anal. Mach. Intell.* **2004,** *26* (9), 1154–1166.

12. Xu, Z.; Wu, J. Intuitionistic Fuzzy C-Means Clustering Algorithms. *J. Syst. Eng. Electron.* **2010,** *21* (4), 580–590.

13. Cannon, R. L.; Dave, J. V.; Bezdek, J. C. Efficient Implementation of the Fuzzy C-Means Clustering Algorithms. *IEEE Transac. Patt. Anal. Mach. Intell.* **1986,** (2), 248–255.

14. Pal, N. R.; Pal, K.; Keller, J. M.; Bezdek, J. C. A Possibilistic Fuzzy C-Means Clustering Algorithm. *IEEE Trans. Fuzzy Syst.* **2005,** *13* (4), 517–530.

15. Dave, R. N. Characterization and Detection of Noise in Clustering. *Patt. Recogn. Lett.* **1991,** *12* (11), 657–664.

16. Dave, R. N. In *Robust Fuzzy Clustering Algorithms*. [Proceedings 1993] Second IEEE International Conference on Fuzzy Systems, Mar 28, 1993; IEEE, 1993, pp. 1281–1286.

17. Chintalapudi, K. K.; Kam, M. In *The Credibilistic Fuzzy C Means Clustering Algorithm*, Insmc'98 Conference Proceedings. 1998 IEEE International Conference On Systems, Man, and Cybernetics (Cat. No. 98CH36218), Oct 14, 1998; Vol. 2, IEEE, 1998, pp. 2034–2039.

18. Tsai, D. M.; Lin, C. C. Fuzzy C-Means Based Clustering for Linearly and Nonlinearly Separable Data. *Pattern Recognition.* **2011,** *44* (8), 1750–1760.

19. Kaur, P. R.; Soni, A. K.; Gosain, A.; India, I. I. Novel Intuitionistic Fuzzy C-Means Clustering for Linearly and Nonlinearly Separable Data. *WSEAS Trans. Comput.* **2012,** *11* (3), 65–76.

20. Subudhi, S.; Panigrahi, S. Use of Optimized Fuzzy C-Means Clustering and Supervised Classifiers for Automobile Insurance Fraud Detection. *J. King Saud Univ.—Comput. Inform. Sci.* **2017,**,32 (5), 568–575.

21. Gosain, A.; Dahiya, S. Performance Analysis of Various Fuzzy Clustering Algorithms: A Review. *Proc. Comput. Sci.* **2016,** *79*, 100–111.

22. Kaur, P.; Soni, A. K.; Gosain, A. Robust Kernelized Approach to Clustering by Incorporating New Distance Measure. *Eng. Appl. Artif. Intell.* **2013,** *26* (2), 833–847.

23. Hu, Z.; Bodyanskiy, Y. V.; Tyshchenko, O. K.; Samitova, V. O. Possibilistic Fuzzy Clustering for Categorical Data Arrays based on Frequency Prototypes and Dissimilarity Measures. *Int. J. Intell. Syst. Appl.* **2017,** *9* (5), 55.

24. Dahiya, S.; Gosain, A.; Mann, S. Experimental Analysis of Fuzzy Clustering Algorithms. In *Inintelligent Data Engineering and Analytics*; Springer: Singapore, 2020; pp. 311–320.

25. Ester, M.; Kriegel, H. P.; Sander, J.; Xu, X. A Density-Based Algorithm for Discovering Clusters in Large Spatial Databases with Noise. *Inkdd* **1996,** *96* (34), 226–231.

26. Dahiya, S.; Gosain, A.; Gupta, S. RKT2FCM: RBF Kernel-Based Type-2 Fuzzy Clustering. Available at SSRN 3577549. 2020 Apr 16.

27. Bal, A.; Banerjee, M.; Chakrabarti, A.; Sharma, P. MRI Brain Tumor Segmentation and Analysis using Rough-Fuzzy C-Means and Shape Based Properties. *J. King Saud Univ.-Comput. Inform. Sci.* **2022,** *34* (2), 115–133.

28. Kaur, P.; Gosain, A. In *Density-Oriented Approach to Identify Outliers and Get Noiseless Clusters in Fuzzy C—Means*, International Conference On Fuzzy Systems, Jul 18, 2010; IEEE, 2010; pp. 1–8.
29. Dahiya, S.; Nanda, H.; Artwani, J.; Varshney, J. Using Clustering Techniques and Classification Mechanisms for Fault Diagnosis. *Int. J.* **2020,** *9* (2), 2138–2146.
30. Gosain, A.; Dahiya, S. A New Robust Fuzzy Clustering Approach: DBKIFCM. *Neural Process. Lett.* **2020,** *52* (3), 2189-2210.

CHAPTER 13

Assessment of Document Clustering and Topic Modeling of Blockchain Adoption by the e-Sports Community

JITENDRA YADAV, MADHVENDRA MISRA, and KULDEEP SINGH

Department of Management Studies, Indian Institute of Information Technology, Allahabad, India

ABSTRACT

The $385.10 million eSports industry in the US offers a lucrative market for the even publishers, organizers, players, and industry shareholders. However, an inequitable distribution of the eSports products such as charging of application programming interface (API) fees and intellectual property (IP) rights have brought discontent among the players, viewers, and investors. Few eSports organizations with the objective of fair supply chain and to preserve the sanctity of eSports have moved toward the adoption of more robust technologies such as blockchain, which promise to offer an environment that restricts unethical practices and aims to bring fairness in the system.

This study focuses on mining the spectator comments on Reddit concerning the discussions of blockchain adoption in the eSports, to unearth the hidden semantic structures through document clustering and topic modeling. One of the most common procedures in machine learning and natural language processing are topic models. Topic models also known as probabilistic models are statistical algorithms that discover less or more abstract topics in selected documents based on their semantic structure. The

Computational Intelligence in Analytics and Information Systems, Volume 2: Advances in Digital Transformation, Selected Papers from CIAIS-2021. Parneeta Dhaliwal, PhD, Manpreet Kaur, PhD, Hardeo Kumar Thakur, PhD, Rajeev Kumar Arya, and Joan Lu (Eds.)

study finds that the spectator's willingness toward blockchain adoption has increased in recent years.

13.1   INTRODUCTION

Sport is an important means of cultural interaction and establishing forms of moral consensus (on law, on how to behave properly, etc.). As a sociological phenomenon, the results of sport are not inherently positive or negative.[1] There has been a dispute between sport as a field of commercial enterprise, subject to business and government legislation and debate, and as an area of physical, moral, and social self-development in civil society. Sport has steadily undergone its profound crises since the turn of the twenty-first century, weakening the confidence in the potential of sport for self-regulation and hence the authority of its leading governing bodies, the Fédération Internationale de Football Association (FIFA) and the International Olympic Committee (IOC). The sports online community has been constantly reporting the ill-practices at various levels in the sports organizations and has also been engaged in proposing technical and general solutions to facilitate fair game.

ESports has been a popular entertainment mode for many people in recent years, and in the online gaming industry, constant, quick growth can be seen. In 2019, Newzoo announced that the market share of eSports is worth US$ 950.60 million and is projected to reach US$ 1 billion for the first time in 2020, excluding sales from streaming networks.[2] Revenues with a volume of US$ 385.10 million in 2020 have described the Asian market as the main eSport market, followed by North America in the second position with overall revenues of US$ 252.80 million.[2] As for attendance, the overall eSports audience is expected to rise to 495 million viewers in 2020. This includes 222.9 million individuals who appear to watch eSports more than once a month.[2] Newzoo estimates that an average of US$ 4.94 will be earned as income from each eSport enthusiast in 2020 (people who watch eSports more than once in a month). That's going to be up 2.8% from 2019.[2]

The rise in the eSports market has attracted the interest of publishers of eSports events, organizers, teams, and industry shareholders due to the profits achieved by eSports.[3] Publishers have entered in the eSports market with the hope of expanding their market share.[4] but have faced various challenges being faced due to the existing distribution channels. Monopolies in the eSports markets are not only limited by extend across the supply chain, thus leading to unfair price distribution among the organizers and publishers.[5] Due the unethical practices in the supply chain, publishers tend to look for more financial possibilities of strategic investment through the use of Intellectual Property (IP) rights.

Recent technologies have been adopted in varied business domains to bring trade fairness and curb unethical practices among the partners. Motivated by the global adoption of blockchain technology in businesses, the study aims to explore the adoption readiness and acceptability of the blockchain in the sports industry.

13.2   REVIEW OF LITERATURE

Professional athletes rely on sports managers to represent them in the business facets of their careers in modern industry experience.[6,7] There have been several organizations interested in trying to regulate agents, but none have been genuinely successful in solving the wide spectrum of issues that have arisen since the late 1970s, despite the implementation of legislation by all of these organizations.[8–10] In addition to the illegal behavior by unscrupulous agents of college athletics, allegations of unethical conduct in the area of sports agencies are common. Incompetent representation, improper financial advice, bribery, larceny, conflicts of interest, unreasonable fee billing, and customer raiding are problems that arise at some frequency.[11–13] Competition against big organizations and by unqualified agents is routinely recognized as a significant contributor to the dishonest and illegal environment that is created by many agents. Previous studies have not only found multiple unethical practices in player selection, sports management, event management at the agency level but also reported ill-practices also at the athlete level.[12–14]

Researchers in the various domains of business operations[15–20] have adopted blockchain technology for combating unethical practices of the stakeholder, thus bringing fairness in trade. Though the concept of blockchain technology is not new and several use cases and multiple publications have been reported in various business domains, the sports researchers have been unable to map the benefits of blockchain technology in proposing efficient sports management techniques and methodologies. An advanced search on Web of Science and Scopus databases with the key "Blockchain AND Sports" led to zero results.

The concentration of the research community on the adoption of blockchain to resolve the issues in the various business domains[17,18,20] and limited studies by the sports researchers acted as the prime motivator for this study. The study being exploratory intends to discover the appetite of the sport's digital community for the probable adoption of blockchain technology in the domain. The study collects the discussions taking place on the social news website (Reddit) as the website restricts the marketers from advertising and thus only the communications taking place among the users can be captured.[21] Initially, a cluster analysis has been conducted on the comments of the users followed by topic modeling that indicated the increase in the frequency of discussions concerning the blockchain adoption in the eSports community.

13.3   METHODOLOGY

13.3.1   DATA COLLECTION

The study through RStudio (version 1.3.1093) scrapped the blockchain discussions in the sports community on Reddit using the package RedditExtractoR[22] that resulted in the collection of 11177 usable user comments. The descriptive of the dataset has been tabulated in Table 13.1.

TABLE 13.1   Descriptive of Reddit Dataset.

Capture dates	March 10, 2013 to September 24, 2020
Authors (thread creators)	186
Users	5291
Subreddits	99
Titles	232
Comments	11177

13.3.2   PREPROCESSING OF DATA

The user comments for the analysis have been preprocessed using the "tm" package in RStudio[23] that eliminated non-ASCII characters, emoticons, URLs, stopwords, digits, punctuations, and unnecessary spaces from the text. The preprocessing of the data has been conducted using the methodology proposed by Yadav et al.[21] This cleaned textual dataset has been transferred for algorithmic evaluation.

13.3.3   ALGORITHMIC EVALUATION

Machine learning algorithms of document clustering and topic modeling[24,25] have been run on the cleaned textual data to fragment sentences into words, thus making a corpus of associated words representing a common topic or sharing a common semantic orientation.

Topic models are sufficient for the analysis of data as an unsupervised machine learning system. The estimation of the topic models aims to determine the proportionate distribution of the topics in the corpus of documents. Based on individual research agendas, the number of parameter selection varies from single to multiple parameters. The most important parameter to specify in advance for parameterized models such as Latent Dirichlet Allocation (LDA) is the number of topics K. It depends on different factors if an ideal K should be chosen. If K is too large, the collection is divided into too many subjects, including those that are scarcely interpretable, which may even overlap. If the value of K is very low, it depicts that the splitting of the collection has been done into a few very general semantic contexts.

13.4   RESULTS

The algorithm segregated topics based on the assigned probabilities. The topics contained in the first three documents have been shown in Figure 13.1, illustrating how topics are distributed in each document.

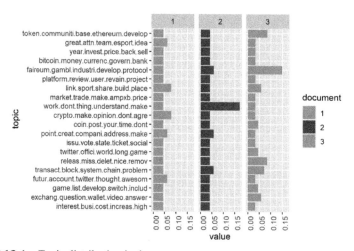

FIGURE 13.1   Topic distribution in documents.

All three documents in the current model represent at least a small proportion of each topic along with identification of few dominant topics in each document. Alpha parameter of the models can be used to regulate the topic distribution in the documents. Higher alpha priors for topics result in an even distribution of topics within a document. Low alpha priors mean that for any document, the inference method distributes the probability mass on a few topics.

The alpha-prior was automatically calculated in the previous model to match the data (highest overall model likelihood). However, the outcomes that one would prefer to see as an analyst do not always lead to this auto-mated calculation. We may be involved in a more peak/even distribution of topics in the model, based on our analytical interest.

Hence, the alpha prior value has been reduced to a lower value and the results have been presented in Figure 13.2. The adjustment of alpha prior values has led to the suppression of the few topics and has extracted the topics that have been frequently used by the Reddit users in their discussions on the website.

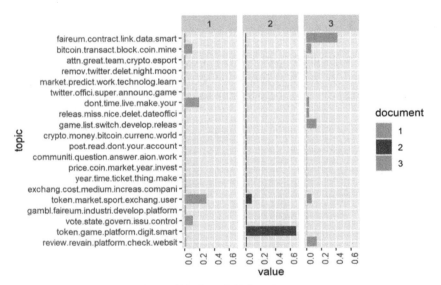

FIGURE 13.2   Topic allocations with adjusted Alpha prior.

The results obtained have been verified by the two approaches of topic ranking by re-ranking the topics in the documents based on a specific score.[25] The first approach allocates probabilities to each topic in the entire document that outlines the most frequently occurring topics in the documents. The second approach is also known as Rank 1 that ranks the topic based on their appearance as a primary topic within the paragraph. Both the topic ranking approaches presented nearly similar results but for demonstration purposes, the output of the second approach has been shown in Table 13.2.

TABLE 13.2 Ranking of Topics based on the Frequency.

Topic	Frequency
attn team great esport crypto	947
post read fuck your account	869
price coin market sell invest	853
communiti question aion answer video	822
year ticket time thing yeah	773
review revain platform check wallet	727
crypto money bitcoin currenc bank	655
token market sport exchang booki	647
token game platform digit smart	603
vote govern state control issu	583
exchang cost medium flight increas	551
gambl faireum industri onlin develop	535
live video your isnt dont	491
bitcoin transact block coin mine	482
releas miss nice delet dateoffici	469
remov twitter delet moon night	419
market predict learn technolog media	315
faireum contract smart link data	299
game list switch releas includ	286
twitter offici announc super relay	87

13.5 DISCUSSION AND CONCLUSION

The topic ranking clearly states that the members of the sports community and enthusiast on Reddit have been actively engaged in discussions about the benefits of blockchain technology and its probable adoption in the sports industry. Apart from the traditional sports, the spectators of esports display a high level of agreement toward the blockchain adoption as can be seen from Table 13.2 where the topic "attn team great esport crypto" has the highest frequency. A timeline analysis has also been conducted to analyze the frequency change of the topics over time as can be seen in Figure 13.3.

The above visualization clearly states the translation of consumer attitude toward the adoption of blockchain technology in the sports industry. Before 2016 the attention toward blockchain technology by the sports community was low but as the use cases in the varied domains increased, the interest in blockchain also increased in the sports community. The region in red color in Figure 13.3 contains the words that are centric to the attention-based reward system for the player (teams) that are possible through the adoption by the adoption of the blockchain technology as practiced by the organizations such as Verasity.

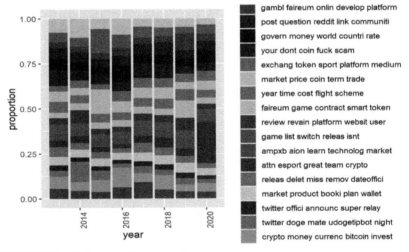

FIGURE 13.3   Topic proportions over time.

The discussion in the year 2020 can be seen to be having a very high frequency of the discussions concerning the use of blockchain technology in the eSports supply chain. The study dictates that the spectators display an increasing interest in the adoption of blockchain in sports and hence further researches need to be conducted on the probable applications of the blockchain technology in sports management, thus creating a decentralized system of fair trade where the rights of the parties are not infringed and the sanctity of the sports events can be maintained.

The study also suffers from few limitations that restrict the generalization of the results. Since blockchain adoption is at a nascent stage in the sports domain, the quantum of data collected is quite low and hence the outcomes may change with the increase in amount of data collected. Also, the study is only indicative that the buzz on the social media concerning the blockchain is significantly high; hence, further studies can adopt a more quantitative approach to the textual analysis of the comments, thus exploring the semantic inclination of the users and identification of the key social media factors forming the sentiments of the social media users.

KEYWORDS

- **blockchain**
- **clustering**
- **latent Dirichlet allocation**
- **machine learning**
- **eSports management**
- **Reddit**
- **topic modeling**

REFERENCES

1. Chatziefstathiou, D.; Henry, I. P. *Discourses of Olympism. From the Sorbonne 1894 to London 2012*; Palgrave Macmillan: London, UK; 2012.
2. Takahashi, D. Newzoo: Global Esports will Top $1 Billion in 2020, with China as the Top Market. Venturebeat, 2020.
3. Rietkerk, R. Newzoo Global Esports Market Report 2020—Light Version, 2020.
4. MarketsandMarkets, Electric Aircraft Market | Industry Analysis and Market Forecast to 2023 | MarketsandMarkets. *www.marketsandmarkets.com* [Online] 2018, https://www.marketsandmarkets.com/Market-Reports/esports-market-123759465.html (accessed Jul 28 2020).
5. Fletcher, A. Following the Money in eSports. *Starters* [Online] 2016, https://blog.starters.co/following-the-money-in-esports-23e00b315cdd (accessed Jul 20, 2020).
6. Gillett, A. G. The Business of Sports Agents. *Bus. Hist.* 2019, *61* (2), 374–375.
7. Shropshire, K. L.; Davis, T. Part I. Background. In *The Business of Sports Agents*; University of Pennsylvania Press: Philadelphia, 2014.
8. Neiman, M. Fair Game: Ethical Considerations in Negotiation by Sports Agents, *SSRN Electron. J.* 2007.
9. Yilmaz, S. Advancing Our Understanding of the EU Sports Policy: the Socio-Cultural Model of Sports Regulation and Players' Agents. *Int. J. Sport Policy Polit.* 2018, *10* (2), 353–369.

10. Commission, E. Study on Sports Agents in the European Union. 2007.

11. Berry, B.; Smith, E. Race, Sport, and Crime: The Misrepresentation of African Americans in Team Sports and Crime. *Sociol. Sport J.* 2000, *17* (2), 171–197.

12. De Marco, N. Corruption in Football—Player Transfers, Agents and the 'Privatisation of Regulation'. *Sports Law Bulletin*, July 4, 2017.

13. The Sport Digest. Corruption. *The Sport Digest* [Online] 2020. http://thesportdigest.com/ethics/corruption/ (accessed Sep 27, 2020).

14. Lipschultz, R. Top 25 Most Corrupt and Scandalous People and Events in Sports | Bleacher Report | Latest News, Videos and Highlights. *Bleacherreport* [Online] Oct 06, 2010. https://bleacherreport.com/articles/483026-top-25-most-corrupt-figures-and-scandals-in-sports-history (accessed Aug 20, 2020).

15. Hughes, L.; Dwivedi, Y. K.; Misra, S. K.; Rana, N. P.; Raghavan, V.; Akella, V. Blockchain Research, Practice and Policy: Applications, Benefits, Limitations, Emerging Research Themes and Research Agenda. *Int. J. Inf. Manage* 2019, *49* (February), 114–129.

16. Dubey, R.; Gunasekaran, A.; Bryde, D. J.; Dwivedi, Y. K.; Papadopoulos, T. Blockchain Technology for Enhancing Swift-Trust, Collaboration and Resilience within a Humanitarian Supply Chain Setting. *Int. J. Prod. Res.* 2020, *58* (11), 3381–3398.

17. Yadav, J.; Misra, M.; Goundar, S. An Overview of Food Supply Chain Virtualisation and Granular Traceability using Blockchain Technology. *Int. J. Blockchains Cryptocurrencies* 2020, *1* (2), 154.

18. Yadav, J.; Misra, M.; Goundar, S. Autonomous Agriculture Marketing Information System Through Blockchain: A Case Study of e-NAM Adoption in India. In *Blockchain Technologies, Applications and Cryptocurrencies*; World Scientific, 2020, pp. 115–138.

19. Rashideh, W. Blockchain Technology Framework: Current and Future Perspectives for the Tourism Industry. *Tour. Manag.* 2020, *80*, 104125.

20. Filimonau, V.; Naumova, E. The Blockchain Technology and the Scope of Its Application in Hospitality Operations. *Int. J. Hosp. Manag.* 2020, *87*, 102383.

21. Yadav, J.; Misra, M.; Singh, K. Sensitizing Netizen's Behavior Through Influencer Intervention Enabled by Crowdsourcing—A Case of Reddit. *Behav. Inf. Technol.* 2022, *41*(6), 1286–1297.

22. Rivera, I. Reddit Data Extraction Toolkit. CRAN, 2019.

23. Feinerer, I. Introduction to the tm Package Text Mining in R. 2019.

24. Schweinberger, M. *Topic Modeling with R*; The University of Queensland: Brisbane, Oct 04, 2020.

25. Grun, B.; Hornik, K. Topicmodels: An R Package for Fitting Topic Models. *J. Stat. Soft.* 2011, *40* (13).

CHAPTER 14

A Novel Hybrid Sampling Algorithm to Deal with Imbalanced Datasets

DEEPIKA SINGH, ANJU SAHA, and ANJANA GOSAIN

University School of Information and Communication Technology, GGSIP University, New Delhi, India

ABSTRACT

Classification of imbalanced dataset is considered challenging in machine learning and data mining community and extensive research has been conducted in the past few decades to overcome imbalanced dataset problem. The classification algorithms show degraded performance for imbalanced datasets. However, there are several other intrinsic features of the dataset that degrades the learning for the classifier on such imbalanced datasets. Thus, it results in a biased classification model that fails to generalize well for the class with a comparatively less number of instances in the dataset. In the literature, there exist a number of metrics to access the intrinsic features of dataset. In this research paper, we present a hybrid preprocessing approach based on *wCM* complexity metric, to preprocess the imbalanced datasets with nonlinear boundaries, overlapping classes, and small disjuncts, which in turn help the classification algorithms to perform well on these datasets. The proposed algorithm combines *wCM* metric to access the difficulty level of the datasets and then accordingly oversamples the minority class data points and undersamples the majority class data points. Experimental results for 23 real-world datasets demonstrate that our algorithm improves

Computational Intelligence in Analytics and Information Systems, Volume 2: Advances in Digital Transformation, Selected Papers from CIAIS-2021. Parneeta Dhaliwal, PhD, Manpreet Kaur, PhD, Hardeo Kumar Thakur, PhD, Rajeev Kumar Arya, and Joan Lu (Eds.)

sensitivity for the minority class without much affecting the specificity for the majority class.

14.1   INTRODUCTION

Many real-world classification problems such as the prediction of frauds in bank transactions, identification of deadly diseases, prediction of software defects involve learning from imbalanced data. In imbalanced data, the distribution of data points in one of the classes (called minority class) is much smaller than the other classes (called majority classes). Traditional machine learning algorithms usually do not work well on imbalanced data as they tend to predict the data points from the majority class correctly, but the data points of the minority class are treated as noise and are usually ignored. This leads to the high misclassification probability of the minority class data points as compared to the majority class.[1]

Nevertheless, the small number of data points in the minority class is not responsible for degraded learning of classifiers. For example when the classes are linearly separable in the input feature space or the imbalance ratio is not very high, it is not difficult to build a proper classification model.[1,9] The degraded performance of the classifiers also depends on other intrinsic data factors such as overlap of classes,[9–11] presence of noise,[12] small disjuncts,[10] etc. There is a common understanding of the researchers[8,11,13] that the dataset factors are more critical, to determine the behavior of classifiers as it has been observed that the accuracy of the classification model (with respect to minority class) degrades when class imbalance occurs together with the other intrinsic data factors.

In literature, there exists a set of data complexity metrics that help to analyze the intrinsic dataset factors. These data complexity metrics are useful to gain the insights for the dataset which proves beneficial to select the proper learning algorithm. Ho and Basu[14] proposed data complexity metrics to measure the complexity of classification tasks. However, in[7,15–17] the authors showed that these complexity metrics do not work well for imbalanced data that suffers from other intrinsic factors such as class overlapping, noise, small disjuncts, etc.

Anwar et al.[17] proposed a new complexity metric that determines the complexity of imbalance datasets. In[18] the authors proposed the weighted complexity metric (*wCM*) to access the difficulty level of a dataset. In this paper, we propose an algorithm for preprocessing the imbalanced datasets using *wCM* metric.[18] We will calculate the *wCM* metric value for an imbalanced dataset and then accordingly apply the proposed preprocessing algorithm. Our proposed algorithm is a hybrid preprocessing approach, which oversamples the minority class datapoints and undersamples the minority class datapoints. The main objectives of this research paper can be stated as:

1. To analyze and compare the relationship between imbalanced data complexity and classification algorithms' performance, thereby contributing further insights into an area that has only been partially studied to date.
2. To preprocess the imbalanced datasets with nonlinear boundaries, overlapping classes, and small disjuncts, to make it a balanced dataset.
3. To analyze the competence of preprocessing methods to deal with particular imbalanced dataset factors such as nonlinear boundaries, overlapping classes, and small disjuncts.

To achieve these objectives, we use the proposed algorithm to balance the dataset intelligently by treating difficult data points. Our hybrid preprocessing algorithm is greatly inspired by the SPIDER method of strong amplification, presented in.[19] Our algorithm gives more promising results for the datasets having intrinsic factors such as imbalance class distribution, overlapping classes, or nonlinear class boundaries. It helps in improving the sensitivity measure value for the minority class without decreasing the specificity measure value for the majority class, hence maintaining the overall accuracy of the classification model. We conducted an experimental evaluation of our hybrid preprocessing algorithm on 23 real-world datasets in MATLAB software, to prove its usefulness. Moreover, we used 4 classifiers such as Decision Tree, *k*-nn, Logistic Regressor, SVM with linear kernel and Gaussian kernel. We compared the proposed algorithm with the 9 preprocessing methods such as Tk-Links (Tk), Condensed Nearest Neighbor (CNN), One Sided Selection (OSS), Neighborhood Cleaning Rule (NCL), Random Undersampling (RUS with 65% undersampling of majority class and RUS with balanced undersampling), SMOTE (SM), BSMOTE (BSM), and SPIDER.

The rest of the paper is organized as follows. Section 14.2 presents the background, describing the state of the art for class imbalance problem and review of the data complexity metrics. In Section 14.3 we have presented our approach based on *wCM* for preprocessing the imbalanced datasets. Section

14.4 shows the experimental study performed and the analysis of the results. Finally, we conclude the paper with Section 14.5.

14.2   RELATED WORKS

Learning from imbalanced dataset is still considered a challenging task. A number of techniques have been proposed to overcome the class imbalance problem. These techniques are majorly grouped into three categories: (i) algorithm-level techniques, which internally make the modification in the classifier bias it in favor of minority class so as to compensate for the class imbalance,[20–22] (ii) data-level techniques, which modify data distribution either by oversampling the minority class (generating new instances from minority class) and/or by under-sampling the majority class (removing instances from the majority class) in order to balance the classes distribution,[23–25] and (iii) cost-sensitive techniques, which assign distinct costs to the classification errors for minority and majority classes.[4] The most popular techniques to deal with the class imbalance problem are data-level techniques, also called data preprocessing techniques. These techniques are further subdivided into under-sampling, over-sampling, and hybrid-sampling techniques.

Under-sampling techniques[26–35] remove the majority class instances so as to balance the class distribution, thus helping the classifiers to learn accurately for the minority class. On the other hand, over-sampling techniques[23,25,24, 36–38] either replicate or generate synthetic instances of minority class to rebalance the class distributions. Moreover, hybrid preprocessing techniques combine the over-sampling and under-sampling techniques, in order to overcome the weaknesses of these two sampling techniques. Some of the hybrid preprocessing techniques include SMOTE-Tk,[39] SMOTE-NCL,[40] Sampling + Ensemble,[41] SMOTE-RSB,[42] SPIDER,[19] SPIDER2.[43]

However, the basic preprocessing methods do not take into consideration the imbalanced data distribution and as a result, they may lead to an increased difficulty of the classification task, for example, in the case in which easily separable subpopulation of the objects (a particular feature subspace) is injected by objects from the opposite class. Therefore, whether we aim to produce new minority class objects or to remove objects from majority class, knowledge about imbalance distribution should guide the resampling procedure. To determine the imbalance distribution of the minority class and majority class instances it is required to investigate the intrinsic dataset properties. These intrinsic dataset properties can be studied using data complexity metrics. The data complexity metrics quantify particular aspects of a dataset, which helps in selecting the appropriate classification algorithm. Ho and Basu,[14] identify data complexity that imposes the difficulty for building classification model for the binary classification problems. Conversely, most studies[7,15–17] have shown that the existing data complexity metrics perform poorly in imbalanced scenarios. Moreover, recently, some of the metrics have been proposed[7,17,18,44,45] for accessing the complexity of imbalanced datasets. A scatter matrix based class separability complexity metric for imbalanced datasets was proposed by Xing et al.[44] Another metric for imbalanced dataset based on k-nn approach was given by Anwar et al.[17] Further, Fernandez et al.[45] suggested a method based on feature selection and instance selection, to overcome class overlap and class imbalance. Victor et al.[7] presented three complexity metrics, adapted from the famous complexity metrics, for imbalanced datasets by regarding each class individually.

14.3 PROPOSED ALGORITHM

This section provides an overview of the proposed hybrid preprocessing algorithm to deal with the class imbalance, nonlinear class boundaries, and class overlapping, which consists of combining *wCM* metric with oversampling and under-sampling techniques. Our approach identifies the data points of minority class that lie in the difficult regions such as borderline areas, overlapped areas, and small disjuncts. Thereafter, it expands the decision borders in favor of the minority class by removing the difficult data points from the majority class. Unlike, ROS (random oversampling) the method does not result in classification model overfitting as it intelligently picks up the minority class points for regeneration.

This algorithm consists of three steps given below:

- **First Step:** First, the algorithm calculates the complexity of each data point in dataset *D* using *wCM* metric[18] and assigns labels to the data point as "*safe*" or "*difficult*" based on its *wCM* metric value. *Safe* data points should be correctly classified by the base classifier, while *difficult* data points are likely to be misclassified and thus need special attention in the second phase. Here, *difficult* data points refer to the borderline data points and data points in small disjuncts, whose majority of neighbors are of the different class and thus likely to be misclassified by the classifier.

- **Second Step:** The second step involves oversampling the minority class data points by replicating all difficult data points from the minority class. The number of copies generated for these minority class points is equal to the number of examples in their neighbourhood from the majority class.

- **Third Step:** In the third step, the algorithm recalculates the complexity of the majority class data points using a new dataset, D', which consists of the old data points as well as the newly generated copies of the minority class. After that, it undersamples "*difficult*" data points from the majority class in D'.

14.4   EXPERIMENTAL SETUP

To analyze the performance of the proposed algorithm and other preprocessing algorithms such as Tk, CNN, OSS, NCL, RUS (with 65% undersampling of majority class and RUS with balanced undersampling), SM, BSM, and SPIDER, we used 4 classifiers such as Decision Tree, k-nn, Logistic Regressor, SVM with Linear kernel and Gaussian kernel. We used 23 datasets in this paper given in Table 14.1. To ensure that the resultant classification model is not an overfitted one, we used the 5 cross-fold validation and took the average of the results obtained from 10 runs of each classifier.

We grouped these datasets on the basis of the *wCM* metric. The grouping of the datasets is done to understand in the better way the effect of dataset complexity on the performance of pre-preprocessing methods and in turn to access the suitability of base classifiers. We used five wCM metric ranges for grouping the datasets (given in Table 14.2), defined as: wCM $\leq$20%, 21 $\leq$ wCM $\leq$ 30%, 31 $\leq$ wCM $\leq$ 40%, 41 $\leq$ wCM $\leq$ 50%, and wCM > 50% respectively. Table 14.3 reports the average results for the Decision Tree classifier (as space complexity results of other classifiers are not shown), obtained by applying the different preprocessing algorithms on the different groups of datasets. For every group the evaluation metrics such as sensitivity, specificity, and overall accuracy have been calculated. Visualization of the experiments is presented in Figure 14.1.

TABLE 14.1 Characteristics of the 23 Datasets Downloaded from UCI and KEEL Repositories.

Dataset	Size	#Attributes	#min/#maj	IR
Ionosphere	351	34	126/225	1.79
Glass1	214	9	76/138	1.82
Ecoli-0_vs_1	220	7	77/143	1.86
Pima	768	8	268/500	1.87
Iris 0	150	3	50/100	2
Glass0	214	9	70/144	2.06
Yeast1	1484	8	429/1055	2.46
Vehicle2	846	18	218/628	2.88
Vehicle1	846	18	217/629	2.9
Vehicle3	846	18	212/634	2.99
Yeast3	1484	8	163/1321	8.1
Haberman	249	3	24/225	9.38
Glass0-1-6_vs_2	192	9	17/175	10.3
Glass2	214	9	17/197	11.59
Balance	625	4	49/576	11.76
Shuttle-c0-vs-c4	1829	9	123/1706	13.87
Yeast-1_vs_7	459	7	30/429	14.3
Glass4	214	9	13/201	15.47
Glass5	214	9	9/205	22.78
Yeast4	1484	8	51/1433	28.1
Yeast5	1484	8	44/1440	32.73
Yeast6	1484	8	35/1449	41.4

TABLE 14.2 Summary of Datasets Divided into Groups based on wCM Metric Value.

Datasets	Group based on *wCM* metric	Complexity
Iris 0 Shuttle-c0-vs-c4 Ecoli-0_vs_1 Vehicle2	<20%	very less complex (traditional classifiers can be applied directly)
Yeast5 Glass0	20–30%	less complex (existing preprocessing methods like OSS,CNN,RUS65, SM performs better)

Yeast3		complex (Proposed Algorithm performs best in terms of both sensitivity and specificity)
Ionosphere	31–40%	
Glass1		
Glass4		
Glass5		highly complex (Proposed Algorithm performs best in terms of both sensitivity and specificity)
Yeast6	41–50%	
Vehicle1		
Yeast1		very highly complex (Proposed Algorithm performs best in terms of both sensitivity and specificity)
Pima		
Vehicle3		
Haberman		
Yeast4	>50%	
Glass0-1-6_vs_2		
Glass2		
Yeast-1_vs_7		
Balance		

14.5   RESULTS AND DISCUSSION

The intrinsic dataset characteristics play an important role in the performance of classifiers. An increase in the complexity of dataset results in the degraded performance of the classifier for minority class. In Table 14.3, for less complex datasets (in group wCM < 20%) the average sensitivity value of the original dataset before applying any preprocessing technique is 0.9262 using the decision tree classifier, which indicates good learning of the classifier for the minority class. Also, the average specificity value for the datasets falling in this category is 0.9795 with an average accuracy value of 96.525%. However, we can notice from the other columns of this table (i.e. for groups 21–30%, 31–40%, 41–50%, and >50%) for OD (first row of Table 14.2), the average sensitivity values start decreasing with the increasing dataset complexity. Hence, we are more concerned for the performance of classifiers for the datasets in these groups.

Moreover, for the datasets in the group 21–30% complexity, even the existing preprocessing methods such as OSS, CNN, NCL, and RUS with 65% balancing show improvement in the sensitivity values without actually degrading the specificity values. On the other hand, for the datasets in the groups 31–40%, 41–50%, and >50%, these existing preprocessing algorithms do not seem to be a good choice; rather SPIDER and our proposed algorithm show good improvement in the sensitivity values. But, the SPIDER algorithm degrades the specificity more as compared to our proposed algorithm. Thus, the proposed algorithm improves the sensitivity without much affecting the specificity.

The results for the k-nn classifier are similar to the DT classifier, whereas the SVM and LR classifiers show less significant improvement in the sensitivity values for the minority class, the reason behind this is that these classifiers are good at learning for linearly separable datasets. Thus, for complex datasets with nonlinear boundaries the performance of SVM (with linear kernel) and LR degrades.

TABLE 14.3 Average Classification Sensitivity, Specificity and Average Values for Decision Tree Classifier (before and after Applying the Preprocessing Algorithms) for the Datasets Grouped based on wCM Metric Value.

Algorithm	Complexity group			
		Sen	Spec	Acc
OD		0.926235	0.979563	96.525
TK		0.922406	0.9856	96.875
CNN		0.960097	0.97169	96.875
OSS		0.914583	0.987175	96.3
NCL		0.943748	0.989439	97.625
RUS65	<20%	0.97	0.99	98.375
RUSBal		0.9775	0.9875	98.25
SM		0.982375	0.974975	97.925
BSM		0.94095	0.979975	96.775
SPIDER		0.97355	0.977525	97.65
PropAlgo		0.965975	0.978625	97.5
OD		0.626786	0.934028	88.85
TK		0.738889	0.903886	88.1
CNN		0.746571	0.893657	95.3
OSS		0.851587	0.921296	88.25
NCL		0.935714	0.943878	94.05
RUS65	21–30%	0.85	0.9155	89.25
RUSBal		0.86	0.81	83.65
SM		0.8789	0.87915	90.5
BSM		0.7251	0.8875	87.65
SPIDER		0.91065	0.91555	93.15
PropAlgo		0.891	0.90815	91.8

TABLE 14.3   *(Continued)*

Algorithm	Complexity group	Sen	Spec	Acc
OD		0.674802	0.904823	87.2
TK		0.728436	0.910611	89.35
CNN		0.716027	0.94126	88.9
OSS		0.759175	0.935747	90.45
NCL		0.697716	0.913772	88.8
RUS65	31–40%	0.711333	0.889667	60.68962
RUSBal		0.7725	0.8245	80.05
SM		0.88785	0.882175	90.8
BSM		0.75265	0.900725	87.875
SPIDER		0.928525	0.905825	93.625
PropAlgo		0.922025	0.91205	92.45
OD		0.586941	0.946801	90.93333
TK		0.630466	0.963321	92.73333
CNN		0.609696	0.935557	89.86667
OSS		0.611419	0.95625	91.76667
NCL		0.711579	0.926965	90.83333
RUS65	41–50%	0.683667	0.838767	78.5
RUSBal		0.756667	0.769	76.43333
SM		0.814633	0.909733	91.73333
BSM		0.5991	0.9159	88.06667
SPIDER		0.913233	0.887067	91.83333
PropAlgo		0.876233	0.903567	91.9
OD		0.29434	0.907961	82.91111
TK		0.390652	0.913418	83.12222
CNN		0.362463	0.924433	83.61111
OSS		0.331601	0.909555	82.81111
NCL		0.477177	0.880106	82.56667
RUS65	>50%	0.507778	0.740556	65.42222
RUSBal		0.685556	0.653222	66.97778
SM		0.724844	0.832256	82.66667
BSM		0.538444	0.863878	81.22222
SPIDER		0.896933	0.7835	86.01111
PropAlgo		0.877967	0.810422	86.1

We have presented the visualizations of the experiment results of Table 14.3 with the help of graphs (refer Figs. 14.1–14.3.). Figure 14.1(a–d) shows the bar graphs for average sensitivity values for different classifiers for original datasets in different complexity groups and balanced datasets after applying different preprocessing algorithms. As can be observed from Figure 14.1(a–d) the behavior of classifiers on less complex data sets is better and more uniform for a minority class than on categories of problems of higher complexity: in the group $wCM < 20\%$ almost all classifiers seem to show the sensitivity values greater than 0.90 for the minority class on the OD (original dataset), whereas for the datasets in the group $wCM > 50\%$ all classifiers are showing the decreased sensitivity values for minority class on the OD. Figure 14.2(a-d) shows the bar graphs for average specificity values for different classifiers. Figure 14.3(a–d) shows the bar graphs for average accuracy values for different classifiers. Figure 14.2 shows the degraded values for the specificity of majority class for the datasets in the groups such as 31–40%, 41–50%, and >50%, because when the preprocessing algorithms try to increase the sensitivity, it in turn penalizes the specificity values. But, the proposed algorithm tries to balance the both sensitivity and specificity.

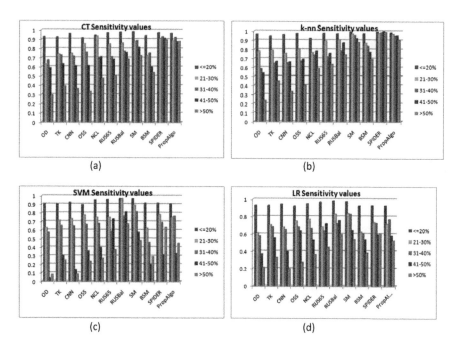

FIGURE 14.1 (a–d)   Sensitivity values for different classifiers on original datasets and on balanced datasets after applying different preprocessing algorithms.

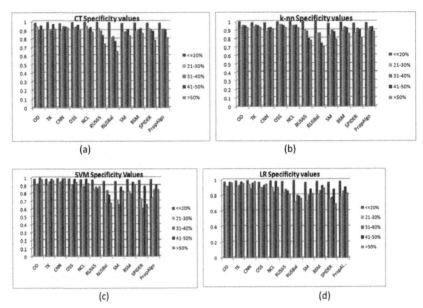

FIGURE 14.2 (a–d)   Specificity values for different classifiers on original datasets and on balanced datasets after applying different preprocessing algorithms.

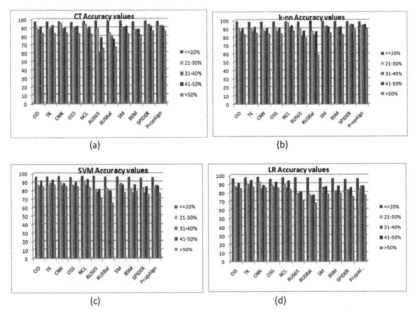

FIGURE 14.3 (a–d)   Accuracy values for different classifiers on original datasets and on balanced datasets after applying different preprocessing algorithms.

14.6 CONCLUSIONS

In this paper we have discussed the issue of creating a classification model from imbalanced datasets coupled with other intrinsic factors such as nonlinear boundaries, borderline examples, and small disjuncts. We have focused on data preprocessing algorithms for alleviating the imbalanced class distribution problem. The limitations of the existing preprocessing methods were discussed. Their main drawback was identified as they do not take into consideration the imbalanced data distribution and as a result, they may lead to an increased difficulty of the classification task. Based on our observations we have introduced a new hybrid preprocessing algorithm for the imbalanced dataset which takes into consideration the other intrinsic factors of the dataset. The proposed algorithm calculates the complexity of minority and majority class datapoints using the *wCM* complexity metric and instead of generating synthetic data points for the minority class it replicates the minority class datapoints. Additionally, it removes the difficult majority class datapoints, but as the removal of majority class datapoints is based on the weighted nearest-neighbor approach this will not distort the actual class boundaries for the majority class. Thus, our algorithm helps the classifier to create a more robust classification model for the minority class without actually sacrificing the majority class performance. The experimental results on the diverse set of datasets proved that our algorithm could be a helpful alternative for the preprocessing algorithms particularly when dealing with difficult imbalanced datasets.

KEYWORDS

- **classification algorithms**
- **class imbalance problem**
- **data complexity metrics**
- **hybrid preprocessing**
- **imbalanced datasets**

REFERENCES

1. Branco, P.; Torgo, L.; Ribeiro, R. P. A Survey of Predictive Modeling on Imbalanced Domains. *ACM Comput. Surv.* **2016,** *49* (2), 1–50.

2. Wozniak, M.; Grana, M.; Corchado, E. A Survey of Multiple Classifier Systems as Hybrid Systems. *Inf. Fusion* **2014,** *16*, 3–17.

3. Czarnecki, W. M.; Tabor, J. Extreme Entropy Machines: Robust Information Theoretic Classification. *Pattern Anal. Appl.* **2017,** 20 (2), 383—400.

4. Ksieniewicz, P.; Grana, M.; Wozniak, M. Paired Feature Multilayer Ensemble-Concept and Evaluation of a Classifier. *J. Intell. Fuzzy Syst.* **2017,** *32* (2), 1427–1436.

5. Gosain, A.; Saha, A.; Singh, D. In *Analysis of Sampling Based Classification Techniques to Overcome Class Imbalancing*, Proceedings of the 10th INDIACom; 2016 IEEE International Conference, 2016, pp. 320–326.

6. Haixiang, G.; Yijing, L.; Shang, J.; Mingyun, G.; Yuanyue, H.; Binge, G. Learning from Class-Imbalanced Data: Review of Methods and Applications. *Exp. Syst. Appl.* **2017,** *73*, 220–239.

7. Barella, V. H.; Garcia, L. P. F.; De Souto, M. P.; Lorena, A. C.; De Carvalho A. In *Data Complexity Measures for Imbalanced Classification Tasks*, Proceedings of the International Joint Conference on Neural Networks (IJCNN), Rio de Janeiro, 2018, pp. 1–8. doi: 10.1109/IJCNN.2018.8489661

8. Jo, T.; Japkowicz, N. Class imbalances versus small disjuncts. *SIGKDD Explor. Newsl.* **2004,** *6* (1), 40–49.

9. Gustavo, E. A.; Batista, P. A.; Prati, R. C.; Monard, M. C. In *Balancing Strategies and Class Overlapping*, International Symposium on Intelligent Data Analysis, 2005, pp. 24–35.

10. Denil, M.; Trappenberg, T. P. In *Overlap versus Imbalance,* Canadian Conference on AI, 2010, pp. 220–231.

11. Gracia, V.; Mollineda, R. A.; Sanchez, J. S. On the k-NN Performance in a Challenging Scenario of Imbalance and Overlapping. *Pattern Anal. Appl.* **2008,** *11* (3), 269–280.

12. Garcia, L. P. F.; De Carvalho, A. C. P. L. F.; Lorena, A. C. Effect of Label Noise in the Complexity of Classification Problems. *J. Neurocomput.* **2015,** *160*, 108–119.

13. Napierala, K.; Stefanowski, J. Types of Minority Class Examples and their Influence on Learning Classifiers from Imbalanced Data. *J. Intell. Inf. Syst.* **2016,** *46* (3), pp. 563–597.

14. Ho, T.; Basu, M.; Law, M. Measures of Geometrical Complexity in Classification Problems. In *Data Complexity in Pattern Recognition Ser. Advanced Information and Knowledge Processing*; Springer: London, 2006, pp. 1–23.

15. Gosain, A.; Saha, A.; Singh, D. Measuring Harmfulness of Class Imbalance by Data Complexity Measures in Oversampling Methods. *Int. Intell. Eng. Inform.* **2019,** *7* (2–3), 203–230.

16. Brun, A. L.; Britto A. S. Jr; Oliveira, L. S.; Enembreck, F.; Sabourin, R. A Framework for Dynamic Classifier Selection Oriented by the Classification Problem Difficulty. *Pattern Recogn.* **2018,** *76*, 175–190.

17. Anwar, N.; Jones, G.; Ganesh, S. Measurement of Data Complexity for Classification Problems with Imbalanced Data. *J. Stat. Anal. Data Min.* **2014,** *7*, 194–211.

18. Singh, D.; Gosain, A.; Saha, A. Weighted k-Nearest Neighbor Based Data Complexity Metrics for Imbalanced Datasets. *J. Stat. Anal. Data Min.* **2020,** *13* (4), 394–404.

19. Stefanowski, J.; Wilk, S. In *Improving Rule based Classifiers Induced by MODLEM by Selective Pre-Processing of Imbalanced Data*, Proceedings of the RSKD Workshop at ECML/PKDD, Warsaw, 2007; pp. 54–65.

20. Anand, R.; Mehrotra, K.; Mohan, C.; Ranka, S. An Improved Algorithm for Neural Network Classification of Imbalanced Training Set. *IEEE Trans. Neural Netw.* **1993,** *4* (6), 962–969.

21. Bruzzone, L.; Serpico, S. Classification of Imbalanced Remote-Sensing Data by Neural Networks. *Pattern Recognit. Lett.* **1997,** *18*, 1323–1328.

22. Oh, S.-H. Error Back-Propagation Algorithm for Classification of Imbalanced Data. *Neurocomputing* **2011,** *74* (6), 1058–1061.

23. Chawla, N. V.; Bowyer, K. W.; Hall, L. O.; Kegelmeyer, W. P. SMOTE: Synthetic Minority Over-Sampling Technique. *J. Artif. Intell. Res.* **2002,** *16*, 321–357.

24. Han H.; Wang, W.-Y.; Mao, B.-H. In *Borderline-SMOTE: A New Over-Sampling Method in Imbalanced Data Sets Learning*, Advances in Intelligent Computing. ICIC 2005. Lecture Notes in Computer Science, 2005; vol. 3644; Huang, D. S., Zhang, X. P., Huang, G, B., Eds.; Springer: Berlin, Heidelberg, 2005; pp. 878–887.

25. Bunkhumpornpat, C.; Sinapiromsaran, K.; Lursinsap, C. In *Safe–Level–SMOTE: Safe– Level–Synthetic Minority Over–Sampling Technique for Handling the Class Imbalanced Problem*, 13th Pacific–Asia Conference on Advances in Knowledge Discovery and Data Mining PAKDD'09, 2009; pp. 475–482.

26. Tomek, I. In *Two Modifications of CNN*, IEEE Transactions on Systems Man and Communications SMC-6, 1976; pp. 769–772.

27. Hart, P. E. The Condensed Nearest Neighbour Rule. *IEEE Transac. Inform. Theory* **1968,** *14*, 515–516.

28. Kubat, M.; Matwin, S. In *Addressing the Curse of Imbalanced Data Sets: One Sided Sampling*, Proceedings of the 14th International Conference on Machine Learninaa, Nashville, TN, 1997; pp. 179–186.

29. Laurikkala, J. *Improving Identification of Difficult Small Classes by Balancing Class Distribution*; Technical Report A-2001-2, University of Tampere, 2001.

30. Provost, F.; Jensen, D.; Oates, T. In *Efficient Progressive Sampling*, Proceedings of the Fifth ACM SIGKDD International Conference on Knowledge Discovery and Data Mining, San Diego, California, United States, 1999; pp. 23–32.

31. Seiffert, C.; Khooshgortaar, T. M.; Van Hulse, J. Napolitano, A. In *RUSBoost: Improving classification when training data is skewed, 2008 19th International Conference on Pattern Recognition,* Tampa, Florida, USA, 2008; pp. 1–4.

32. Zhang, Y. P.; Zhang, L. N.; Wang, Y. C. In *Cluster-based Majority Under-Sampling Approaches for Class Imbalance Learning*, IEEE International Conference on Information and Financial Engineering (ICIFE), 2010, pp. 400–404.

33. Chen, S.; He, H. In *Sera: Selectively Recursive Approach Towards Non Stationary Imbalanced Stream Data Mining*, International Joint Conference on Neural Network (IJCNN), June 2009; pp. 522–529.

34. Chen, S.; He, H.; Li, K.; Desai, S. In *Musera: Multiple Selectively Recursive Approach Towards Imbalanced Stream Data Mining*, International Joint Conference on Neural Networks (IJCNN), July 2010; pp. 1–8.

35. Chen, S.; He, H. Towards Incremental Learning of Non Stationary Imbalanced Data Stream: A Multiple Selectively Recursive Approach. *Evolv. Syst.* **2011,** *2*, 35–50.

36. Hu, S.; Liang, Y.; Ma, L.; He, Y. In *MSMOTE: Improving Classification Performance when Training Data is Imbalanced*, 2nd International Workshop Computer Sci. Eng., 2009; Vol. 2, pp. 13–17,.

37. Bunkhumpornpat, C.; Sinapiromsaran, K.; Lursinsap, C. DBSMOTE: Density-Based Synthetic Minority Over-Sampling Technique. *Appl. Intell.* **2012,** *36* (3), 664–684.

38. Haibo, H.; Yang, B.; Garcia, E. A.; Shutao, L. In *ADASYN: Adaptive Synthetic Sampling Approach for imbalanced learning*, International Joint Conference on Neural Networks (IJCNN), 2008; pp. 1322–1328.

39. Batista, G. E. A. P. A.; Prati, R. C.; Monard, M. C. A Study of the Behaviour of Several Methods for Balancing Machine Learning Training Data. *SIGKDD Explor.* **2004,** *6* (1), 20–29.

40. Sun, Y.; Liu, F. In *SMOTE-NCL: A Re-Sampling Method with Filter for Network Intrusion Detection*, 2016 2nd IEEE International Conference on Computer and Communications (ICCC), Chengdu, 2016, pp. 1157–1161. doi: 10.1109/CompComm.2016.7924886

41. Gao, J.; Ding, B.; Fan, W.; Han, J.; Yu, P. S. Classifying Data Streams with Skewed Class Distributions and Concept Drifts. *IEEE Internet Comput.* **2008,** *12* (6), 37–49.

42. Ramentol, E.; Caballero, Y.; Bello, R. Francisco Herrera: SMOTE-RSB*: A Hybrid Preprocessing Approach based on Oversampling and Undersampling for High Imbalanced Data-Sets Using SMOTE and Rough Sets Theory. *Knowl. Inf. Syst.* **2012,** *33,* 245–265.

43. Napierala, K.; Stefanowski, J.; Wilk, S. In *Learning from Imbalanced Data in Presence of Noisy and Borderline Examples*, 7th International Conference on Rough Sets and Current Trends in Computing (RSCTC'10), Lecture Notes on Artificial Intelligence, 2010; Vol. 6086, pp. 158–167.

44. Xing, Y.; Cai, H.; Cai, Y.; Hejlesen, O.; Toft, E. In *Preliminary Evaluation of Classification Complexity Measures on Imbalanced Data*, Proceedings of Chinese Intelligent Automation Conference, 2013, pp. 189–196.

45. Fernandez, A.; Jesus, M. J. D.; Herrera, F. Addressing Overlapping in Classification with Imbalanced Datasets: A First Multi-Objective Approach for Feature and Instance Selection. In *Intelligent Data Engineering and Automated Learning - IDEAL Lecture Notes in Computer Science*; Vol. 9375; Jackowski, K., Burduk, R., Walkowiak, K., Wozniak, M., Yin, H., Eds.; 2015, pp. 36–44.

CHAPTER 15

A Study on Analysis of E-Commerce Application on Online Healthcare

RAJIB NAG, NILOY DEV, and RIYA SIL

Department of Computer Science & Engineering, Adamas University, Kolkata, India

ABSTRACT

The global pandemic outbreak of COVID-19 had led to a great scope of improvement in the field of electronic healthcare systems. Visible changes have been found in the healthcare system as the patients have to follow isolation and social distancing to cut off the chain leading to virus transmission. In this global pandemic situation, advanced technology-based communication, information-based websites, and applications are used to deliver online healthcare consultations to patients. In this chapter, the authors have studied the existing work of researchers on e-healthcare. The survey aims to preserve a log-file of the significant researches performed till date on e-healthcare and discuss about the technologies used. Further, the authors have conferred about their proposed model, termed advaity.in. It is an Indian online healthcare web application that provides several e-healthcare facilities including online doctor's consultation, medical tests facilities, and medical services for patients and vendors in a single platform. Moreover, the web application has four client-side views consisting of doctors, hospitals and diagnostics, vendors, and users. The clients can work simultaneously in this web application without any interruption.

Computational Intelligence in Analytics and Information Systems, Volume 2: Advances in Digital Transformation, Selected Papers from CIAIS-2021. Parneeta Dhaliwal, PhD, Manpreet Kaur, PhD, Hardeo Kumar Thakur, PhD, Rajeev Kumar Arya, and Joan Lu (Eds.)

15.1   INTRODUCTION

Various problems have been created in our day-to-day life due to the global pandemic outbreak of COVID-19.[1] India, being one of the major Information Technology hubs, has increased in digitization to cut off the contamination of the deadly virus. This practice is mostly visible in the communication field. Online communication[2] helps to break through the transmission of virus in the society. One of the most common fields of online consultation and information retrieval is healthcare. Nowadays, e-healthcare[3] has been a regular phenomenon to avoid the spread of coronavirus. It has provided immense assistance to doctors as well as patients with medical facilities,[4] online doctor's consultation, and many more. In this paper, the authors have discussed two most significant topics: (i) Survey on online healthcare, (ii) proposed model of E-healthcare web application (Advaity.in). The survey related to online medical application provides a clear view of the significant research works performed on different e-healthcare applications[5] and their technologies. In the second part, the authors have discussed the proposed model of advaity.in which is a web application that offers online medical services consisting of online doctor's consultation, medical test services, and online pharmaceutical services.

The authors have organized this paper in the following structure. Section 15.2 discusses the origin of the work. Section 15.3 focuses on the basics of Online Healthcare System. Section 15.4 focuses on survey related to online medical applications. The proposed model advaity.in is implemented in section 15.5. Section 15.6 concludes the paper and also discusses about the future scope of online e-healthcare system.

15.2   ORIGIN OF THE WORK

Online healthcare came into existence in the year 1999 that described "a new term needed to describe the combined use of electronic communication and information technology in the health sector... the use in the health sector of digital data—transmitted, stored and retrieved electronically—for clinical, educational and administrative purposes, both at the local site and at distance."[6] According to Mitchell, in one of his research works,[7] he stated that "e-health can be considered to be the health industry's equivalent of e-commerce," and thus it can be one of the major key factors to understand the e-health system.[8]

15.3 ONLINE HEALTHCARE SYSTEM

In the recent outbreak of coronavirus, the use of e-healthcare has increased drastically leading to the dependence of medical services at a higher rate to follow the rules of lockdown and maintain social distancing to break through the chain of COVID-19. The ease of access, proximity, quality information, and immediacy has made the Internet the most popular source for getting information regarding healthcare. Furthermore, according to a survey, in the year 2016,[9] out of 9,086 smartphone users in ten Asian developing countries such as China (79%), Philippines (80%), Indonesia (85%), Vietnam (86%), and others, the number of people exploring online healthcare information is huge. E-healthcare has been one of the key factors in maintaining, improving, and recovering health.[10]

15.4 SURVEY ON ONLINE MEDICAL APPLICATIONS

The authors have created a table in this paper, highlighting the different technologies used and hence comparing the existing work done till date on the e-healthcare system. Table 15.1 shows the cervical cancer statistics.

TABLE 15.1   Comparison of Various Technologies used in Online Healthcare System.

SL. no.	Paper title	Technology used	Description
1	Web-based long distance appointment registered system[11]	ASP.NET, SQL server 2000	The website is built using the ASP.NET technology feature for online booking of patients or users to view hospital, experts, or specialist and many others to seek expert guidance.
2	Automated patient appointment reminder for cross platform mobile application[12]	IOT mobile application, JMS, JAVA MOM	It is a mobile application that provides a cross-platform for patients, medical staffs, and doctors to manage their appointment using IoT technology in an easier and more reliant manner.
3	E-Health Appointment Solution, A web-based approach[13]	WebRTC TECH., XMPP protocol, JMS, ACTIVEMQ, JAVA MOM	It provides an online platform for both doctors and patients so that they can have consultation through video chat services according to the time slots of the physician.

TABLE 15.1   *(Continued)*

SL. no.	Paper title	Technology used	Description
4	A web application to support recovery and shared decision-making in psychiatric medication clinics[14]	Common Ground, Web-based technology	The Common Ground offers a singular platform for the psychiatrists and the patients to have online sessions to share decisions and treatments.
5	Heuristic-based user interface evaluation of the mobile centralized doctor appointment system[15]	CDAS, Web-based technology	The online mobile-application platform is designed using CDAS (Centralized Doctor Appointment System) technology to help the people in Turkey have an online mode to get appointment of doctors with less error and easy-to-use technology systems.
6	Near Field Communication based Patient appointment[16]	NFC, Android-enabled mobile application, NFC hardware, PHP, MySQL, Android SDK	It is a mobile application platform that not only allows patients to take online appointments for doctors but also works on the priority level of patients to avoid queue in the healthcare or hospital systems bringing ease for the doctors and the patients in a more time-efficient manner.
7	Medkwick-An E-commerce Mobile Application Based on Online Medicine Shopping[17]	Android OS, Android SDK	It is an android application that offers a medicine buying facility. It has an extra feature of a chatbot that has artificial intelligence for replying customer queries. This software has feature to help customers to choose alternative drugs.
8	An e-Commerce portal for online Medicine trading[18]	Demand analysis, B2B and B2C transactions; XML, CXML, EDI Technology.	It is an online portal where users can check the available list of medicine stock in shops next to them. They can order medicine online, according to their need. Here individual shopkeepers can update their shop's online stock availability list without interrupting other shopkeepers. This portal provides 24×7 online medicine purchase facility and thus helps the rural area users to buy online medicine.
9	Android Application for Medicine Based Smart E-commerce Site[19]	An android phone, Android Studio, Weka, XML, Java, SQLite, Python	This project is based on android that is having a motive of selling online medicine. There users can buy medicine after verifying the prescription. At the time of unavailability of medicine in this application, it will automatically show the alternative medicine as a suggestion

TABLE 15.1　*(Continued)*

SL. no.	Paper title	Technology used	Description
10	Research on Pharmaceutical E-Commerce Enterprises: A Case Study of Jxdyf. Com[20]	ASP+SQL system, web2.0 system	Jxdyf is a Chinese company that is based on e-commerce. It is one of the largest and well-known companies that have more than 60 million users on their website. They offer above 10,000 kinds of medicine everyday with good customer service facility and health-related information.
11	Analysis of e-commerce application in pharmaceutical enterprises—A case study of Yaofang. cn[21]	Analysis, pharmaceutical enterprises, application	Yaofang.cn is the first medicine e-commerce website in China. Beijing Jing Wei Yuan Hua Pharmaceutical Technology Co. Ltd built it in Dec, 2005. It provides online medicine-buying facility with many health products.
12	BOOKAZOR-an Online Appointment Booking System[22]	CSS, HTML, JavaScript, Firebase, NodeJS, Angular	BOOKAZOR is an online appointment system where users can book not only for doctor's appointment but also for architects, plumbers etc. The appointments will be based on user's geographical region.

15.5　PROPOSED MODEL OF ADVAITY.IN

Advaity.in is a web-based application for online medical services. It provides facilities that include online doctor's consultation, medical test services, and online pharmaceutical service. The following sections analyze the running model of advaity.in comprehensively from the perspective of operating model, technology, management, and functions of the proposed web application.

15.5.1　OPERATING MODEL OF ADVAITY.IN

The proposed model of advaity.in provides the society with three distinct features consisting of online doctor's consultation, medical tests, and medical services. As an online platform providing all types of medical needs to our consumers, our website features with advanced facilities designed with Python-Django technology to get the services they need with ease.

Advaity.in is designed to avail the patients to get appointment of any doctor according to their convenience and booking slots available. This website also acknowledges the user about the best doctors either in clinic or in hospital present in their specific locality depending upon the patient's syndrome. Patients are also benefitted to browse doctor's profiles and select doctor accordingly. They can consult with the specific doctor by chat facility provided in our website advaity.in, so that they can register their issues. The web application also provides help to the patients to go for a medical test booking through our website. The patients can book for medical test to any medical diagnostic-center near them to know about the cause of their illness and take necessary steps accordingly. Moreover, the patients can also browse about the best pathology examining center nearby to their respective location as per their need. The feedback facility of our application helps to attain more knowledge about the center. Lastly, advaity.in has provided the facility of buying medicine for the user according to their requirement. It also provides image-recognition AI facility by which users can address his or her prescription picture and accordingly the medicine will be delivered to their doorstep. Customers can also avail to browse through our medicine page and order any medicine as per their need.

After the login/signup procedure, the website offers to the users a three-way service where the customer can select if they want to go for doctor's consultation, book for medical test, or buy medicines. After the user makes their respective choice, a search facility will be availed to them about the specific choice. They will be also acknowledged about the best services or centers available to their locality in case of doctor's appointment or medical check-up. In case of medicine-shopping they will be advised to upload prescription and will also be provided with search facility. An MLP is a feed-forward neural network consisting of an input layer, an output layer, and at least one hidden layer, as shown in Figure 15.1.

15.5.2   TECHNOLOGY USED

We are living in an era of technological revolution, where technology is advancing with each passing day. To keep pace with the time, we need to use modern technologies for making secure and efficient web-application.

As our project is a web-based application, we have used the following tools and technologies: (i) HTML5, (ii) CSS, (iii) JavaScript, (iv) Python3, (v) SQL, (vi) MySql, (vii) Django, (viii) phpMyAdmin. HTML5, CSS,

JavaScript have been used for front-end part, Python3 language has been used for the back-end logic, and the Django web framework is used to boost the performance and efficiency of our web application.

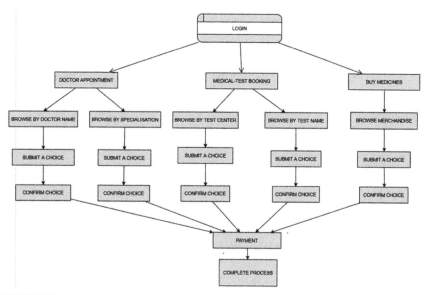

FIGURE 15.1   Proposed model of advaity.in.

15.5.3   FUNCTIONING OF THE MODEL

For proper functioning of the proposed model, the following are required:

- Project manager: Has all over control of all the departments and designs plan and strategy for the future. Final caller for all kinds of management level work of each department.
- Web application developer: Develops the website and provides with new innovative ideas on the basis of business requirement.
- Database administrator: Monitors the database performance, takes timely backup and recovery, maintains data integrity, and helps to support clients' and admins' database.
- Security administrator: To ensure security access, provides protection against unauthorized access, troubleshooting network security, delivers staff training to prevent unexpected loss.
- Business head: All the sales and marketing sections of all departments need to take approval of business head to execute any plan.

The following functions are required for doctor's consultation section:

- Department Manager: To manage the workflow of patient–doctor interaction. Department Manager has to make plan and strategy for upcoming future.
- Department developer: To maintain web application, provides with necessary development for more user-friendly and faster working appointment booking system.
- Marketing section: All online marketing-related work regarding doctor's appointment is controlled by this section.
- Tech section: To maintain a fluent network between client-side and server-side.
- Recruitment section: Recruits employee and trains them on the basis of work requirement.
- Customer care: Appointment booking-related problems and solutions.

Below are the tasks required for the Medical Test Booking Department:

- Department Manager: To manage the workflow of hospital–patient interaction. Plan and strategy for future aspect of health test booking are also done.
- Department developer: Development for medical test booking website is done.
- Marketing section: All online marketing of this department is controlled by this section.
- Tech section: Maintenance of client-side and server-side of this department.
- Customer care: Problems and solutions for medical test booking.

The required functions for the department of medicine e-commerce are:

- Department Manager: Manages the online medicine store.
- Department developer: Makes the section more user-interactive on the basis of customer's need and maintenance of the department.
- Sales section: All the sales-related work including all kinds of offers and market management.
- Marketing section: Involves marketing and advertisement in the online world.
- Tech section: Efficiently maintains the server-side interlinked with client-side.
- Recruitment section: Recruiting and training is the work of this section.

- Business section: To manage the price of medicines, vender's profit, delivery-related charge, and all kinds of financial work of this department.
- Transportation section: This section is made for all kinds of medicine delivery and return.
- Customer care: To give proper solution of query related to products before and after sales.

15.6 CONCLUSION

In this chapter, the authors have preserved a logfile of the significant research that has been performed till date in the field of e-healthcare and their technologies. The proposed model, advaity.in, is a healthcare web application that provides several e-healthcare facilities such as the online doctor's consultation, medical tests, and medical services. The general purpose of advaity.com is to serve the society and to uplift them to a better version of tomorrow. The online platform breaks up the restrictions of place and time. Consumers can be facilitated with the advantages of e-commerce, e-services, and much more. Instant communication and online call service delivery provides customer with more satisfaction.

Further, in the future the authors will be adding extra feature of chatbot having artificial intelligence for booking purposes and replying to customer queries.

ACKNOWLEDGMENT

The authors would like to convey their heartiest thanks to the reviewers for their comments and insight.

KEYWORDS

- **e-healthcare**
- **web-application**
- **doctor's appointment**
- **e-commerce**
- **medical test**
- **pharmaceutical**

REFERENCES

1. Velavan, T. P.; Meyer, C. G. The COVID-19 Epidemic. *Trop. Med. Int. Health* **2020,** *25* (3), 278.
2. Valkenburg, P. M.; Peter, J. Online Communication among Adolescents: An Integrated Model of Its Attraction, Opportunities, and Risks. *J. Adolesc. Health* **2011,** *48* (2), 121–127.
3. Mukherjee, A.; McGinnis, J. E-Healthcare: An Analysis of Key Themes in Research. *Int. J. Pharm. Healthc. Mark.* **2007,** *1,* 349–363.
4. Das, S. R.; Kinsinger, L. S.; Yancy, W. S. Jr; Wang, A.; Ciesco, E.; Burdick, M.; Yevich, S. J. Obesity Prevalence among Veterans at Veterans Affairs Medical Facilities. *Am. J. Prevent. Med.* **2005,** *28* (3), 291–294.
5. Ali, M.; Mosa, A. H.; Al Machot, F.; Kyamakya, K. In *EEG-based Emotion Recognition Approach for e-Healthcare Applications,* Eighth international conference on ubiquitous and future networks, **2016**; pp. 946–950.
6. Della Mea, V.; What is e-Health (2): The death of telemedicine? *J. Med. Internet Res.* **2001,** *3* (2), e22.
7. Mitchell, J. Increasing the Cost-Effectiveness of Telemedicine by Embracing e-Health. *J. Telemed. Telecare* **2000,** *6* (1 suppl), 16–19.
8. Alvarez, R. C. The Promise of e-Health—a Canadian Perspective. *Ehealth Int.* **2002,** *1* (1), 4.
9. Wang, X.; Shi, J.; Kong, H. Online Health Information Seeking: A Review and Meta-Analysis. *Health Commun.* **2021,** *36* (10), 1163–1175.
10. Cao, W.; Zhang, X.; Xu, K.; Wang, Y. Modeling Online Health Information-Seeking Behavior in China: The Roles of Source Characteristics, Reward Assessment, and Internet Self-Efficacy. *Health Commun.* **2016,** *31* (9), 1105–1114.
11. Hang, B. In *Web based Long-Distance Appointment Registered System,* International Conference on Computer and Communication Technologies in Agriculture Engineering, 2010; Vol. 3; pp. 232–235.
12. Chaiwongsai, J.; Preecha, P.; Intem, S. In *Automated Patient Appointment Reminder for Cross-Platform Mobile Application,* International Symposium on Intelligent Signal Processing and Communication Systems, 2016; pp, 1–6.
13. Cola, C.; Valean, H. In *E-Health Appointment Solution, A Web-based Approach,* E-Health and Bioengineering Conference, 2015; pp. 1–4.
14. Deegan, P. E. A Web Application to Support Recovery and Shared Decision Making in Psychiatric Medication Clinics. *Psychiatr. Rehabil. J.* 2010, *34* (1), 23.
15. Inal, Y. Heuristic-based User Interface Evaluation of the Mobile Centralized Doctor Appointment System. *Electron. Libr.* **2019,** *37* (1), 81–94.
16. Mey, Y. S.; Sankaranarayanan, S. In *Near Field Communication-based Patient Appointment,* International Conference on Cloud & Ubiquitous Computing & Emerging Technologies, 2013; pp. 98–103
17. Sunarsono, R. J.; Hartini, S.; Soedarto, T. In *The E-Servicescape of Mobile-based Online Shopping Application Assessment: An Indonesian M-Commerce Fact,* Proceedings of the International Conference on Science and Technology, 2018.
18. Chatterjee, S.; Gupta, S.; Saha, T. An e-Commerce Portal for Online Medicine Trading. *Int. J. Eng. Appl. Sci.* **2017,** *4* (11).

19. Fahim, M.; Islam, A.; Shoab, M. Android Application for Medicine Based Smart E-commerce Site. *DSpace Rep.* **2020**.
20. Tian, L.; Wang, X.; Li, L. In *Research on Pharmaceutical E-Commerce Enterprises: A Case Study of Jxdyf.com*, In International Conference on Information and Management Engineering, 2011; pp 241–246.
21. Tian, L.; Wang, X.; Xue, W. In *Analysis of e-Commerce Application in Pharmaceutical Enterprises—A Case Study of YAOFANG*, International Conference on Future Information Technology and Management Engineering, 2010; Vol. 2, pp. 96–99.
22. Akshay, V.; Kumar, A.; Alagappan, R. M.; Gnanavel, S. In *BOOKAZOR-an Online Appointment Booking System*, International Conference on Vision Towards Emerging Trends in Communication and Networking, 2019; pp. 1–6.

CHAPTER 16

A Computational Approach to Detect the Incipient Cracks of Bearing in the Magnetic Particle Inspection Process

JUNAID ALI[1], VANSH KHERA[2], and ANUDRUTI SINGHA[3]

[1]*Department of Mechanical Engineering, Indian Institute of Technology Madras, Tamil Nadu, India*

[2]*Department of Mechanical Engineering, Rajasthan Technical University, Kota, India*

[3]*Department of Biomedical Engineering, School of Electronics Engineering, Vellore Institute of Technology, Vellore, India*

ABSTRACT

Manufacturing industries across the world are using various heat treatment processes to supply hardened steels for various applications such as industrial machines, bearings, automotive chassis. Many manufacturing industries, from a quality perspective, use Magnetic Particle Inspection (MPI) machine to detect the cracks on the surface of the metal body generated during heat treatment. MPI is a manual process where a workman is required to carry inspection operation on the machine. The underlying with manual operation of this process is direct exposure of workman of chemicals and fumes generated in the process as well as prolonged UV exposure during a visual inspection of parts causes vision impairment in long run. Various attempts have already been made by researchers during this field to integrate machine

Computational Intelligence in Analytics and Information Systems, Volume 2: Advances in Digital Transformation, Selected Papers from CIAIS-2021. Parneeta Dhaliwal, PhD, Manpreet Kaur, PhD, Hardeo Kumar Thakur, PhD, Rajeev Kumar Arya, and Joan Lu (Eds.)

vision with the conventional MPI process. However, it is always worthy to utilize the latest algorithms to improve the efficiency of the process. We have made a comparative study of different machine learning methods for image processing (with computer vision) to choose the best possible model for MPI machine.

16.1   INTRODUCTION

With the advent of Industry 4.0, manufacturing industries are shifting their attention to incorporate the automation complexities in their factories to walk together with engendering advancement of technology.[1] Automotive industries are currently integrating automation techniques with traditional manufacturing processes to achieve optimum process efficiency. The growing demand of product requires a smooth and robust manufacturing process with least downtime. To provide for required production capacity, condition monitoring of machines is required to predict failure before their occurrence to prevent unnecessary downtime loses. Computer vision is prevailing in visual inspection of rollers, super-finish bearing components etc.[2] Collectively, these efforts are diligently put toward improving the quality of product which is going to be used in any basic or advanced machinery. Quality of a bearing is of prime concern for any bearing manufacturer; any kind of defect or design limitation in bearing can cause catastrophic failure at end application or sometimes may even lead to fatal accidents. Bearing failures such as brinelling, smearing, abrasive wears, dents, scratches, fretting, or chatter happen due to surface irregularities or inclusion of any foreign particle on the bearing surface that during application run results in catastrophic failure. Likewise, surface cracks during fitment, material chip-off during mounting/unmounting, inner ring crack during cornering of wheel, transmission bearing failure due to track damage happen due to incipient cracks present in bearing which develop due to residual stresses in heat treatment processes.[3] The engineering characteristics of bearing parts such as dimensional stability, fatigue life, distortion, and wear resistance could get affected by residual stresses. For example, excessive residual stress retained in metal from heat treatment can increase the machining cost, and the re-equilibration of the remaining residual stress can distort the geometry of bearing components. As a result, the bearing industry is making good efforts to closely monitor residual stresses and minimize their generation during the manufacturing process, using methods such as tempering. However, sometimes, surface cracks develop due to critical stress development in bearing during heat treatment process. These cracks, however, not visible to naked eye, as shown in Figure 16.1, can be seen with the help of Magnetic Particle Inspection method.[4-7]

Our scope of problem is so far limited to bearing industries due to simplicity of product geometry and high impact of process automation on OEE. The industries are using a manual methodology to perform the Magnetic Particle Inspection of bearing surface cracks. The problem with the manual process is mostly because of workman's exposure to chemicals that are used in the process and because chemical fumes generated in the process can cause serious skin problems. Also, the MPI process is done under UV light lamp in a dark room. The operator looks closely over thousands of parts in day and on a longer run this causes problems such as vision impairment in workman. So, the problem is basically about the safety of a workman and improving the OEE of process because a machine can work more efficiently and reliably than a human being in repetitive tasks such as visual inspection.

16.2   BASIC PRINCIPLE OF MAGNETIC PARTICLE INSPECTION PROCESS

Magnetic particle inspection (MPI) is used to highlight defects that are not normally visible to a human eye. The process involves magnetizing a component on a magnetizer, after which, closed-loop magnetic field lines align itself around circumference of bearing surface as shown in Figure 16.2. As per concept of magnetism, the flux lines do not traverse the cracks or crevices on the surface of bearing ring due to air medium. Now, the bearings are showered with ferromagnetic particles—either suspended in a fluid or in a powder form. If a crack or crevice exists in the component, the particles will be attracted by the magnetic poles, which are present on each side of the crack or crevice, where the flux leaks in to the air as shown in Figure 16.1.

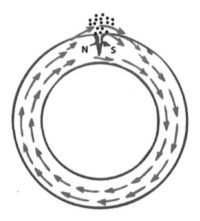

FIGURE 16.1   Cracked metal surface allowing magnetic flux leakage.

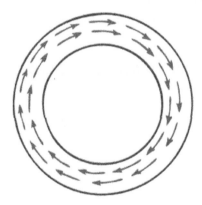

FIGURE 16.2   Noncracked metal ring without magnetic flux leakage.

Basically, micro-particles are suspended in a fluid or coolant, which supports the mobility of the particles in the crevasses on the metal surface. The difference between the component surface, dark background, and the micro-particles along the crack is not high enough that a human eye can see the defect, but with some strain, which leads to a high possibility of human error in the inspection process. Therefore, maximum contrast between defect and rest of surface can be achieved by using micro-particles coated with a fluorescent chemical, which will glow when illuminated under ultraviolet light. Therefore, it is not necessary to closely inspect the component, since the illuminated defect indications catch the workmen's eye and the workmen will quarantine the defective material lot.[8]

16.3 IMAGE PROCESSING

For a human eye there are certain limitations and boundaries that fortunately machines take care of through some devices. Similarly, in this experiment we are not just limiting our algorithm to process images, rather we are applying filters and masking to adjust the contrasts and focus area for better analysis of image captured.[9] After the ultraviolet light exposure on the bearing, the reduced pixel intensity of the surrounding metal particles, leaving the cracked region, makes it more convenient for the algorithm to detect the crack smoothly. The image is captured by the camera after the UV light exposure and the captured image is transferred to the system for processing. The image is converted into a gray scale for better visibility under UV lighting. Then the image is converted into a binary form, setting a threshold of 0.4. The image is resized and cropped using an image resizing factor of 0.5 for the enhanced subject identification.[10] The area of the cropped region is calculated. A median filter is applied over the image, as we need to detect the cracked regions. Hence, it is necessary to acquire the median pixel intensity values of the cracked regions. A clip limit of 0.05, with an exponential distribution over the entire image, is set. Contrast adjustment and masking of the regions other than the cracked regions are done to further improve the visibility of the cracked edges. Gaussian blurring is done to enhance the crack regions' visibility over background noise. The polarity of the pixel values in the image foreground is set to an adaptive mode with an adaptive threshold of 0.5 to 0.7. The morphological openings and the closing of the crack are detected as shown in Figures 16.3 and 16.4.

FIGURE 16.3 Raw image of defective part with surface cracks visible under ultraviolet light in the MPI process.

FIGURE 16.4   Processed image after contrast setting and masking.

After processing input images from our training set and converting into histogram of oriented gradients for enhancing visibility of each pixel of image to bring defect edges in contrast with background elements of image as shown in Figures 16.5 and 16.6. To import the image input dataset to train the machine learning model we created a feature matrix of image dataset through conversion of multidimensional array into 3D array using the RGB function. The conversion of an m-D array into a 3D array is the most crucial step to prepare a ready-to-feed dataset for our machine learning model. Otherwise, the model will not be able to train on provided dataset due to dimensionality error. Finally, to fit and transform the standard matrix we called for Principal Component Analysis function. Then the Data-Frame was split into training and test set on which we will train our machine learning models.

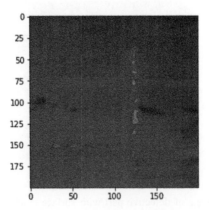

FIGURE 16.5   Cropped image of defective crack on surface of bearing.

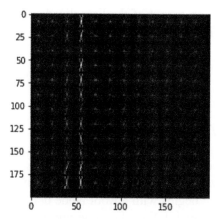

FIGURE 16.6   Histogram of oriented gradient conversion of image.

This preprocessing is the fundamental requisite for further proceedings in this study. The next step in this experiment is to test the above-processed dataset by splitting training and test set respectively to perform predictions on various Machine Learning Algorithm and Computer Vision assisted with Convolution Neural Networks. The major challenge in attempting this problem was unavailability of MPI dataset for bearings on online repositories. To prepare the dataset we manually clicked photographs of MPI process parts with the help of industry.

16.4   MATHEMATICAL MODELING

16.4.1   *SUPPORT VECTOR MACHINE CLASSIFICATION (SVMC)*

Support Vector Machine is a classical model to perform classification tasks and we will be testing this power algorithm over our image dataset.

$$\varnothing_\gamma \left(x,l\right) = exp\ exp\left(-\gamma \left\| x - l \right\|^2\right) \qquad (16.1)$$

where γ is our regularization hyper parameter to optimize our model to prevent over-fitting and under-fitting? Gaussian RBF kernel trick saves us from the computational complexity especially on large dataset. It bolsters the model optimization and the similarity feature function shown in eq 6 prevents over-computing from repeated computations of similar features in dataset.

The final prediction output of the kernelized support vector machine is computed by the following equation:

$$\hat{h} = \sum_{i=1}^{m} \hat{\alpha}^{(i)} t^{(i)} K\left(x^{(i)}, x^{(n)}\right) + \hat{b}, \text{ where } \hat{\alpha}^{(i)} \neq 0 \text{ and } \hat{b} \text{ is bias term} \qquad (16.2)$$

16.4.2   RANDOM FOREST (RF)

RF is an ensemble of multiple Decision Trees working together to produce an output that is a weighted sum average of total number of trees in the forest or structure. The tree begins with a Root Node defined by eq 1, and further split into two nodes which follow the same rule as given in eq 1.

$$n_{j \in Nodes\ in\ Tree} = w_j G_j - w_{left(j)} G_{left(j)} - w_{right(j)} G_{right(j)} \qquad (16.3)$$

where $w_{right/left(j)}$ is the weight factor that is a ratio of instances in class (k) of right and left nodes to the total number of instances of the subset of the node and $G_{right/left(j)}$ is the impurity factor of right and left nodes which basically depicts the mixing of other class instances in the subset of each node. If $G = 0$ then the node is purely of same instances, but if $G > 0$ then there is some amount of impurity meaning other class instances in the nodal subset. The fundamental equation given to calculate the impurity of the jth node in the tree structure is as follows:

$$G_j = 1 - \sum_{k=1}^{n} p_{j,k} 2 \qquad (16.4)$$

pj,k is the ratio of k ϵ prediction classes' instances among the training instances in the jth node of the tree. The n is the total number of classes which is two in our case (Cracked or Smooth Surface). The above equation sets fundamental ground for defining our model in the RF algorithm. By the nature of the algorithm, it works on Gini impurity which is faster in computation of results; however in our case the input dataset is small, and we have computational power to run more stabilized trees to predict the results with higher accuracies. We will define the *Entropy* hyper-parameter for our model in place of Gini Impurity.

$$H_j = -\sum_{k=1}^{n} p_{j,k} \log_2\left(p_{j,k}\right) \qquad (16.5)$$

$$p_{j,k} \neq 0.$$

16.4.3 ADABOOST BOOSTING ALGORITHM

AdaBoost Classifier with Decision Tree Classifier is used to train extracted feature data-frame of images and to make predictions on the training set. Let $w^{(i)}$ be the input instance, $\hat{y}_j^{(i)}$ be the prediction of model over the jth training instance of data-frame. The below equation is the weighted error rate of the model.

$$r_j = \frac{\sum_{i=1}^{m} w^{(i)}}{\sum_{i=1}^{m} w^{(i)}} \, where \, \hat{y}_j^{(i)} \neq y^{(i)} \tag{16.6}$$

After computing the weighted error rate of the model, we need to assign predictor weight α_j. The concept works on the fundamental principle of weighted average; as per the learning rate hyper parameter φ the more accurate will be the predictor then more will be its weight to contribute to overall weighted average of predictions.

$$\alpha_j = \varphi \, loglog \, \frac{1-r_j}{r_j} \tag{16.7}$$

If $\hat{y}_j^{(i)} \neq y^{(i)}$ the instance prediction weight will be updated with $\hat{y}_j^{(i)} \neq y^{(i)}$, whereas if the prediction $\hat{y}_j^{(i)} = y^{(i)}$ then the respective weights will be upgraded as per multiplication factor $w^{(i)}$

Finally, the AdaBoost algorithm computes the prediction values and individual weights to result in final output which is our actual prediction. The predictions are performed based on the following equation, where N is the number of predictors in the model.

$$\hat{y}(x) = argmax_k \sum_{j=1}^{N} \alpha_j, where \, \hat{y}_j(x) = k \tag{16.8}$$

16.4.4 CONVOLUTION NEURAL NETWORK ALGORITHM

A convolution neural network is a deep-learning-based algorithm currently deployed for various modern techniques such as self-driving cars, tagging people in images on Facebook, recognizing hand-written texts. In this paper, we have used a combination of CNN and ANN model to process the MPI images to detect the incipient cracks on taper roller bearing. The input image from the MPI machine, considered a 3D array of pixels (size from 0 to 255), was processed through feature detectors to return convolutional layer or feature map. The major role of Feature detector is to reduce the size of input image by keeping important features of image. The convoluted feature map is then passed through ReLU (Rectifier activation function) filter to remove any kind of linearity in the given image. Then comes the pooling process in which size of each convoluted layer is reduced by almost 75% to focus only on key features of image (suitable enough for its prediction), which helps in minimizing the processing efforts and reduces chances of overfitting. We have used pool size of 2 × 2 and no of strides as 2. In the next step, these pooled layers are flattened out and converted into linear vector carrying the important relevant features of our input image.

To improve our prediction accuracy, we further used the ANN model with its input layer as output from the CNN model. The hidden layers used are fully connected type with 128 units of neurons. The output is in the form of binary prediction (categorical variable type) with sigmoid function as an activation function. The complete model was trained using the back-propagation technique, in which "Cross-entropy function" was used to measure error in the output and "Adam" as the optimizer.

16.5   RESULT AND DISCUSSION

The results of machine learning algorithm on performing image classification tasks are encouraging. These models are clearly representing the primitive period of machine learning when we did not have the tools like CNN for image classification, which are so readily available now. Among all three models, surprisingly Adaboost Classifier has shown an accuracy of 85% against the F1 Score of 83% for true negative and 86% for true positive which are defective and nondefective images respectively. Similarly, the support vector classifier and the random forest model have shown an accuracy score of 86% both and F1 scores of 86% equally as shown in the ROC analysis curves in Figure 16.7.

Among all three models, surprisingly Adaboost Classifier has shown an accuracy of 85% against the F1 Score of 83% for true negative and 86% for true positive which are defective and nondefective images respectively. Similarly, the support vector classifier and the random forest model have shown an accuracy score of 86% both and F1 scores of 86% equally as shown in the ROC analysis curves in Figure 16.7.

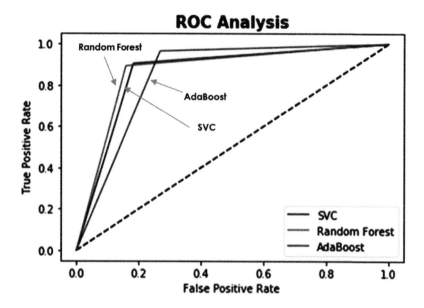

FIGURE 16.7   ROC curve analysis of machine learning models.

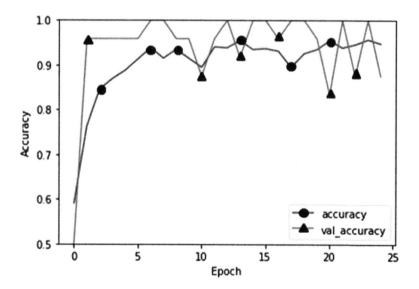

FIGURE 16.8   Epochs plotted against training and accuracy.

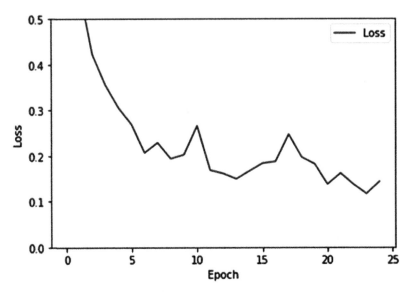

FIGURE 16.9   Epochs plotted against loss.

In each epoch process, the error was measured and optimized with the back propagation method to improve an output prediction accuracy. At the end of 25 epochs, the model has achieved an accuracy of 87% as shown in Figure 16.8. With increase in epochs number the model losses are decreasing whereas the accuracy score for training as well as validation set has shown significant rise with rising epochs as shown in Figure 16.8. After 0.87 accuracy index the epoch vs accuracies curves have shown resistance in Figure 16.9 which signifies further increase in epoch will result in model over-processing. Perhaps increasing the dataset will increase the accuracies which are currently 87% for both training and validation with loss as 40%. Overall, the model has performed up to the mark with the provided dataset. We recommend a bigger dataset of around 10,000 images to achieve higher efficiencies of model. S. Y. Chaganti et al. performed similar comparative analysis with SVM and CNN for image classification. The respective models achieved an accuracy score of 83% and 93.57%.[11] Our SVM model performed much better here due to proper image processing before providing input to the model. However, the efficiency of CNN is very less comparatively. The possible reason for low model accuracy is dataset. Since we have built this particular dataset manually the number of images was limited. However, with a limited number of images we can use some model optimization techniques in CNN to reduce the error within 10%.

On the same dataset we increased the number of layers by 5 and integrated a sigmoid activation function. Further, we decreased the sloping constant alpha to 0.002 from 0.5 to allow model to read each pixel in greater detail. We made a trade-off between model speed and efficiency by decreasing the sloping constant. Through this we were able to achieve an accuracy score of 93% which is well within the error limit of 10% as shown in Figures 16.10 and 16.11. We can declare our predicted results as reliable. However, these are still not viable for industrial use. Efficiency can be further increased through big dataset for higher accuracy scores. However, our aim was just to provide a proof of concept for this problem which could benefit the industries specially bearing manufacturers in a long run.

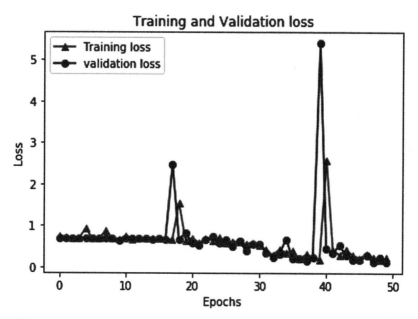

FIGURE 16.10 Optimized model loss vs epochs.

16.6 CONCLUSION

Fault diagnosis of surface defects through computer vision is mostly found integrated with all surface machining-related processes. In the bearing manufacturing process, apart from structural dimensionality

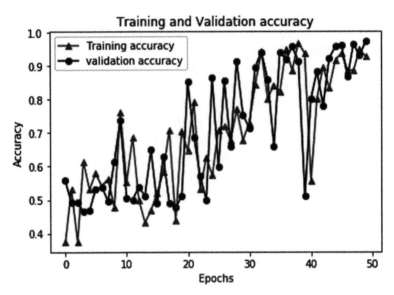

FIGURE 16.11   Optimized model accuracy vs epochs.

of the product, surface cosmetics plays a key role in quality and performance of bearing. Therefore, surface defects prognostics are trending in bearing manufacturing sector and to horizontally deploy the idea of prognosis we have integrated the computer vision technique in the MPI process. We have optimized the image parameters, by detecting the morphological openings and closings of the bearings in the image, further optimizing the pixel intensity and normalizing it with median filter and some image-processing tools. The processed images are compiled into dataset on which machine learning models such as Support Vector Classifier, AdaBoost Classifier, Random Forest Classifier, and Convolution Neural Networks are applied. We have achieved nearly similar prediction accuracy for all three machine learning models; however, the convolution neural network model provided best results, that is, 95% after optimizing the model parameters. The nobility of the problem is the area of its application which is overlooked in most manufacturing process automation attempts. Our aim is to highlight this problem to the research community so that with more advance modeling techniques in Computer Vision we can reach efficiencies up to 99%. The above models are proven and implemented in many industries applications of automatic visual inspection. However, very less work was published in the domain of MPI with computer vision integration to solve the problem of human health hazard and increasing the processing efficiency with Industry 4.0 tools.

ACKNOWLEDGMENT

We would like to show our sincere gratitude to National Engineering Industries Ltd. for supporting us in providing the dataset for our project.

KEYWORDS

- **computer vision**
- **magnetic particle inspection**
- **industry 4.0**
- **machine learning**
- **bearings**
- **neural networks**

REFERENCES

1. Kronos Incorporated. *The Future of Manufacturing: 2020 and Beyond.* Industry Week Special Research Report, 2016, p. 12.
2. Ghorai, S.; Mukherjee A.; Gangadaran, M.; Dutta, P. K. In *Automatic Defect Detection on Hot-Rolled Flat Steel Products*, IEEE Transactions on Instrumentation and Measurement, March 2013; vol. 62, no. 3, pp. 612–621, doi: 10.1109/TIM.2012.2218677.
3. Dai, J.; Li, Y.; He, K.; Sun, J. In *R-FCN: Object Detection via Region-based Fully Convolutional Networks*, Proceedings of the 30th International Conference on Neural Information Processing Systems (NIPS'16), Curran Associates Inc., Red Hook, NY, USA, 2016. pp. 379–387.
4. Prabuwono, A. S.; Sulaiman, R.; Hamdan, A. R.; In *Hasniaty, A. Development of Intelligent Visual Inspection System (IVIS) for Bottling Machine*, TENCON 2006–2006 IEEE Region 10 Conference, Hong Kong, 2006, pp. 1–4, doi: 10.1109/TENCON.2006.343887.
5. Ravikumar, S.; Ramachandran, K. I.; Sugumaran, V. Machine Learning Approach for Automated Visual Inspection of Machine Components. *Expert Syst. Appl.* **2011**, *38* (4), 3260–3266.
6. Dimiduk, D. M.; Holm, E. A.; Niezgoda, S. R. Perspectives on the Impact of Machine Learning, Deep Learning, and Artificial Intelligence on Materials, Processes, and Structures Engineering. *Integr. Mater. Manuf. Innov.* **2018**, *7*, 157–172.

7. Lin, Y. Z.; Nie, Z. H.; Ma, H. W. Structural Damage Detection with Automatic Feature-Extraction through Deep Learning. *Comput. Civ. Infrastruct. Eng.* **2017,** *32,* 1025–1046.

8. Jia, F.; Lei, Y.; Guo, L.; Lin, J.; Xing, S. A Neural Network Constructed by Deep Learning Technique and Its Application to Intelligent Fault Diagnosis of Machines. *Neurocomputing* **2017,** *272,* 619–628.

9. Hou, W.; Wei, Y.; Guo, J.; Jin, Y.; Zhu, C. Automatic Detection of Welding Defects using Deep Neural Network. *J. Phys. Conf. Ser.* **2017,** *933,* 012006.

10. Wang, P.; Fan, E.; Wang, P. Comparative Analysis of Image Classification Algorithms based on Traditional Machine Learning and Deep Learning. *Pattern Recogn. Lett.* **2021,** *141,* 61–67.

11. Chaganti, S. Y.; Nanda, I.; Pandi, K. R.; Prudhvith, T. G. N. R. S. N.; Kumar, N. In *Image Classification using SVM and CNN,* 2020 International Conference on Computer Science, Engineering and Applications (ICCSEA), Gunupur, India, 2020; pp. 1–5, doi: 10.1109/ICCSEA49143.2020.9132851.

PART II

Computational Intelligence in Network Technologies

CHAPTER 17

Comparison of Novel STE-AMM and EDES-ACM Frameworks with a Standard Cryptography Mechanism

SAMEER AND HARISH ROHIL

Department of Computer Science & Applications, Chaudhary Devi Lal University, Sirsa, Haryana, India

ABSTRACT

One of the tremendous services that the cloud environment offers is data sharing and storage. However, one of the prime concerns encountered in the cloud is security. It also provides a flexible and a convenient method to share the data. Since the data is confidential, users are reluctant to store the data directly in cloud. Hence a security should be provided by cryptographic means. Hence there is need to improve the security mechanism of the system. In this paper, a comparative study is established among the proposed secret twisted encryption-based access mechanism model and enigma diagonal encryption standard access control model. Also, a study of the existing mechanism of data sharing in an effective method to enhance the security of data sharing in the cloud environment is also done. The proposed scheme is evaluated and validated with the existing method.

Computational Intelligence in Analytics and Information Systems, Volume 2: Advances in Digital Transformation, Selected Papers from CIAIS-2021. Parneeta Dhaliwal, PhD, Manpreet Kaur, PhD, Hardeo Kumar Thakur, PhD, Rajeev Kumar Arya, and Joan Lu (Eds.)

17.1   INTRODUCTION

Cloud processing framework is the novel rendition of utility figuring that has subbed its territory at various data centers. The customers have wide-running admittance to data innovation abilities and offices, which is conveyed through the Web and has conveyed a glorious variety in the cycles of IT enterprises. It likewise assisted the IT enterprises with less foundation speculation other than support.[1] "The IT world is looking forward to the services delivered and consequently enhancing the growth of cloud computing."[2]

Utilizing the cost-viability improvements in the computational innovation and huge scope organizations, sharing data through the others end up being harmoniously more suitable.

In the interim, cloud information-sharing requirements off-premises foundation that specific associations commonly held, far off capacity is someway scary classification of information proprietors. Thusly, implementing the security of individual.[3]

"The essential objective in security is to supply a cryptographic system that is computationally infeasible for attackers to realize the proper use of the system. For example, the issue of number factorization is a technique used in RSA. The discrete logarithm is favored in DH Key Exchange, Digital Signature algorithm, elliptic curve cryptography, etc."[4] These natives are established on hard AI problems.

The problem of instantaneously attaining fine-grainedness, usual data confidentiality of cloud data sharing, and high effectiveness on the data owner's sideremain vague. There is no constituency among the data synchronization besides data storage. It is essential to enhance the system security mechanism.

The proposed decisional bilinear diffie-factorial prime elliptic curve hellman cryptographic data sharing in cloud computing is to secure the sharing of data in cloud computing. It also focuses on all the type of attacks in the area of cloud computing. It is also used to prevent the data from brute force attack, dictionary attack, SQL injection attack, collusion attacks, and side-channel attacks.

The fragmentations of the paper are divided as follows: Section 17.2 explains about the Literature review of the study. Section 17.3 presents the research methodology of the current work and is about the overview of the proposed algorithms. Section 17.4 deals with detailed results along with discussion and finally the conclusion in the 5th Section.

17.2 LITERATURE SURVEY

This part aims to introduce an outline of existing articles related with secure information sharing inside the Cloud. We characterized the condition of workmanship articles in two perspectives: information sharing and Cloud security. There have been some journals on privacy and security in the Cloud.[5,6] Xiao and Xiao recognized the five areas of Cloud computing; accountability, availability, privacy, confidentiality, and integrity and thoroughly analyzed the threats to a piece of the concerns in addition to protection strategies.[7]

Chen and Zhao outlined the necessities for attaining privacy as well as safety in the Cloud and also concisely summarized the necessities for safe sharing of the data in the Cloud environment.[8] Shen et al. proposed an audit on protection notwithstanding security in the Cloud focusing on the way in which security laws should likewise take into concern. Cloud computing and how work may be dealt with deflect protection to security breaks of one's private data inside the Cloud.[9] Wang et al. explored issues that affect managing information security in Cloud computing. It clarified the essential security requirements for enterprises to realize the dynamics of information security in the Cloud.[10] Mitchley described the benefits of data sharing from a banking perspective and emphasized the privacy concerns still affecting it.[11]

Athena et al. implemented effective methods. The elliptic curve D-H for the secret key generation and ID attribute-based encryption for enhancing data security in the cloud.[12] Geoghegan was effectively implemented.[13] The protocol could resist forgery attack beneath the assumption that the D-H problem was hard suggested Moreover, the suggested protocol is already compared with further ID-based auditing protocols.[12]

Initially, the CSP, data owner, and data user create the secret key for the data using implementing the DH Algorithm; formerly the Third Party Auditor authenticated the generated secret information.[9] A protected information bunch sharing was proposed on trait-based and coordinated delivery restrictive ID-based transmission PRE.[14] It includes a determinant that licenses access power over encoded data utilizing access techniques and credited ascribes among private keys and ciphertexts. Particularly, "Ciphertext-Policy Attribute-Based Encryption permits data owner to describe the access policy over a universe of attributes in which the user desires to possess to decode the ciphertext, by which the confidentiality and access control of data can be assured."[15] Then again, current arrangements generally focus while in transit to manage the cost of secure information read for clients, none of these works thinks that few clients may likewise compose the encoded data cooperatively in cloud computing. "In order to provide privacy to sensitive data, a Modified Elliptic Curve Cryptography algorithm was proposed."[16] An effective encryption technique based on Elliptic Curve Cryptography was proposed,[17] which used the DES, modified Feistel algorithm to encrypt the data or decrypt the data.

17.3   RESEARCH METHODOLOGY

17.3.1   ADVANCED ENCRYPTION STANDARD

The AES is the one of the standard symmetrical cryptography that are utilized to encrypt and decrypt the information in the cloud climate. In general, the AES algorithm operates with matrix and involves for steps for both encryption and decryption of data. The steps in AES are given in Figure 17.1.

Sub bytes—This form the first step in AES, a value among the 16 inputs in the matrix is replaced with the value of another matrix. It can be achieved through multiplicative inverse followed by affine transformation.

Permutation—The next step in the AES is the shifting of the rows of the input matrix into column. It is performed over all the rows except the first row. It is generally achieved through shift left.

Mixing—In this step, the shifted matrix is generally multiplied with the common polynomial. This process will yield the new matrix with 16 different input values.

Add Round key—It is the final step of AES; it involves the bitwise XOR function over the two subkeys in the similar state.

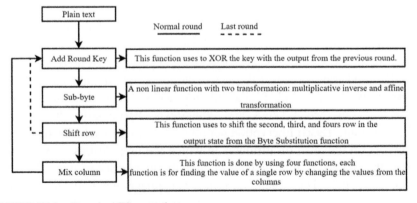

FIGURE 17.1   Steps in AES cryptology.

17.3.1.1 *RSA*

RSA uses asymmetric cryptography that allows the usage of two different keys for encoding and decoding of data, respectively. This avoids the same key for both decoding and encoding, which can be potential threat for data. The RSA algorithm by and large based on the choice of two unique numbers P,Q and RSA receives just the prime numbers.[18,19]

"After selecting two prime numbers L and M, the following steps are followed for key generation

Estimate $N = L \times M$

Estimate $\varphi\,(N) = (L - 1)\,(M - 1)$

Choose integer e

$GCD\,(\varphi\,(N), e) = 1; 1 < e < \varphi\,(N)$

Calculate d

$de \bmod \varphi\,(N) = 1$

Public key PUKR = $\{e, n\}$

Private key KR = $\{d, n\}$" (Padmaja and Priyanka)

17.3.1.2 *PROPOSED ALGORITHMS*

For sharing the data among the user in the cloud to novel frameworks are introduced and are termed as Enigma Diagonal Encryption Standard Access Control Model (EDES-ACM) and Secret Twisted Encryption-based access mechanism model (STE-AMM). Both the framework involves the distinct signature and encryption algorithm. Both the frameworks fundamentally adopt the traditional AES algorithm and Diffie Hellman technique for encryption and signature generation. The EDES-ACM framework involves inverse decisional Diffie Hellman for signature generation whereas STE-AMM involved the Square Decisional Diffie Hellman.[20] In both frameworks, the key generated through the AES algorithm is processed through the secret twisting matrix. In both system, the client is at first added to the cloud through the particular digital signature and private key. The client was given the digital signature to get to the cloud and the key to obtain the first information from the encrypted information.

17.4   RESULTS AND DISCUSSION

The proposed Frameworks generated the digital signature for user. The time considered for both the generation and approval of the client digital signature increment with increment in the number of clients in the group. The obtained time over the generation and proofing of the signature is given in Figures 17.2 and 17.3, which showed that the proposed framework is effective than the existing standard frameworks.

In general, the cryptic mechanism over the cloud data is observed over the different size data. Figures 17.4 and 17.5 indicated that there is increment in encryption and decryption time with increment file size. However, the proposed frameworks are better than the existing cryptographic algorithms.

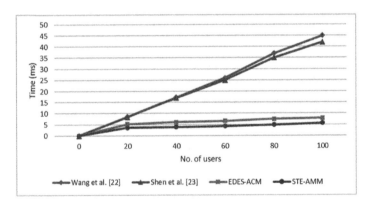

FIGURE 17.2   Comparison on signature generation.

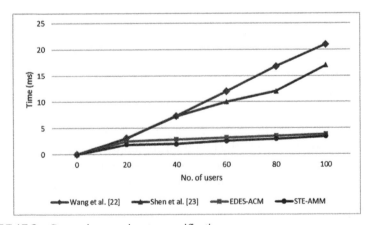

FIGURE 17.3   Comparison on signature verification.

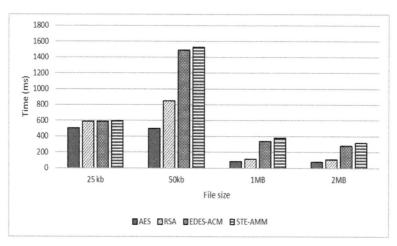

FIGURE 17.4 Encryption time over different file size.

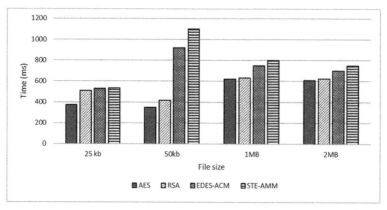

FIGURE 17.5 Decryption time over different file size.

17.5 CONCLUSION

Cloud computing provides a great convenience for people to store their data. Data can also be shared over the internet. However, one of the predominant concerns encountered in cloud is the security aspects. It should provide a flexible and a convenient method to share the data. Since the data was confidential, users were reluctant to store the data directly in cloud. Hence a security model was proposed by cryptographic means to improve the security mechanism of the system. Hence research work was carried out to solve such security issues. In this paper, a comparative study over the proposed and existing framework to secure the sharing of data in cloud computing. Additionally, an investigation of the current system of information sharing was done successfully to improve the security of information partaking in cloud computing. The proposed technique was assessed and contrasted with the current strategy.

KEYWORDS

- **cloud computing**
- **data sharing**
- **security**
- **secret twisted encryption-based access mechanism model**
- **enigma diagonal encryption standard access control model**

REFERENCES

1. Shawish, A.; Salama, M. Cloud Computing: Paradigms and Technologies. In *Inter-Cooperative Collective Intelligence: Techniques and Applications. Studies in Computational Intelligence*; Xhafa, F., Bessis, N., Eds.; vol 495; Springer: Berlin; 2014, pp. 39–67.
2. Swathi, T.; Srikanth, K.; Reddy, S. R. Virtualization in Cloud Computing. *Int. J. Comput. Sci. Mobile Comput.* **2014**, *3*, 540–546.
3. Shaikh, A.; Pathan, R.; Patel, R.; Rukaiya, A. P. S. Implementation of Authentication using Graphical Password for Cloud Computing. *Int. Res. J. Eng. Technol.* **2018**, *5*, 3293–3297.
4. Sharma, A.; Mittal, S. K. Attacks on Cryptographic Hash Functions and Advances, *Int. J, Inform. Comput. Sci.* **2018**, *5*, 89–96.
5. Prasad, K.; Poonam, J.; Gauri, K.; Thoutam, N. C. In *Data Sharing Security and Privacy Preservation in Cloud Computing*, International Conference on Green Computing and Internet of Things (ICGCIoT), 2015.
6. Zhang, L.; Cui Y.; Mu, Y. Improving Security and Privacy Attribute Based Data Sharing in Cloud Computing. *IEEE Syst. J.* **2020**, *14*, 387–397.
7. Xiao, Z.; Xiao, Y. Security and Privacy in Cloud Computing. *IEEE Commun. Surv. Tutor.* **2012**, *99*, 1–17.
8. Chen, D.; Zhao, H. In *Data Security and Privacy Protection Issues in Cloud Computing. In Computer Science and Electronics Engineering (ICCSEE),* 2012 International Conference, 2012; *1*, pp. 647–651.
9. Shen, J.; Zhou, T.; Chen, X.; Li, J.; Susilo, W. Anonymous and Traceable Group Data Sharing in Cloud Computing. *IEEE Trans. Inform. Foren. Sec.* **2018**, *13*, 912–925.

10. Wang, J. S.; Liu, C. H.; Lin, G. T. In *How to Manage Information Security in Cloud Computing. In Systems, Man, and Cybernetics (SMC)*, IEEE International Conference, 2011, pp. 1405–1410.

11. Mitchley, M. Data Sharing: Progress or Not. *Credit Manage* **2006**, 10–11.

12. Athena, J.; Sumathy, V.; Kumar, K. An Identity Attribute-based Encryption using Elliptic Curve Digital Signature for Patient Health Record Maintenance. *Int. J. Commun. Syst.* **2018**, *31*, 34–39.

13. Geoghegan, S. The Latest on Data Sharing and Secure Cloud Computing. *Law Order* **2012**, 24–26.

14. Cui, H.; Wan, Z.; Deng, R. H.; Wang, G.; Li, Y. Efficient and Expressive Keyword Search Over Encrypted Data in Cloud. *IEEE Trans. Dependable Secure Comput.* **2018**, *15*, 409–422.

15. Rahulkrishnan, C. Prime Factorization: A New Approach. 2014.

16. Thangapandiyan, M.; Anand, P. M. R.; Sankaran, K. S. In *Enhanced Cloud Security Implementation Using Modified ECC Algorithm*, 2018 International Conference on Communication and Signal Processing (ICCSP), 2018, pp. 1019–1022.

17. Young-Sil, L.; Esko, A.; Hoonjae, L. An Efficient Encryption Scheme using Elliptic Curve Cryptography (ECC) with Symmetric Algorithm for Healthcare System. *Int. J. Secur. Appl.* **2014**, *8*, 63–70.

18. Padmaja, N.; Priyanka K. Providing Data Security in Cloud Computing using Public Key Cryptography. *Int. J. Eng. Sci. Res.* **2013**, *1*, 1059–1063.

19. Kalpana, P.; Sudha, S. Data Security in Cloud Computing using RSA Algorithm. *Int. J. Res. Comput. Commun. Technol.* **2012**, 2278–5841.

20. Diffie, W.; Hellman, M. New Directions in Cryptography. *IEEE Trans. Inf. Theory* **1976**, *22*, 644–654.

CHAPTER 18

Privacy Protection in Personalized Web Searches Using Anonymity

KRISHAN KUMAR[1], MUKESH KUMAR GUPTA[1], and VIVEK JAGLAN[2]

[1]Suresh Gyan Vihar University, Jaipur, India

[2]Graphic Era Hill University, Dehradun, India

ABSTRACT

Personalized Web Search is a one-stop solution for everyone to get answer of day-to-day questions. Web Search Engines are storing individual information creating user profiles to get better results. This storage of information creates very serious privacy concerns as the data stored online can be transferred or leaked, which can reveal user's personal information and interests. We have proposed a system that can maintain anonymity of individual and reveal partial information to get benefits of personalization as well. The proposed system is using well-defined protocols and implemented on proxy level with privacy protection.

18.1 INTRODUCTION

Personalized Web Search (PWS) is a good way to get better web search results that need collection and aggregation of information about the user to be more effective, which pose severe privacy infringement threats for users. It is found that if personalization is performed on the client machine, better

Computational Intelligence in Analytics and Information Systems, Volume 2: Advances in Digital Transformation, Selected Papers from CIAIS-2021. Parneeta Dhaliwal, PhD, Manpreet Kaur, PhD, Hardeo Kumar Thakur, PhD, Rajeev Kumar Arya, and Joan Lu (Eds.)

results can be achieved than the existing server-side PWS in terms of privacy protection.[1] "One size fits all" is a big drawback of existing search engines as they are not tailored as per the privacy need of individual users. Search engine record individual search query logs, location information, click-through history, user cookies, browsing history, IP address, and conduct user profiling. The collection of personally identifiable information (PII) by the search engine about the user is considered as tracking. This information is collected from the user while interacting with web search engine to provide personalization and user profiling but at the same time web search engine use this information for targeted advertisement to get monetary benefits and improving search quality. But once the information is revealed individual's privacy can be compromised because it is no longer under their own control, how and by whom it is used. Although some web search engine organization online publish the privacy policies about their practices for the sake of public knowledge. But these policies are full of legal and technical terms which are difficult to understand for the users. most of the users are worried about monitory of their activities. Some users try to avoid this monitoring by using tools to anonymize their queries and by rejecting cookies. users register themselves on web search engines and enhance services by personalizing and customizing as per their needs. Beside this users require sides to garner data to their end.

To fill the bridge off conflicting requirements, we developed a system that manage anonymity while sharing information with the web search engines. This web-based framework takes care of privacy concerns while using web search engines and balance personalized web services and privacy concerns. In this system, masks are used as anonymity barriers between user's private data and web search engine. It also controls the information flow between web search engine and user. Mask act as a filter that prevents exposure of user's information and allow service personalization. It does not allow third parties to create user profiles on the basis of click-through and privacy issue at data collection are well addressed.

18.2   RELATED WORK

Anonymity of Twitter users is analyzed[2] to check user anonymity and correlation with the sensitive content. It was observed that the people were supporting, fighting, sharing, and discussing on the topics like sexual orientations, marital and relationship issues, health-related issues, personal experience and feelings, social anxieties, depression, suicidal tendencies, and disclosing their own. Anonymity can provide them an opportunity to solicit support.

In the recent times, users are providing their personal information to get excellent web services. This personal information generally contain name of the user, contact number, address, social, IDs credit card numbers, etc. privacy of the user can be compromised, because the web services can provide it to some third parties which may not be obliged to keep the privacy protected. Companies generally implement anonymization or de-identification techniques on the users data to keep the privacy intact. Anonymized data cannot be associated with individual users in any way.[3] Anonymization is a way of converting open personal information of the user into aggregated data. Few techniques of anonymization are suppression, encryption, generalization, and perturbation. These techniques are combined to make the data anonymous. Data anonymization models includes k-anonymity,[4–6] l-diversity,[7] t-closeness,[8] b-likeness, etc. But all the techniques are implemented after storing information about the user. We are working on a system that does not allow web service providers to store user personal information.

Nowadays privacy can be breached in many ways like hackers can steal data from email, computers, user groups, and online service providers can also steal habits and user activity. Service providers also garner personal information about the user to personalize websites, which also create big concerns in the minds of users. It may vary from user to user how much privacy they want to give up when they are making their personal information publicly available. Beside this it is totally different how much information they reveal while interacting with web search engine. One more question how much information users are interested in order to obtain better services. It may vary person to person how much privacy they want to protect, or we can say privacy can be determined individually. We cannot decide on privacy needs, which may fit to all users.

18.3 LEVELS OF PRIVACY PROTECTION IN PWS

Everyone has different requirement of privacy protection so the level of privacy protection can be decided as per individual need and there is trade-off between personalization and privacy protection. In the given below table, four levels of privacy protection in PWS as discussed.

18.3.1   *LEVEL I: PSEUDO IDENTITY*

The user identity ID(U) is not used directly rather a pseudo identity IDp(U) is created, which contains less personal information about the user and used.

TEXT (N, i) can be aggregated according to IDp(U) at server side.

Identification and classification of user are safeguarded. Pseudo profile can be mapped with user information like queries and click through. User profile can be exploited to PWS. AOL replaced IP addresses of users with a pseudo Id in August, 2006 User log release.[9] A lady was identified in Lilburn, Georgia by New York Times Reporter with this log.

18.3.2   *LEVEL II: GROUP IDENTITY*

(a) Some users can create a group and identity for the whole group is treated as single user identity ID(U).
(b) The description of information needs TEXT(N; i) for the users of group is aggregated to ID(U).

In this technique, a proxy for a group of users is created and users of whole group communicate with web search engine through proxy. So the identity and descriptions of user information needs mixed with group users and it is made very difficult to identify an individual user.

18.3.3   *LEVEL III: NO IDENTITY*

(a) The user identity ID(U) is completely hidden from the search engine.
(b) Information needs TEXT(N; i) for the user are also not be aggregated on the search engine side, not even at the group level.

Here, user profile can be kept on the local machine and personalization of search results at local user personal computer by re-ranking the results. Anonymous networks like Torpark are used to communicate with web search engine.

18.3.4   *LEVEL IV: NO PERSONAL INFORMATION*

(a) User identity ID(U) and information need TEXT(N) of the user are not provided to the web search engine.

To achieve level IV of privacy protection Cryptography techniques can be used. For example, the user does not send any query directly to the web search engine but it sends the query to the trusted third party and the third party perform the search operation on behalf of client and send back search results to client. Government agencies also can force search engine companies not to store any sort of data which can avail level IV privacy protection to the user.

18.4   SOFTWARE ARCHITECTURE FOR PERSONALIZED SEARCH

On the basis of location of PII about the user and way of exploitation for personalization, the architectures are divided into three categories as given below table.

18.4.1   SERVER-SIDE PERSONALIZATION

Personal information $P(U)$ of the user is stored and updated on server side using user-specified interests (explicitly) and queries, click-through history (implicitly), etc. Information collected implicitly is a richer way of data collection although both ways require an account to store information.

In current scenario, most of the personalized search systems like Google, Yahoo use server-side personalization, which have some advantages like resources of search engine (e.g., common search patterns, document index) can be used in personalization algorithms without any requirement of changes at client-side software. Although Search Engines store and hold PII of user with his/her consent used for personalization and claim first level of privacy. But still many users are doubtful about the potential privacy threats by the search engine so the adoption of this architecture is hindered by some users.

If search engine replaces identity of the user $ID(U)$ by a pseudo identity $IDp(U)$, then it is possible to achieved level I privacy. Then search logs can be shared with corporate partners, public, or researchers with pseudo-identity and it is possible to achieve level I privacy.

In current scenario, level II of privacy cannot be achieved even if user communicate through proxy and use group profile technique. Because search engines use the user login ID and locale machine address (MAC address and IMEI numbers) to aggregate the user information not only the IP address. Level III and level IV privacy protection cannot be attained with this architecture.

18.4.2 CLIENT SIDE-PERSONALIZATION

Personal information of user $P(U)$ is stored on client machine. Client-side personalization agent makes changes in the query at the time of submission and re-ranks the search results as per the requirements of the user after receiving results from the search engine. In this architecture, user search behavior, contextual activities, page viewed, browser bookmarks, and emails also can be considered to personalize the user profile. Sensitive information, computation, and storage of user profiles are distributed among various client machines and no more overhead of server but there is a drawback also that is algorithms available at server side for personalization cannot be used.

18.4.3 CLIENT SERVER COLLABORATIVE PERSONALIZATION

In this case, all the information about the User profile is kept on client machine only, and it is not shared with the server. Client only submits contextual information extracted from the user profile with the query to the web search engine. Server performs personalization on the contextual information received from user and provide the results to the user. Advantage of this architecture is to utilize the resources of server and drawback is only contextual information is not sufficient for good search results as compare to the profile. This architecture cannot provide better level of privacy as the server can keep storing the contextual information received from the client and provides almost same privacy as obtained from server-side personalization

18.5 ANONYMITY

Meaning of anonymity is personas identity unknown or namelessness, which originated from Greek word "anonymia." In other words, we can say person is nonidentifiable, untrackable, or unreachable. Other similar terms like identity, pseudonymity, and privacy also come up with time.

First of all, we need to determine what type of anonymity service we are concerned with in personalized web search. As discussed by[10] Anonymity can be segregated into parts data anonymity and connection anonymity. data anonymity is de-identification of data which means removing identity linkage or filtering any personal identifiable information from the data. So de-identification is an issue related to privacy-preserving data mining and carried out on data sets.[11] Whereas connection anonymity deals with the issue of stealing identities during the interaction. So in privacy protection in personalized web search, we are concerned with connection anonymity.

Further, we can define three types of anonymity. First one is environmental anonymity, which can be defined by external factors like number of users, diversity of the users, and their prior knowledge. Second one is procedural anonymity, which is defined by underlying protocol, intrinsic qualities, and design of the system. It can be discussed to improve the privacy of the system. Third one is content-based anonymity, which deals with mitigating contextual information in the data transfer.

Different levels of anonymity can be defined on the basis of properties which can be defined as follows. Identifiability is case of possibility of revealing PII or identity of user during the communication with the system when actual data exchange take place. Traceability is the case of obtaining PII about the user by observing the communication context. Unlikability means that two or more items of interest are no more and no less related to each other than to apriori knowledge. Identifiability and traceability are almost identical terms, the way information is collected makes them different. Recognizability is a common term which means collection of PII irrespective of how information is observed. Every user wants to hide identity but at the same time fraudsters should be held accountable for their actions, which creates strong conflict of interest over unrecognizability. So we can say unlikability and unrecognizability is not required to provide anonymity.

PII can be of two types—direct PII and indirect PII. Direct PII do not need any external assistance to trace individual user whereas indirect PII needs third-party involvement to access PII records. Whereas unresolvable PII cannot be revealed with third party as well. This is highest level of anonymity. Pseudo-anonymity or Pseudonym is a single identifier which associate with an individual user. Public pseudonyms are a class of direct PII whereas nonpublic pseudonyms can be considered as indirect or unresolvable PII. Group anonymity precludes unconditional recognizability and link ability, which involves trusted and dedicated group manager who is responsible for removing or adding members and reveal identities in case of disputes.

18.6 PRIVACY CONCERNS IN WEB SEARCH

Let us suppose a User (U) submitted a query (q) to a Search Engine (S) that returned Results ($R = \{R1, ..., Rn\}$) back to the user. Then User selects Ri

ε R and then, Search Engine provided the content of Ri to the user. In this whole process between user and search engine, the user reveals potential personal information that can be inferred as:

1. User Identity: This can be IP address of user machine or personal user ID if user has registered account with search engine.
2. Queries: Queries submitted by the user.
3. Viewed Search Results: Web pages viewed by the user. (Click through, Time spent, url, footprints, etc)

All the submitted Queries and viewed search results are about to pose serious privacy concerns for the user. Abbreviations are mentioned in Table 18.1.

TABLE 18.1 Abbreviations Used.

Abbreviation	Description
U	User
S	Search Engine
q	Query submitted to search Engine
$R = \{R1, ..., Rn\}$	Search results from search engine for query q
Ri ε R	Chosen to view Result Ri by the user
ID(U)	Some ID revealed about user like user ID or IP address
TEXT(N)	Text description of information need N of user e.g. viewed results and/or related queries
$P(U)$	Personal Information of User U.

So sensitive personal information a user can reveal while conducting k search activities can be expressed as follow:

$$P(U) = \{ \text{ID}(U,i), \text{TEXT}(N, i)\} \text{ where } i = 1, ..., k$$

So $P(U)$ is what a search engine needs to personalize web search for user U. The challenge is to protect user privacy in PWS to exploit $P(U)$ to improve services for user (U) but to protect $P(U)$ to keep identity of user safe from outer world.

18.7 PRIVACY PROTECTION STEPS

We have an idea of six steps to implement personalized privacy protection. Users can improve and enhance their privacy by following these six steps. It will be totally up to the user how much information it want to expose through their actions and situation. In other words, we can say users can select information disclosure as per time place or some other entities involved. Each step is independent of the other one and existence of each step doesn't affect others like previous or next. However, if more than one step is not available they're still available in the same fashion and order.

18.7.1 STEP 1: AWARENESS

Users can provide information to the web search engine voluntarily or involuntarily. When user fill form and submit information about itself, we call it voluntarily. But when web search engine collect information about user and its activities without user consent, we call it involuntarily. The information collected from the user without its consent during the interaction for the web services is considered as a privacy risk. Many users are not aware that they can block cookies to enhance privacy but they have to sacrifice personalization for this task. Many of them do not know that web server is storing their each click, website searched, and creating their profile to provide personalized results. The best and easiest way to enhance the privacy is to aware the user about these privacy risks. Privacy Critics[12] is a privacy protection tool, which helps user while interacting with the Internet and issues warnings and suggestions. It is considered as first step privacy protection and spreads awareness among users about privacy risks and help them to understand their exposure with the web. However, it is not protecting privacy of the user by itself. It just informs and suggest the user.

18.7.2 STEP 2: CONTROL

Step 2 help users to define a mechanism that can fight against privacy invasion, which support user behavior analysis like History file access, Web Bugs, and Third Party Cookies. The major platform to interact with the interact is Web Browser, which help user with the help to reject and filter-out undesired data collection techniques. Hackers use malicious codes to collect information about history files and can easily reveal to third party about the webpages traversed, which is considered as a privacy breach. So web browsers should delete this information automatically or provide a facility to the user to delete these files. Cookies, hidden form fields, session Ids, URL rewriting, and Web Brower Ids are different techniques to track user and collect information about it. Web conglomerates generally collect user information on one platform and use it to create profile and can use it on other web platform. Emails, News sites, web search engines, Shopping sites, and Social sites can be used to track user and create profile web search engine is not the only platform. Most of the web browser provide facility to reject cookies, even it is cumbersome task for the user and only conscious user opt it and it may stop some desired services. Filters can also be used to block cookies advertisements and web bugs but there is disadvantage with filters that they block all the cookies and which lose access to personalized services also. it is true that filters can only lower down chances of privacy invasion but cannot guarantee hundred percent privacy. Still geographical location, interaction time, and IP address can be used to track the user.

18.7.3   STEP 3: PRIVACY IMPROVING TOOLS

In step 3, privacy protection tools are used to enhance user privacy. In this step location of privacy protection mechanism also matters which make it different from step 2 as well. Privacy specialists say that a user should not trust privacy policies laid down by website but should control privacy with own tools and techniques.

Pseudonyms are virtual names, individually or as part of a collective, used to maintain anonymity while interacting with internet. Generally, it is not easy to associate a real user with the pseudonym but a groups of messages can be associated if they carry PII about the user. The Anonymizer act as a proxy and submit queries on behalf of user. In this case, Web services cannot trace user's IP Address but there are some drawbacks also like web server or search engine cannot get information about the real user and so cannot provide personalization and customization.

Lucent Personalized Web Assistant[13] is a pseudonym-based tool, which allow user to interact with web site for identification-based services without revealing actual identity. But there is drawback with this system also, if real identity of user is revealed, all past action are exposed.

Unlike Lucent Personalized Web Assistant and Anonymizer that involve third parties to interact with internet, Crowds[14] and Onion[15] are using groups to hide identity of user. Onion has a static path defined on other hand Crowds have dynamic path. Just like other tools these also do not provide personalization facility.

18.7.4   STEP 4: PRIVACY POLICIES

This step is about the privacy policies laid down by the websites, how they collect personal information of the user. It is mandatory for the websites to publicly disclose how the information collected from the users is handled and also describe their privacy preferences. Privacy preference Project (P3P) of World Wide Web Consortium-enabled website need to provide information in a format that can be read by machine. P3P-enabled web browsers can easily read this information and can perform comparative analysis with the privacy preferences of the user. Generally, web browser continue requisition of the web pages if the policy match with security configuration of the user else agent notify the user about the disparity. P3P does not monitor sites for their minimum standard, user have to trust them and sites can change their privacy policy also.

18.7.5   STEP 5: PRIVACY AND TRUST CERTIFICATION

On the basis of Huaiqing Wang and Colleagues, taxonomy website are graded. This grading takes in consideration access, collection, monitoring, analysis, transfer, solicitation, and storage of the user data. Nowadays, consumers and businesses are very sensitive about privacy policies and approach privacy certification very cautiously. Bankrupt companies transfer users private information and assets to other companies and these purchasing companies are generally not obliged to keep the user information safe and private.

18.7.6   STEP 6: PRIVACY PROTECTION LAWS

In many countries, laws to regulate privacy are discussed and proposed. A mechanism to take action against companies and individuals for breaking rule is created. But until these laws are enforced universally, companies hardly respect and protect user privacy. One of the major reason is, user is not even aware that there privacy can be violated and behavior on web is very tough to control. Another issue is to create international laws, which is dependent on diverse culture and political will. Still we can address some common concerns of privacy invasion like-

(1) Use data should not be collected and analyzed without user consent
(2) User data should be used the way it has been consented.

(3) Use data should not be disclosed or sent to others without permission and knowledge.

Even after implementing international laws, some countries may not follow those and we can say that only laws cannot protect user data and user should trust some mechanism which can be trusted to protect the data.

18.8   MULTIPLE PROXY SERVER

Steps 5 and 6 cannot be implemented in any mechanism as these steps belong to different countries. But we are proposing a system that implements first three steps of privacy protection. The proposed system has proxy servers, consent-based distributed privacy architecture. Multiple proxies use Network Address Translation to improve security and deal with IP address shortage. A proxy is a temporary identification used to interact with the internet. The proxy is selected on the basis of user's area of interest in or a particular site. When a user interact with a website, website store information about the proxy instead of visitor. Users can interact with a site through different proxies depending on interest at a given time.

As shown in Figure 18.1, multiple proxy server has two main components—proxy servers and privacy and security agents (PSA). Proxy servers work between user and websites, whereas PSA work in coordination with web browser. PSA warn users about privacy invasion, allow users to configure proxies and cipher user request to avoid eavesdropping. It filters and blocks general privacy violations like web bugs and cookies. PSA can allow to directly interact with internet by giving up anonymity. It provide privacy protection that belong to the first two steps.

Multiple proxy servers can be deployed on locations like- intranet or ISP proxy. User request goes to the group selector, which decide to which group the request should be forwarded based on semantic context of user request. Every group represents a different area of interest. Groups then forward the request to any of the proxy servers randomly. Proxy servers forward the request to the web search engine and individual identity is hidden but interest are shown, which help in personalization and protect privacy of the user.

Role of group selector is very important. A user can have diverse interest in a session and it is very difficult to predict its behavior, so group selector choose a group on the basis of each request which makes it very difficult for the adversary to track the user. Multiple proxy server does not store any information about the user, which makes almost impossible for the web search engine to detect sequence of requests from different proxies belong to individual or group of people with common area of interest.

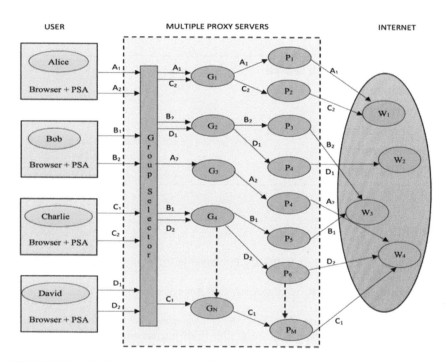

FIGURE 18.1 Multiple proxy server architecture.

18.9 CONCLUSION

Multiple proxy servers can provide a number of benefits including spreading awareness among the user about the privacy risks involved while using the internet. The system can control the amount of private information to be shared with the internet. Anonymity is the basic feature behind the system to preserve user privacy. Unlike other privacy tools, multiple proxy servers can disclose partial information about a group of users, which can personalize services without profiling single user. It stores only one request and multiple request can use different groups and proxies that does not allow adversary to relate queries with each other. Users can select exposure level also which make the system more transparent. Complex data mining techniques and clustering algorithms are avoided and simple data structures like lists, trees used to enhance efficiency. HTTP and TCP protocols are used to communicate and no special protocols are created.

KEYWORDS

- **personalized web search**
- **anonymity**
- **privacy,**
- **personalized web search**
- **anonymity**
- **obfuscation**

REFERENCES

1. Shen, X.; Tan, B.; Zhai, C. Privacy Protection in Personalized Search. *ACM SIGIR Forum* **2007**, *41* (1), 4–17.
2. Peddinti, S. T.; Ross, K. W.; Cappos, J. User Anonymity on Twitter. *IEEE Secur. Priv.* **2017**, *15* (3), 84–87.
3. Liu, K.; Kuo, C.; Liao, W.; Wang, P. In *Optimized Data De-Identification using Multidimensional k-Anonymity*, 2018 17th IEEE International Conference on Trust, Security and Privacy in Computing and Communications/12th IEEE International Conference on Big Data Science And Engineering (TrustCom/BigDataSE), 2018; no. 2, pp. 1610–1614, 2018.
4. Man, N.; Li, X.; Wang, K. In *A Privacy Protection Model Based On K-Anonymity*, International Conference Advanced Engineering and Technology research, 2018; vol. 153, no. Aetr 2017, pp. 15–19, 2018.
5. Domingo-Ferrer, J.; Torra, V. In *A Critique of k-Anonymity and Some of Its Enhancements*, ARES '08: Proceedings of the 2008 Third International Conference on Availability, Reliability and Security, May 2014; pp. 990–993, 2008, doi: 10.1109/ARES.2008.97.
6. El Emam, K.; Dankar, F. K.; El Emam, K.; Dankar, F. K. Protecting Privacy Using k-Anonymity. *J. Am. Med. Informatics Assoc.* **2008**, *15* (5), 627–637.
7. Machanavajjhala, A.; Gehrke, J.; Kifer, D.; Venkitasubramaniam, M. In *l-Diversity : Privacy Beyond k-Anonymity*, Proceedings of 22nd International Conference on Data Engineering, 2006; vol. 1.
8. Domingo-Ferrer, J.; Soria-Comas, J. From t-Closeness to Differential Privacy and Vice Versa in Data Anonymization. *Knowl. Based Syst.* **2015**, *74*, 151–158.
9. Barbaro, M.; Zeller, T. A Face is Exposed for AOL Searcher No. 4417749. *New York Times* [Online] 2006, no. 4417749, pp. 1–3. http://papers3://publication/ uuid/33AEE899-4F9D-4C05-AFC7-70B2FF16069D.
10. Díaz, C.; Seys, S.; Claessens, J.; Preneel, B. Towards Measuring Anonymity [Online]. http://www.esat.kuleuven.ac.be/cosic/ (accessed: Dec 09, 2020).

11. Aggarwal, C. C.; Yu, P. S. A General Survey of Privacy-Preserving Data Mining Models and Algorithms.

12. Aekerman, M. S.; Cranor, L. *Privacy Critics: UI Components to Safeguard user's Privacy*, Conference on Human Factors in Computing Systems—Proceedings, 1999; pp. 258–259, doi: 10.1145/632716.632875.

13. Kristol, D.; Gabber, E.; Gibbons, P. Design and Implementation of the Lucent Personalized Web Assistant (LPWA), *Submitt. ...*, [Online] **1998**, http://citeseerx.ist.psu.edu/viewdoc/download?doi=10.1.1.53.5909&rep=rep1&type=pdf

14. Reiter, M. K.; Rubin, A. D. Crowds: Anonymity for Web Transactions. *ACM Trans. Inf. Syst. Secur.* **1998,** *1* (1), 66–92.

15. Reed, M. G.; Syverson, P. F.; Goldschlag, D. M. Anonymous Connections and Onion Routing. *IEEE J. Sel. Areas Commun.*, **1998,** *16* (4), 482–493.

CHAPTER 19

Performance Study of Various Routing Protocols in Opportunistic IoT Networks

S. P. AJITH KUMAR[1,2] and HARDEO KUMAR THAKUR[3]

[1]*Manav Rachna University, Faridabad, Haryana, India*

[2]*Bhai Parmanand Institute of Business Studies, New Delhi, India*

[3]*Department of CST, Manav Rachna University, Faridabad, Haryana, India*

ABSTRACT

Opportunistic Internet of Things (OppIoT) networks have been one of the effective evolutions of delay tolerant networks. OppIoTs are different from IoT network as end-to-end routing path may not be available from the source to the destination. It operates in an intermittent, mobile communication topology, employing hops on a store-carry-forward manner, and peer-to-peer transmission. In this network, routes are building dynamically, whenever messages are routed from the source to destination(s), any potential node will act as the next hop, bringing the message nearer to the destination. This is necessary to develop routing protocols that can maximize the message delivery possibility and minimize the delivery failure possibility. Many protocols like Epidemic, PROPHET, Spray and Wait, MLPROPH, KNNR, GMMR, etc… used in OppIoT networks. Most of these protocols suffer from overheads like higher power and memory requirements, large delays, generalization in their approach in a dynamic, mobile environment,

Computational Intelligence in Analytics and Information Systems, Volume 2: Advances in Digital Transformation, Selected Papers from CIAIS-2021. Parneeta Dhaliwal, PhD, Manpreet Kaur, PhD, Hardeo Kumar Thakur, PhD, Rajeev Kumar Arya, and Joan Lu (Eds.)

misrepresentation of the node attributes in the wrong cluster, etc. Machine learning (ML) is a tool for learning from histories used to select the next hop to forward message under store-carry-forward scheme to reach the message to destination. The trained ML model leverages information on delivery predictability with respect to buffer availability, success rate, transmission speed, node strength, and message live time.

19.1   INTRODUCTION

Opportunistic networks[1] are the foremost emerging current and fascinating developments of the MANETs prototype. They have all the challenges and problems faced by MANETs and they have also some new challenges. In opportunistic networks, when there is no path exists from source to endpoint the message routing is constructed based on opportunistic contacts through the intermediate nodes are called Store-Carry-Forward technique and it happens local forwarding from one to another node. Since opportunistic networks derived several observations from delay tolerant networks (DTNs)[2] generally known as subclass of DTNs. In Opportunistic Internet of Things (OppIoT) networks, the source to destination end-to-end path never happens or may happen only for a very small and volatile duration of time. The construction of routes in these networks is dynamic in nature and the source node picks any node from the cluster of neighbors as the succeeding hop thinking that it may carry the data to the end node.   Internet of Things (IoT)-based technologies[22] majorly include a system of computing devices with analog and digital machines added with the capacity to transfer data into the network without significant human participation. With the latest technologies, there have been challenging approaches in the development domain in terms of various overhead costs and, at the same time, in terms of the functionality of the IoT-based device. These techniques are mainly based on AI and machine learning (ML) to improve the decisive power in order to develop an action plan in the routing and processing phases of these devices. Trends show that these devices are becoming more mobile in nature and these mobile IoT devices are prevailing in the form of portable or man-made technologies. Due to this nature of the devices, we often experiment their mobility model following the mobility of their human host directly or indirectly leading to a routing based on social concepts that is exploited in the development of the proposed regime. Often, such devices communicate in groups or work as part of a larger group, creating an IoT network. This network is comprised of heterogeneous IoT devices that have the capacity to communicate and route data packets over the network.

In opportunistic networks, nodes will be either static or movable like pedestrian users and vehicles, normally mobile in nature. It uses all the communication medias such as Wi-Fi,[5] Bluetooth,[4] cellular,[6] etc. to contact and communicate with each other. Every OppNet starts from a seed node. Initially, it will start with single node called seed node and extend this into a large network by inviting link to the near nodes, node clusters that are close to system are capable to make contact.

An IoT network comprises of nodes that are embedded in network for sensing, actuation, and communicating with various communication protocols such as Internet, Wi-Fi, Bluetooth, M-bus, etc. These protocols provide connectivity between nodes within network. The communication network provides connectivity to remote area networks. To enable the communication between remote networks gateways are used. In IoT data is composed in the cloud and accessed by cloud applications like remote diagnosis, enterprise applications, management applications, analytics applications, etc.

19.1.1 CHARACTERISTICS OF OPPIOT NETWORKS

Some of the most important characteristics of OppIoT networks are[3]:

OppIoT networks are derived from DTN. Usually it is a light network. Generally, its scenario has fewer intermittent Contacts. In most cases, no end-to-end links are available in this type of network. It uses Store-Carry-Forward Mechanism in Routing. These networks would use infrastructure-less protocols. The link performance is highly variable. It makes smart things. OppIoT networks build effective business intelligence and real-time analyzing by connecting all the relevant things.

19.1.2 ARCHITECTURE OF OPPIOT NETWORKS

Figure 19.1 elucidates the hybrid OppIoT network architecture. This hybrid means confluence of both elements of DTN and IoT-based systems. The architecture is designed to serve disruptions and intermittent connectivity in a network that has the infrastructure to handle this heterogeneity.

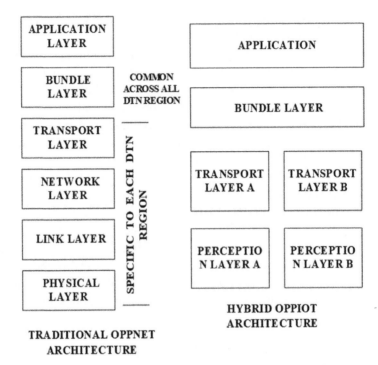

FIGURE 19.1   OppIoT architecture.

There are numerous schemes, and each has a somewhat different semantic, a group of protocol-centric convergence layer adapters facilitates the utility to transmit the data units known as bundles according to the corresponding protocols. The end-to-end connection is known as the bundle layer that is placed below the application layer and above the transport layer. Here, the role of IoT devices that implement the work. This essentially exists as an overlay that utilizes storage that is persistent and manage intermittent connectivity. Also, this involves a hop-by-hop transfer to ensure reliable delivery with end-to-end recognition capacity. Diagnostic functions are included to ensure interoperability and usability of semantics. In addition, security nodes may also be integrated into this architecture as designated nodes to avoid unauthorized use.[23]

19.1.3   *OPPORTUNISM IN MOBILE IOT NETWORKS*

In OppIoT, enormous delays in propagation and irregular queues can cause breakdowns, and that adds to the problems because traditional protocols implicitly require rapid recognition, which means they 'do not work in these situations. There are asymmetrical data rates and a high error rate in transmission involving sparsely spaced networks. The solution to this obstacle lies in the very thing that provokes the mobile nature of the devices.[23] One way to improve the aforementioned barrier is to use the mobile nature of nodes within the network and the ability to transfer data locally. When opportunistic contacts are established, the intermediary nodes can transmit the data successively and in order to route them to the destination. This is called the store-carry-forward mechanism, which is common in OppIoT networks. OppIoT networks are belonging to range of DTNs. In such cases, contacts, also referred to as opportunities, are intermittent. Connectivity or permanence of links is extremely volatile and end-to-end connectivity is for a short and unpredictable time, so the classic suite of Internet Protocol will not work in this scenario.[18] This has necessitated a confluence between the devices, IoT manages a large amount of information across networks that are intrinsically heterogeneous. In principle, OppIoT assigns similar delay tolerance properties compared with conventional opportunistic networks. This is very useful in many scenarios where the network architecture is deficient, key configuration information is missing and nodes follow random mobility patterns.[25] Transmission carried out here in a manner like opportunistic networks, when more than one node meet at a communicating distance, message is forwarded by a decision-making paradigm based on probability of delivery. The decision whether to transfer to the node is referred as the next-hop selection.

19.1.4 APPLICATION AREAS OF OPPIOT NETWORKS

OppIoT networks applications are[1,8]:

OppIoT networks are used for message exchanges in developing areas. These networks assist in scientific monitoring of wildlife to track animal movements, habitat use, population demographics, catch and poaching incidents, and outbreaks. Emergency communication in disaster areas makes this network very commendable. Quality of the environment such as weather, pollution, etc can be monitor using this network. Other applications are healthcare, Sensor networks, Smart Home, Smart City, Industrial Internet, connected vehicle, intelligent supply chain, intelligent retail, intelligent agriculture, etc.

19.2   LITERATURE SURVEY ON ROUTING IN OPPIOT NETWORKS

To understand the routing in OppIoT networks in a better way, the different types of routing protocols existing in the opportunistic networks and IoT were studied. This chapter presents the brief literature survey.

19.2.1   OPPIOT ROUTING

OppIoT networks functions in an intermittent mobile communication topology. In OppIoT network nodes behaving as hosts and routers transfer messages to the gateways. In OppIoT network, the traditional protocol means TCP/IP will not work due to long transmission delays and intermittent in nature. There is no assurance that the network will construct end-to-end route from start to end. This issue is resolved by OppIoT by transmitting the message from source to end node through intermediate nodes and finally the message will reach close to the destination.

In view of the intermittent communication topology of OppIoT Networks, the intermediate nodes may not meet nodes in the route consistently or frequently.[9] Sometime to take data nearer to the destination there might not be appropriate intermediate node, in this situation data may be delivered directly to the destination. For this, nodes have to keep the packet long period in the buffer.

Suppose there is no forwarding chance towards the endpoint directly, it uses Store-Carry-Forward technique through the intermediate nodes to move the packet. The intermediate nodes may encounter with other nodes in the destination path because the network is dynamic in nature. In this way, the intermediate node forwards the data more close to the destination.

Figure 19.2, explains how the Store-Carry-Forward technique and node's mobility can be used to deliver a data to the end node. Let "S" be a source node having a data to be delivered to the end node "D, " but there is no path among "S" and "D." The movement of nodes allows the data to be transmitted to node 3 at time t1, then transmitted to node 4, which comes in contact with time t2 at node 3 and then finally to node "D" which comes in contact with time t3 at node 4.

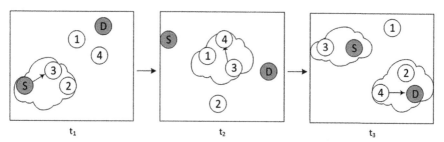

FIGURE 19.2 A data is sent from node "S" to "D" via nodes 3 and 4 through the mobility of nodes.

19.2.2 REVIEW OF ROUTING PROTOCOLS

A performance study of some routing protocols in OppIoT networks presented in Table 19.1

TABLE 19.1 Analysis of Opportunistic IoT Networks Protocols.

Research paper name	Description	Algorithm(s) used	Limitations
Routing in a delay tolerant network.[10]	First Contact Protocol: Randomly sends the messages to any neighbor node. The path chosen randomly to forward the message from all the available contacts. Suppose no path is available to send the message to the neighbor, the message will wait till it gets a path.	Dijkstra's Algorithm.	Delivery ratio is poor due to path looping and one copy of the message retained by protocol.
Single-copy routing in intermittently connected mobile networks.[11]	Direct Contact Protocol: In this protocol, the message is not transmitted to the intermediate nodes through the originating node, but the originating node retains the message until it establishes direct contact with the ending node. The message is transmitted directly to the final destination. Hence every message is transmitted only one time. So both the resource utilization and usage of bandwidth are less for message transferring in this protocol method.	Single-copy routing algorithms.	If the starting node never encounters the ending node then the delivery delay is boundless. Hence this protocol has long delays for delivering the message.

TABLE 19.1   *(Continued)*

Research paper name	Description	Algorithm(s) used	Limitations
Epidemic routing for partially connected ad hoc networks[12]	Epidemic routing Protocol: This protocol has two buffers in each node. A unique and single identification is attached to every message. A directory of message identification numbers is contained in its buffer and is maintained by each node. This list or directory is called the summary vector. As soon as any two nodes meets, they swap their summary vectors between them. By means of collating the two summary vectors, the nodes collate those messages that they haven't contained with them. Once the process of message collection is finished, the nodes will begin to exchange the messages.	Epidemic algorithm	Creates huge quantity of message redundancy in the network. Some nodes still carry on sending the same message even if the target node obtain the same message, waste the resources.
Spray and wait: An efficient routing scheme for intermittently connected mobile networks.[13]	Spray and Wait protocol: It has two phases. First one is called spray phase and second is wait phase. In first phase starting node transmits message to a fixed number of neighbor nodes and will wait for some time to reach message to the end node. In the wait phase suppose the information not reached to the end node, leads each intermediate node which contain message will act as source node. Using fixed number of flooding in wait phase this protocol limit the flooding level.	Spray and wait routing algorithm.	The output of the protocol depending on the value of L. The larger value of L proceeds it like Epidemic protocol and smaller value of L proceed it like Direct delivery protocol.

TABLE 19.1   *(Continued)*

Research paper name	Description	Algorithm(s) used	Limitations
Probabilistic routing in intermittently connected networks.[14]	PROPHET: Each node before sending the message in PROPHET computes delivery predictability. The delivery predictability is prepared according to the history of visit to particular location or history of encounters between nodes. If two nodes meet frequently then these two nodes have higher delivery predictability and both are good forwarder for each other. Therefore if a node is willing to forward message to next node will select neighbor node which is having higher delivery predictability.	PROPHET algorithm.	In PROPHET, hop selection is made according to delivery predictability of the node. The nodes with delivery better predictability than a fixed threshold are marked as 'best' by the source node, the set of these 'best' forwarder nodes select from crisp Set.
A Machine Learning-Based Protocol for Efficient Routing in Opportunistic Networks.[20]	MLProph protocol is probabilistic metric based approach for routing in opportunistic situations applying machine learning. It uses a both machine learning and neural network to determine the probability of successful message delivery.	Decision Tree Machine Learning algorithm and Neural Network Machine Learning algorithm.	ML model may suffer from the absence of generalization in their approach in a dynamic and mobile environment, under represented topological aspects involved, therefore not giving an optimal solution.

TABLE 19.1   *(Continued)*

Research paper name	Description	Algorithm(s) used	Limitations
KNNR:K-Nearest Neighbor-based Routing Protocol for Opportunistic Networks.[19]	KNNR protocol having two phases: first is training phase and corresponding is application phase. In the first phase KNN classifier is trained using the node encounter history dataset of the network. At each node encounter, the protocol assesses whether the intermediate node is similar to the dataset and finds the nearest instances that resembles intermediate node. By Using the characteristics of past network behavior nodes and the data from the routing process to shortlist the intermediate nodes towards the destination.	K-Nearest Neighbor algorithm.	KNNR employs a hard clustering technique, known as K-means clustering. Hard clustering segregates the nodes into non-overlapping partitions of the network topology. This will lead to erroneous presentation of node attributes or even erroneous group allocation by neglecting other parameters.
GMMR: A Gaussian Mixture Model Based Unsupervised Machine Learning for opportunistic IoT.[27]	GMMR employs a soft clustering Technique, It allows overlapping of clusters, with each node being free to exhibit multiple prominent characteristics.	Expectation Maximization algorithm.	It not take into consideration about the degree of representation of each cluster of which the node is part, therefore, being unable to quantify the representation that each cluster has toward the behavior of a node.

TABLE 19.1 *(Continued)*

Research paper name	Description	Algorithm(s) used	Limitations
A Machine Learning Approach Using Classifier Cascades for Optimal Routing in Opportunistic Internet of Things Networks.[26]	Machine learning based scheme namely classifier cascades for the OppIoT networks which termed as CAML. It extracts the relevant data from the network nodes and then uses a pre-trained classifier to determine the value of the likelihood of delivery.	Algorithm-1: CAML (Training Phase), Algorithm-2: CAML Routing Protocol.	Computationally heavy and impractical in cases where training must be more frequent.
RLProph: A reinforcement learning approach for optimal routing in opportunistic IoT networks[28]	The RLProph involves OppIoT networks from Reinforced Learning (RL). In RLProph the agent selects certain actions from the previous time stamp based on the reward obtained and the environmental states. The optimum routing process is achieved as a result of the resolution of the Markov (MDP) decision process using policy iteration.	Reinforced Learning algorithm	Any time the system inputs increases leads to handling a large number of inputs cause the system to slow down.

19.3 DESCRIPTION OF STUDY

Due to the obscure quality and uneven performance of the nodes, routing, and forwarding may be a hard task in OppIoT networks. A lot of analysis done in OppIoT networks routing and forwarding region. In OppIoT, a very important task is finding proper routes towards the desired destination. Thus, designing a new routing protocol in this situation is much in demand in the OppIoT. The protocol must be consuming less power and be energy efficient while forwarding the messages. The aim of the protocol is to decrease the communication delay and increase the successful data delivery rate to the target. Going from core development of healthcare to finance, IoT-based technologies are emerging.[22] Without much human intervention, these technologies usually involve a system of computing equipment in addition to analog and digital machines equipped with the capability to exploit data transfer in the network. But with new trends and interdisciplinary approaches to development, this definition has become broader and encompassing. With the emerging of technologies, there have been competing approaches in the development sphere to minimize various overhead and simultaneously increase the functionality of these IoT-based devices. These techniques are mainly based on artificial intelligence and ML to enhance decisive power so as to draw up an action plan in the routing and processing phases of these IoT devices.

Trends suggest that these devices are increasingly mobile in nature and these mobile IoT devices are prevailing in the form of portable or human-related technologies. Due to this nature of the devices, we often experiment with their mobility model emulating the mobility of their human host directly or indirectly resulting in a routing based on social concepts, which is operated in developing the proposed scheme. Often these devices communicate in groups or work as part of a bigger group, creating an IoT network. The network consists of heterogeneous IoT devices that, without interaction between humans or machines, have the ability to communicate and route data packets across the network. Its device-based networks are increasingly popular and often replace their current wireless sensor networks rather than increased functionality.[24] In addition, they are used together with more complex and heterogeneous devices to enable distributed computing with parallel processing for better efficiency.

ML is one of the latest research topics in trending. OppIoT network is a network where source to endpoint path is missing to route messages. Therefore, to transmit message from one to another node uses store-carry-forward concept is used where intermediate nodes carry message to the destination. Selection of best intermediate node, i.e., next hop who carries message will be decided by ML algorithm. KNNR[19] and MLPROPH[20] opportunistic routing protocols use ML technique to select next hop. To control flooding of messages in intermediate nodes we may use clustering technique, krop[21] opportunistic network routing protocol uses K-means clustering to control flooding of messages.

19.4   OBJECTIVES OF THE STUDY

OppIoT networks suffer from various things like lack of end-to-end route definition, intermittent connectivity, resource restrictions and uncertainties arising from the dynamic behavior of topology, and many more.

Many ML paradigms have been proposed like KNNR, MLPROPH, and GMMR for computational intelligence in the field. This work aims at designing and analyzing novel schemes and algorithms to improve routing efficiency in infrastructureless OppIoT networks. It aims at developing an efficient routing protocol in future work that can easily be applied to OppIoT networks and provide efficient functionality even in the existing constraints.

- Classify the previously proposed routing algorithms and describe the main properties of the most popular algorithms for infrastructure-less OppIoT networks.
- A new routing protocol will be developed in future for infrastructure-less OppIoT networks and its advantages and disadvantages will be compared with already existing protocols.
- The nodes of OppIoT Network have limited energy resources therefore any new technique used for communication defined should keep this constraint in mind like frequent disconnection and re-connection, Intermittent contacts, long delays, etc. normally add complexity to routing and result in the reducing of energy of the device. Hence, energy efficiency of the routing technique may also be explored in pursuing work.
- The new protocol should be implemented with acknowledgment-based technique for the guaranteed information delivery in OppIoT networks.
- As the intermediate nodes use buffer to store the message, a buffer management system is desired. Hence, the buffer management technique will also be considered.
- Secure opportunistic routing is needed to provide a safety shield for the secure communication among the nodes in infrastructure-less OppIoT networks. It is necessary to design a protocol against various types of security threats underlying this environment. Hence, secured routing technique will also be explored.

19.5   METHODOLOGY TO BE ADOPTED

The OppIoT model works well on the conjuncture over the capability of the constituting entities to be able to interact freely, learn from these interactions and make intelligent decisions for message routing based on the knowledge gained from such interactions. The earliest propositions in opportunism that lays the foundation of the advancing field of OppIoT are history-based algorithms, as introduced in the text earlier. Building on such a basis of operations, various learning paradigms have been used in the past to emulate topological knowledge into decision making strategy.

- For minimal overhead usage, the ML technique in an OppIoT network is one of the effective solutions, like MLPROPH. However, they may suffer from the absence of generalization in their approach in a dynamic and mobile environment, under represented topological aspects involved, therefore not giving an optimal solution.
- The lack of generalization can be addressed by comparing likelihood with the ideal solution rather than ranking the best candidate locally. Clustering gives us the opportunity to find such similarity in characteristics to that of the ideal solution. Clustering may happen with hard or soft boundaries.
- Hard clustering separates nodes into nonoverlapping partitions from network topology. Such segregation leads to the combination of the node with a single cluster. This will lead to a false representation of the node attributes or even a wrong cluster attribution by neglecting the other parameters that must be well in order to shape the node behavior.
- In soft clustering technique, clusters are allowed to overlap, each node being free to display multiple prominent features, being represented by several clusters at once. However, this decision-making paradigm does not consider the level of representation of each cluster of which the node is part, thus, being unable to quantify the representation that each cluster has toward the behavior of a node.
- In fuzzy logic scheme partial participation of entities into different sets are possible, allowing a better representation of real-world entities. Here, I propose the use of a fuzzy clustering scheme for routing in the OppIoT scenario, combining the ability of fuzzy logic to enable a quantified representation of network topology characteristics by the various topological partitions. These partitions are based on the behavior of network topology and nodes, shaped by the different interactions and the historical behavior of nodes during such interactions. Fuzzy clustering is a soft clustering technique that uses fuzzy logic to signify the degree of association of a node to the all existing topological partitions.

In order to obtain the results of the protocol, compare with some already existing latest protocols. For the purpose of evaluation, make use of the following performance metrics.

- Message Delivery Probability: These metric amounts to messages that successfully reached the delivery destination. A higher delivery probability is a positive indicator and signifies a higher delivery capability of the scheme. The values ranges between 0 and 1.

- Average Hop Count: Average number of nodes in-between traveled by a message to meet its destination. A hop count lower in magnitude is an indicator of a better routing scheme in OppIoT scenario.
- Network Overhead Ratio: This is delta between the total number of transmitted messages and delivered messages. A lower value of Overhead Ratio indicates lesser processing time hence the objective of the routing proposed protocol is to minimize this quantity for more optimized performance.
- Time to live: This metric indicates how much time a message lives in a network and deliver messages before they get decays or dies.

19.6 CONCLUSION

A literature survey on routing techniques like First Contact, Direct Delivery, Spray and Wait, Epidemic, PROPHET, MLPROPH, KNNR, CAML, GMMR, and RLProbh to send data from source to destination in OppIoT network has been done, tabulated description with routing algorithms and limitations. The performance of some routing protocols in OppIoT network have been equated with each other by using some performance calculating elements like average hop count, number of messages delivered, average buffer occupancy time, average delay, and time to live field. As future work, a new approach suggested by the authors in this paper aims to improve the data distribution model in an OppIoT network using a fuzzy clustering-based approach. Although this paper not evaluated and addressed security and privacy as key areas of consideration. Inherently, IoT devices owing to their nature (heterogeneous) in networks of this type become increasingly vulnerable to security vulnerabilities and attacks like black hole attacks, Gray hole attacks, Sybil attacks, and so on. This requires the protocol to have a strong encryption and trust scheme to avert this problem.

KEYWORDS

- **opportunistic internet of things**
- **delay-tolerant networks**
- **store-carry-forward**
- **machine learning**

REFERENCES

1. Lilien, L.; Gupta, A.; Yang, Z. In *Opportunistic Networks for Emergency Applications and their Standard Implementation Framework, 2007 IEEE International Performance, Computing, and Communications Conference*, 2007; vol. 1; pp. 588–593, 2007.

2. Fall, K. In *A Delay-Tolerant Network Architecture for Challenged Internets*, SIGCOMM '03: Proceedings of the 2003 Conference on Applications, Technologies, Architectures, and Protocols for Computer Communications, August 2003; pp. 27–34, 2003.

3. Chen, L.; Yu, C.; Tseng, C.; Chu, H.; Chou, C. A Content-Centric Framework for Effective Data Dissemination in Opportunistic Networks. *IEEE J. Select. Areas Commun.* **2008,** *26* (5).

4. Bluetooth, The Bluetooth Specification, v.1.0B (referred 2000/03/15).

5. http://www.bluetooth.com/developer/specification/specification.asp.

6. WiFi, http://www.wifinotes.com

7. *Cellular networks.* http://www.cellular.co.za/cellular networksoverview.htm

8. Scopigno, R.; Spirito, M.; Korpeoglu, I.; Ulucinar, A. R.; Moustakas, A. L.; Galluccio, L.; Leonardi, A.; Fabbri, F.; Verdone, R.; Chiasserini, C. F.; Zanella, A.; Zorzi, F.; Ferrus, R.; Novillo, F.; Boc, M.; Dias de Amorim, M.; Riihijarvi, J.; Brunstrom, A.; Cavalcanti de Castro, M. State of the Art of Research on Opportunistic Networks, and Definition of a Common Framework for Reference Models and Performance Metrics. *NEWCOM++ 216715, DR.11.1.* p. 54.

9. Pelusi, L.; Passarella, A.; Conti, M. Opportunistic Networking: Data Forwarding in Disconnected Mobile ad Hoc Networks. *IEEE Commun. Maga.* **2006,** *44*, 134–141.

10. Huang, C.-M.; Lan, K.-C.; Tsai, C.-Z. In *A Survey of Opportunistic Networks*, Proceedings of the 22nd International Conference on Advanced Information Networking and Applications (WAINA), Biopolis, Mar. 25–28 2008; Okinawa, Japan, 2008.

11. Jain, S.; Fall, K.; Patra, R. In *Routing in a Delay Tolerant Network*, Proceedings of SIGCOMM 2004; pp. 145–158, 2004.

12. Spyropoulos, T.; Psounis, K.; Raghavendra, C. S. In *Single-Copy Routing in Intermittently Connected Mobile Networks*, Proceedings of Sensor and Ad Hoc Communications and Networks (SECON), Oct. 2004; pp. 235–244, 2004.

13. Vahdat, A.; Becker, D. *Epidemic Routing for Partially Connected ad hoc Networks*; Technical Report CS-2000-06; Department of Computer Science, Duke University: Durham, NC, 2000.

14. Spyropoulos, T.; Psounis, K.; Raghavendra, C. S. In *Spray and Wait: An Efficient Routing Scheme for Intermittently Connected Mobile Networks*, Proceedings of ACM SIGCOMM Workshop on Delay-Tolerant Networking (WDTN '05), 2005; pp. 252–259, 2005.

15. Lindgren, A.; Doria, A.; Schelen, O. Probabilistic Routing in Intermittently Connected Networks. *ACM SIGMOBILE, Mobile Comput. Commun. Rev.* **2003,** *7* (3), 19–20.

16. Burgess, J.; Gallagher, B.; Jensen, D.; Levine, B. N. In *Maxprop: Routing for Vehicle-Based Disruption-Tolerant Networks*, Proceedings of IEEE INFOCOM, 2006; pp. 1–11, 2006.

17. Nordrum, A. Popular Internet of Things Forecast of 50 Billion Devices by 2020 Is Outdated. *IEEE Spectrum: Technology, Engineering, and Science News*, 2016.

18. Jain, A.; Crespo, R.; Khari, M. *Smart Innovation of Web of Things*; 1st ed.; CRC Press: Boca Raton, 2020, pp. 21–51.

19. Dorsemaine, B.; Gaulier, J.; Wary, J.; Kheir, N.; Urien, P. In *Internet of Things: A Definition & Taxonomy*, 9th International Conference on Next Generation Mobile Applications, Services and Technologies; 2015.

20. Sharma, D.; Aayush, Sharma, A.; Kumar, J. In *KNNR: K-Nearest Neighbour Classification Based Routing Protocol for Opportunistic Networks*, Tenth International Conference on Contemporary Computing (IC3), 2017.

21. Sharma, D.; Dhurandher, S.; Woungang, I.; Srivastava, R.; Mohananey, A.; Rodrigues, J. A Machine Learning-Based Protocol for Efficient Routing in Opportunistic Networks. *IEEE Syst. J.* **2018,** *12* (3), 2207–2213.

22. Sharma, D. K.; Dhurandher, S. K.; Agarwal, D.; Arora, K. Krop: k-Means Clustering based Routing Protocol for Opportunistic Networks. *J. Ambient Intell. Humaniz. Comput.* **2018,** 1–18.

23. Bhardwaj, K.; Banyal, S.; Sharma, D. Artificial Intelligence Based Diagnostics, Therapeutics and Applications in Biomedical Engineering and Bioinformatics. *Internet Things Biomed. Eng.* **2019,** 161–187.

24. Liu, K.; Chen, Z.; Wu, J.; Wang, L.; FCNS: A Fuzzy Routing-Forwarding Algorithm Exploiting Comprehensive Node Similarity in Opportunistic Social Networks. *Symmetry* **2018,** *10* (8), 338.

25. Chakchouk, N. In *A Survey on Opportunistic Routing in Wireless Communication Networks*, IEEE Communications Surveys & Tutorials, 2015; vol. 17, no. 4, pp. 2214–2241, 2015.

26. Sok, P.; Tan, S.; Kim, K. In *PRoPHET Routing Protocol Based on Neighbor Node Distance Using a Community Mobility Model in Delay Tolerant Networks*, 2013 IEEE 10th International Conference on High Performance Computing and Communications & 2013 IEEE International Conference on Embedded and Ubiquitous Computing, 2013.

27. Vashishth, V.; Chhabra, A.; Sharma, D. In *A Machine Learning Approach Using Classifier Cascades for Optimal Routing in Opportunistic Internet of Things Networks*, 16th Annual IEEE International Conference on Sensing, Communication, and Networking (SECON), Boston, MA, USA, 2019; pp. 1–9, 2019.

28. Vashishth, V.; Chhabra, A.; Sharma, D. GMMR: A Gaussian Mixture Model based Unsupervised Machine Learning Approach for Optimal Routing in Opportunistic IoT Networks. *Comput. Commun.* **2019,** *134*, 138–148.

29. Sharma, D.; Rodrigues, J.; Vashishth, V.; Khanna, A.; Chhabra, A. RLProph: A Dynamic Programming based Reinforcement Learning Approach for Optimal Routing in Opportunistic IoT Networks. *Wireless Networks* **2020,** *26* (6), 4319–4338.

CHAPTER 20

On AES S-boxes with Variable Modulus and Translation Polynomials

CHAMAN PRAKASH ARYA, RAM RATAN, and NEELAM VERMA

Scientific Analysis Group, Defence Research and Development Organisation, Delhi, India

ABSTRACT

Translation polynomials used in the construction of advanced encryption standard (AES) S-box are computed for each modulus polynomial and carry out the analysis based on the nonprimitive and primitive modulus polynomials. These translation polynomials are judiciously selected so that there are no fixed points and conjugate fixed points in the S-boxes constructed. Varying a translation polynomial in the algebraic construction of standard AES S-box leads to different S-boxes with same cryptographic properties as of original AES S-box. The translation polynomials are studied by varying modulus polynomials for various bias parameters of the S-boxes constructed. The reported new results indicate that the AES can be implemented to achieve dynamic encryption for real applications of information security.

20.1 INTRODUCTION

Security of an information is one of the paramount requirement to safeguard the vital information from adversaries. It can be obtained by providing the confidentiality to the messages through cryptographic technique. In the cryptographic

Computational Intelligence in Analytics and Information Systems, Volume 2: Advances in Digital Transformation, Selected Papers from CIAIS-2021. Parneeta Dhaliwal, PhD, Manpreet Kaur, PhD, Hardeo Kumar Thakur, PhD, Rajeev Kumar Arya, and Joan Lu (Eds.)

approach, an encryption algorithm transforms a plain message into an encrypted message. Normally, the plain messages appear intelligible but the encrypted messages appear unintelligible and random. An encryption algorithm may be based on the symmetric key cryptography or asymmetric key cryptography. A symmetric key cryptography uses the same key for encryption as well as decryption. An asymmetric key cryptography uses two keys, one key for encryption and another key for decryption. An symmetric key cryptography is known as secret-key cryptography and an asymmetric key cryptography is known as public-key cryptography.[1,2] The encryption algorithms based on symmetric key cryptography are widely used since long back because of their computational advantages. A data encryption standard (DES) algorithm based on the symmetric key cryptography was recommended and used for message security but due to the advancement in computing technology and power rendered the DES algorithm insecure. The DES algorithm was replaced temporary by the Triple-DES but a need for more secure and efficient algorithm was prevailing. After four years of rigorous testing against five finalists, block cipher Rijndeal was selected as an Advanced Encryption Standard (AES) by the National Institute of Standards and Technology. At present, AES algorithm is being widely used by various agencies with the purpose to keep their data secure and safe from adversaries.

Rijndeal was developed by Joan Daemen and Vincent Rijmen.[3,4] It is a symmetric block cipher supporting key size of 128, 192 and 256-bit length.[5-6] However, there is constraints on data length and it allows 128-bit. The output of AES is 128-bit. The description of AES algorithm is available in.[4] Input 128 bits are written in a matrix 4×4, called as the "state," and all calculations are performed in a Galois Field $GF(2^8)$. Attempts have been made to customize AES to make it more secure by changing its structure in a way that its original strength remains intact and it becomes strong against known attacks being new to the attackers.[7,8] Cryptographic primitives such as Boolean functions and Substitution boxes play a vital role in designing strong encryption algorithm.[9-11]

In AES, the S-box is known as the backbone, which provides confusion and nonlinearity. This makes AES very strong against various known attacks. The AES S-box has beautiful algebraic construction using the Galois field. The AES S-boxes can be generated by changing different parameters.[5,6,12] Relevant work related to the S-box is reported in.[13-19] In,[14,1517-24] the key-dependent S-boxes in place of standard AES S-box have been studied. The generation of AES S-box with modulus and additive constant has been studied in.[12] The optimization and generation of some methods of S-boxes have been studied in.[25-28]

In this paper, translation polynomials are obtained by varying a modulus polynomial. These translation polynomials are used in the algebraic construction of AES S-box to avoid fixed point and conjugate fixed point. Furthermore, the analysis of these translation polynomials is carried out based on the primitive or nonprimitive modulus polynomials. The security analysis of S-boxes generated from these translation polynomials is also done and it has found to be strong as original AES S-box.

In the paper, Section 20.2 discusses the algebraic construction of AES S-box and their characteristics. Section 20.3, discusses the computation of translation polynomials. Section 20.4 presents the results and observations on S-box construction of translation polynomial based on modulus polynomial. Last section concludes the paper followed by references.

20.2 CONSTRUCTION OF AES S-BOX AND ITS PROPERTIES

20.2.1 CONSTRUCTION OF AES S-BOX

A byte in AES algorithm is the basic data unit for all the cipher operations. A byte is interpreted as a finite field element represented by the polynomial $p(x)$ given in the below equation

$$m(x) = \sum_{i=0}^{7} a_i x^i \qquad (20.1)$$

Where a_i belongs to the Galois Field GF(2) and each byte b belongs to the GF(2^8). The construction of the field GF(2^8) is based upon Theorem 20.1:

Theorem 20.1 Let m be a nonzero element of a Principal Ideal Domain (PID) R then, R/m will be a field if and only if m is irreducible.[29]

As $Z_p[x]$ is a PID, where p is a prime and $m(x)$ is an irreducible polynomial of degree n. So Zp[x]/(m(x))= GF(pn) will be a field that contains polynomials of degree less than n. In AES, the Galois field GF(2^8) is constructed by taking an irreducible polynomial $m(x) = x^8 + x^4 + x^3 + x + 1$ (11B in Hex) as modulus polynomial and $p = 2$. Considering this underlying field, the S-box is designed as a function given below

$$f : GF(2^8)\ GF(2^8), f(x) = x^{-1} \bmod(m(x)) \qquad (20.2)$$

It is composed with the affine transformation $F(x) = Af(x) + C$ where A is an affine matrix belongs to the General Linear group $GL_8(Z_2)$, (Z_2 is a field) and C is translation polynomial belongs to $GF(2^8)$. Both A and C are fixed in AES and are given in below equation

$$A = \begin{bmatrix} 1 & 0 & 0 & 0 & 1 & 1 & 1 & 1 \\ 1 & 1 & 0 & 0 & 0 & 1 & 1 & 1 \\ 1 & 1 & 1 & 0 & 0 & 0 & 1 & 1 \\ 1 & 1 & 1 & 1 & 0 & 0 & 0 & 1 \\ 1 & 1 & 1 & 1 & 1 & 0 & 0 & 0 \\ 0 & 1 & 1 & 1 & 1 & 1 & 0 & 0 \\ 0 & 0 & 1 & 1 & 1 & 1 & 1 & 0 \\ 0 & 0 & 0 & 1 & 1 & 1 & 1 & 1 \end{bmatrix}, C = x^6 + x^5 + x + 1 \tag{20.3}$$

There are the following 30 irreducible polynomials (in Hex) of degree 8 and anyone can be taken as modulus polynomials.[30]

| 11B | 139 | 13F | 177 | 17B | 18B | 19F | 1A3 | 1B1 | 1BD | 1D7 | 1DB | 1F3 | 1F9 | 11D |
| 12B | 15F | 163 | 165 | 169 | 1C3 | 1E7 | 171 | 1A9 | 1F5 | 18D | 14D | 12D | 187 | 1CF |

AES S-box can be generated by different modulus polynomial, affine matrix, and the translation polynomial without affecting its algebraic properties. The affine matrix is an element of a general linear group $GL_8(Z_2)$. The order of $GL_8(Z_2)$ is given in the below equation

$$o(GL_8(Z_2)) = \prod_{k=0}^{7} (2^8 - 2^k) = 5.3581 \times 10^{18} \tag{20.4}$$

There are a number of affine matrixes (nonsingular matrices) that can be used in the construction of AES S-box. On changing a affine matrix in AES S-box, the strength of the S-box can be studied by computing the bias parameters. As there are 30 irreducible polynomials of degree 8, so there are 30 options of modulus polynomial in the construction of the S-box.

On changing the modulus polynomial in S-box, the strength of S-box is studied by computing bias parameters. It is observed that the strength of all the S-boxes varies in terms of the bias parameters if a modulus polynomial is changed.[12] The best suitable modulus polynomial can be selected on the basis of these parameters.

There is no change in the bias parameters of S-boxes if a translation polynomial is varied along with fixing affine matrix and modulus polynomial in the construction of S-box. The translation polynomial is used to avoid fixed point and conjugate fixed point in the construction of S-box. On varying translation polynomial in the construction of S-box for fixed, affine matrix, and modulus polynomial, the strength of S-box remains unchanged. All the translation polynomials are not suitable or valid for fixed affine matrix and modulus polynomial. A suitable translation polynomial is computed for all 30 modulus polynomial by taking affine matrix same as that in the AES S-box. Theorem 20.2 gives an insight about the values of parameters on S-box constructed by varying translation polynomial C.

Theorem 20.2 The characteristic properties of S-box are independent of the choice of C in S-box $S(x) = AF(x) + C$.[5]

This theorem shows that only a translation polynomial C is being changed and all bias values will be the same as that of standard AES S-box. Hence, the strength of all the S-boxes constructed by varying C is equivalent.

20.2.2 S-BOX CHARACTERISTICS

The cryptographic parameters used to analyze the strength of S-box are the nonlinearity, propagation criteria bias, correlation immunity bias, and the input/output bit-to-bit entropy termed as the characteristics of S-boxes.[5] To analyze S-box, it is realized as a vector Boolean function $F : Z_p^n \to Z_p^m$, where $n \geq m$ In AES, $p = 2$, $n = m = 8$, and $F : Z_2^8 \to Z_2^8$. Following are the characteristics considered for analysis of constructed S-box:

Nonlinearity: Let $f : Z_2^n \to Z_2$ be an arbitrary Boolean function, and let A_n denote the collection of all the Affine Boolean functions, i.e., function $g : Z_2^n \to Z_2$ of the form $g(x_1, x_2, ..., x_n) = \sum_{i=1}^{n} a_i x_i$, $a_i \in Z_2$. The A_n is also known as the first-order Reed–Muller code of length 2^n.[19,31] The nonlinearity of a function f means the parameter: $N(f) = \min_{g \in A_n} d(f, g)$, where $d(f, g)$ is the hamming distance. If $F : Z_2^n \to Z_2^n$ is a function so that $F(x) = (f_1(x), f_2(x), ..., f_n(x))$ then the nonlinearity of F is given by $N(F) = \min_{1 \leq i \leq n} N(f_i)$.

Input/output bit-to-bit Entropy: Let $F : Z_2^n \to Z_2^n$ be a S-box with $F(x) = (f_1(x), f_2(x), ..., f_n(x))$. Then for each $i, j = 1, 2, ..., n$ compute the

$(i, j)^{th}$ input/output bit-to-bit entropy $H(x_i/f_j(x))$, and define the parameter:
$$H = \min_{i,j=1,2,\dots,n} H(x_i/f_j(x)) .[5]$$

Propagation Criterion: A Boolean function $f : Z_2^n \to Z_2$ satisfies the propagation criterion of degree k, if for each $\alpha \in Z_2^n$ of weight $w(\alpha) = 1,2,\dots,k$ the function $f(x) \oplus f(x \oplus \alpha)$ is balanced.[5] Precisely, f satisfies propagation criterion of degree k if $\sum_{x \in Z_2^n} f(x) \oplus f(x \oplus \alpha) = 2^{n-1}$. The propagation criterion of degree 1 is also called the strict avalanche criterion.

Propagation Criterion Bias (PCB): Let $f : Z_2^n \to Z_2$ be a Boolean function. The propagation criterion bias of degree k and order m is given by:
$$PCB_f(k,m) = \max_{a \in A, g \in B} \left| \sum_{x \in Z_2^n} (g(x) \oplus g(x+\alpha)) - 2^{n-m-k} \right|,$$

where $A = \{\alpha \in Z_2^n : w(\alpha) = 1,2,\dots,k\}$ and B is the set of Boolean functions obtained from f by fixing any m input bits.[5] The propagation criterion bias of order k and degree m of S-box $f : Z_2^n \to Z_2$ is given by
$$PCB_k(k,m) = \max_{i=1,2,\dots,m} \{PCB_{f_i}(k,m)\}.$$

Correlation Immunity Bias (CIB): The correlation immunity bias of order m for the Boolean function f is defined by $CIB_f = \max_{g \in B} \left| 2^m.w(g) - w(f) \right|$. The correlation immunity bias of order m for S-box $F : Z_2^n \to Z_2^n$ is given by $CIB_F(m) = \max_{i=1,2,\dots,m} \{CIB_{f_i}(m)\}$ as the value of standard parameters for each of the 34 S-boxes.[5]

20.3 COMPUTATION OF TRANSLATION POLYNOMIALS

The translation polynomial C plays a crucial role in the S-box construction. The purpose of using a translation polynomial C is to avoid fixed and conjugate fixed points in S-box. A $x \in Z_p^n$ is called fixed point of F, if $F(x) = x$ and conjugate fixed point of F, if $F(x) = x^c$, where x^c is the complement of vector x. The presence of such points in S-box renders it weak.

As $C \in GF(2^8)$ and the order of $GF(2^8)$ is 2^8, there are 256 different choices. So keeping the affine matrix and modulus polynomial fixed, if C is varied over a field $GF(2^8)$ then the 256 different S-boxes can be constructed including standard AES S-box. However, some of these

S-boxes contain the fixed points and conjugate fixed points. Therefore, C is to be judiciously computed to avoid these points. We construct different translation polynomials by taking the affine matrix same as in AES S-box for each modulus polynomial. As an illustration, the translation polynomials (in Hex) for the modulus polynomials 11B (AES)[32] and 171 are given in Tables 20.1 and 20.2, respectively, where TP indicates a translation polynomial and CTP indicates a complement translation polynomial of TP.

TABLE 20.1 Translation Polynomials for Modulus Polynomial 11B (AES).

TP	05	07	08	15	1D	20	30	37	38	3B	3D	49	52	56	5D	63(AES)	76
CTP	FA	F8	F7	EA	E2	DF	CF	C8	C7	C4	C2	B6	AD	A9	A2	9C	89

TABLE 20.2 Translation Polynomials for Modulus Polynomial 171.

TP	02	07	0F	1C	22	23	2C	2E	3A	3E	41	48	4B	56
CTP	FD	F8	F0	E3	DD	DC	D3	D1	C5	C1	BE	B7	B4	A9
TP	57	5A	64	68	6B	6C	6E	70	73	75	77	7E	7F	
CTP	A8	A5	9B	97	94	93	91	8F	8C	8A	88	81	80	

Total number of translation polynomials for 11B and 171 modulus polynomials with fixed affine matrix of standard AES S-box are 34 and 54, respectively. The translation polynomial can be obtained and listed for all the modulus polynomials for a fixed affine matrix. Similarly, for different can be obtained for other affine function.

20.4 RESULTS AND OBSERVATIONS

For fixed affine matrix and modulus polynomial in the AES, there are only 34 translation polynomials C out of the 256 which give 34 S-boxes without fixed and conjugate fixed points. For each modulus polynomial, a number of translation polynomials are computed by taking affine matrix same as AES S-box as given in Tables 20.3 and 20.4 for different nonprimitive and primitive modulus polynomials. From Tables 20.3 and 20.4, the number of translation polynomials for different irreducible and primitive modulus polynomials varies in a range from 22 to 46 and 26 to 54, respectively. The minimum number of translation polynomials obtained are 22 for irreducible modulus polynomial 1D7 (in Hex) and maximum number of translation polynomials are 46 for 1DB and 1F9. Similarly, the minimum number of translation polynomials obtained are 26 for primitive modulus polynomial 165 (in Hex) and maximum number of translation polynomials are 56 for 171 (in Hex).

TABLE 20.3 Number of Translation Polynomials Corresponding to Nonprimitive Irreducible Polynomials.

Modulus polynomial (In Hex)	11B (AES)	139	13F	177	17B	18B	19F	1A3	1B1	1BD	1D7	1DB	1F3	1F9
Number of translation polynomial	34	34	38	32	40	30	32	34	34	40	22	46	38	46

TABLE 20.4 Number of Translation Polynomials Corresponding to Primitive Polynomials.

Modulus polynomial (In Hex)	11D	12B	15F	163	165	169	1C3	1E7	171	1A9	1F5	18D	14D	12D	187	1CF
Number of translation polynomial	40	34	42	46	26	32	40	40	54	30	36	40	44	34	38	32

It is observed that the number of translation polynomials corresponding to the nonprimitive irreducible polynomials are less in comparison to the primitive polynomials. Hence the number of S-boxes would be more in the case of primitive polynomial. So it is better to use the primitive polynomial as modulus polynomial for the construction of S-boxes and the encryption algorithm in which the S-boxes are used dynamically to encrypt the messages. Theorem 20.3 gives the relationship between the fixed point and the conjugate fixed point with respect to the translation polynomial and its complement.

Theorem 20.3 If a function $S : GF(2^8) \rightarrow GF(2^8)$ defined as $S(x) = Ax^{-1} + C$, where A is the invertible matrix of size $n \times n$, has no fixed point and conjugate fixed point for a given C then the function $S : GF(2^8) \rightarrow GF(2^8)$ defined as $S(x) = Ax^{-1} + \overline{C}$ also has no fixed point and conjugate point, where $\overline{C}$ is the complement of C.

Proof Suppose $S(x) = Ax^{-1} + \overline{C}$ has a fixed point then $x = Ax^{-1} + \overline{C}$. This implies $\overline{x} = Ax^{-1} + C$. It shows that S has a conjugate fixed point, which is the contradiction.

This theorem says if a translation polynomial C in the construction of S-box is chosen such that it has no fixed point and conjugate fixed point then S-box has also does not have any fixed point and conjugate fixed point in case a translation polynomial is replaced by its complement. It has been verified by computing the list of translation polynomials for each modulus polynomial.

Moreover, it has been observed that the number of valid translation polynomials is the even for each modulus polynomial and half of the translation polynomials are the complement of other translation polynomials. It is also observed that a primitive polynomial (171 in Hex) has highest number of translation polynomials and it produces S-box with cryptographic strength and properties equivalent to original AES S-box. This polynomial is the best suitable polynomial for generating the dynamic S-boxes by varying translation polynomial. The security of S-boxes is not compromised by varying translation polynomial in the construction of AES S-box.

Further, the cryptographic characteristics of S-boxes corresponding to some different modulus polynomials and a fixed translation polynomial $C = 63 = x^6 + x^5 + x + 1$ are shown in Table 20.5.

TABLE 20.5 Values of the Cryptographic Characteristic Parameters for AES S-box.

Modulus polynomial (In Hex)	Cryptographic criteria				
	Nonlinearity	PCB(1,0)	PCB(1,1)	CIB(1)	Entropy H
11B	112	16	20	16	0.989
1B1	112	16	20	14	0.991
12D	112	16	20	16	0.994

Table 20.5 indicates that the values of different cryptographic parameters vary for different modulus polynomials. Such characteristics can be seen in[12] for some affine matrices and all modulus polynomials. It has also been seen that a change of translation polynomial has no change in cryptographic parameters of s-box.

20.5   CONCLUSION

The customization of AES for multiple S-boxes to use dynamically has been studied for construction of AES S-boxes by changing affine matrix, modulus polynomial, and translation polynomial. Translation polynomial has been used in the construction of S-box to avoid fixed point and conjugate fixed point with same cryptographic strength. It has been observed the following:

(i)   Strength of S-box remains unchanged for a fixed affine matrix and modulus polynomial. It will vary for different modulus polynomials and affine matrices.

(ii)   There are different number of translation polynomials corresponding to different modulus polynomials. Number of translation polynomial is more for primitive modulus polynomial.

(iii) The S-box for a translation polynomial replaced by its complement also has no fixed point and conjugate fixed point if a S-box for a translation polynomial has no fixed point and conjugate fixed point.

(iv) Number of translation polynomials are even and half of the translation polynomials are complement of other translation polynomials for each modulus polynomials.

(v)   Strength of S-box generated by changing translation polynomial for different bias parameters for a fixed modulus polynomial and has found equivalent to original AES S-box.

The construction of AES S-box by varying a translation polynomial is the safest way to obtain multiple S-boxes of equal strength that can be used in the dynamic encryption of vital massages in various applications of information security.

KEYWORDS

- **information security**
- **cryptography**
- **encryption**
- **block cipher**
- **S-box**
- **advanced encryption standard (AES)**
- **cryptographic properties**

REFERENCES

1. Menezes, A.; Vanstone, S.; Van Oorschot, P. Handbook of Applied Cryptography; CRC Press: Boca Raton, 1996.
2. Dubey M. K.; Ratan, R.; Verme, N.; Saxena, P. K. In Cryptanalytic Attacks and Countermeasures on RSA, Proceedings of the Third International Conference on Soft Computing for Problem Solving. Advances in Intelligent Systems and Computing; Pant, M., Deep, K., Nagar, A., Bansal, J., Eds.; Springer: New Delhi, vol 258; pp. 805–819, 2014..
3. Advanced Encryption Standard (AES). Federal Information Processing Standards Publications (FIPS 197), Nov 26, 2001.
4. Daemen, J.; Rijmen, V. The Design of Rijindeal: AES—The Advanced Encryption Standard; Springer, 2002.
5. Grosek, O.; Mangliveras, S. S.; Tapuska, T.; Wei, W. Is Rijndeal Really Independent of the Field Polynomial. Tatra Mt. Math. Publ. **2006**, 33, 51–69.
6. Stallings, W. Cryptography and Network Security, 4th ed.; Pearson Education, 2003.
7. Tiessen, T; Knudsen, L. R.; Kibble, S.; Lauridsen, M. M. In Security of the AES with a Secret S-box, Fast Software Encryption. FSE 2015. Lecture Notes in Computer Science, 2015; Leander, G., Eds.; vol. 9054. Springer: Berlin, Heidelberg.
8. Hamdy, N.; Shehata, K.; Eldemerdash, H. Design and Implementation of Encryption Unit Based on Customized AES algorithm. Int. J. Videos Image Process. Netw. Sec. **2011**, 11 (1), 33–40.
9. Ratan, R. In Applications of Genetic Algorithms in Cryptology, Proceedings of the Third International Conference on Soft Computing for Problem Solving. Advances in Intelligent Systems and Computing; Springer, Vol. 258, pp. 821–831; 2014.
10. Asthana, R.; Verma, N.; Ratan, R. In Generation of Boolean Functions using Genetic Algorithm for Cryptographic Applications, *IEEE International Advance Computing Conference (IACC)*, 2014; pp. 1361–1366.
11. Kadhim, A. F.; Kamal, Z. A. Generating Dynamic S-box based on Particle Swarm Optimization and Chaos Theory. Iraq J. Sci. **2018**, 59 (3C), 1733–1745.
12. Sinha, S. D.; Arya, C. P. Algebraic Construction and Cryptographic Properties of Rijndael Substitution Box. Def. Sci. J. **2012**, 62 (1), 32–37.
13. Farahan, A. K.; Ali, R. S.; Yasein, H. R.; Al-saidi, N. M. G.; Majeed, G. H. A. A New Approach to Generate Multi S-Boxes based on RNA Computing. Int. J. Innovat. Comput. Inform. Control **2020**, 16 (1), 331–348.
14. Das, S.; Uz Zaman, J. K. M. S.; Ghosh, R. Generation of AES S-Boxes with Various Modulus and Additive Constant Polynomial and Testing their Randomization. Procedia Techol. **2013**, 10, 957–962.
15. Juremi, J.; Mahmod, R.; Sulaiman, S.; Ramli, J. Enhancing Advanced Encryption Standard S-box Generation based on Round key. Int. J. Sec. Digit. Forens. (the Society of Digital Information and Wireless Communication) **2012**, 1 (3), 183–188.
16. Seghier, A.; Li, J.; Sun; D. Z. Advanced Encryption Standard based Key Dependent S-box Cube. IET Inform. Sec. **2019**, 13 (6), 552–558.
17. Katiyar, S.; Jeyanthi, N. Pure Dynamic S-box Construction. Int. J. Comput. **2016**, 1, 42–46.
18. Krishnamurthy G. N.; Ramaswamy, V.; Making AES Stronger: AES with Key Dependent S-Box. IJCSNS Int. J. Comput. Sci. Network Sec. **2008**, 8 (9), 388–398.

19. Fammy, A.; Shaarawy, M.; El-Hada, K.; Salma, G.; Hassanain, K. In A Proposal for a Key-Dependent AES, 3rd International Conference: Sciences of Electronic, Technologies of Information and Telecommunications, 2005.

20. Tiangong, A. O.; Rao, J.; Dai, K.; Zon, X. Construction of High Quality Key-Dependent S-Box. IAENG, Int. J. Comput. Sci. **2017**, 44 (3), 337–344.

21. Kazlauskas, K.; Vaicekauskas, G.; Smaliukas, R. An Algorithm for Key Dependent S-box Generation in Block Cipher System. Informatica **2015**, 26 (1), 51–65.

22. Vaicekauskas, G.; Kazlauskas, K.; Smaliukas, R. A Novel Method to Design S-boxes based on Key-Dependent Permutation Schemes and Its Quality Analysis. Int. J. Adv. Comput. Sci. Appl. **2016**, 7 (4), 93–99.

23. Nadu, S. T. A Block Cipher Algorithm to Enhance the Avalanche Effect using Dynamic Key-Dependent S-box and Genetic Operations. Int. J. Pure Appl. Math. **2018**, 119 (10), 399–418.

24. Thinn, A. A.; Thwin, M. M. S. In Modification of AES Algorithm by using Second Key and Modified Subbytes Operation for Text Encryption, Computational Science and Technology. Lecture Notes in Electrical Engineering; Alfred, R., Lim, Y., Ibrahim, A., Anthony, P., Eds.; vol. 481; Springer: Singapore, 2019; pp. 435–444.

25. Rodinko, M.; Oliynykov, R.; Gorbenko, Y. Optimization of the High Nonlinear S-box Generation Method. Tatra Mt. Math. Publ. **2017**, 70, 93–105.

26. Ali, K. M.; Khan, M. Application based Construction and Optimization of Substitution Boxes over 2D Mixed Chaotic Maps. Int. J. Theor. Phys. **2019**, 58 (9), 3091–3117.

27. Zahid, A. H.; Al-Solami, E.; Ahmad, M. A Novel Modular Approach based Substitution-box Design for Image Encryption. IEEE Access **2020**, 8, 150326–150340.

28. Ali, K. M.; Khan, M. A New Construction of Confusion Component of Block Ciphers. Multimed. Tools Appl. **2019**, 78 (22), 32585–32604.

29. Artin, M. Algebra. Massachusetts Institute of Technology, Mathematics Department; Prentice Hall Inc.: Cambridge, USA, 1991.

30. Lidl, R.; Niederreiter, H. Introduction to Finite Fields and their Applications; Cambridge University Press: New York, 2012.

31. Kontak, M.; Szmidt, J. Nonlinearity of the Round Function. Cont. Cybernet. **2007**, 36 (4), 1037–1044.

32. Liu, H.; Kadir, A.; Xu, C. Cryptanalysis and Constructing S-Box based on Chaotic Map and Backtracking. Appl. Math. Comput. **2020**, 376, 125153.

CHAPTER 21

On-Demand Link and Energy-Aware Dynamic Multipath Routing for Mobile Nodes in Wireless Sensor Networks

S. SUMA and B. HARSOOR

Department of Information Science and Engineering, Poojya Dodappa Appa College of Engineering, Kalaburagi, India

ABSTRACT

Extensive research approaches have offered (Mobile ad-hoc network) MANET to build wireless network connectivity of mobile nodes, which does not require centralized infrastructure for operation. In simple words, MANETs are self-generated and self-configuring battery-operated mobile nodes, which collaborate with each other and provide robust data transfer through wireless transmission to whole network. Since nodes are mobile in nature, change in network topology occurs frequently. Dynamic topology leads to link failure, decreased bandwidth due to unstable link that degrades the network efficiency and decreases QoS. Reliable wireless communication mainly depends on stable link, available bandwidth, and nodes energy. The existing MANET's routing scheme is based on multipath routing that considers optimal hop count and any link failure results in packet loss, and thus increase in delay

Computational Intelligence in Analytics and Information Systems, Volume 2: Advances in Digital Transformation, Selected Papers from CIAIS-2021. Parneeta Dhaliwal, PhD, Manpreet Kaur, PhD, Hardeo Kumar Thakur, PhD, Rajeev Kumar Arya, and Joan Lu (Eds.)

and energy consumption for retransmission. To address these issues, this paper proposes an on-demand link and energy aware dynamic multipath (O-LEADM) routing scheme for MANETs. The proposed scheme discovers nodes link quality by link estimation indicator (LEI) that decides whether the link is stable or unstable. The O-LEADM scheme selects neighbor nodes by determining nodes residual energy and makes a multipath routing decision by maintaining link stability, reliability, and prolonged network lifetime. Simulation is performed using (NS2) and performance of O-LEADM scheme is compared with existing dynamic routing schemes and performance results are evaluated in terms of packet delivery ratio, energy consumption, delay, throughput, and overhead.

21.1   INTRODUCTION

Advances in mobile computing applications have shown tremendous prospect in proving wireless communication and Internet services.[1] MANETs[2] and VANETs[3] have become popular wireless communication technology for upcoming smart computing networks due to their decisive performance on vast application areas. MANET's features and function-alities have offered wider reach for upcoming wireless 5G networks.[4] MANETs are self-organized, self-configured, and self-controlled mobile nodes used for wireless communication in infrastructure networks.[5] Nodes in MANETs can freely move in and out at any direction and network can admit node at any time depending on energy resource and nature of network topology. Mobile nodes cooperate with each other and serve as router to forward packets.[6] In Figure 21.1 nodes forward packets take through single or multihop incorporating routing functions. In single hop node communicates directly to other nodes that are within the transmission range. Intermediate nodes act as relay nodes for forwarding packets if the node is out of communication range in multihop. Since nodes are dynamic, frequent link breaks occur between nodes which degrade the link quality resulting in packet loss.[7] An efficient and stable route is determined by discovering nodes with stable link, high residual energy nodes, signal strength, and mobility patterns. Due to topology changes and link failures in MANETs, it is a challenging task for proving reliable routing.[8-12] In this paper we propose an on-demand link and energy aware dynamic multipath (O-LEADM) routing scheme for MANET's an adaptation of AODV (Adhoc on Demand Routing) protocol. This scheme mainly concentrates on finding stable links between nodes using link estimation indicator (LEI) which indicates the signal strength of the nodes and ensures stable links between nodes, whenever node disjoints occur which may pose link failure. To ensure reliable data transfer O-LEADM selects forwarding nodes based on high residual energy aware to regulate fair usage of bandwidth and to balance energy among nodes. The contributions are as follows:

- Link estimation indicator (LEI) ensures high quality signal strength received from media access control (MAC) and estimates the radio connection stability of individual node link.
- Energy aware ensures available link bandwidth for high-quality communication at specific time and incorporating high residual energy increases network lifetime and efficient data transmission.

The rest of this paper is organized as follows. Section II describes problem statement and motivation. Section 21.3 describes the related works. The proposed mechanism scheme is described in Section 21.4. Section 21.5 describes results and evaluation. Section 21.6 describes the comparison results. Conclusion on the proposed scheme is drawn in Section 21.7.

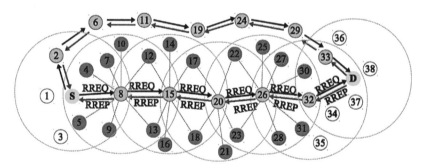

FIGURE 21.1   Routing process.

Source: Reprinted from Ref. [30]. © 2018 The Authors. https://creativecommons.org/licenses/by-nc-nd/4.0/

21.2   PROBLEM STATEMENT AND MOTIVATION

In practical MANET is designated to constant change in network topology, and does not rely on any fixed or centralized infrastructure. Mobile nodes coordinate with each other, act as router and hosts, and establish connection between source and destination. During route establishment between a pair of nodes, it is necessary to determine the status of the intermediate nodes before routing. Dynamic behavior of MANETs experiences frequent route breakages affecting factors such as bandwidth, energy resource, mobility, and channel fading. It is required to maintain the stability of the link between two nodes for reliable communication. Characteristics of low power wireless links have been studied over decades and these links are error prone, asymmetric, and unreliable due to hardware and environmental factors. Estimating stability of link quality is problematic due to dynamic change in topology. Link quality estimation or path stability is an essential requirement to increase the routing performance. Determining the path stability is a challenging task, this motivates us to propose a scheme where the link stability is measured between two participating nodes while establishing path between source and destination. Path stability is determined by measuring the link quality of participating nodes by link estimation indicator (LEI) and remaining energy of nodes. Link stability is estimated by received signal strength from MAC layer and available bandwidth ensures high-quality communication and achieves QoS parameters such as increased throughput, more packet delivery ratio, and low computational overhead. Energy aware nodes are selected as forwarder nodes for reliable data transfer and to improve network lifetime.

21.3   RELATED WORKS

In[13] the author proposed an LQEAR protocol that discovers nodes disjoints links across multiple paths to improve network lifetime. LQEAR uses the link quality indicator to estimate the link quality and residual energy metric and selects better one hop forwarding nodes to offer reliable transmission. However this protocol fails to estimate link quality accurately and provides limited attributes of wireless links that are not sufficient for routing performance. In[14] the author proposed a routing protocol aiming to increase network lifetime called energy-efficient multipath routing (AOMR-LM) which harvests energy and balances nodes energy consumption. Multipath selection is done through calculating nodes residual energy, parameters such as threshold energy and coefficient are analyzed to ensure energy harvesting. This protocol extends network lifetime and improves routing performance of MANETs, but it does not concentrate on channel fading due to link failures. In[15] the author proposed an power-efficient AODV routing scheme (EPA-AODV). In this scheme residual energy field information is added to route request packet header (RREQ). Intermediate node manipulates route request packet (RREQ) on arrival and checks for residual energy, if residual energy is above the specified threshold value then it is considered a qualified neighbor for forwarding data. In[16] the author proposed dynamic energy-efficient adhoc on demand distance vector protocol (DE-AODV) to minimize the average end-to-end delay and increase network lifetime. This protocol supplies dynamic external energy through battery and selects nodes with trustworthy and energy-efficient nodes. External battery energy is supplied dynamically whenever link failures occur, thus reducing the nodes energy consumption and prolonging network lifetime. In[17] the author defines link stability of a reliable path that is determined by the strength of the received signal which calculates link expiry time of every node with other links in a path. In[18] the author proposed zone-based routing that includes link availability computation and reducing RREQ broadcast packets. In zone-based routing, communication range for each node is split into inner, middle, and outer zones based on RSSI and threshold. Middle-zone nodes are involved in the route discovery process. The link availability ratio calculates the neighboring links through localization and angular sector within the communication range. This technique suffers from packet loop and takes more number of hops increasing routing overhead. In[25] the author proposed prediction of link failure before its occurrence to improve the QoS. Stability of the link predicts the availability of routes. In this scheme the author proposed Newton divided difference interpolation to estimate the link stability and predict the link failure. An alternate path is built when the link failure occurs between two nodes proactively. Related works mainly concentrated on prediction of link failure and link disjoint techniques that required more computation functions to find the alternate routes and consume more energy by retransmitting packets to destination which leads to increase in delay. It is essential for the routing protocol to find the best path to destination and aware of the link stability, which reduces the retransmission delay and increases overall network lifetime.

21.4 PROPOSED MECHANISM

21.4.1 NETWORK MODEL

The network consists of mobile nodes that are deployed randomly in an area and each node has neighbor nodes within its transmission range. Communication between nodes in the network can be represented as graph $G_n = (V_n, L_n)$, where V_n is the number of nodes and L_n is link between nodes. The source node s_n and destination node d_n and their link is represented as (s_n, d_n), that is, $(s_n, d_n) \in V_n$. Source node s_n can directly communicate with destination node d_n if it is within communication range through single hop, else it takes multihop if destination d_n is out of communication range. Dynamic nature of nodes makes frequent topology changes occur in an unreliable manner. In such a dynamic movement two nodes do not share stable link due to variable speed at which the node is moving. Node's speed is considered an important criterion in forming a reliable link as the node speed is irrespective of its time and position. Nodes moving at lower or medium speed form stable link rather than nodes moving at higher speeds. Mobile node V_n moving at a variable speed is computed as total distance traveled in a given time that is evaluated as in[19]:

$$V_{n_{speed}} = \left(distance_{V_n} / time_{V_n} \right) mps$$

Distance traveled by mobile node V_n is computed from the Euclidean distance formula that is given as in[20]:

$$D_{V_{n_a}, V_{n_b}} = \sqrt{\left(y_i - y_j \right)^2 + \left(x_i - x_j \right)^2}$$

The routing cost function calculation is done during the route discovery phase for selecting the forwarding node within the transmission range r for two nodes V_{na} and V_{nb} with coordinates (x_i, y_i) and (x_j, y_j) of 1-hop neighbor node of V_{na} represented as V_{Na} that is calculated as

$$V_{N_a} = \left(V_{n_b} \mid D_{V_{n_a}, V_{n_b}} \leq r \right)$$

The nodes transmission range r can be computed using RSSI (received signal strength indicator) threshold value and error probability which is assumed to be 10^{-3} given in[21,22] expressed as bit error rate (BER).

21.4.2   MOBILITY MODEL

In a real scenario the nodes are equipped with GPS that provide accurate location of node within the transmission area along with nodes speed and velocity. Localization algorithm provides information of mobile nodes speed, current location, and direction at each time Δt. Nodes movement in a network is unpredictable, random waypoint model (RWP) periodically estimates nodes mobility, link failure, and link stability. In our scheme the nodes move randomly in a network area with minimum and maximum velocities along with pause time which are configured using the RWP model. The dynamic topology is formed by nodes moving at their velocities range $\left[v_{n_{max}}, v_{n_{min}}\right]$ and node direction, δ, between $[0,1]$. If the node current location V_{ni} at time instant, t_n is $(x_i(Vt_{ni}), y_i(Vt_{ni}))$ then the new location of the node after the increment in time interval Δt is determined as

$$\begin{cases} x_i\left(t_n + \Delta t\right) = x_i\left(t_n\right) + \Delta t * v_i\left(t_n\right) \cos\delta_i\left(t_n\right) \\ y_i\left(t_n + \Delta t\right) = y_i\left(t_n\right) + \Delta t * v_i\left(t_n\right) \cos\delta_i\left(t_n\right) \end{cases}$$

Speed of node is denoted as $v_i(t_n)$ and node direction of motion is represented as $\delta_i(t_n)$ for the ith node at time instant t_n. The value of $\delta_i(t_n)$ is 0 if node velocity is maximum and 1 if the node velocity in minimum.

21.4.3 LINK STATUS AND STABILITY

Nodes link status can be determined by computing Euclidean distance $DV_{n_{ij}}$ between pair of nodes V_{n_i}, V_{n_j} at time t_n and estimating RSSI transmission range $r\tau_i$ or $r\tau_j$ of mobile nodes for link status $L_{n_{ij}}(t_n)$ as

$$DV_{n_{ij}} = \sqrt{\left(y_i\left(t_n\right) - y_j\left(t_n\right)\right)^2 + \left(x_i\left(t_n\right) - x_j\left(t_n\right)\right)^2}$$

$$L_{n_{ij}}\left(t_n\right) = \begin{cases} 1, if\ DV_{n_{ij}}\left(t_n\right) \leq r\tau_i\ or\ r\tau_j \\ 0, \qquad otherwise \end{cases}$$

Therefore, the network at any time instant t_n between the source and the destination can be represented by a matrix of $V_N \times V_N$ with link status elements to determine connectivity. If the connectivity exists between the pair of nodes at time t_n it is denoted as "1;" otherwise it is "0."

21.4.4 LINK ESTIMATION INDICATOR (LEI)

Link estimation indicator estimates the stablity of link between pair of nodes for time period. LEI is expressed as a time duration of two mobile nodes V_{n_i}, V_{n_j} which know its initial location $s(x_i, y_i)$ and (x_j, y_j) and are within the transmission range $r\tau$ with velocities v_{n_i} and v_{n_j} and phase angles δ_i and $\left(0 \leq \delta_i, \delta_j \leq 2\pi\right)$ respectively will remain connected. Stable link quality between two mobile nodes V_{n_i}, V_{n_j} can be estimated as

$$LEI_{V_{n_{ij}}} = \frac{-(ab+cd)+\sqrt{(a^2+c^2)r\tau^2-(ad-bc)^2}}{(a^2+c^2)}$$

where $a = v_{n_i}\cos\delta_i - v_{n_j}\cos\delta_j$: $b = (x_i - x_j)$: $c = v_{n_i}\sin\delta_i - v_{n_j}\sin\delta_j$: $d = (y_i - y_j)$
A stable link will exist when $v_{n_i} = v_{n_j}$ and $\delta_i = \delta_j$ where a and c become zero and nodes will be connected throughout when the value of $LEI_{V_{n_{ij}}} = \infty$ if two nodes moving at the same speed and direction. Since nodes can move in any direction and with different mobility speeds the stability of the link for two nodes is proportional to the $LEI_{V_{n_{ij}}}$ value. The link stability form can be given as

$$LS_{V_{n_{ij}}} = 1 - e^{\frac{-LEI_{V_{n_{ij}}}}{\alpha}}$$

where α is a constant, In the proposed method we add RSSI parameter to link state to predict link failure. While route discovering the Hello message time interval T has to be reduced to avoid out of date information of next hop node since T is inversely proportional to $LEI_{V_{n_{ij}}}$. Therefore, the equation can be written as

$$LF_{V_{n_{ij}}} = 1 - e^{\frac{RSSI(V_{N_a}).LEI_{V_{n_{ij}}} V_{ND}}{\alpha.T}}$$

where $LF_{V_{n_{ij}}}$ indicates the link failure prediction. $LEI_{V_{n_{ij}}}$ is computed to find the stable link, RSSI gives the received signal strength for nodes within the transmission range which is computed during route cost function for 1-hop neighbor V_{N_a}. T is Hello time interval and V_{ND} represents the node density.

21.4.5 ENERGY CONSUMPTION

To prolong network lifetime, nodes energy consumption has to be optimized and energy-efficient intermediate nodes have to be selected for reliable data transfer. Routing protocol discovers multiple paths and establishes communication between nodes to perform data transfer. Few nodes fail in network due to energy drain. In the proposed scheme the intermediate nodes are selected by monitoring the available residual energy which is capable for reliable transmission of data successfully. To estimate nodes energy consumption at different states, all nodes are assigned same initial energy as the network is homogeneous. The initial energy of intermediate node V_{n_i} at time instant t_n is denoted by e_{int} and e_{res} denotes residual energy of node V_{n_i}. The residual energy of node V_{n_i} for time period Δ is calculated as

$$e_{res}\left(t_n+\Delta\right)=e_{int}\left(t_n\right)-e_{cons}\left(t_n+\Delta\right)$$

where $e_{cons}\left(t_n+\Delta\right)$ is consumed energy of node V_{n_i} for time period of Δ for transmitting, receiving, and computing internal operations of nodes. In the proposed scheme the energy consumed by node for forwarding data along with the energy included to overcome link fluctuation of unstable links due to channel fading is given as

$$e_{t_x}\left(t_n+\Delta\right)=d_s\times p_{t_x}\left(t_n+\Delta\right)$$

where $p_{t_x}\left(t_n+\Delta\right)$ is the total power consumed during transmitting of d_s data packets sent and exchange of control message with intermediate node at time Δ measured in Watts per second. Similarly, the receiving nodes energy during receiving state for sent packet is calculated as

$$e_{r_x}\left(t_n+\Delta\right)=d_r\times p_{r_x}\left(t_n+\Delta\right)$$

$p_{r_x}\left(t_n+\Delta\right)$ denotes the power consumed for receiving data packets d_r at time $(t_n+\Delta)$. Energy is consumed when the node does internal computation such as processing digital signal, updating encoding, and decoding at time period Δ and is denoted as $e_{comp}(t_n+\Delta)$. The total amount of energy consumed by a node V_{n_i} at time period Δ for its transmission, reception, and computation is given as

$$e_{cons}\left(t_n+\Delta\right)=e_{t_x}\left(t_n+\Delta\right)+e_{r_x}\left(t_n+\Delta\right)+e_{comp}\left(t_n+\Delta\right)$$

Therefore nodes residual energy is calculated as

$$e_{res}\left(t_n+\Delta\right)=e_{int}\left(t_n\right)-\left\{e_{t_x}\left(t_n+\Delta\right)+e_{r_x}\left(t_n+\Delta\right)+e_{comp}\left(t_n+\Delta\right)\right\}$$

The proposed O-LEADM routing scheme selects nodes with higher residual energy for forwarding data packets efficiently.

21.4.5.1 O-LEADM ALGORITHM

Step 1: Set_RTR_PROT = OLEADM
Step 2: Set_node = V_{n_i}

Step 3: Set_Source = V_{n_s}

Step 4: Set_Dest = V_{n_d}

Step 5: OLEADM_method( ) {

Step 6: Proc broadcast Hello $\left(V_{n_{ij}}\right)$ to find neighbor

Step 7: Initialize route discovery process

Step 8: Calculate RSSI (Received signal strength) distance between nodes:

$$RSSI = -(10 \times log_{10}\left(dV_{n_{ij}}\right) - A$$

$$dV_{n_{ij}} = 10^{\frac{RSSI-A}{-10*n}}$$

where $dV_{n_{ij}}$ is distance between nodes V_{n_i} and V_{n_j} : $n = 2$ for propagation-free space model : $A = -32$ (dBm) signal strength between two nodes.

Step 9: Get_Link_Status of two nodes by $L_{n_{ij}}\left(t_n\right)$

Step 10: Predict link failure and estimate link quality by $LEI_{V_{n_{ij}}}$

Step 11: Update routing information in routing table

Step 12: Update energy levels of the nodes in the network

Check

If $\left(e_{res}\left(t_n + \Delta\right) >= High \ \&\& \ dist <= low \ \&\& \ hop\,count <= low\right)$

Select route for communication

else

check link stability

end if

21.5   RESULTS AND EVALUATION

21.5.1   SIMULATION PARAMETERS AND MODEL

The performance of the proposed O-LEADM scheme is evaluated for two different scenarios and compared with the existing AODVLP scheme. The scenario includes varying the node speed and simulation time by keeping node size of 50. Simulation is carried out on network simulator tool (NS2). Constant bit rate (CBR) traffic is utilized, the nodes are randomly deployed in an network area of 1000 × 1000 mts. Nodes are mobile and topology change occurs frequently as nodes move in different velocities and speed. The node transmission range is set to 250 m and nodes are assigned with initial energy of 100 joules. The threshold energy level is set to 50 joules, the performance of the proposed scheme was evaluated on two scenarios. In the first scenario the node speed is varied as (10, 20, 30, 40 m/s) by keeping the simulation time and packet size (100 sec and 512 bytes). For all runs other parameters are considered the same. In the second scenario the simulation time is varied to (50, 100, 150, 200 sec) by keeping fixed node speed as 30 m/s and packet size of 512 bytes. The simulation parameters used are presented in Table 21.1.

TABLE 21.1 Simulation Parameters.

Parameters	Value
Nodes	50
Mobility speed	10,20,30,40 m/s
Queue size	50
MAC	802.11
Simulation time	50,100,150,200 sec
Node deployment	Random
Network area	800×800 mts
Packet size	512 bytes
Transmission range	250 mts
Protocols	OLEADM and AODVLP
Traffic type	CBR
Initial energy	100 Joules

21.5.1.1 PERFORMANCE METRICS

Packet Delivery Ratio: It is the ratio of the transmitted packet from the source to the received packets at the receiver to destination.[23] This metric indicates a routing protocol's reliability in its transmission of data packets from source to destination. The higher the ratio, the better the routing protocol efficiency will be.

$$PDR = \frac{number\ of\ received\ packets}{number\ of\ transmitted\ packets} \times 100$$

Throughput: It is defined as the number of bits obtained successfully at destination. It is expressed as kilobits per second (Kbps).[24] Routing protocols efficiency is measured by receiving data packets at destination. Throughput is calculated as

$$Throughput = (total\,received\,bytes \times 8/time) \times 1000\,Kbps$$

End-to-end Delay: It is defined as delay time required receiving the transmitted data packet and retransmitting to other nodes across the network[26]

$$E2E = \sum T_1 - T_2 / N$$

where T_1 is the first data packet arrived time, T_2 is time first packet sent by source, and N is total number of packets sent.

Energy Consumption: It is defined as total amount of energy spent by nodes in network within simulation time. Node's consumed energy is calculated as initial energy assigned at the start time to the difference of energy spent at the end of simulation time. It is expressed as

$$E_{cons} = \sum_{i=1}^{n} \left(ini(i) - ene(i) \right)$$

21.6   SIMULATION RESULTS

21.6.1   PACKET DELIVERY RATIO

Figure 21.2(a) shows the packet delivery ratio variation for AODVLP and OLEADM. The X-axis indicates node speed in m/s and the Y-axis indicates percentage of packet deliver ratio. In this scenario the node speed is varied to 10, 20, 30, and 40 m/s. As the node speed increases the chance of link failure is higher and packet drop occurs when the link breaks resulting in low packet delivery to destination. As the node speed is varied it can be observed that at a lower speed the packet delivery ratio in the AODVLP scheme is higher, once the node reaches its maximum speed the OLEADM delivers higher packets to destination. OLEADM selects an optimal route with high residual energy and estimates the link stability and dynamically selects an alternate route for reliable data transfer.

Figure 21.2(b) shows the effect of varying the simulation time on the packet delivery ratio. The X-axis indicates time in sec and the Y-axis indicates percentage of packet delivery ratio. In this scenario the simulation time is varied for 50, 100, 150, and 200 sec and checked for PDR. As the simulation time is increased the packet delivery ratio is increased. As it is seen in the plot both the schemes are delivering the same ratio of packets at 50, 100, and 150 sec. At 200 sec it is observed that the OLEADM scheme delivers a high packet ratio than AODVLP. The results clearly demonstrate that OLEADM performs better with increased simulation time as it selects better routes to deliver data traffic to destination.

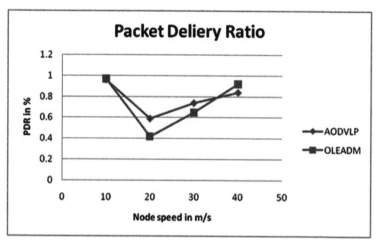

FIGURE 21.2 (A)   Packet delivery ratio variation for AODVLP and OLEADM.

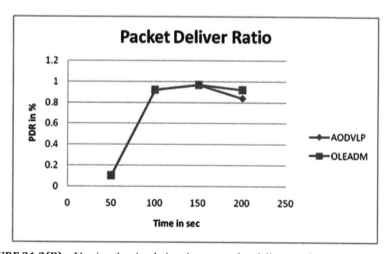

FIGURE 21.2(B)   Varying the simulation time on packet delivery ratio.

21.6.2   THROUGHPUT

Figure 21.3(a) shows the throughput graph, the X-axis indicates node speed in m/s, and the Y-axis indicates throughput in kbps. In this scenario the node speed is varied to 10, 20, 30, and 40 m/s. The simulation results demonstrate the throughput variation of AODVLP and OLEADM. It is observed that OLEADM has higher throughput than AODVLP at different speeds. In this scenario the node moves randomly in different directions, OLEADM selects next hop neighbor by calculating link status through RSSI and forwards the data to the next node and selects more stable paths by estimating the quality of links between nodes.

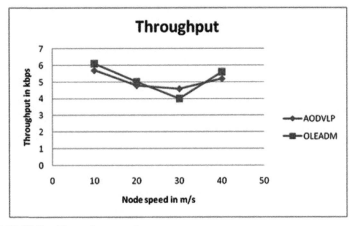

FIGURE 21.3(A)   Throughput graph.

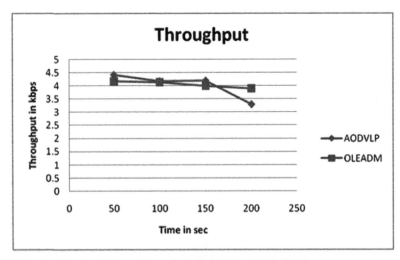

FIGURE 21.3(B)   Variation on throughput by varying simulation time.

Figure 21.3(b) shows variation on throughput by varying simulation time. The X-axis indicates simulation time in sec and the Y-axis indicates throughput in kbps. In this scenario the simulation time is varied from 50, 100, 150, 200 sec and throughput is evaluated for AODVLP and OLEADM. Since the simulation time is varied the performance of OLEADM is better than AODVLP. Increase in simulation time helps in finding more stable and strong routes to destination by minimizing packet drops. The route selected by OLEADM has a higher energy level with a stable link quality based on LEI and diverts the packet to the active nodes that have better link quality.

21.6.3   END-TO-END DELAY

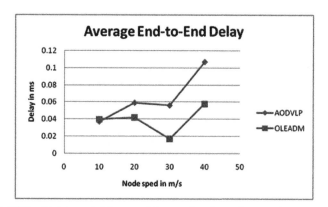

FIGURE 21.4(A)   End-to-end delay graph by varying the nodes speed.

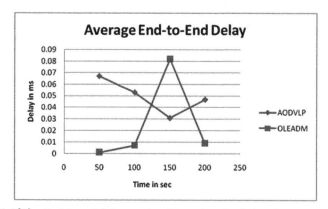

FIGURE 21.4(B)   End-to-end delay graph with varying simulation time.

Figure 21.4(a) shows the average end-to-end delay graph by varying the nodes speed. The X-axis indicates node speed in m/s and the Y-axis indicates delay in milliseconds. It is observed that AODVLP does not consider the energy levels of intermediate nodes while selecting the optimal route to destination, therefore increasing the delay at nodes moving at a higher mobility speed. The OLEADM scheme selects an optimal route and intermediate nodes based on the mobility speed, LEI, and energy level parameters, respectively. Therefore, it stabilizes the dynamic network and controls end-to-end delay in network. Figure 21.4(b) shows the average end-to-end delay graph with varying simulation time. The X-axis indicates simulation time in sec and the Y-axis indicates delay in milliseconds. As the time increases OLEADM delay increases compared to AODVLP, at 200 sec OLEADM delay decreases by selecting the routes with minimum hop distance and consumes less time to transmit packets over the network.

21.6.4   ENERGY CONSUMPTION

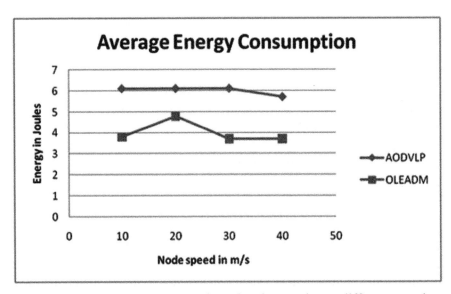

FIGURE 21.5(A)   Energy consumption of nodes moving at different speeds.

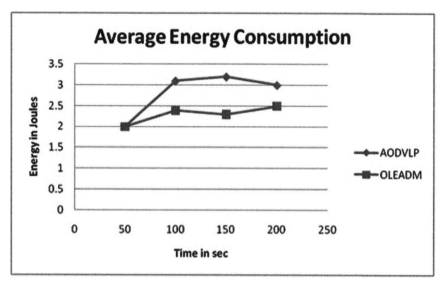

FIGURE 21.5(B)   Energy comparison with varying simulation time.

Average energy consumption network operation is shown in Figure 21.5(a) and 21.5(b). Figure 21.5(a) shows the average energy consumption of nodes moving at different speeds. The X-axis indicates node speed in m/s and the Y-axis indicates energy consumption in joules. Route computation of network topology becomes more complex when mobility speed increases. Higher average nodes participating in routes reduce retransmission and re-route discovery process, save time, and prolong network lifetime. Simulation results show the OLEADM scheme reduces energy consumption compared to AODVLP. The OLEADM scheme is able to maintain route stability, effective energy balance that ensures finding relay or intermediate nodes with higher residual energy to transmit packet. Because of route reconstruction and sending more number of RREQ packets to find alternate route consumes more energy in AODVLP. Figure 21.5(b) shows the energy comparison with varying simulation time; OLEADM classifies routes and selects nodes according to high-energy levels from source to destination. The X-axis indicates simulation time in sec and the Y-axis indicates energy in joules. As simulation time increases the energy consumption of nodes in network increases, simulation results show OLEADM selects energy-efficient routes to deliver data packets and prolongs network lifetime compared to AODVLP.

21.7   CONCLUSION

By integrating routing features into mobile nodes, mobile ad hoc networks (MANETs) are intended to enable efficient and stable mobile wireless network operation. MANETs perform multihop communication among nodes distributed in network. Moving nodes causes frequent topology change and link failure which results in link disjoints among nodes and reduces overall network performance. The objective is to maintain path stability and find optimal multipath from source to destination. For efficient data transfer MANETs do not depend on single parameter, MANETs experience problems such as packet loss, frequent link breaks, energy, and bandwidth. This paper proposes an on-demand link and energy aware dynamic multipath (O-LEADM) routing scheme for MANETs to enhance the communication quality by finding the stable link between two nodes. LEI (Link estimation indicator) indicates the quality of link and finds the nodes with higher residual energy for reliable data transfer. The proposed O-LEADM scheme is simulated in NS2 by varying node mobility speed, simulation time and compared with AODVLP. Performance evaluation is carried out for network parameters such as packet delivery ratio, throughput, average end-to-end delay, and energy consumption. Simulation results show OLEADM outperforms better than AODVLP. Comparison results show OLEADM gains more throughput, less delay, high packet delivery, and less energy consumption than AODVLP. As a future enhancement several scenarios could be explored and implemented to study the nodes behavior while routing data, since nodes can experience packet drops when attackers attack the node. An efficient trust-based routing scheme that assures secure routing to destination by analyzing the trust values of nodes can improve in achieving QoS parameter.

KEYWORDS

- **disjoint links**
- **dynamic topology**
- **link quality**
- **MANETs**
- **routing**

REFERENCES

1. Yazıcı, V.; Kozat, U. C.; Sunay, M. O. A New Control Plane for 5g Network Architecture with a Case Study on Unified Handoff, Mobility, and Routing Management. *IEEE Commun. Mag.* **2014**, *52*, 76–85.
2. Wang, X.; Li, J. Improving the Network Lifetime of Manets through Cooperative Mac Protocol Design. *IEEE Trans. Parallel Distrib. Syst.* **2015**, *26*, 1010–1020.
3. Huang, C.-F.; Chan, Y.-F.; Hwang, R.-H. A Comprehensive Real-Time Traffic Map for Geographic Routing in Vanets. *Appl. Sci.* **2017**, *7*, 129.
4. Agiwal, M.; Roy, A.; Saxena, N. Next Generation 5G Wireless Networks: A Comprehensive Survey. *IEEE Commun. Surv. Tutor.* **2016**, *18*, 1617–1655.
5. Helen, D., Arivazhagan, D. Applications, Advantages and Challenges of Ad Hoc Networks. *J. Acad. Ind. Res.* **2014**, *2* (8), 453–457.
6. Wang, D.-L.; Sun, Q.-Y.; Li, Y.-Y.; Liu, X.-R. Optimal Energy Routing Design in Energy Internet with Multiple Energy Routing Centers using Artificial Neural Network-based Reinforcement Learning Method. *Appl. Sci.* **2019**, *9*, 520.
7. Cao, Y.; Sun, Z. Routing in Delay/Disruption Tolerant Networks: A Taxonomy, Survey and Challenges. *IEEE Commun. Surv. Tutor.* **2013**, *15*, 654–677.
8. Kuipers, F.; VanMieghem, P. Conditions that Impact the Complexity of Qos Routing. *IEEE/ACM Transac. Network.* **2005**, *13* (4), 717–730.
9. Yang, D.; Xia, H.; Xu, E.; Jing, D.; Zhang, H. An Energy-Balanced Geographic Routing Algorithm for Mobile Ad Hoc Networks. *Energies* **2018**, *11*, 2219.
10. Xu, L.; Wang, J.; Liu, Y.; Yang, J.; Shi, W.; Gulliver, T. A. In *Outage Performance for IDF Relaying Mobile Cooperative Networks*, 5G for Future Wireless Networks. 5GWN 2017. Lecture Notes of the Institute for Computer Sciences, Social Informatics and Telecommunications Engineering, 2017; Long, K., Leung, V., Zhang, H., Feng, Z., Li, Y., Zhang, Z., Eds.; . Springer: Beijing, China, vol. 211, pp. 395–402, 2017.
11. Baccour, N.; Koubâa, A.; Mottola, L.; Zúñiga, M. A.; Youssef, H.; Boano, C. A.; Alves, M. Radio Link Quality Estimation in Wireless Sensor Networks: A Survey. *ACM Trans. Sensor Netw. (TOSN)* **2012**, *8* (4), 34.
12. Barroca, N.; Borges, L. M.; Velez, F. J.; Chatzimisios, P. In *IEEE 802.15.4 MAC Layer Performance Enhancement by Employing RTS/CTS Combined with Packet Concatenation*, 2014 IEEE International Conference on Communications (ICC), 2014; IEEE; pp. 466–471..
13. Aswale, S.; Ghorpade, V. R. LQEAR: Link Quality and Energy-Aware Routing for Wireless Multimedia Sensor Networks. *Wireless Pers. Commun.* **2017**, *97* (1), 1291–1304.
14. Smail, O.; Cousin, B.; Mekki, R.; Mekkakia, Z. `A Multipath Energy Conserving Routing Protocol for Wireless Ad Hoc Networks Lifetime Improvement. *EURASIP J. Wireless Commun. Netw.* **2014**, *2014*, 139.
15. Mafirabadza, C.; Makausi, T.; Khatri, P. In *Efficient Power Aware AODV Routing Protocol in MANET*, International Conference on Advances in Information Communication Technology & Computing; ACM: Bikaner, India, 2016.
16. Deepa, J.; Sutha, J. A New Energy based Power Aware Routing Method for MANETs. *Cluster Comput.* **2019**, *22*, 13317–13324.

17. Singal, G.; Laxmi, V.; Gaur, M. S.; Lal, C. In *LSMRP: Link Stability based Multicast Routing Protocol in MANETs*, 2014 IEEE Seventh International Conference on Contemporary Computing, 2014; pp. 254–259.
18. Malwe, S. R.; Taneja, N.; Biswas, G. P. Enhancement of DSR and AODV Protocols using Link Availability Prediction. *Wireless Pers. Commun.* **2017,** *97* (3), 4451–4466.
19. Lin, Y.-W.; Huang, G.-T. In *Optimal Next Hop Selection for VANET Routing*, Proceedings of Seventh International ICST Conference on Communications and Networking in China (CHINACOM), 2012; pp. 611–615.
20. Kumar, R.; Rao, S. V. In *Directional Greedy Routing Protocol (DGRP) in Mobile Ad-Hoc Networks*, 2008 International Conference on Information Technology, pp. 183–188; 2008.
21. Goldsmith, A.; Chua, S.-G. Variable-Rate Variable-Power MQAM for Fading Channels. *IEEE Trans. Commun.* **1997,** *45* (10), 1218–1230.
22. Kalansuriya, P.; Tellambura, C.; Network, A. D. F. C. In *Performance Analysis of Decode-and-Forward Relay Network under Adaptive M-QAM*, Proceedings of Communications Society, 2009; pp. 3393–3399.
23. Ali, S.; Madani, S. A.; Khan, A. U. R.; Imran, A. K. Routing Protocols for Mobile Sensor Networks: Acomparative Study. *Comput. Syst. Sci. Eng.* **2014,** *29* (2), 183–192.
24. Otero, A. S.; Atiquzzaman, M. Adaptive Localized Active Route Maintenance Mechanism to Improve Performance of VoIP Over Ad Hoc Networks. **2011,** *J. Commun.* *6* (1), 68–78.
25. Yadav, A.; Singh, Y. N.; Singh, R. R. Improving Routing Performance in AODV with Link Prediction in Mobile Adhoc Networks. *Wireless Pers. Commun.* **2015,** *83*, 603–618.
26. Gujral, R. K.; Grover, J.; Rana, S. In *Impact of Transmission Range and Mobility on Routing Protocols over Ad Hoc Networks*, International Conference on Computing Sciences, 2012, pp. 201–206.
27. Suma, S.; Harsoor, B. Congestion Control Algorithms for Traffic and Resource Control in Wireless Sensor Networks. In *Advances in Decision Sciences, Image Processing, Security and Computer Vision. Learning and Analytics in Intelligent Systems*; Satapathy, S. C., Raju, K. S., Shyamala, K., Krishna, D. R., Favorskaya, M. N., Eds.; vol. 3; Springer: Cham, 2020.
28. Suma, S.; Harsoor, B. In *An Effective Congestion Control Approach through Route Delay Estimation Using Packet Loss in Wireless Sensor Network*, Proceedings of the Second International Conference on Emerging Trends in Science & Technologies for Engineering Systems (ICETSE-2019), May 17, 2019; SSRN: https://ssrn.com/abstract=3511452 or http://dx.doi.org/10.2139/ssrn.3511452
29. Suma, S., Harsoor, B. Congestion Control for Multihop Transmission in WSN using Contention Window. *Int. J. Adv. Sci. Tech.* **2020,** *29* (5), 13697–13603.
30. Aswale, S., Ghorpade, V. R. Geographic Multipath Routing based on Triangle Link Quality Metric with Minimum Inter-path Interference for Wireless Multimedia Sensor Networks, Journal of King Saud University – Computer and Information Sciences, *33*(1), 2021. https://www.sciencedirect.com/science/article/pii/S1319157817303920?via%3Dihub

CHAPTER 22

An Optimized Multi-Server Queuing Model for Transportation Problems

AMIT BHATNAGAR and ARVIND KUMAR SHUKLA

School of Computer Science & Applications, IFTM University, Moradabad, India

ABSTRACT

We provide a process to solve the real-time transportation problem which is basically related to the organization. For this, we use an optimized multi-server queuing model to find the optimum number of unloading and loading service centers and minimum total cost of the ready product. We provide the comparison graph that shows the optimized multi-server queuing model provides a better result instead of the existing model. In this manuscript, we make an attempt to achieve an effective and minimum cost of the ready product for the organization.

22.1 INTRODUCTION

Every organization wants to raise their bussiness but the cost of the product is a major problem; it should be minimum. In this paper, we make an effort to solve such a problem. We show the expected structure of organization in Figure 22.1. For this, first, we calculated product cost according to various

Computational Intelligence in Analytics and Information Systems, Volume 2: Advances in Digital Transformation, Selected Papers from CIAIS-2021. Parneeta Dhaliwal, PhD, Manpreet Kaur, PhD, Hardeo Kumar Thakur, PhD, Rajeev Kumar Arya, and Joan Lu (Eds.)

constraints within the organization. We know the best suitable probability distribution like logistic distribution, based on the inter-arrival time and service time for unloading and loading service centers. After that we used an optimized multi-server queuing model for calculating waiting cost and service cost of different numbers of unloading service centers and used an effective model for cost to find out waiting cost per vechicle and service cost per vechicle of the different number of unloading service centers. When we increse the number of service centers then cost is also increased. This is a major problem. Regarding such a problem, we calculated the total cost of a ready product on different numbers of unloading centers and then we find the optimum number of unloading service centers on which the total cost of the ready product is minimum. Again, we apply the same process for the loading service centers; we find the optimum number of loading service centers on which the total cost of ready product is minimum within the organization.

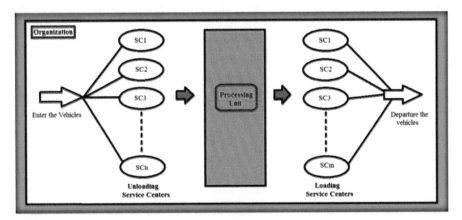

FIGURE 22.1   Expected structure of oraganization.

This Chapter deals with the following sections:

Section 22.2 explains about the methodology related to finding the optimum number of unloading and loading service centers and minimum cost of the ready product for the organization, finding will be disscussed in Section 22.3, and the final conclusion will be discussed in Section 22.4, Finally, Section 22.5 provided future work in this manuscript.

22.2 METHODOLOGY

In this chapter, research methodology is to analyze the data that is provided by the organization like inter-arrival time among the vehicles, services cost of the service centers, waiting cost as penalty, average number of vehicles in queue, average number of vehicles in waiting area, number of service centers, cost of product, etc based on the existing model. We find the total cost of the product and optimum number of loading and unloading service centers by using the optimized multi-server queuing model. For a comparative study and result verification we collected the data from an origination. This is as follows.

22.2.1 DETAILS FOR UNLOADING SERVICE CENTERS BASED ON EXISTING MODEL

According to the organization, the current length of the queue of vehicles is 50 and maximum waiting time for vehicles is 44 hrs and the service centers for unloading and loading are 2 each only. Every service center has 10 persons as labor. We have average queue length and average waiting time of the vehicles for unloading service centers using the model-I and also have unloading service center that serves 01 vehicle per 45 minutes.

Mean arrival rate = 04 per 60 minutes
Mean service rate = 01 per 45 minutes

TABLE 22.1   Given Avg. Queue Length and Average Waiting Time by the Organization.

Number of unloading service center	Queue of vehicles in system (L_s) (approx.)	Average queue length (L_q) (approx.)	Average waiting time (W_q)
2	42	40	28.50

TABLE 22.2   Calculated Service Cost and Total Cost of Ready Products per Day.

Number of unloading service centers	Labor cost	Penalty cost for waiting of vehicle	Electricity cost	Total service cost	Total cost of ready products before loading per day
2	6000	47,520.00	42	53,562.00	36,53,562.00

We show the average waiting time by the organization in Table 22.1 and also show total cost of ready products per day before loading in Table 22.2.

By the existing model, minimum total cost of ready product before unloading service is 11.1488 Rs with 02 unloading service centers.

22.2.2 DETAILS FOR LOADING SERVICE CENTERS BASED ON EXISTING MODEL

According to the organization, the current length of the queue of vehicles is 50 and maximum waiting time for vehicles is 40 hrs. We have average queue length and average waiting time of the vehicles for unloading service centers. The loading service center serves 02 vehicles per 60 minutes.

    Mean arrival rate = 04 per 45 minutes

    Mean service rate = 02 per 60 minutes

TABLE 22.3   Given Avg. Queue Length and Average Waiting Time by the Organization.

Number of loading service center	Queue of vehicles in system (L_s) (approx.)	Average queue length (L_q) (approx.)	Average waiting time (W_q)
2	44	36	25.50

TABLE 22.4   Calculated Service Cost and Total Cost of Ready Products per Day.

Number of loading service centers	Labor cost	Penalty cost for waiting of vehicle	Electricity cost	Total service cost	Total cost of ready products per day
2	6000	42,628.00	42	48,670.00	36, 48,670.00

We show the average waiting time for loading by the organization in Table 22.3 and also show total cost of ready products per day in Table 22.4. By the existing model, the minimum total cost of a ready product is 11.1351 Rs with 02 loading service centers.

22.3 PROPOSED MODEL

In this manuscript, we write the detail provided by the organization based on the existing model and then we used optimized multi-server queuing model (Model-I) to find the number of vehicles in queue, waiting time of vehicles in queue, optimum number of service centers, and total cost of ready product.

22.3.1 OPTIMIZED MULTI-SERVER QUEUING MODEL (MODEL-I)

The following formulae of model-I is used for finding the length of queue and average waiting time in the queue:

$$P_0 = \left[\sum_{n=0}^{(c-1)} \frac{(\lambda)^n (\mu)^{-n}}{n!} + \frac{(\lambda)^c (\mu)^{-c}}{c!} + \frac{c\mu}{(c\mu - \lambda)} \right]^{-1} \qquad (22.1)$$

$$L_s = \left[\frac{(\lambda)^{(1+c)} (\mu)^{(1-c)}}{(c-1)! \cdot (c\mu - \lambda)} P_0 + (\lambda)^1 \cdot (\mu)^{-1} \right] \qquad (22.2)$$

$$L_q = \left[L_s - (\lambda)^1 \cdot (\mu)^{-1} \right] \qquad (22.3)$$

$$W_q = \left[\frac{(\lambda)^c (\mu)^{1-c}}{(c-1)! \cdot (c\mu - \lambda)^2} \cdot P_0 \right] \qquad (22.4)$$

22.3.1.1 FOR UNLOADING SERVICE CENTERS

According to the organization, the current length of the queue of vehicles is 50 and maximum waiting time for vehicles is 44 hrs and the service centers for unloading and loading are 2 each only. The average waiting time of vehicles into the organization for unloading is 25.53 hrs. We calculated average queue length and average waiting time of the vehicles for unloading service centers using the multi-server queuing model formulae. We considered each unloading service center that serves 01 vehicle per 50 minutes.

Mean arrival rate = 2/3 per 50 minutes
Mean service rate = 01 per 50 minutes

TABLE 22.5 Calculated Avg. Queue Length and Average Waiting Time using Model-I.

Number of unloading service centers	P_0	Queue of vehicles in system (Ls) (approx.)	Average queue length (L_q) (approx.)	Average waiting time (W_q)
3	0.1738	45	44	22.50
4	0.1326	19	17	8.5
5	0.1123	10	08	4.6
6	0.0823	06	04	2.7
7	0.0712	04	02	1.12
8	0.0632	03	01	0.64

If the number of unloading service centers will increase then the cost of the product will also increase and the profit will be decreased. So we selected best number of unloading service centers according to the minimum total cost of the product. We can show the calculated average waiting time in Table 22.5. We calculated waiting cost as penalty to the organization because the waiting time problem is a concern to the organization, not for transportation company (TC). TC decided 4 Rs per ton if the waiting time of the vehicle is more than 2.5 hrs, otherwise 0 Rs and maximum weight of raw material on the vehicle is 12 ton only. We used the following formula of an effective model for cost:

- Waiting cost per vehicle for number of unloading service centers = waiting time × weight of raw material × penalty.

TABLE 22.6   Calculated Waiting Cost Per Vehicle with Different Numbers of Unloading Service Centers.

Number of unloading service centers	Waiting cost per vehicle (in Rs)
3	1080.00
4	408.00
5	220.80
6	129.60
7	00
8	00

Again, we calculated the service cost of the product according to the different number of unloading service centers. The rate of raw material of product is 18 Rs per kg. We show the waiting cost per vehicle for unloading in Table 22.6.

$$\text{Number of ready product per day} = \left(\frac{\text{Total raw material}}{\text{material required per product}} \right)$$

$$\frac{18 \times 500 \times 50 \times 1000}{1250}$$

$$= 3.60,000 \text{ pieces}$$

We considered unloading centers with 03 persons labor to provide the service at each service center. Every vehicle has the 500 packets of raw material and each person carries only one packet at a time and the weight of a single packet is 50 kg. We used the following formulae:

- Labor cost = number of centers × one person per day cost × number of persons at each center
- Penalty cost for waiting of vehicle = waiting cost of vehicle for service centers × number of vehicles in queue
- Electricity cost = Total power unit consumption per day of service centers × rate of per unit
- Error margin = 1000 Rs
- Total service cost = Labor cost + penalty cost for waiting of vehicle + electricity cost + error margin
- Total cost of ready product before loading service per day = Number of ready products per day × processing cost + service cost

TABLE 22.7 Calculated Service Cost and Total Cost of Ready Products per Day.

Number of unloading service centers	Labor cost	Penalty cost for waiting of vehicle	Electricity cost	Total service cost	Total cost of ready products before loading per day
3	2700	47,520.00	63	51,283.00	36,51,283.00
4	3600	6,936.00	84	11,620.00	36,11,620.00
5	4500	1,766.40	105	7,371.40	36,07,371.40
→6	5400	518.40	126	6,584.40	36,06,584.40
7	6300	00	147	7447	3,607,447.00
8	7200	00	168	8368	36,08,368.00

$$\text{Cost of ready product} = \frac{36,06,584.40}{3,60,000}$$
$$= 10.0182 \text{ Rs}$$

By using model-I, the minimum total cost of ready product before loading service is 10.0182 Rs with 06 unloading service centers. So, the optimum number of unloading service centers is 06.

22.3.1.2 FOR LOADING SERVICE CENTERS

Again, we used model-I to find number of vehicles in queue in loading service centers and also calculated waiting time of vehicles in queue. According to the organization, the current length of queue of vehicles is 50 and maximum waiting time for vehicles is 40 hrs and the service centers for loading are 2 only. Average waiting time of vehicles into the organization for loading is 20.22 hrs. We calculated the average queue length and the average waiting time of the vehicles within the organization with different numbers of loading service centers using the model-I formulae. We considered each loading service center serves 01 vehicle per 06 minutes.

Mean arrival rate = 1/2 per 60 minutes
Mean service rate = 01 per 60 minutes

TABLE 22.8 Calculated Avg. Queue Length and Avg. Waiting Time using Model-I.

Number of loading service centers	Probability (P_0)	Queue of vehicles in system (L_s) (approx.)	Average queue length (L_q) (approx.)	Average waiting time (W_q)
3	0.2314	38	36	18.6
4	0.1734	14	12	6.3
5	0.1268	09	07	3.8
6	0.0868	07	05	2.3
7	0.0613	05	03	1.45
8	0.0542	03	01	0.67

We selected best number of loading service centers according to the minimum total cost of product and also calculated waiting cost as penalty to the organization because the waiting time problem is a concern to the organization, not for transportation company (TC). We show the average waiting time in Table 22.8. TC decided 4 Rs per ton if the waiting time of the vehicle is more than 2.5 hrs, otherwise 0 Rs, and maximum weight of raw material on the vehicle is 12 ton only. We used the following formula of an effective model for cost:

- Waiting cost per vehicle for number of loading service centers = waiting time × weight of raw material × penalty

TABLE 22.9 Calculated Waiting Cost Per Vehicle with Different Numbers of Loading Service Centers.

Number of loading service centers	Waiting cost per vehicle (in Rs)
3	892.80
4	302.40
5	177.60
6	134.40
7	00
8	00

Again, we calculated the service cost of the product according to the different number of loading service centers. We show the waiting cost per vehicle for loading in Table 22.9.

The rate of raw material of the product is 18 Rs per kg. We considered loading center with 03 persons to provide the service at each loading service center. Every vehicle could be loaded 500 carton of ready product and each person carries only one carton at a time and the weight of a single carton is 30 kg.

(i) Labor cost = number of service centers × one person per day cost × number of persons at each center

(ii) Penalty cost for waiting of vehicle = waiting cost of vehicle for service centers × number of vehicles in queue

(iii) Electricity cost = Total power unit consumption per day of service centers × rate of per unit

(iv) Error margin =1000 Rs

(v) Total loading Service Cost = Labor cost + Penalty cost for waiting of vehicle + Electricity cost + Error Margin

(vi) Total cost of ready product = Number of ready products per day × processing cost + service cost

TABLE 22.10 Calculated Service Cost and Total Cost of Ready Products per Day.

Number of loading service centers	Labor cost	Penalty cost for waiting of vehicle	Electricity cost	Total service cost	Total cost of ready products per day
3	2700	32,140.80	63	35,903.80	36,35,903.80
4	3600	3,628.80	84	8312.80	36,08,312.80
→5	4500	1243.20	105	6848.20	36,06,848.20
6	5400	672.00	126	7198.00	36,07,198.00
7	6300	00	147	7447.00	36,07,447.00
8	7200	00	168	8368.00	36,08,368.00

$$\text{Cost of ready product} = \frac{36,06,848.20}{3,60,000}$$

$$= 10.0190 \text{ Rs}$$

By using model-I, the minimum total cost of a ready product is 10.0190 Rs with 05 loading service centers. So, the optimum number of loading service centers is 05. So, the optimum number of loading service centers is 05 in Table 10.

22.4   RESULT AND DISCUSSIONS

Figure 22.2 shows that the optimized multi-server queuing model provides an optimum number of unloading service centers with minimum total minimum cost of ready product.

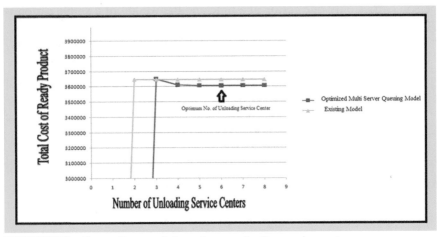

FIGURE 22.2   Comparison graph for optimum unloading service centers.

- By using model-I, the minimum total cost of a ready product before loading service is 10.0182 Rs with 06 unloading service centers.
- By the existing model, the minimum total cost of a ready product before loading service is 11.1488 Rs with 02 unloading service centers.

According to the above, our optimum multi-server queuing model provides approximately 11 percent better results on the comparison of the existing model for unloading service centers. Figure 22.3 shows that the optimized multi-server queuing model provides an optimum number of loading service centers with a minimum total minimum cost of a ready product.

- By using model-I, the minimum total cost of a ready product is 10.0190 Rs with 05 loading service centers.
- By the existing model, the minimum total cost of a ready product is 11.1351 Rs with 02 loading service centers.

According to the above, our optimum multi-server queuing model provides approximately 11 percent better results on the comparison of the existing model for loading service centers.

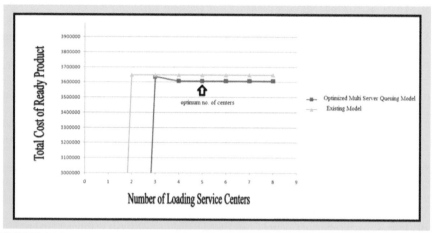

FIGURE 22.3   Comparison graph for optimum loading service centers.

22.5   CONCLUSION

In this paper, we used the optimized multi-server queuing model to achieve the optimum number of unloading and loading service centers and minimum total cost of the ready product. The comparison graphs show that the optimized multi-server queuing model provides a better result instead of the existing model. So we used 06 unloading and 05 loading service centers to achieve the minimum cost of a ready product within the organization.

KEYWORDS

- **multi-server queuing model**
- **queues**
- **waiting time**
- **service cost**

REFERENCES

1. Cooper, R. B. Queues with Ordered Servers that Work at Different Rates. *Opsearch* **1976**, *13*, 69–78.
2. Cooper R. B. *Basicintroduction to Queuing Theory*; North-Holland: New York, 1981.

3. Trivedi K. S. *Probability and Statistics with Queuing, Reliability and Computer Science application*; Duke University: North Carolina, Prentice Hall of India: New Delhi, 1998.
4. Diaz, J. A.; Perez, I. G. In Optimization and Simulation of Sugarcane Transportation in Season of Harvest, *Proceedings of Winter Simulation Conference*, 2000.
5. Morabito, R.; Morales, S. R.; Widmer, J. A. Loading Optimization of Palletized the Products on Trucks. *Transport. Res.*
6. Hawwa, M. A.; Menon, A. Airflow Assisted Ramp Loading And Unloading of Sliders in Hard Disk Drives, United States Patent, 2002.
7. Goodchild, A. V.; Daganzo, C. F. Double Cycling Strategies for Container Ships and Effect on Ship both Loading and Unloading Operations. *Transp. Sci.* **2006**, *40* (4), 473–483.
8. Montazer, A. A.; Mishra, D. P. A Single Server Poission Queuing Systems with Delayed Service. *Int. J. Oper. Res.* **2008**, *3*.
9. Zeng, Q.; Yang Z. Integrating Optimization and Simulation to Schedule Loading Operations in Container Terminals. *Comput. Oper. Res.* **2009**, *36*, 1935–1944.
10. Jose, K. Application of Control Chart Based Reliability Analysis in Progress Industries. *IJMET* **2012**, *3* (1).
11. Dachyar, M. Simulation and Optimization of Services at Port in Indonesia. *Int. J. Adv. Sci. Technol.* **2012**, *44*.
12. Saxena, A. Rescheduling of Railways Timetable based on Circulation Scheme. *Int. J. Appl. Math.* Sci. **2013**, *6*.

CHAPTER 23

Forming the Cluster in the RFID Network for Improving the Efficiency and Investigation of the Unkind Attacks

M. THURAI PANDIAN[1] and P. DAMODHARAN[2]

[1]Department of Computer Science and Technology, Manav Rachna University, Faridabad, India

[2]Department of Computer Engineering, Marwadi University, Rajkot, Gujarat

ABSTRACT

Security is a major issue of the present world. Radio frequency identification (RFID) is the strategy for following the vehicles utilizing intelligent transportation system and furthermore protection, medical and human identification. RFID innovation is utilized for following the moving or steady items. Minor RFID tags and the readers were taking an interest in tracking objects. In this paper, we learn about the different assaults and the clustering mechanism of the RFID framework. This paper will give the proposal to improve the security from the attacks and furthermore improve the presentation of the correspondence between the RFID Tags and the Readers.

23.1 INTRODUCTION

Radio frequency identification (RFID) innovation is quickest developing innovation. The RFID framework is anything but difficult to follow the moving or stable articles. The RFID framework is utilized for following the

Computational Intelligence in Analytics and Information Systems, Volume 2: Advances in Digital Transformation, Selected Papers from CIAIS-2021. Parneeta Dhaliwal, PhD, Manpreet Kaur, PhD, Hardeo Kumar Thakur, PhD, Rajeev Kumar Arya, and Joan Lu (Eds.)

vehicles, medicinal shop, Internet of Things, and so forth. These days use of RFID framework is expanded massively. America gave an announcement for securing their arms and powers utilizing the RFID-tracking framework.[1] Shanghai Grid Project will follow the moving vehicles utilizing RFID tag and Reader by the assistance of HERO (Hierarchical Exponential Region Organization) convention.[4] A large number of assaults are conceivable to break the RFID framework and the performance of the correspondence between the Tag and Reader is additionally influenced.[2,3] Clustering instrument is accustomed to improving the correspondence between the Tag and the Reader.[12] The clustering component is well appropriate for tracking frameworks. It is improving the exhibition of the quality correspondence. At the point when we are expanding the Readers, naturally the presentation of the tag and reader's correspondence will get diminished. To beat this issue the clustering component is utilized. Every one of the hubs is gathered with the cluster head. The bunch head will convey to the servers and with one another.

Semi-passive tags are utilized for Indoor Positioning framework (IPS) to recognize the places of the articles.[5] The Kalman Filtering Algorithm is guaranteed for the indoor positioning system.[7] The IPS framework may likewise be influenced by the infection assault impact.[6] In this paper we depict the investigation of the RFID innovation and working standards, assault notice and proposed a strategy to improve the nature of the correspondence between the tag and the reader.

23.1.1 SURVEYING ON RFID

RFID tag assumes the significant job of the RFID framework. Each RFID tag has its one of a kind id, which conveys the data about the item. Where the tag has been fixed, the RFID tag discharges the radio frequency signal. This sign contains the data of the articles. RFID semi-passive tag's radio frequency distance is 46 m.[8]

Semi-passive tag's range is little in case of contrasted and dynamic tag. Its range is 1 meter.[9] These sorts of tags are intelligent or bar controlled. Dynamic tag's range is huge in case of contrasted and semi-passive tag. Its range is 300 meter.[9] These tags are transmitting the sign utilizing microchip circuit. It is communicating the sign to all readers. Semi-passive tags work when the power is off. This tag has inner memory as read just and read compose.

23.1.2 WORKING PRINCIPLES

The RFID tag and the reader are utilized for confinement and following. The tag contains the data, where it is secure inside the item. The reader gets the sign and calculates the Received Signal Strength (RSS) which is discharged by the tag. Every one of the readers is communicated with the server. The server has the conveyed database and stores the data in the database.

The RSS is estimated as dbm (represented by 1 MW).[9] We can send the reader as known spots and they got the RSS from the tag. The reader screens intermittently by sending the parcels. The tags discharged the sign consistently. At the point when the tags enter the scope of the readers it produces the sign. This sign contains the data of the items. At the point when the readers read the sign, it sends back to the server and the server answers back as an acknowledgment to the reader.

Figure 23.1 itemizes the working approach of the RFID framework. This kind of framework has not been verified. The assailant may effortlessly break the framework. In the event that the middle of the road can follow the correspondence of the tag and the reader, the all-out framework will be influenced. T1, T2, T3, and Tn are the tags and R1, R2, Rn is the reader.

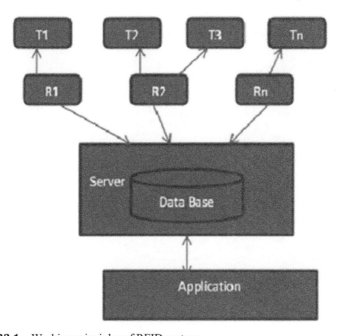

FIGURE 23.1 Working principles of RFID system.

The LAND MARK framework[10] contains two kinds of tags, reference tags and the tracking tag. Reference tags are utilized uniquely for finding the tag. However, the tracking tags will follow the article where it is found and revealed.

23.2 RELATED WORKS

The Shanghai Grid venture was produced for following the vehicles utilizing smart transportation framework. The HERO convention[4] assumes the significant job of that venture. The RFID readers are sent in the overlay structure. In the overlay structure they are conveyed in the genuine street system and every one of the hubs is comprehended by their neighbors. The HERO composes the reader in the chain of command association structures. Figure 23.2 portrays that there are 3 regions R1, R2, and R3. The outer circle consists of region R1. The middle circle consists of R2 region. The inner circle consists of region R3. R1 is the inward district and it contains some neighborhood hubs in it. The following R2 is the center district. Moreover, it covers the inward district hubs. R3 is the external region; it has part of hubs in the external district. It covers the internal and center regional hubs.

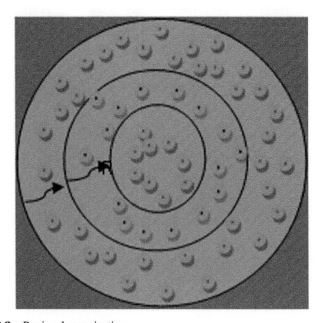

FIGURE 23.2   Regional organization.

At the point when the vehicles are moving inside their district, the area is refreshed and it includes just in the little arrangement of hubs. At the point when the vehicles are moving from R1 to R2, the area refreshing is stretched out to center locale. At the point when the vehicles are moving to external district the area data is refreshed to the internal and center locale.

At the point when we need to follow the vehicle, simply infuse the question to the specific reader. The reader reads the question and is steered to the closeby hubs to the specific vehicles areas and returna legitimately to the hub. This venture covers just the Shanghai city. Be that as it may, we need to develop the framework the unpredictability at high and the exhibition of the correspondence among reader and tag is exceptionally low. This undertaking is appropriate just for the restricted topographical territory. Be that as it may, in the enormous scale RFID framework[12] we can include progressively number of readers. The huge scale RFID framework utilizes bunch idea for diminishing the multifaceted nature and improving the exhibition between the tag and the reader's correspondence.

23.3 ATTACK NOTIFICATION

Various assortments of RFID assaults are conceivable such as spying, snooping, swapping assault, and questionable tag. The aggressor can effectively take on the appearance of another by distorting information and consequently increasing an ill-conceived advantage.

23.3.1 RFID ATTACKS

The RFID attacks[13-17] are advised beneath.

23.3.1.1 BASIC RFID ATTACKS

23.3.1.1.1 Tag/Reader Damage

By the regular cataclysms or by the human the tag can be broken. At the point when the tag has broken the correspondence between the tag and readers would detach.

23.3.1.1.2   Duplicate tag

The assailant may copy the tag rather than the legitimate one. When the tag is copied the bogus data will be refreshed in the server.

23.3.1.1.3   Impersonate Tag

The aggressor may have inbuilt phony data in the tag. At the point this kind of tag would speak with the reader and give the phony data.

23.3.1.1.4   Security Attack

Someone can break the security calculation utilized in the RFID system and furthermore change the data that is put away in the server.

23.3.1.2   SKIMMING ATTACK

The radio beneficiary identifies and peruses the radio signs received from the labels, which are far away from the transmitter. On the off chance that the transmission way is not ensured appropriately, there is an opportunity of getting to the RFID tag by the unapproved clients. The attacker may use their own RFID reader and examine the tags by using the lacking and insufficient communication strength to read the tags. Regardless of whether the labels are ensured, the traffic investigation devices are used to anticipate the label reactions. The joining and breaking down cycle of information can be used in the field of social associations, monetary exchanges, and picture developments. The abuse of the traffic investigation may cause a straight effect on security.

23.3.1.3   DESYNCHRONIZATION ATTACK

There should be some mystery data that is known by the tag just and not the others utilized for verifying a tag. Utilizing this mystery data, the tag can register an extraordinary reaction and show its verification to the reader. At the framework arrangement time, rundown of aliases is created for each tag. These qualities are additionally put away at the back-end worker, and partner with the tag ID. The tag can answer with the following pen name to every reader's inquiry and the reader will coordinate with the information base to locate the genuine tag ID. In any case, issues emerge when a tag leaves the nom de plumes. Regularly, it might require some investment before this occurs, yet the assailant can dispatch a desynchronization assault by questioning the tag over and again. Since the label will consistently answer with the following nom de plumes, sort of assault will influence the tag out of synchronization with the reader. Ultimately, the label will debilitate every one of its nom de plumes the reader cannot validate this tag any longer. Henceforth, a desynchronization assault can prompt a DoS assault.

23.3.1.4 SPOOFING ATTACK

The interloper can trick the RFID framework by the caricaturing substantial tags and change the tag's personality for acquiring the undetected preferred position. At the point when the shrewd tags are not appropriately ensured, a product bundle called RFdump will run on the individual advanced help and PC has permitted the client to peruse and compose the assignment. This product permits the interlopers to overwrite on the current RFID tag data with caricature information. The attacker may change the RFID tag data, for example, while purchasing the costly products attacker may change the RFID sticker price as less expensive.

23.3.1.5 RELAY ATTACK

RFID is particularly powerless against hand-off assault. This is one of the incredible assaults and requires no cryptographic information to dispatch such an assault. The assailant who does this assault will go about as a tag to confirm and record the test sent from the reader. The aggressor comes up short on the mystery data that is needed to figure a right reaction to the test; it should locate an authentic tag as the assault target. At the point when an assault target shows up, this test is handed off to the objective by the assailant and the substantial reaction from the objective is sent back to the reader. At last the aggressor can swindle the reader from accepting that it reader a genuine tag yet it was the assailant really.

23.3.1.6   MIDDLE MAN ATTACK

A middleman attack puts her between a tag and a reader, interfacing them as a center man where typically the reader's signal reach cannot reach to the tag. This implies all the correspondences between the tag and the reader need to experience the attacker. The attacker may adaptively supplant, trade, and postpone the correspondence content. This may require some cryptographic information. The middle man attack has adequately desynchronized this tag creating a DoS to the tag temporary, which prompts tag location.

23.3.2   SERVER FAULT

In the RFID framework the server and the database will assume the significant job for backend work. In the event that the server may get the shortcoming and the deficiencies resistance is limit its server will goes defective condition because of server issue. The unapproved tag is perceived and prompts to transmit the phony transmission. The time restricted designation convention[11] will include with the reader during the legitimate inquiry exchange.

Sending the inquiry demand rub, we can check the server. On the off chance that the server won't react inside the timespan, the reader will speak with their neighbors by communicating the message.

23.3.3   FORMING THE GROUP AND CLUSTER HEAD

The huge scale RFID framework[12] utilizes the cluster idea for improving the system productivity. The huge scale RFID framework pursues the organized conditions. The space division technique is pursued for organization of readers.

Figure 23.3 details the clustering mechanism of the RFID network. In the specific region of gathering, readers are grouped. These readers can speak with one another inside the group. Each group has the group head (CH). The group head is chosen by their vitality levels. The hub that has high vitality level is chosen by the group head. The hub-to-hub correspondence between the clusters by the group head as it were. At the point when the hub needs to send the data to the next group the cluster head will take the reaction to send the data between clusters. The cluster head can transmit the data to the next group head. The cluster head will discuss the data with their group's hub.

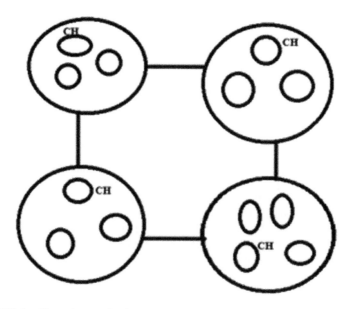

FIGURE 23.3   Clustering mechanism.

23.4   CONCLUSION

In this paper we have a little investigation of the RFID framework and its working standards. Additionally, the potential assaults are point by point and the impacts of the assaults are reviewed. This article is proposing a technique as a grouping component for improving the correspondence between the tag and the readers and for diminishing the multifaceted nature of the enormous RFID frameworks. We finish up this examination paper that will help the future research and improve the RID framework interchanges.

KEYWORDS

- **RFID**
- **attack**
- **security**
- **cluster**
- **objects**

REFERENCES

1. Li, Y.; Ding, X. In *Protecting RFID Communications in Supply Chains*, ASIACCS '07: Proceedings Of The 2nd ACM Symposium On Information, Computer And Communications Security, March 2007; Singapore; 2007; pp. 234–241.
2. Zuo, Y. Survivable RFID Systems: Issues, Challenges, and Techniques. *IEEE Trans. Syst. Man. Cybern. C Appl. Rev.* **2010**, *40* (4), 406–418.
3. Zuo, Y. Survivability Experiment and Attack Characterization for RFID. *IEEE Trans. Depend. Sec. Comput.* **2012**, *9* (2), 289–302.
4. Zhu, H.; Zhu, Y.; Li, M. HERO: Online Real-Time Vehicle Tracking. *IEEE Trans. Parallel Distrib. Syst.* **2009**, *20*, 740–752.
5. Saad, S. S.; Nakad, Z. S. A Standalone RFID Indoor Positioning System Using Passive Tags. *IEEE Trans. Indus. Electron.* **2011**, *58*, 1961–1970.
6. Rieback, M.; Crispo, B.; Tanenbaum, A. In *Is Your Cat Infected with a Computer Virus? Fourth Annual IEEE International Conference on Pervasive Computing and Communications (PERCOM'06)*, Mar. 2006; pp. 179–189.
7. Sarkka, S.; Viikari, V. V.; Huusko, M.; Jaakkola, K. Phase-based UHF RFID Tracking with Nonlinear Kalman Filtering and Smoothing. *IEEE Sens. J.* **2012**, *12* (5), 904–910.
8. Ilie-Zudor, E.; Kemeny, Z.; Egri, P.; Monostori, L. *The Rfid Technology and its Currents Applications*; Computer and Automation Research Institute, Hungarian Academy of Science Kend u.13-17,1111: Budapest.
9. Ni, L. M.; Zhang, D.; Souryal, M. R. RFID-based Localization and Tracking Technologies. *IEEE Wirel. Commun.* **2011**, *18* (2), 45–51.
10. Nietal, L. M. In *LANDMARC: Indoor Location Sensing Using Active RFID, Proceedings of the First IEEE International Conference on Pervasive Computing and Communications, 2003. (PerCom 2003)*, 2003; pp. 407–415.
11. Molnar, D.; Soppera, A.; Wagner, D. A Scalable, Delegable Pseudonym Protocol Enabling Ownership Transfer of RFID Tags. *Lecture Notes Comput. Sci.* **2006**, *3897*, 276–290.
12. ThuraiPandian, M.; Sukumar, R. RFID: Enhanced Performance Using Clustering Mechanism in Large Scale RFID System. *Transylv. Rev.* **2016**, *24* (10).
13. ThuraiPandian, M.; Sukumar, R. In *RFID: An Appraisal of Malevolent Attacks on RFID Security System and its Resurgence*, IEEE International Conference in MOOC, Innovation and Technology in Education (MITE), 2013.
14. Ai, X.; Chen, H.; Lin, K.; Wang, Z.; Yu, J. Nowhere to Hide: Efficiently Identifying Probabilistic Cloning Attacks in Large-Scale RFID Systems. *IEEE Trans. Inf. Forensics. Secur.* **2020**, *16*, 714–727.
15. Lounis, K.; Zulkernine, M. Attacks and Defenses in Short-Range Wireless Technologies for IoT. *IEEE Access* **2020**, *8*, 88892–88932.
16. Zhao, B. Q.; Wang, H. M.; Liu, P. Safeguarding RFID Wireless Communication Against Proactive Eavesdropping. *IEEE Int. Things J.* **2020**, *7* (12), 11587–11600.
17. Wang, G.; Cai, H.; Qian, C.; Han, J.; Shi, S.; Li, X.; Ding, H.; Xi, W.; Zhao, J. Hu-Fu: Replay-Resilient RFID Authentication. *IEEE/ACM Transac. Network.* **2020**, *28* (2), 547–560.

CHAPTER 24

Traffic-Aware Quality of Service Routing in SDIoT Using Ant Colony Optimization Algorithm

DHARAMENDRA CHOUHAN, L. KAVYASHREE, P. K. UDAYAPRASAD, J. SHREYAS, N. N. SRINIDHI, and DILIP KUMAR S. M.

Department of Computer Science and Engineering, University Visvesvaraya College of Engineering, Bangalore, India

ABSTRACT

Internet of Things (IoT) is a network of smart objects connected over the Internet. With the rapid reduction in the cost of sensors and the availability of high-speed wireless connectivity, there is an extensive increase in the usage of IoT devices. With a high incoming of data from billions of IoT devices, there is an increasing demand on the current Internet infrastructure. An optimized routing technique is required to cater to the quality-of-service (QoS) demands of the existing and future applications in the IoT network. Designing a traffic-aware QoS routing scheme has become a major challenge in the Software-Defined Internet of Things (SDIoT) network. Many works have been proposed addressing the delay-sensitive and loss-sensitive flow-based QoS routing in the IoT network. Due to the increase in usage of real-time applications such as video conferencing, video surveillance, health care, jitter has to be considered in addition to delay and packet loss. This paper proposes an ant-inspired traffic-aware quality of service routing scheme for the SDIoT network. Simulation of the proposed solution is done

Computational Intelligence in Analytics and Information Systems, Volume 2: Advances in Digital Transformation, Selected Papers from CIAIS-2021. Parneeta Dhaliwal, PhD, Manpreet Kaur, PhD, Hardeo Kumar Thakur, PhD, Rajeev Kumar Arya, and Joan Lu (Eds.)

in MATLAB and the proposed solution is found to reduce the end-to-end delay by 5%, jitter by 4%, and packet loss by 7%.

24.1   INTRODUCTION

IoT is a network of smart heterogeneous objects connected over the Internet.[1] Routing plays a major role in any network as it traverses data from source to destination. Since billions of IoT devices are getting added to the network, the best effort transmission mechanism designed for the current network does not guarantee the various applications' QoS requirements in the future. An optimized routing technique is required to cater to the QoS demands of the existing and future applications in the IoT network.

The Software-Defined Networking (SDN)[2] approach abstracts the control logic from network devices, enabling simplified network management with a centralized SDN controller. The programmable SDN controller has the overall view of the network which improves QoS by reducing traffic interference. The drawback of the existing solutions that used SDN for QoS Management was that it focused mainly on particular applications such as video streaming.[3] The selection of a single metric or a linear combination of different QoS metrics failed to satisfy individual QoS requirements.[4]

Recent developments on SDN in QoS routing management have utilized the flow-based SDN nature to fulfill the QoS requirements such as delay-sensitive (ds) and loss-sensitive (ls) for ingress traffic from end-devices within the network.[5] But, with the rapid increase in real-time applications in IoT networks, jitter is also an important parameter to be considered in QoS routing.

Jitter is the inter-arrival time between the packets and it influences the viewing or hearing quality of services at the receiver. This paper considers jitter sensitive (js) flows, besides delay-sensitive (ds) and loss-sensitive (ls) flows in the IoT network. This approach differs from the other works in two angles. First, it uses the programmable feature of SDN to route IoT traffic using Ant-inspired K shortest path algorithm and QoS-based path selection to find the optimal forwarding path for application-centric requirements, i.e., delay-sensitive, loss-sensitive, or jitter-sensitive. Second, the impact of SDN rule-capacity on QoS routing is taken into consideration in this work.

The main idea of the Ant Colony Optimization (ACO)[6] algorithm is to mimic the cooperative behavior of ants to find the shortest path from their colony to the food source and vice versa. This artificial intelligence technology is implemented to identify the shortest path in the proposed work.

The contributions of the work include:

(1) A software-defined network architecture with a centralized controller is proposed to manage network devices at a single point.
(2) A traffic-aware QoS routing method is proposed by splitting the flows into the delay, packet loss, and jitter sensitive.
(3) The proposed work integrates the Ant Colony Optimization algorithm to get the QoS-based routing path.

24.2 LITERATURE SURVEY

Recent studies show the advantages of flexible centralized Software Defined Network in IoT. Tang et al.[7] proposed a novel deep learning approach for load prediction and assigning the partially overlapped channel to maximize the channel utilization in SDN-IoT. A convolution neural network is used to train the model in a centralized control system for periodic and bursty IoT traffic and for allocating the channel with less interference. This approach showed better results compared to the conventional approach in terms of throughput, packet loss, and when there is an increase in the number of nodes. The QoS requirement of flows is not taken into consideration while allocating the channel.

A recent research trend shows that using bio-inspired artificial intelligent algorithms in the IoT network achieves notable results in QoS routing. Janabi et al.[8] proposed a centralized routing protocol using SDN for I-IoT to decrease the power consumption of IoT devices and to increase the lifespan of the network. AI-based particle swarm optimization and genetic algorithms are used to achieve energy-efficient routing in the I-IoT network. The results prove that the proposed work increases the lifespan of the network with reduced delay in I-IoT. Other QoS parameters such as throughput, jitter, etc. constrained are not considered in the proposal.

Verma et al.[9] proposed an ant clustering technique to find optimal path routing in wireless networks. The clustering technique is used to handle a huge amount of data on large-scale networks. The combination of clustering and ACO has achieved a higher probability of finding the optimum path with a high coverage rate. The results show that individual QoS parameters are used to enhance performance. The capabilities of the SDN controller can be explored with the proposed technique to achieve higher performance to meet QoS requirements.

Sendra et al.[10] implemented the use of an intelligent algorithm using reinforcement learning for distributed routing in SDN. They have considered QoS parameters such as delay, jitter, and packet loss for routing. This scheme is compared with the traditional OSPF routing method. The proposed method shows a better result compared to the traditional method. The main disadvantage is the rule capacity constraint is not considered for switches.

Jing et al.[11] proposed the novel method that is the combination of both genetic algorithm and ant colony for routing in a power communication network using SDN. The proposed scheme takes the advantage of both algorithms to find the best path efficiently with minimum execution time. While finding the best path parameters like delay, link utilization is not considered.

24.3   PROBLEM STATEMENT AND OBJECTIVES

The problem considered in the proposed work is to formulate a novel routing paradigm for SDIoT by finding the best path by reducing the delay, packet loss, and jitter to fulfill application-dependent QoS requirements for each flow with a minimal hop count. To accomplish the research goal the following are the objectives set forth.

(1) To deploy a topology with higher diversity of communication links in IoT networks using MATLAB integrated development environment.

(2) To assign priorities to delay, jitter, and loss-sensitive flows depending on the requirement. This can be achieved by specifying the number of flows to be processed for each flow type in an iteration.

(3) To design an efficient QoS routing scheme for a Software-Defined IoT network to find a path with allowable delay, loss, and jitter, along with rule capacity constraint.

(4) To improve the Quality of Service for each flow depending on the application-dependent requirements.

24.4   SYSTEM MODELS

24.4.1   ARCHITECTURE

We are considering the ubiquitous connectivity model for the proposed work where IoT devices are part of the Internet. This model contains a different type of resource constraint networks. They are connected to the Internet via IoT gateways using the hybrid communication architecture. For load balancing on the core network and bringing processing close to the end devices, IoT gateways and SDN-enabled switches are used as fog nodes. Considering the SDN network as graph $Gp = (Sw, Lk)$ where Sw denotes switches and $Lk = \{(a, b) \mid (a, b) \subset S \times S, a \neq b\}$ link between two switches a and b. Open flow Application Programming Interfaces (API) are used for communication between SDN controllers and switches and northbound APIs are between the application layer and controllers.

24.4.2 ROUTING METRIC SELECTION

Mathematically the flow is represented as

$$F = \{f_k \mid k \in N\}, f_k = (s_k, t_k, \theta_k, q_k) \qquad (24.1)$$

where S_k is the source, t_k is the destination, q_k is the QoS demand, and sk θ_k is the type of flow—either delay, loss, or jitter.

Consideration of multiple metrics affects the complexity of QoS routing. So we are considering multiple single metrics to achieve QoS routing. For a given network, each link $(a,b) \in L$, has its own associated QoS metric like delay, packet loss, jitter, and bandwidth. Delay is an additive metric, and delay for a path can be

$$d_p = d(a,b) + d(c,d) + \ldots + d(i,j) \qquad (24.2)$$

and the packet success rate can be calculated by

$$l_p = l(a,b) + l(c,d) + \ldots + l(i,j) \qquad (24.3)$$

where the success rate of each link is calculated by $l(a,b) = log(1-pl(a,b))$. where $pl(a, b)$ is the probability of each link's packet loss. The jitter is the difference between delays between two packets and the jitter of the path can be

$$j_p = j(a,b) + j(c,d) + \ldots + j(i,j) \qquad (24.4)$$

The available bandwidth can be calculated by

$$c_p = min\{c(a,b), c(c,d), \ldots, c(i,j)\} \qquad (24.5)$$

The residual bandwidth is the remaining bandwidth within the link after all the flows f_k are routed. It is given as

$$c_{res}(a,b) = c(a,b) - \sum_{f_k \in F} q_k^{bandwidth} x_k(a,b) \qquad (24.6)$$

for any path $p = \{a, b, c,..., i, j\}$. Consideration of multiple single metrics offers better performance compared to single-metric-based solutions. The programmatic reconfiguration capability of SDN can be used to separate multiple flows based on QoS requirements and on the type of traffic that can process in parallel.

Each open flow switch has TCAM (Ternary Content Addressable Memory) which allows fast lookup on multiple fields, with high power consumption. The total number of rules inserted is restricted by TCAM. Active links are chosen over the inactive link to minimize energy consumption. When the number of rules exceeds in a switch, the inactive link is activated and thus increasing the power consumption.

24.5   IMPLEMENTATION

24.5.1   ALGORITHM FOR ANT-INSPIRED TRAFFIC-AWARE ROUTING

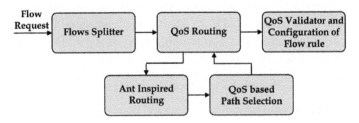

FIGURE 24.1   Proposed controller architecture.

The proposed controller architecture is given in Fig. 24.1. The Flow Splitter module splits the incoming flows into Delay/Loss/Jitter flows and provides to the corresponding flow processor to find the route for the flow. The QoS routing module uses the ant-inspired pathfinder to find the K shortest path and from that, it finds the path that satisfies the QoS conditions specified in the flow request and gives the best path as a reply. The QoS validator module verifies if the route satisfies the Delay/Loss/Jitter QoS conditions specified in the flow request and configures the flow rule. After the flow is routed with the best path, the rule capacity constraint and bandwidth are updated.

To Algorithm 24.1 network scenario is given as input with allowable delay, loss, and jitter of each link, with a batch of flows. The priority for each type of flow can be defined by the user. The input flows are handled in a round-robin fashion to give equal opportunity to each type of flow.

Algorithm 24.1: QoS Route computation algorithm for delay(dsf), loss(lsf) and jitter (jtf) flows

Inputs:

Directed Graph, Gp

A batch of flows Fl with their corresponding specifications for QoS

Maximum rules can be inserted at a switch- Rm

C1←delay-sensitive flow priority, C2←loss-sensitive flow priority, and C3←jitter sensitive flow priority

Output:

QoS satisfied path on which each flow can be routed

1: for each switch k in Graph Gp

2: Initialize maximum rule-capacity

3: while all Flows are not processed do

   //For dsf, lsf and jtf, round robin scheduling is used for fair distribution

4: if dsf not routed then

5: for a ← 1 to C1 do

6: QoSsatisfiedpath ← getPath(source,destination,demand,delay-sensitive)

7: if lsf not routed then

8: for b ← 1 to C2 do

9: QoSsatisfiedpath ← getPath(source,destination,demand, loss-sensitive)

10: if jtf not routed then

11: for c ← 1 to C3 do

12: QoSsatisfiedpath ← getPath(source,destination,demand, jitter-sensitive)

function getPath(src, targ, QoSdemand, flowtype)

13: if flowtype = dsf then

14: for each path in Ant Inspired K shortest path(src, targ, fd) do

15: if ValidateQoS (path, QoSdemand) then

16: QoSsatisfiedpath ← path

17: else if flowtype = lsf then

18: for each path in Ant Inspired K shortest path (src, targ, fl) do

19: if ValidateQoS (path, QoSdemand) then

20: Qossatisfiedpath ← path

21: else if flowtype = jtf then

22: for each path in Ant Inspired K shortest path (src, targ, fj) do

23: if ValidateQoS (path, QoSdemand) then

24: QoSsatisfiedpath ← path

25: return QoSsatisfiedpath

26: function ValidateQoS (path, demand)

27: if(Delay and Loss And Jitter is less than the demand and satisfies Bandwidth and satisfies Rule Capacity) then

28: return 1

29: return 0

The main idea of the ACO technique is to mimic the cooperative behavior of ants to find the shortest path from their colony to the food source and vice versa. Initially, many forager ants start from the colony to find food. Each ant leaves a quantity of pheromone while reaching the food. The ant finding the best path returns to the colony leaving a higher level pheromone quantity than other ants. Thus, other ants follow a path with a higher pheromone value to find food.

In the proposed method artificial ant agents are used in identifying the path from the source switch to the destination switch in an SDN network as it has a global view of the network. Here, the ant colony is the source switch and the food source is the destination switch. The type of flow determines the value to be considered for visibility. Minimum value of delay, packet loss, or jitter that are stored in SDN gives higher visibility.

Tabu search uses the short-term memory to avoid the ant to choose the switch that is already visited. By using the tabu search method in the proposed work, it can avoid the creation of cycles while searching for the path from the source switch to the destination switch. If the artificial ant finds the path to the destination switch the pheromone concentration matrix is updated for the path, otherwise not. From the second iteration onward probability is considered for choosing the next neighboring node. After a constant number of iterations for m number of ants, the K number of shortest paths can be drawn from the pheromone concentration matrix depending upon the type of flow.

24.6   EXPERIMENTAL SETUP AND PERFORMANCE ANALYSIS

24.6.1   SETTINGS FOR SIMULATION

The proposed work is simulated using the MATLAB platform. All studies were performed on an Intel® CoreTM i5 CPU PC, 2.60 GHz processors, and 8 GB of RAM. As tabulated in Table 24.1, different simulation parameters are considered. The Goodnet and AttMpls network topology from the Internet Topology Zoo[12] is used for simulation.

TABLE 24.1   Parameters Considered for Simulation.

Parameter	Value
Topology	Goodnet, Attmpls
Number of switches	17, 25
Number of links	31, 56
Bandwidth	1 kpbs–10 kpbs
Delay of a flow	1–50 ms
Packet loss	0–30%
Jitter of flow	1–30 ms

24.6.2   PERFORMANCE EVALUATION

To compare the performance of the ant-inspired K shortest path algorithm, the following performance metric is used: End-to-end delay, packet loss ratio.

(1) Average delay: The average delay is calculated by considering the delay value of all the flows. The maximum number of optimal routing is achieved by alternating the flows as delay, packet loss, and jitter flows. Indirectly, the total QoS violated flows and the number of hop counts are related to the delay. The proposed algorithm tries to minimize the QoS violated flows with a minimum number of hop counts. The figure depicts that the proposed algorithm performs better than the Sway by reducing the delay by 5%. The below figure (Fig. 24.2a and 24.2b) shows the comparisons. The X-axis represents the number of flows considered and the Y-axis is the average delay.

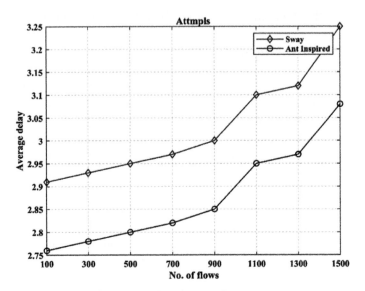

FIGURE 24.2 A   Average delay comparison in Attmpls.

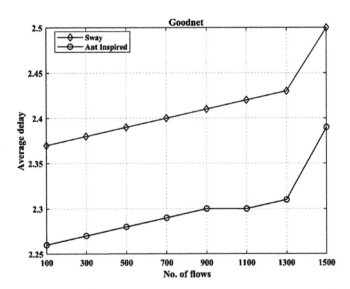

FIGURE 24.2 B   Average delay comparison in Goodnet.

(2) Average packet loss: The average packet loss is calculated by considering the packet loss of all the flows. The proposed scheme tries to find the optimum path having less packet loss probability. The figure

depicts that the proposed algorithm performs better than the Sway by reducing the packet loss by 7%. The below figures (Fig. 24.3a and 24.3b) show the comparisons. The X-axis represents the number of flows considered and the Y-axis is the average packet loss.

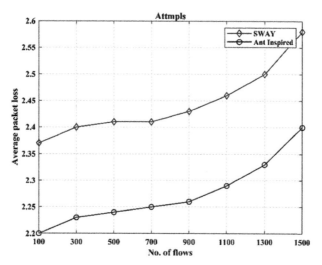

FIGURE 24.3A   Average packet loss in Attmpls.

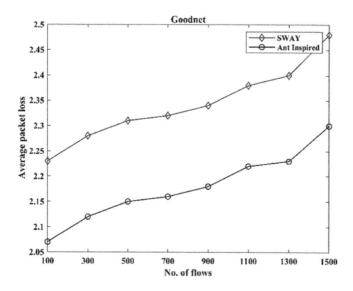

FIGURE 24.3B   Average packet loss in Goodnet.

(3) Average jitter: The average jitter is calculated by considering the jitter of all the flows. The total QoS-violated flows and the number of hop counts are proportional to the jitter. The proposed algorithm tries to minimize the QoS-violated flows with a minimum number of hop counts. The figure (Fig. 24.4) depicts that the proposed algorithm performs better than the Sway by reducing the jitter by 4%. The X-axis represents the number of flows considered and the Y-axis is the average jitter.

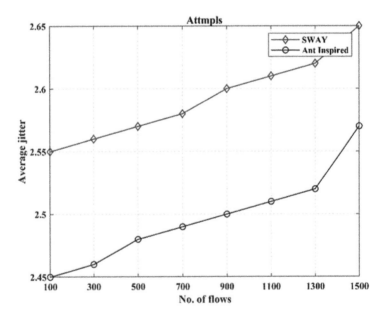

FIGURE 24.4   Average jitter in Attmpls.

24.7   CONCLUSION

In the software-defined IoT network, we proposed an ant-inspired traffic-aware QoS routing strategy, taking into account the different QoS requirements of heterogeneous flows such as delay, loss, or jitter sensitive. The proposed work uses a meta-heuristic approach to find the shortest path using an Ant inspired algorithm to find the best possible routing path. Overall network performance is maximized with minimum resource utilization by dealing with delay-sensitive, loss-sensitive, and jitter-sensitive flows.

Ant-inspired K shortest path routing and QoS-based path selection is employed to find the optimal path satisfying the application-specific QoS requirements. Simulation of the proposed solution is done in MATLAB and the proposed solution is found to reduce the end-to-end delay and percentage of flows violating the QoS constraints. Comparing the existing solutions, the proposed solution can satisfy all three types of flows and reduce the number of QoS violations.

KEYWORDS

- **software-defined networking (SDN)**
- **internet of things (IoT)**
- **quality-of-service (QoS)**
- **ant colony optimization (ACO)**

REFERENCES

1. Shreyas, J.; Jumnal, A.; Kumar, S.; Venugopal, K. Application of Computational Intelligence Techniques for Internet of Things: An Extensive Survey. *Int. J. Comput. Intell. Stud.* **2020,** *9* (3), 234.
2. McKeown, N.; Anderson, T.; Balakrishnan, H.; Parulkar, G.; Peterson, L.; Rexford, J.; Shenker, S.; Turner, J. Openflow. *ACM SIGCOMM Comput. Commun. Rev.* **2008,** *38* (2), 69–74.
3. Shreyas, J.; Singh, H.; Bhutani, J.; Pandit, S.; Srinidhi, N. N.; D. Kumar S. M. In *Congestion Aware Algorithm using Fuzzy Logic to Find an Optimal Routing Path for IoT Networks*, 2019 International Conference on Computational Intelligence and Knowledge Economy (ICCIKE), 201, pp. 141–145.
4. Wang, Z.; Crowcroft, J. Quality-of-Service Routing for Supporting Multimedia Applications. *IEEE J. Select. Areas Commun.* **1996,** *14* (7), 1228–1234.
5. Saha, N.; Bera, S.; Misra, S. Sway: Traffic-Aware Qos Routing in Software-Defined IoT. *IEEE Trans. Emer. Topics Comput.* **2021,** *9* (1), 390–401.
6. Pei, Y.; Wang, W.; Zhang, S. In *Basic Ant Colony Optimization*, 2012 International Conference on Computer Science and Electronics Engineering, 2012.
7. Tang, F.; Fadlullah, Z.; Mao, B.; Kato, N. An Intelligent Traffic Load Prediction-based Adaptive Channel Assignment Algorithm in SDN-Iot: A Deep Learning Approach. *IEEE Int. Things J.* **2018,** *5* (6), 5141–5154.
8. Al-Janabi, T.; Al-Raweshidy, H. A Centralized Routing Protocol with a Scheduled Mobile Sink-Based AI For Large Scale I-Iot. *IEEE Sens. J.* **2018,** *18* (24), 10248–10261.
9. Verma, A.; Vashist, P. In *Enhanced Clustering Ant Colony Routing Algorithm Based on Swarm Intelligence in Wireless Sensor Network*, 2015 International Conference on Advances in Computer Engineering and Applications, 2015.

10. Sendra, S.; Rego, A.; Lloret, J.; Jimenez, J.; Romero, O. In *Including Artificial Intelligence in a Routing Protocol Using Software Defined Networks*, 2017 IEEE International Conference on Communications Workshops (ICC Workshops), 2017.

11. Jing, S.; Muqing, W.; Yong, B.; Min, Z. In *An Improved GAC Routing Algorithm Based on SDN*, 2017 3rd IEEE International Conference on Computer and Communications (ICCC), 2017.

12. Knight, S.; Nguyen, H.; Falkner, N.; Bowden, R.; Roughan, M. The Internet Topology Zoo. *IEEE J. Select. Areas Commun.* **2011,** *29* (9), 1765–1775.

CHAPTER 25

ML-BBFT: ML-Based Bonding-Based Forwarding Technique for Social OppIoT Networks

RITU NIGAM[1] and SATBIR JAIN[2]

[1]Division of Computer Engineering, University of Delhi (Netaji Subhas Institute of Technology), New Delhi, India

[2]Department of Computer Engineering, Netaji Subhas University of Technology, New Delhi, India

ABSTRACT

Message routing is a critical problem in the Social Opportunistic Internet of Things Networks (OppIoTs) because of the intermittent connection and nonexistent end-to-end path. Recently, much work has been done in machine learning (ML) and is now introduced as a tool to automate the message routing in the social opportunistic networks (SONs), which are similar in aspects to social OppIoTs. This paper utilized a feed-forward artificial neural network to improve an existing protocol named BBFT and proposed the ML-BBFT algorithm. Simulation results through ONE simulator demonstrate that the proposed ML-BBFT performs superior to MLProph and ProPhet on various performance metrics such as delivery probability, overhead ratio, average latency, and average buffer time.

Computational Intelligence in Analytics and Information Systems, Volume 2: Advances in Digital Transformation, Selected Papers from CIAIS-2021. Parneeta Dhaliwal, PhD, Manpreet Kaur, PhD, Hardeo Kumar Thakur, PhD, Rajeev Kumar Arya, and Joan Lu (Eds.)

25.1 INTRODUCTION

Social opportunistic IoT Networks (Social OppIoTs)[1] are a class of social opportunistic networks (SONs).[2] The OppIoTs are basically introduced to overcome the geographic boundaries of the IoT networks-based applications. The network infrastructure of social OppIoTs is distinct from conventional IoT networks; no end-to-end connection exists from the source to the destination node. Hence, devices incorporate the fundamental law, store-carry-forward, which means that nodes store the data packets in their buffer space. Whenever any node comes in their communication range, opportunistically forward the data to those nodes for successful data forwarding. Therefore, designing a routing protocol with a high message delivery rate suitable for intermittently connected and random infrastructure-based networks is challenging.[3,4] Researchers also observed that the data routing behavior of the social OppIoTs and SONs is similar that allows designing the same routing scheme to both the networks. More immediate works such as BBFT[5] and PeopleRank[6] have employed the concept of average separation period, and people rank centrality to advance routing decisions in the social OppNets. Few machine learning techniques-based routing protocols MLProph and KNNR routing protocols are designed to automate the routing-based decision-making in SONs.[7]

This paper introduces a new routing protocol called ML-BBFT for social OppIoTs to automate the routing decisions of the BBFT protocol. ML-BBFT uses a machine learning technique, the feed-forward artificial neural network (FNN), to train itself based on various node characteristics such as buffer space, hop count, energy, speed. Using former routing data, the FNN model is trained, which results in a formula that predicts the node's forwarding capability.

The remaining part of the paper is set up as follows. Section 25.2 discusses the literature review accomplished in routing in the Social OppIoTs. Section 25.3 explains the proposed ML-BBFT scheme; Section 25.4 presents the simulations and results. Finally, the conclusion part is discussed in Section 25.5.

25.2 LITERATURE REVIEW

Various message transmission schemes for OppIoTs have been introduced in recent times. The HBPR[8] protocol converted the network area into equal size of cells. The node's context information such as speed, home location, and movement direction are exploited to predict the future next-hop to improve the message forwarding. The PRoPHET[9] is a crucial protocol that applies the node's frequency of interaction and concept of transitivity. This combination measures a probabilistic assessment of whether forwarding the message to an appropriate next-hop will boost the delivery process. The MLProph[10] protocol applied MLP neural networks and decision trees using prophet probability and other context information of the nodes to make next-hop decisions intelligently. The KNNR protocol[11] employed the K-nearest neighbor classifier to propose a routing model. The proposed KNN model is trained on several significant node's characteristics to produce better routing. The BBFT protocol used the bonding metrics, which utilized the average detachment period and variance between any two network nodes. The direct and indirect bonding among the nodes is considered to select the best relay nodes for message forwarding in social OppNets. The NSRP protocol[12] employed the nature-inspired algorithm named NSGA-II for making optimal routing decisions in social OppNets. NSRP worked on multiple conflicting parameters such as average forwarding delay degree and the collaboration probability to obtain the nondominated solutions for message transmission.

25.3 PROPOSED WORK

25.3.1 SYSTEM MODEL

The proposed ML-BBFT protocol employs a feed-forward artificial neural network (FNN) to implement the routing in the social OppIoTs. Suppose a node has a message in its buffer, and a connection is established between the sender and neighbor nodes in the communication range. A decision is then required to decide relay nodes with high delivery probability among these neighbor nodes to directly or indirectly send the message to the target node. Frequent transmission of the message replicas may cause extreme packet loss and massive overhead. Contrarily, less frequent transmission leads to fewer delivered messages. There are various factors involved to enhance the probability of successful transmission based on the history and capability of nodes. In the proposed ML-BBFT approach, the relay node's determination is performed by a trained FNN model that includes the following node's characteristics: BBFT's direct bonding metrics, buffer occupancy, successful transmissions, success ratio, speed, energy, distance, and current hop count.

This trained FNN model computes the forwarding probability of the nodes called NN probability represented by Fm. Fm is compared with the Fr of the node, which is the direct bonding metric of the BBFT protocol. The sender node's message is only forwarded if Fm > Fr.

25.3.2   *FEED-FORWARD NEURAL NETWORK MODEL (FNN)*

This paper proposes a routing model that uses a feed-forward artificial neural network that works on multiple hidden layers. Many input parameters $(x_1, x_2, ..., x_{11})$ are assigned to the FNN model, which forms an input layer; an output layer contains the results p1 and p2, which are the probabilities of successful and unsuccessful message delivery. The p1 value represents the predicted probability of successful delivery based on given values of input parameters, called FNN probability Fm. In the FNN model, each node contains the predicted neural networks probability Fm value, a linear aggregate of node values in the previous layer called the feed-forward process. The value at node R_i is given as

$$R_i = A\left(\sum_{j=1}^{n} x_j \cdot w_{ji} \right) \tag{1}$$

$$h_1 = F\left(w_{11}x_1 + w_{21}x_2 + w_{31}x_3 + ... + w_{111}x_{11} \right) \tag{2}$$

where x_j is the value of the jth node of the previous layer, A is the activation function, and w is the weight matrix.

25.3.3   *ML-BBFT ALGORITHM*

Algorithm 25.1 ML-BBFT routing algorithm
1: Input: Initialization of the feed-forward neural network (FNN) in the network
2: Output: best relay nodes
3: Begin
4: Phase I: Initialization
5: initialize the hash map of all the nodes.
6: Calculate the direct bonding weight of each neighbor node of the sender node.

7: Create the new training dataset by performing a simulation on the training scenario.

8: Obtain the feature set F. $F = (x_1, x_2, ..., x_{11})$

9: Initialize the FNN on default settings.

10: Phase II: Build FNN

11: Call Build Neural Network for creating and training the FNN.

12: Calculate the message delivery rate for each message.

13: if Fm > Fr, then

14: Message is forwarded to the selected neighbor nodes.

15: else

16: discard the node.

17: end if

18: End

25.4 SIMULATION AND RESULTS

25.4.1 SIMULATION SETUP

The proposed ML-BBFT protocol is assessed on ONE simulator[13] against the MLProph and ProPhet forwarding protocols. For the training and deploying of the FNN-based learning model to implement ML-BBFT, the Weka ML library[14] is used. The simulation environment consists of different groups such as pedestrians, cars, and trams. The configuration of these groups is distinct in terms of node speed, a number of nodes, wait time, movement model, to name a few. A few parameters such as buffer size, time to live, transmit range, and transmit speed are typical for every group. Table 25.1 presents the main configuration settings.

TABLE 25.1 Default Simulation Parameters.

Value	Value
Total time of simulation	43200 s
Simulation area	43200 s
Message TTL	100 minutes
Total number of nodes	126

TABLE 25.1   *(Continued)*

Value	Value
Buffer space	10 MB
Message size	1 kB–5 MB
Transmission speed	250 kBps
Transmission range	10 m
Message generation interval	25–35 s
Range of speed	0:5–1:5 m/s

For training the ML model, data is generated using the default simulation settings of the BBFT protocol. After that, gathered data is used to train the FNN-based learning model with the help of the Weka library. As a result, the trained FNN model is then further used to build simulation settings that are compared against the other protocols. The buffer sizes of the node groups are varied from 40 MB, 60 MB, 80 MB, 100 MB to test the ML-BBFT protocol. The matrics considered for performance evaluation are: delivery probability, overhead ratio, average latency, and average buffer time.

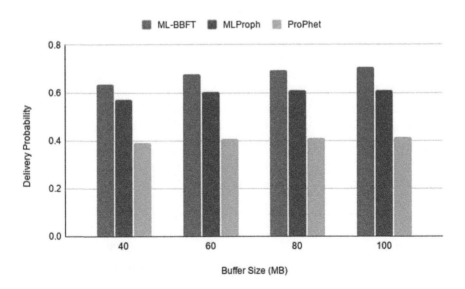

FIGURE 25.1   Buffer size vs. delivery probability.

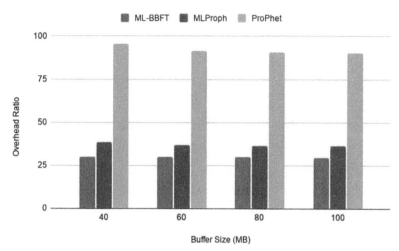

FIGURE 25.2   Buffer size vs. overhead ratio.

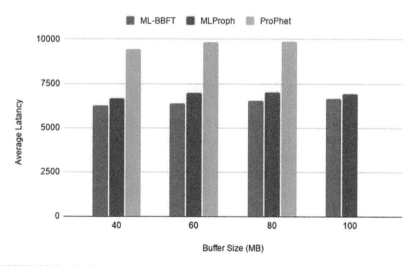

FIGURE 25.3   Buffer size vs. average latency.

25.4.2   RESULTS

This section discusses the results acquired through regressive simulations on the ML-BBFT protocol by utilizing the ONE simulator.

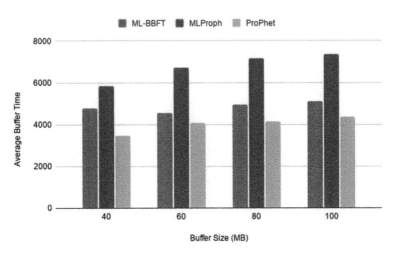

FIGURE 25.4   Buffer size vs. average buffer time.

25.4.2.1   *VARYING THE BUFFER SIZE*

When buffer size is increased steadily from 40 MB to 100 MB, the nodes' capacity to carry messages is profoundly enhanced, improving the message routing toward the target. Figure 25.1 illustrates the analogous progress in delivery probability with the evenly growing buffer size. As the ML-BBFT utilizes the FNN model, a rise in the buffer size increases smart next-hop selection, enhancing the message routing. The ML-BBFT protocol proves its supremacy in terms of the delivery probability over compared protocols. On average, the delivery probability of ML-BBFT is 67.43% and 13.29% higher than ProPhet, and MLProph, respectively.

Figure 25.2 represents the variation in overhead ratio with changing buffer sizes, and the overhead rate drops with growing buffer size. Overhead increases when the source nodes find more suitable next-hop nodes and quickly results in more replicas. The ML-BBFT protocol is significantly better than MLProph and ProPhet in terms of overhead ratio. Concurrently, ML-BBFT produces fewer message replicas that cause less overhead. The overhead ratio of ML-BBFT is 19.45% lower than MLProph and 67.64% lower than ProPhet.

Figure 25.3 depicts the increase in average latency as the buffer size is incremented. The ML-BBFT protocol managed the minimum average latency compared to ProPhet and MLProph. The intelligent routing decisions are made based on the FNN model, resulting in no more delayed message buffering, better delivery probability. The average latency of ML-BBFT is 6.36% and 33.55% lower than MLProph and ProPhet, respectively.

Figure 25.4 graphically shows that the proposed ML-BBFT protocol significantly performs better than MLProph but performs lower than the ProPhet. The average buffer time of ML-BBFT is 28.49% lower than MLProph and 20.65% higher than Prophet, respectively.

25.5 CONCLUSION AND FUTURE WORK

In ML-BBFT work, a neural network model is used to perform intelligent forwarding in social OppIoT networks. The simulations' results illustrate that the ML-BBFT is superior over MLProph and ProPhet with respect to the discussed metrics. In the future, we will use real mobility traces to simulate ML-BBFT; other ML classifiers such as SVM will be explored to make the opportunistic routing efficient.

KEYWORDS

- **machine learning**
- **feed-forward artificial neural network**
- **social OppIoTs**
- **BBFT**
- **internet of things (IoT)**

REFERENCES

1. Guo, B.; Zhang, D.; Wang, Z.; Yu, Z.; Zhou, X. Opportunistic IoT: Exploring the Harmonious Interaction between Human and the Internet of Things. *J. Network Comput. Appl.* **2013,** *36* (6), 1531–1539.
2. Guan, P.; Wu, J. Effective Data Communication based on Social Community in Social Opportunistic Networks. *IEEE Access* **2019,** *7,* 12405–12414.
3. Radenkovic, M.; Grundy, A. In *Congestion Aware Forwarding in Delay Tolerant and Social Opportunistic Networks*, 2011 Eighth International Conference on Wireless On-Demand Network Systems and Services, IEEE, 2011; pp. 60–67.
4. Singh, A.; Mahapatra, S. Network-based Applications of Multimedia Big Data Computing in IoT Environment. In *Multimedia Big Data Computing for IoT Applications*; Springer, 2020; pp. 435–452.

5. Nigam, R.; Sharma, D. K.; Jain, S.; Gupta, S.; Ghosh, S. Bonding based Technique for Message Forwarding in Social Opportunistic Network. *Scalable Comput. Practice Exp.* **2019,** *20* (1), 1–15.

6. Mtibaa, A.; May, M.; Diot, C.; Ammar, M. In *Peoplerank: Social Opportunistic Forwarding*, 2010 Proceedings IEEE INFOCOM, IEEE, 2010; pp. 1–5.

7. Cuka, M.; Elmazi, D.; Bylykbashi, K.; Spaho, E.; Ikeda, M.; Barolli, L. Implementation and Performance Evaluation of Two Fuzzy-Based Systems for Selection of IoT Devices in Opportunistic Networks. *J. Ambient Intell. Humaniz. Comput.* **2019,** *10* (2), 519–529.

8. Dhurandher, S. K.; Sharma, D. K.; Woungang, I.; Bhati, S. In *Hbpr: History based Prediction for Routing in Infrastructure-Less Opportunistic Networks*, IEEE 27th International Conference on Advanced Information Networking and Applications (AINA), IEEE, 2013; pp. 931–936.

9. Lindgren, A.; Doria, A.; Schelen, O. Probabilistic Routing in Intermittently Connected Networks. *ACM SIGMOBILE Mobile Comput. Commun. Rev.* **2003,** *7* (3), 19–20.

10. Sharma, D. K.; Dhurandher, S. K.; Woungang, I.; Srivastava, R. K.; Mohananey, A.; Rodrigues, J. J. A Machine Learning-based Protocol for Efficient Routing in Opportunistic Networks. *IEEE Syst. J.* **2016,** *12* (3), 2207–2213.

11. Sharma, D. K.; Sharma, A.; Kumar, J.; et al. In *Knnr: K-Nearest Neighbour Classification based Routing Protocol for Opportunistic Networks*, 2017 Tenth International Conference on Contemporary Computing (IC3), IEEE, 2017; pp. 1–6.

12. Nigam, R.; Sharma, D. K.; Jain, S. Routing Protocol based on Nsga-Ii for Social Opportunistic Networks. In *Data Analytics and Management*; Springer, 2021; pp. 489–496.

13. Keranen, A.; Ott, J.; Karkkainen, T. *The One Simulator for DTN Protocol Evaluation*, Proceedings of the 2nd International Conference on Simulation Tools and Techniques, 2009; pp. 1–10.

14. Holmes, G.; Donkin, A.; Witten, I. H. In *Weka: A Machine Learning Workbench*, Proceedings of ANZIIS'94-Australian New Zealand Intelligent Information Systems Conference, IEEE; 1994; pp. 357–361.

15. Kukreja, D.; et al. GASER: Genetic Algorithm-based Secure and Energy Aware Routing Protocol for Sparse Mobile Ad Hoc Networks. *Int. J. Adv. Intell. Paradig.* **2019,** *13* (1-2), 230–259.

16. Sharma, D. K.; et al. Supernode Routing: A Grid-based Message Passing Scheme for Sparse Opportunistic Networks. *J. Ambient Intell. Humaniz. Comput.* **2019,** *10* (4), 1307–1324.

CHAPTER 26

Eff-MANet: A Systematic Approach for Feature Extraction in Unstructured Road Scene Scenarios

ANAMIKA MAURYA and SATISH CHAND

School of Computer and Systems Sciences, Jawaharlal Nehru University, New Delhi, India

ABSTRACT

The most popular convolutional neural networks (CNNs) centered encoder–decoder architecture captures several redundant and analogous low-level features at various layers and various scales. Also, these architectures are not able to model long-range dependencies efficiently. This results in nonoptimal representations of discriminative features related to every semantic class in the final segmented outputs. In this paper, for the unstructured driving scenario, we suggest a new approach by using a global and a local context block on high-level features for capturing global and multi-scale contextual knowledge, respectively. Thereafter, we use a channel-wise attention block to weigh multi-scale higher-level features. This strategy enhances the feature representation of specific semantic by improving channel dependencies. Experimental results evaluate that our proposed approach achieves 0.756 mIoU and 0.846 dice score on the validation set of the India Driving Lite Dataset (IDD Lite) and proves its superiority over other state-of-the-art approaches including Eff-UNet, winner of NCVPRIPG 2019 competition.

Computational Intelligence in Analytics and Information Systems, Volume 2: Advances in Digital Transformation, Selected Papers from CIAIS-2021. Parneeta Dhaliwal, PhD, Manpreet Kaur, PhD, Hardeo Kumar Thakur, PhD, Rajeev Kumar Arya, and Joan Lu (Eds.)

26.1   INTRODUCTION

In computer vision, road scene segmentation is critical for various applications, namely, autonomous driving, lane detection, and pedestrian detection, etc. With the rapid advancement of automatic driving systems, a steady and authentic road scene analysis gets fundamental for a protected driving surrounding. The deep learning-centered semantic segmentation seems the finest solution since it is adequately robust in investigating the complex driving surroundings.

Recently, the encoder–decoder-based architectures are famous for segmentation. The encoder is normally a classification architecture, such as VGGNet,[1] ResNets,[2] DenseNet,[3] etc. It contains a series of convolutional and pooling operations to encode the information. However, these operations significantly condense the meticulous spatial knowledge which is vital for segmentation tasks. To address this issue, the decoder is considered to recuperate the lost spatial information by utilizing the multiple up-sampling processes with skip-connections. Some works have improved the representation power of these architectures by utilizing multi-scale features.[4-6] In[4] a subregion average pooling method is proposed to capture features at multiple scales. Another approach has exploited dilated convolutions at different rates for producing contextual multi-scale information.[6] These methods assist in capturing features at a different range in the image.

On the other hand, attention-based techniques have been broadly studied in deep learning for several computer vision tasks. The important benefits of the attention module are that it not only helps the model to emphasize the most relevant features but also improves the representation of features that are advantageous for a particular problem. Semantic segmentation also benefitted from attention modules and produced improved models for pixel-wise recognition tasks.[7-9]

In this research paper, we suggest a novel approach named Efficient Multiple-scale Attention Network (Eff-MANet) for semantic segmentation of unstructured road scenario which systematically incorporates global and local context knowledge together along with the attention mechanism in a single framework. The newly proposed approach performs better for the IDD Lite[10] dataset than Eff-UNet[11] and other existing approaches in terms of mIoU and dice score. The remainder of the research paper is prepared as follows: Different CNN-related segmentation approaches are reviewed in Section 26.2. Our newly proposed approach is discussed in Section 26.3.

Next, segmentation results are discussed along with dataset and implementation details. Lastly, there is a conclusion in Section 26.5.

26.2 RELATED WORKS

Fully convolutional networks (FCNs)[12] based strategies have gained incredible advancement in semantic segmentation. But these methods produce coarsely segmented outputs. To overcome this drawback, encoder–decoder-type architecture was proposed where the pooled indices from the encoder along with an up-sampling process are used to get segmented maps.[13] But these indices do not keep spatial information. To further boost the accuracy, the feature representations from various convolutional layers of the encoder have been used to get final prediction maps.[14] These are simple yet effective methods. There are a few model variations[4-6,15] proposed to upgrade the context information as it plays an important role in scene understanding. For example, a pyramid pooling method was suggested in[4] to gather contextual data of various scales. Another interesting approach named atrous spatial pyramid pooling (ASPP) based on atrous convolution was introduced to implant contextual knowledge where dilated convolutions are used at different rates.[6] Although these approaches are very effective, they cannot define the relationship between different objects which is also vital for segmentation.

Second, the attention mechanisms that have great capability to select relevant features and to filter undesired information are being successfully involved in various computer vision tasks. This mechanism shows the greater capability to capture long-range dependencies with more accuracy. PSANet connects the local features with others and aggregates long-range contextual knowledge in an adaptive manner with the help of a self-attention module.[7] In[16] a different attention selection mechanism is used to fill the void of a grouping of lower-level and higher-level features. DANet[9] incorporates both local and global features by using two different attention mechanisms. Specifically, they have used two different position and channel attention blocks on the top of the ResNet-50 model to explore the connections in the spatial and channel dimensions. But it did not incorporate multi-scale features. In[17] a global attention method and a spatial pyramid pooling method are exploited to extract accurate dense features. Eff-UNet[11] has used pretrained EfficientNet architecture as the encoder for feature extraction with UNet decoder for the reconstruction of segmented maps for unstructured road images. But this model did not pay attention to multi-scale information. All the above-discussed strategies have not systematically studied global and local multi-scale knowledge with an attention mechanism in a single architecture specifically for unstructured road scene scenarios. In this research paper, we suggest an approach that uses a global context block for global knowledge, an ASPP block for multi-scale knowledge, and a channel-attention block for unstructured road scenarios.

26.3   PROPOSED METHOD

In this section, we will discuss the proposed encoder–decoder-type framework for road scene segmentation. The whole framework can be viewed in Figure 26.1. Generally, the encoder module comprises a CNN that is utilized for learning the different feature representations from the given input. For the encoder part, we have used the layers of a pretrained EfficientNet B4[18] model that outperforms the existing state-of-the-art models. Next, the features of the last layer are used as input to the global context block and the modified ASPP block. Both outputs are then combined and fed to the channel-wise attention block.

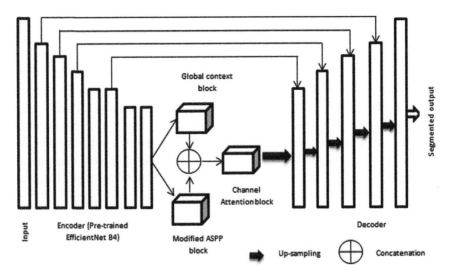

FIGURE 26.1   The newly proposed approach for unstructured road scene segmentation.

From here decoder part starts its working process. The decoder comprises several upsampling layers that help to recover the spatial information during the downsampling of the image. In our research work, we use similar decoder architecture as used in the UNet[14] neural network designed for biomedical image segmentation.

26.3.1 MODIFIED ASPP

Since road scene images exhibit various objects in different sizes, shapes, and positions, multi-contextual knowledge becomes very important in semantic segmentation. An atrous convolution-based ASPP approach that properly encodes multi-contextual information has shown impressive results in this regard.[6] We modify the ASPP approach by introducing 1 × 1 convolution to decrease the channel dimension of the final layer of EfficientNet B4[18] before applying atrous convolution with various dilation rates set at 3, 6, 12, and 18. After the atrous convolutions, all the features are concatenated and again followed by 1 × 1 convolution for dimension reduction as shown in Figure 26.2.

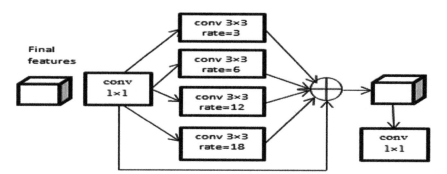

FIGURE 26.2   Modified ASPP block for catching multiple-scale information with different dilation rates.

26.3.2 GLOBAL CONTEXT BLOCK

This block is utilized to specify the spatial or position dependencies of the feature maps that are very important for global context information. We have adopted the global context module proposed in[17] with a little modification by using the sigmoid function instead of softmax as shown in Figure 26.3.

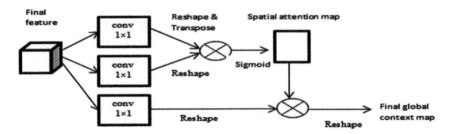

FIGURE 26.3   Global context block with a sigmoid activation function.

First, to decrease the channel dimension of the last layer of EfficientNet B4, a 1×1 convolution operation is applied and three copies (K, L, M) are generated and reshaped into (H × W, C). One copy (K) is transposed and further multiplied by the other copy (L). Thereafter, the resultant feature map is fed to the sigmoid activation function for producing the final spatial attention map. Last, it is multiplied by the M to obtain a weighted feature map by global spatial interdependencies and reshaped to the original size (H × W × C).

26.3.3   CHANNEL-WISE ATTENTION BLOCK

Since we know that the different channels of any features give different semantic responses, that is, "what" is meaningful information, we employ a similar channel-wise attention block suggested in[19] to assign a large weight to that channel which provides the better semantic meanings. The arrangement of this block is illustrated in Figure 26.4.

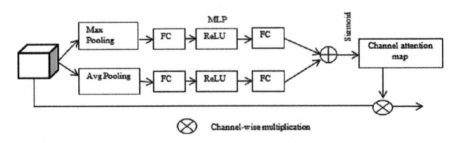

FIGURE 26.4   The structure of channel-wise attention block.

For this block, we use multi-scale learned features from the modified ASPP module as an input. To efficiently compute channel-based attention, we employ average and max-pooling to get different spatial contextual descriptors, that is, D_{avg} and D_{max} respectively. Both descriptors are then fed separately as an input to a multilayer perceptron (MLP) having only one hidden layer to obtain two different channel-wise attention maps. We then merge both attention maps using element-wise summation followed by sigmoid activation function (θ) to produce the final channel attention vector (V_{cam}). This activation function is utilized to get a flatten output with a score value between 0 and 1 signifying the importance of a particular region in the image. Shortly, we can formulate the above method as in eq 26.1:

$$V_{cam} = \theta(W_i\left(W_h\left(D_{avg}\right)\right) + (W_i\left(W_h\left(D_{max}\right)\right)) \tag{26.1}$$

where $W_h \in R^{C/r, C}$ and $W_i \in R^{C, C/r}$ are the shared weight of the hidden and input layers of the MLP. Besides, we apply channel-wise multiplication between multi-scale features and V_{cam} to explore channel dependency that has been proved important for segmentation tasks.

26.4 RESULTS AND DISCUSSION

To the finest of our information, India driving dataset (IDD)[20] is the primary dataset for unstructured driving scenarios, especially in Asian countries. It contains images of less sophisticated road networks in urban and rural driving environments. The IDD Lite dataset,[10] a subsampled variant of IDD, was used in the semantic segmentation online challenge of the 7th NCVP-RIPG in 2019 in India. IDD Lite is a small-scale segmentation dataset with a resolution of 320 × 227 and 7 labels. It contains 1404 training, 204 validation, and 408 testing road scene images with 7 different classes: drivable, non-drivable, road side objects, living things, cars, sky, and far objects. The proposed architecture is designed in Tensorflow 2.0. For 12 epochs of the training process, 320 × 224 size images are used with a batch estimate of 8. The previously learned weights of EfficientNet B4 are finetuned according to the IDD Lite dataset. Since training data is very small, we used heavy augmentation techniques such as rotation, flip, brightness, contrast, shear, to avoid overfitting. The learning rate is fixed to 0.0001 for the Adam optimizer. The efficacy of our proposed approach is dignified by mean Intersection over Union (mIoU) or Jaccard Index (JI) and Dice score (DS). We have used a summation of binary cross-entropy and JI as a function of loss. For a single class, IoU and DC can be formulated with the help of true positive (TP) pixel, false positive (FP) pixel, and false negative (FN) pixel as in eqs 26.2 and 26.3 respectively:

$$IoU = \frac{TP}{TP + FN + FP} \tag{26.2}$$

$$DS = \frac{2TP}{2TP + FN + FP} \tag{26.3}$$

It is evident from Table 26.1 that the performance of the newly proposed approach is superior to other state-of-the-art models including Eff-UNet,[11] UNet,[14] DeepLabV3.[6] All the approaches are trained on the IDD Lite dataset. For the validation set, Eff-MANet achieves 0.756 mIoU and 0.846 dice-score which are the highest among other tested approaches.

TABLE 26.1   Results Evaluation in Terms of mIoU and Dice Score on IDD Lite Validation Dataset.

Method	mIoU	Dice score
DeepLabV3[6]	0.603	0.710
UNet[14]	0.654	0.763
Eff-UNet[11]	0.729	0.804
Eff-MANet (ours)	0.756	0.846

Other methods such as UNet[14] extracted features through only downsampling layers and did not consider multiscale context information that was very crucial for complex images such as road scenes. DeepLabV3[6] has considered the ASPP module to capture different scaled objects. But because of the lack of some fine details, the segmented maps have false edges. Eff-UNet[11] that adopted Efficient-Net B7 for feature extraction also did not perform well because it did not incorporate global and local multi-scale features. To remove the drawbacks of the above-tested approaches, our newly proposed approach has exploited a stronger feature extractor, that is, EfficientNet B4, and also incorporates both global and local multi-scale features to cope with different scaled objects. To further improve the accuracy, our approach even used channel-wise attention block by exploiting channel dependencies. From Figure 26.5, it is already visible that our proposed approach produces better segmented maps than the other tested frameworks.

26.5   CONCLUSION

This paper highlights the importance of local and global contextual information as well as attention modules for long-range dependencies in the segmentation task. We have suggested a new approach that incorporates both global context information and local multi-scale information for the segmentation of complex unstructured driving scenarios. The global context block captures global dependencies in spatial dimension, while the modified ASPP block gathers multi-scale features to cope with variable size objects. Moreover, we have utilized channel-wise attention block to demonstrate long-range contextual knowledge that further enhances the segmented outputs. The experimental findings verified the superiority of the proposed Eff-MANet approach over other models on the IDD Lite dataset. In the future, we will evaluate the performance of the proposed approach on the full IDD dataset.

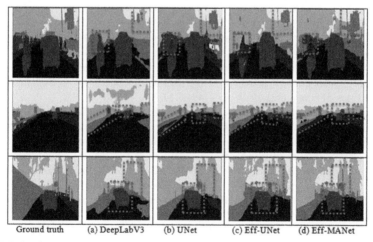

| Ground truth | (a) DeepLabV3 | (b) UNet | (c) Eff-UNet | (d) Eff-MANet |

FIGURE 26.5   A comparison of few predicted outputs of different state-of-the-art frameworks with the newly proposed approach on the validation set of IDD Lite.

KEYWORDS

- **road scene segmentation**
- **attention module**
- **multi-scale contextual knowledge**
- **global contextual knowledge**

REFERENCES

1. Simonyan, K.; Zisserman, A. Very Deep Convolutional Networks for Large-Scale Image Recognition. 2014, arXiv:1409.1556.
2. He, K.; Zhang, X.; Ren, S.; Sun, J. In *Deep Residual Learning for Image Recognition*, Proceedings of the IEEE Conference on Computer Vision and Pattern Recognition, 2016; pp. 770–778.
3. Huang, G.; Liu, Z.; Maaten, L. V. D.; Weinberger, K. Q. In *Densely Connected Convolutional Networks*, Proceedings of the IEEE Conference on Computer Vision and Pattern Recognition, 2017; pp. 4700–4708.
4. Zhao, H.; Shi, J.; Qi, X.; Wang, X.; Jia, J. In *Pyramid Scene Parsing Network*, Proceedings of the IEEE Conference on Computer Vision and Pattern Recognition, 2017; pp. 2881–2890.
5. Liu, W.; Rabinovich, A.; Berg, A. C. Parsenet: Looking Wider to See Better, 2015, arXiv:1506.04579.
6. Chen, L.-C.; Papandreou, G.; Schroff, F.; Adam, H. Rethinking Atrous Convolution for Semantic Image Segmentation, 2017, arXiv:1706.05587.
7. Zhao, H.; Zhang, Y., Liu, S.; Shi, J.; Loy, C. C.; Lin, D.; Jia, J. In *Psanet: Point-Wise Spatial Attention Network for Scene Parsing*, Proceedings of the European Conference on Computer Vision (ECCV), 2018; pp. 267–283.
8. Li, H.; Xiong, P.; An, J.; Wang, L. Pyramid Attention Network for Semantic Segmentation, 2018, arXiv:1805.10180.
9. Fu, J.; Liu, J.; Tian, H.; Li, Y.; Bao, Y.; Fang, Z.; Lu, H. In *Dual Attention Network for Scene Segmentation*, Proceedings of the IEEE/CVF Conference on Computer Vision and Pattern Recognition, 2019; pp. 3146–3154.
10. Mishra, A.; Kumar, S.; Kalluri, T.; Varma, G.; Subramaian, A.; Chandraker, M.; Jawahar, C. V. In *Semantic Segmentation Datasets for Resource Constrained Training*, National Conference on Computer Vision, Pattern Recognition, Image Processing, and Graphics; Springer: Singapore, 2019; pp. 450–459.
11. Baheti, B.; Innani, S.; Gajre, S.; Talbar, S. In *Eff-Unet: A Novel Architecture for Semantic Segmentation in Unstructured Environment*, Proceedings of the IEEE/CVF Conference on Computer Vision and Pattern Recognition Workshops, 2020; pp. 358–359.
12. Long, J.; Shelhamer, E.; Darrell, T. In *Fully Convolutional Networks for Semantic Segmentation*, Proceedings of the IEEE Conference on Computer Vision and Pattern Recognition, 2015; pp. 3431–3440.
13. Badrinarayanan, V.; Kendall, A.; Cipolla, R. Segnet: A Deep Convolutional Encoder-Decoder Architecture for Image Segmentation. *IEEE Trans. Pattern Anal. Mach. Intell.* **2017,** *39* (12), 2481–2495.
14. Ronneberger, O.; Fischer, P.; Brox, T. In *U-Net: Convolutional Networks for Biomedical Image Segmentation*, International Conference on Medical Image Computing and Computer-Assisted Intervention; Springer: Cham, 2015; pp. 234–241.
15. Yu, F.; Koltun, V. Multi-Scale Context Aggregation by Dilated Convolutions, 2015, arXiv:1511.07122.
16. Fan, L.; Wang, W.-C.; Zha, F.; Yan, J. Exploring New Backbone and Attention Module for Semantic Segmentation in Street Scenes. *IEEE Access* **2018,** *6*, 71566–71580.

17. Lin, C.-Y.; Chiu, Y.-C., Ng, H.-F.; Shih, T. K.; Lin, K.-H. Global-and-Local Context Network for Semantic Segmentation of Street View Images. *Sensors* **2020,** *20* (10), 2907.

18. Tan, M.; Le, Q. In *Efficientnet: Rethinking Model Scaling for Convolutional Neural Networks*, International Conference on Machine Learning; PMLR, 2019; pp. 6105–6114.

19. Woo, S.; Park, J.; Lee, J.-Y.; Kweon, I. S. In *Cbam: Convolutional Block Attention Module*, Proceedings of the European Conference on Computer Vision (ECCV), 2018; pp. 3–19.

20. Varma, G.; Subramanian, A.; Namboodiri, A.; Chandraker, M.; Jawahar, C. V. IDD: In *A Dataset for Exploring Problems of Autonomous Navigation in Unconstrained Environments*, 2019 IEEE Winter Conference on Applications of Computer Vision (WACV); IEEE, 2019; pp. 1743–1751.

CHAPTER 27

Quantum Error Correction Technique for Quantum-Based Satellite Communication

VEENU YADAV[1], DEEPSHIKHA AGARWAL[1], and
KRISHNA KANT AGARWAL[2]

[1]Amity University, Lucknow, India

[2]ABES Institute of Technology, Ghaziabad, India

ABSTRACT

QKD is performed to secure quantum communication between the ground stations and satellite. To implement the quantum channel, better security and output are required. QKDP is a successful way for satellite quantum communications for secure networks. In this paper, we discuss error correction schemes and their comparison, quantum communication procedures A, D, and M represent encoding, decoding, and performed measurement operations. A/P represents classical bit to quantum conversion. We also present the proposed model designed for a quantum channel to improve the performance of QKD protocol satellite-based communication under problem-environmental noise, adversary attacks, atmospheric turbulence.

27.1 INTRODUCTION

The satellite communication system is used to provide communication between two parties using artificial satellites in space. It involves microwave

Computational Intelligence in Analytics and Information Systems, Volume 2: Advances in Digital Transformation, Selected Papers from CIAIS-2021. Parneeta Dhaliwal, PhD, Manpreet Kaur, PhD, Hardeo Kumar Thakur, PhD, Rajeev Kumar Arya, and Joan Lu (Eds.)

communication to happen. The major advantages of this system are the large coverage area and reliability of communication. However, it suffers from severe propagation delay due to its distance from the earth. Also, microwave signals suffer from tremendous noise from space and the earth's atmosphere. Quantum communication and encryption is the recent buzzword in communication. Quantum communication is based on the use of light photons for carrying information. Due to this communication media, the propagation delay is supposed to be negligible. Also, quantum encryption provides a very high level of security due to its major principle of entanglement. It is said that it is nearly impossible to eavesdrop on the quantum communication system.

In this paper, we propose a new model of satellite communication based on quantum communication and present a detailed discussion of the components. As security requirement in satellite communication is a very important factor, we try to present some discussion on the security aspect also. The distinguishing feature of such a system is its ability to do the successful transmission of qubits under noisy environments. Space communication has various techniques used such as frequency hopping detection spread spectrum, quality of service routing methods, and game theory on varies spread spectrum methods..[1-4]

27.2   QUANTUM KEY DISTRIBUTION PROTOCOL

Quantum Key Distribution is a methodology that is used for secure communication between the end parties located on earth. It is distributed and generates a random secret key that is implemented on a cryptographic protocol.[26]

The secret key is used to encrypt and decrypt the message for the sender (Alice) and receiver (Bob). Efficient quantum error correction and detection methods implemented by Quantum Key distribution method for secure satellite-based communication system under some condition.[11,13] The BB84 protocol was implemented by the classical-quantum key distribution.[8] This law follows the quantum mechanics; they can find that nobody had found or knew before the existence of an eavesdropper, which provides unconditional security for satellite communication,[6] since the excogitation of BB84 protocol in 1984.[8] Recently, many researchers have to implement wireless networks such as optical network and satellite networks for secure satellite communication.

Recently, May 2019, a group led by Hong Guo at Peking University and Beijing University of Posts and telecommunication reported and implemented a continuous-variable Quantum Key Distribution System using commercial fiber networks that cover the distance of 3002 km (12.49 dB) and 49.90 km (12.21 dB).[14]

27.2.1 QUANTUM KEY DISTRIBUTION (QKD) FOR SATELLITE NETWORKS

0 bit and 1 bit is the basic unit to represent the information of classical communication. A quantum bit is a collection of photons and electrons, the quantum bit is the basic unit to represent the quantum information for communication.

|0>, and |1> in the form of Dirac notion using mathematics notion: These are the superposition of quantum states. Classical information is represented by 0 and 1 respectively.

Representation of the Qubit as

$$|\Psi>=\alpha|0>\beta|1> \tag{27.1}$$

where α and β are the complex coefficients of the quantum state, associate probabilities of output becomes |0> and |1> are $\alpha|2|$, $\beta|2$ associate probabilities of outcomes $|0\rangle$ and $|1\rangle$ are $|\alpha|2$, and $|\beta|2$ as well as

$$|\alpha|2+|\beta|2=1$$

The security of the encryption is based on the law of quantum mechanics in quantum key distribution.

The third-party eavesdropping attempt is reduced that is found by measuring the law of quantum mechanics. Quantum bit and classical bit channel has been implemented by the quantum key distribution.[10]

27.3 OPERATION FOR QUANTUM-BASED SATELLITE COMMUNICATION

However, we have to discuss the quantum error correction methods to reduce the noisy effect for satellite communication and improve the quantum results. We can improve efficiency, better throughput in real field applications to get better quantum error correction techniques.

According to our model the nonideal quantum channel by Vθ has been proposed. Due to the noisy environment, the error that will be generated can be written in the form of an angle $\theta \in [0,2\prod]$. We have to take one example of the satellite communication use mode in the angular motion.

$$| \theta >=\cos |0>+j \sin | 1>, \tag{27.2}$$

$$V\theta = \cos \acute{M} + j \sin \underset{.}{N}, \tag{27.3}$$

where N and N are identify and Pauli operators, reshown on

$$| h> = V\theta | \Psi > = \alpha | 0>+\beta|1>, \tag{27.4}$$

The communication between the sender (Alice) to the receiver (Bob) to share the quantum state $| \Psi >$ is to convert to a damaged state. Further the $| h >$ quantum state we have to use by $V\theta$ from one station to another station. The receiver (Bob) receives the input quantum state $| \Psi >$ and then matches the damaged state $| h >$, this quantum state is different. This type of problem is generated due to the noisy quantum channel for transmitting data. So we have to apply an effective quantum error correction method.[20] This method is also called the pilot-based quantum error correction method.

27.4 QUANTUM ERROR CORRECTION METHOD IN QUANTUM BASED ON SATELLITE COMMUNICATION NETWORKS

According to the instruction the redundancy-free error correction and detection methods are introduced on the basis the size and dada qubit. We developed different redundancy error correction-free solutions for space quantum communication networks that are required for successful error correction.

Here P, Q, and M represent encoding and decoding of the data and then operated. Here P/Q performed the classical to quantum bit conversion. These models show that we can realize quantum communication over intercontinental distance. However, after analyzing many error detection and redundancy-free solution for free-space satellites based on quantum communication methods most are not able to tackle the issue raised in this paper. In this model, we have to provide secure communication and a large amount of data transfer via satellite. Quantum cryptography provides better security during the communication networks to accurately transmit qubits and obtain better keys, as shown in Figures 27.1 and 27.2.

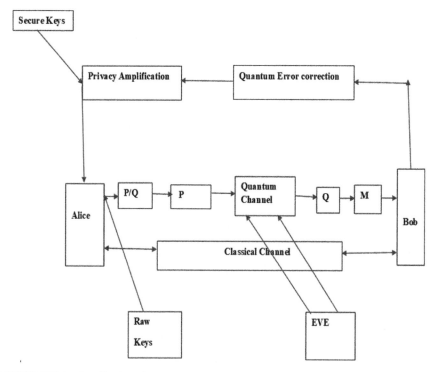

FIGURE 27.1   Satellite based on quantum communication procedure.

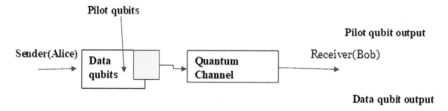

FIGURE 27.2   Quantum error correction and detection methods.

In quantum-based satellite communication networks accept that Vθ is a constant for a *T* time interval.

In quantum-based satellite communication, we assume that Uθ is a constant for a time interval *T*. Hence, considering its effect, we receive the output pilot qubit state shown as follows.

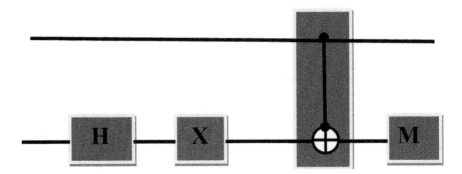

FIGURE 27.3   Satellite-based quantum error correction circuit.

Here H, X, and M show Hadamard gate, Pauli X gate, and measurement operator in the above figure. Here the M (measurement) applies the receiver (Bob) to achieve the qubit state | 0 > or | 1 >. We have to apply the tensor product from the receiver (Bob) to correct the error for transmitting the data. In this circuit, we have to achieve and improve the performance by applying the multiple pilot qubit string for quantum security satellite-based communication.

27.5   PERFORMANCE ANALYSIS ON QUANTUM-BASED SATELLITE COMMUNICATION

However, after analyzing and obtained secure key transmitted via. Show that a Low Earth Orbit (LEO) quantum-based satellite communication. Time interval T is constant during free space channel, the value of T = 0.5. We have to use the number of pilot states to reduce the redundancy and get the success probability (Ps) as shown in Figure 27.4.[21,22]

27.6   CONCLUSION

According to our results in quantum key distribution, satellite-based quantum communication networks perform the classical-quantum error correction methods and then achieve a better outcome and improved efficiency.

The pilot-based quantum error correction methods to reduce the noisy quantum channel that some consequence during in quantum-based satellite communication networks. We have to propose a quantum error detection circuit-based quantum key distribution scheme over satellite networks and then get the graphs.

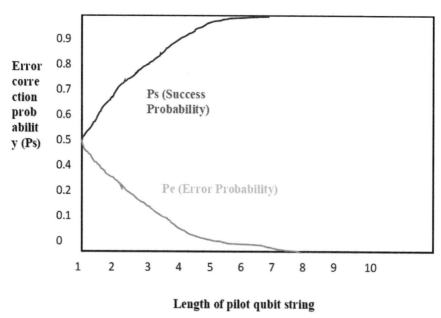

Length of pilot qubit string

FIGURE 27.4 It shows the performance and compares between the (Ps) error correction probability-length of the pilot qubit.

KEYWORDS

- **satellite quantum communication**
- **quantum key distribution cryptography**
- **encoding**
- **decoding**
- **measurement operations**

REFERENCES

1. Sharma, V.; Shukla, C.; Banerjee, S.; Pathak, A. Controlled Bidirectional Remote State Preparation in a Noisy Environment: A Generalized View. *Quantum Inf. Process.* **2015,** *14* (9), 3441–3464.

2. Sharma, V.; Thapliyal, K.; Pathak, A.; Banerjee, S. A Comparative Study of Protocols for Secure Quantum Communication under Noisy Environment: Single-Qubit Based Protocols versus Entangled-State-Based Protocols. *Quantum Inf. Process.* **2016,** *15* (11), 4681–4710.

3. Sharma, V. Effect of Noise on Practical Quantum Communication Systems. *Def. Sci. J.* **2016,** *66* (2), 186–192.

4. Sharma, V.; Shrikant, U.; Srikanth, R.; Banerjee, S. Decoherence can Help Quantum Cryptographic Security, **2017,** arXiv:1712.06519.

5. Sharma, V.; Sharma, R. Analysis of Spread Spectrum in Matlab. *Int. J. Sci. Eng. Res.* **2014,** *5* (1), 1899–1902.

6. Johnson, J. S.; Grimaila, M. R.; Humphries, J. W.; Baumgartner, G. B. Ananalysis of Error Reconciliation Protocols used in Quantum Key Distribution Systems. *J. Def. Model. Simul.* **2015,** *12* (3), 217–227.

7. Gyongyosi, L.; Imre, S. In *Pilot Quantum Error Correction for Global-Scale Quantum Communications*, 2013 IEEE Symposium on Swarm Intelligence (SIS); IEEE, **2013;** pp. 125–132.

8. Sharma, V.; Banerjee, S. Analysis of Atmospheric Effects on Satellite Based Quantum Communication: A Comparative Study, **2017,** arXiv:1711.08281.

9. Dixon, R. C. *Spread Spectrum Systems: With Commercial Applications*; Vol. 994; Wiley: New York, 1994.

10. Han, Z.; Dusitniyato, W. S.; Başar, T.; Hjørungnes, A. *Game Theory in wireless and Communication Networks: Theory, Models, and Applications*; Cambridge University Press, 2012.

11. Wright, T. H.; Ziarno, J. J. Wireless, Frequency-Agile Spread Spectrum Ground Link based Aircraft Data Communication System. U.S. Patent 6,047,165, April 4, 2000.

12. Wootters, W. K.; Zurek, W. H. A Single Quantum Cannot be Cloned. *Nature* **1982,** *299* (5886), 802–803.

13. Bennett, C. H. In *Quantum Cryptography: Public Key Distribution and Cointossing*, Proceedings of IEEE Conference on Computers, Systems and Signal Processing, 1984.

14. Zhang, Y.; Li, Z.; Chen, Z.; Weedbrook, C.; Zhao, Y.; Wang, X.; Huang, Y.; Xu, C.; Zhang, X.; Wang, Z.; Li, M.; Zhang, X.; Zheng, Z.; Chu, B.; Gao, X.; Meng, N.; Cai, W.; Wang, Z.; Wang, G.; Yu, S.; Guo, H. Continuous-Variable QKD Over 50 km Commercial Fiber. *Quantum Sci. Technol.* **2019,** *4,* 035006.

15. Bacsardi, L.; Galambos, M.; Imre, S. *Modeling and Analyzing the Quantum based Earth-Satellite and Satellite-Satellite Communications*; International Astronautical Congress: Prague, 2010.

16. Imre, S.; Ferenc, B. *Quantum Computing and Communications: An Engineering Approach*; Wiley, 2005.

17. Schmitt-Manderbach, T.; et al. Experimental Demonstration of Free-Space Decoy-State Quantum Key Distribution Over 144 km, *Phys. Rev. Lett.* **2007,** *98,* 010504.

18. Bacsardi, L. Satellite Communication over Quantum Channel. *Actaastronautica* **2007,** *61* (1–6), 151–159.

19. Andrews, L C.; Phillips, R. L. *Laser Beam Propagation Through Random Media*; SPIE Press Book, 2005.

20. Villoresi, P.; Jennewein, T.; Tamburini, F.; Aspelmeyer, M.; Bonato, C.; Ursin, R.; Pernechele, C.; Luceri, V.; Bianco, G.; Zeilinger, A.; et al. Experimental Verification of

the Feasibility of a Quantum Channel Between Space and earth. *N. J. Phys.* **2008,** *10* (3), 033038.

21. Gyöngyösi, L.; Imre, S. Pilot Quantum Error-Correction for Noisy Quantum Channels, 2011.
22. Kamilbrádler, P. H.; Touchette, D.; Wilde, M. M. Trade-Off Capacities of the Quantum Hadamard Channels. *Phys. Rev. A* **2010,** *81* (6), 062312.
23. Brandão, F. G.; Oppenheim, J.; Strelchuk, S. When does Noise Increase the Quantum Capacity? *Phys. Rev. Lett.* **2012,** *108* (4), 040501.
24. Gyongyosi, L.; Imre, S. In *Quantum Polar Coding for Noisy Optical Quantum Channels*, APS Division of Atomic, Molecular and Optical Physics Meeting Abstracts, 2012.
25. Gyongyosi, L.; Imre, S. In *Classical Communication with Stimulated Emission Over Zero-Capacity Optical Quantum Channels*, APS Division of Atomic, Molecular and Optical Physics Meeting Abstracts, 2012.
26. Gyongyosi, L.; Imre, S. Pilot Quantum Error-Correction for Noisy Quantum Channels. 2011.

PART III

Computational Intelligence in Software Engineering

CHAPTER 28

A Study on an Education-Based Interactive Automated Agent

JALY DASMAHAPATRA[1], MILI DASMAHAPATRA[2], DEBOJIT DHALI[2], NAYAN GARAIN[2], and RIYA SIL[2]

[1]Department of Computer Science & Engineering, College of Haldia Institute of Technology, West Bengal, India

[2]Department of Computer Science & Engineering, Adamas University, Kolkata, India

ABSTRACT

The use of interactive automated agents has increased drastically in the past few decades in various sectors. Education-based interactive automated agents can help education administrators and human educators in achieving great potential. Various interactive automated agents have been developed for years in the field of education. These interactive automated agents can answer any educational-based queries anytime that can be either artificial intelligence-based or rule-based. In this paper, for better understanding, the authors have studied the existing education-based interactive automated agents and discussed the similarities and dissimilarities among the techniques related to educational-based agents. A basic model of an education-based interactive automated agent has been designed by applying artificial neural network that focuses on communication to provide a suitable answer.

Computational Intelligence in Analytics and Information Systems, Volume 2: Advances in Digital Transformation, Selected Papers from CIAIS-2021. Parneeta Dhaliwal, PhD, Manpreet Kaur, PhD, Hardeo Kumar Thakur, PhD, Rajeev Kumar Arya, and Joan Lu (Eds.)

28.1   INTRODUCTION

Michael Mauldin has proposed the term Chatbot in 1994 to describe conversational programs. The Chatbot is a computer program that can interact with humans using natural language or chat through artificial intelligence.[1] A Chatbot is a program used to organize any conversation via text or text-to-speech. Nowadays, people are surrounded by smart devices (e.g., smartphones, smartwatches, and IoT devices). Chatbots are capable of interacting with the user and they provide useful services. A user can ask questions by an interactive automated agent and get the response to the requested action. Some educational institutions are trying to enhance their campuses to provide novel, smart services to the students and their parents that make everyday activities much easier. An interactive automated agent can solve numerous problems and simultaneously gather required information despite its location. On various websites, sometimes users are unable to find the required information.[2] In such a scenario, smart environments designed by Artificial Intelligence and Machine Learning for a better understanding of the environment therefore do the needful for the society. Despite the great presence of assistants such as Amazon-Alexa, Apple-Siri, Google-Assistant, Microsoft-Cortana, there is still a request for technologies to develop campus virtual assistants that can be fully trained and specialized for specific applications. An education-based virtual assistant must be designed to support students of the universities to move around inside the campus easily (e.g., by locating buildings, classrooms, and other relevant points). It answers common university-related questions (such as scholarships, enrolments, fees structure, courses, and many others). It can further enhance by communicating with other related frameworks to perform more intricate assignments, such as recognizing a free spot in the university campus and providing the temperature. The other information of that particular area is with the help of IoT gadgets.

In this paper, the authors have organized the remainder of the paper as follows. Section 28.2 discusses the origin of the work, Section 28.3 focuses on the basic structure of Chatbot, and Section 28.4 focuses on different surveys on the education-based interactive automated agents. In Section 28.5 the proposed work is discussed. Section 28.6 concludes the paper and discusses the future scope of education-based interactive automated agents.

28.2 ORIGIN OF THE WORK

Chatbots are assumed to have a critical job as human–computer interfaces. A Chatbot is very quick, it can work 24 × 7. It is not like a client assistant specialist,[3] and it does not take any break from work or goes offline. It is a computerized program and a conversational specialist that can have a conversation with any human in any field by using Natural Language Processing. With Chatbots, organizations can support customers 24 × 7.

28.3 BASIC STRUCTURE OF CHATBOT

To design, any efficient Chatbot needs to divide the model into parts for improved development. There are two parts of a Chatbot (Fig. 28.1): (i) One that works in the backend and (ii) The other one is the user interface that interacts with the user.

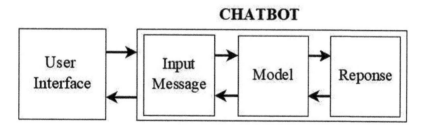

FIGURE 28.1 Chatbot Basic Structure.

28.3.1 *OTHER FEATURES*

Chatbots have many other features that assist people in many ways.[4] Chatbots have several features that include the following.

28.3.1.1 *HUMAN-LIKE APPROACH*

The Chatbots have used machine learning techniques for better learning. The Chatbot's reply depends on the input of the client or the user. It replies to any conversation in a way such that the client undoubtedly believes that they are having a conversation with humans rather than an interactive automated agent.

28.3.1.2   *PREDICTIVE IN NATURE*

The Chatbot always drives the discussion forward. It would consider proposing activities that would provide additional utility. The Chatbot keeps the user updated and helps them move forward with a significant amount of data.

28.3.1.3   *SIMPLE UI/UX*

Chatbots are normally text-driven, with proper pictures and widgets, which provide smooth interaction with the user. It assists by moving from UI filled with graphics to a UI of simple texts. Finally, Chatbots bring a new experience of messaging and Graphic User Interface.

28.3.1.4   *CHATBOT SERVICE*

Chatbots should have the option to mechanize day-to-day events in our daily life (e.g., reserving a hotel, ordering goods, and so on). It saves time and decreases human efforts.

28.3.2   **TYPES OF CHATBOT**

There are mainly two types of Chatbot mentioned in Figure 28.2; one is a Rule-Based Chatbot and the other one is an AI-Based Chatbot.

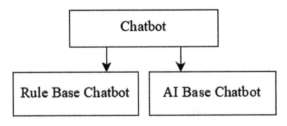

FIGURE 28.2   Types of Chatbots.

28.3.2.1 RULE-BASED CHATBOTS

Rule-based Chatbots essentially work for user support as interactive frequently asked questions (FAQs). This sort of Chatbot[5] has an absence of adaptability and analytics capability of an individual. They are programmed to perceive certain terms and patterns from which they can react with preset answers. This bot is limited and it can respond to only specific types of commands. Unknown questions are not understood.

28.3.2.2 AI-BASED CHATBOTS

This bot has an artificial brain that understands languages and not just commands. One does not need to be strangely explicit when conversing with it. This Chatbot continuously learns from its previous conversations and gets smarter.

28.4 SURVEY ON EDUCATION-BASED AUTOMATED AGENT

Based on the research work done, the authors of this paper have created a table (Table 28.1) to highlight the comparison between the technologies used in the existing Chatbots and their respective solutions.

28.5 PROPOSED MODEL OF EDUCATION-BASED INTERACTIVE AUTOMATED AGENT

The authors of this chapter have built an education-based interactive automated agent for a University Campus environment (i.e., Adamas University). The architecture of our model (Fig. 28.3) answers the inquiries posted by the user. The Chatbot works in the following process:

TABLE 28.1 Comparison of Technologies used in Existing Chatbots and their Solutions.

SL. no.	Paper title	Technology used	Description
1	Home Automation using IoT and a Chatbot using Natural Language Processing[6]	Software Used: Raspbian Python WebIOPi Natural Language Toolkit (NLTK) Microsoft Azure Server IFTTT Hardware Used: Raspberry Pi with Wi-fi PIR Motion Detector and Relay Board Electrical Lock Temperature Sensor DHT11 Router	In this paper, the client can connect with the framework utilizing either a web application or a Chatbot with the help of a PC or a handheld gadget. The web application used to enable home automation likewise has a security highlight that enables certain clients to get to the application.
2	Enabling Intelligent Environment by the Design of Emotionally Aware Virtual Assistant: A Case of Smart Campus[7]	Speech-to-texts, word embedding is the input of long-short term memory recurrent neural network (RNN-LSTM), deep convolutional neural network (CNN), unity 3D game engine, AR	In this paper, Deep Convolutional Neural Network (CNN) and Long Short-Term Memory in Recurrent Neural Network (RNN-LSTM) are used. For short sentence feeling acknowledgment, the most extreme precision is 95.6%. This exploration utilizes the Unity 3D model to execute AR-relevant discourse robots.
3	Extracting Chatbot Knowledge from Online Discussion Forums[8]	Cascaded Hybrid Model, Support Vector Machines (SVM)	In this paper, the principal approach is to make a more effective and explicit domain Chatbot contrasted and manual information development strategies.

TABLE 28.1 (*Continued*)

SL. no.	Paper title	Technology used	Description
4	Freudbot: An Investigation of Chatbot Technology in Distance Education[9]	AIML (Artificial Intelligence Mark-up Language)	In this paper, Freudbot was built utilizing the open-source design of AIML.
5	The Study of the Application of a Keywords-based Chatbot System on the Teaching of Foreign Languages[10]	HTTP Server, Speech synthesis technology of Microsoft Agent.	Online human PC dialog system discoveries by this paper report with natural language on the educating of foreign languages. With the examination of the keywords or example coordinating instrument utilized in this Chatbot, it very well may be inferred. As a teaching assistant program, this sort of framework cannot fill in foreign language learning.
6	A Tool of Conversation: Chatbot[11]	Eclipse software, Java applets use to create a dialog box, Artificial Intelligence	This paper depends on the text-only Chatbot to perceive the client contribution by utilizing pattern matching, access data to give a predefined acknowledgment. General-purpose Chatbot should be straightforward and easy to understand. It should be effectively perceived and the information base should be reduced.
7	Chatbot for University Related FAQs[12]	AIML (Artificial Intelligence Mark-up Language)	In this paper, we have proposed and executed an interactive Chatbot for the university climate using AIML. This Chatbot can be used by any university to answer FAQs to curious understudies in an intuitive manner.

TABLE 28.1 *(Continued)*

SL. no.	Paper title	Technology used	Description
8	A New Chatbot for Customer Service on social media[13]	LSTM neural networks, Word Embedding, word2vec	In this work, another conversational framework makes for client support via online media. State-of-the-art deep learning techniques such as Long Short-Term Memory (LSTM) networks are first applied to produce reactions for client support demands via web-based media. Seen that a deep learning-based framework had the option to take recorded as hard copy styles from a brand and move them to another.
9	Survey on Chatbot Design Techniques in Speech Conversation Systems[14]	Speech recognition, Natural Language Toolkit (NLTK), AIML, SQL, and relational database	In this paper, the writing survey has covered a few chosen papers that have focused explicitly on Chatbot plan methods in the most recent decade. The Chatbots intended for exchange frameworks in the chose studies are, by and large, restricted to specific applications. Universally useful Chatbots need upgrades by planning more extensive information bases.
10	A Deep Reinforcement Learning Chatbot[15]	Deep Learning, Reinforcement Learning, Natural Language	For the discourse framework system, the large-scale ensemble is utilized for the Amazon Alexa Prize rivalry. This framework uses an assortment of machine learning techniques, including deep learning and reinforcement learning.
11	Chatbot Using A Knowledge in Database[16]	Relational Database Management System (RDBMS), Artificial Intelligence Mark-up Language (AIML), Java language	In this paper, Chatbot information is put away in the database. In the Relational Database Management Systems (RDBMS) the Chatbot comprises the core and interface. Pascal and Java are utilized to assemble the interface.

TABLE 28.1 *(Continued)*

SL. no.	Paper title	Technology used	Description
12	Programming challenges of Chatbot: Current and Future Perspective[17]	Natural Language Processing (NLP), Machine learning, Artificial Intelligence (AI)	This paper gives a review of cloud-based Chatbots advances alongside the programming of Chatbots and the difficulties of programming in the current and future era of the Chatbot.
13	Goal-Oriented Chatbot Dialog Management Bootstrapping with Transfer Learning[18]	Transfer learning, Deep Reinforcement Learning, Natural Language	In this paper, the **Transfer learning** (TL) Technique can be effectively applied to support the exhibitions of the Reinforcement Learning-dependent on goal-oriented Chatbots. Finally, the transfer learning approach is corresponding to extra preparation, for example, a warm beginning.
14	Chatbot using Data Sciences for Educational Institutions[19]	AIML, XML, Java programming language, Data Science-based corpus modules	This paper depends on the content exclusively Chatbot which recognizes the client input still as, by abuse pattern matching, access information to deliver a predefined affirmation upheld the sentence given by the client.
15	Chatbot: An automated conversation system for the educational domain[20]	Ensemble learning-based random forest, python along with telegram API, NLTK package, and WordNet lexicon	To plan the Chatbot, we have arranged training data from the crawled information. The Chatbot can react to the greater part of the inquiries with a precision of 88.60%. Finally, the proposed framework is a type of telegram bot.

TABLE 28.1 *(Continued)*

SL. no.	Paper title	Technology used	Description
16	JAICOB: A Data Science Chatbot[21]	Natural Language Interface (NLI), Machine Learning	This work targets exploring the utilization of psychological figuring in blended learning conditions. This framework has been actualized as an individual specialist to help students in Learning Data Science and Machine Learning procedures. The experiment confirms that the framework can answer successfully. It can give experiences and tackle questions about Data Science.
17	Doly: Bengali Chatbot for Bengali Education[22]	Bengali Natural Language Processing (BNLP), Dialogue and Corpus, Naïve Bayesian algorithm, Natural Language Toolkit, Dictionary Based Search by Removing Affix (DBSRA)	This exploration is a pioneering work in the field of the discourse framework in Bengali. The primary test of this work is to make a Chatbot dependent on a precise information base. The Chatbot is 88% accurate. This Chabot chats with the client dependent on the pattern matching algorithm and will improve its presentation measure by gaining from the communication.
18	AI and Web-Based Human-Like Interactive University Chatbot (UNIBOT)[23]	Machine Learning, PHP language, HTML, CSS and jQuery, SQL, Natural language	In this paper, insights concerning the plan, the algorithm utilized, and the execution of the Unibot are introduced. The client does not have to assemble data by visiting sites or universities. The Project GUI is like a Messaging Application.

TABLE 28.1 *(Continued)*

SL. no.	Paper title	Technology used	Description
19	Expression Tracking with OpenCV Deep Learning for a Development of Emotionally Aware Chatbots[24]	Deep Learning which implemented Tensorflow	It tends to be demonstrated that the reaction of Chatbot can be set off by interactants' facial expression and it can help in making Chatbots sincerely aware. It can follow 17 expressions with the fixed subjects and 14 expressions with the nonfixed subjects in a range of 30 seconds.
20	A Question Answering and Quiz Generation Chatbot for Education[25]	Artificial Neural Networks (ANN), NLP	The Chatbot can accept a transferred archive as input and empower the student to ask inquiries from the content or quizzes to test his or her intelligence. The transferred report is changed over into an information base through data cleaning and preprocessing steps.

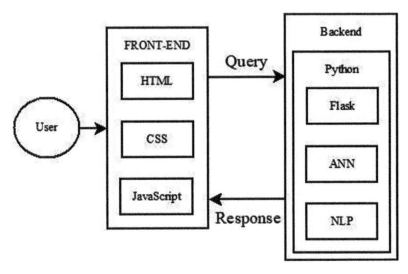

FIGURE 28.3   Diagram of a Chatbot.

28.5.1   *CONVERSATIONAL AND ENTERTAINING*

The Chatbot reactions are a route that is well known to the user. The discussion follows a Basic English language and collaborates in an easy-to-understand way. The discussion between the user and the Chatbot resembles a conversation similar to humans. The conversation working flow is shown in Figure 28.4.

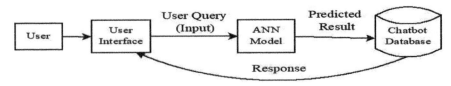

FIGURE 28.4   Sequence Diagram of the Chatbot.

28.5.2 DATABASE CREATION

Multidimensional python dictionary and array are applied to build a database (Fig. 28.5) where three keys are present (i.e. "tag," "pattern," "response") with their respective values being available.

```
{
    'data': [
            {'tag':'t1',
            'pattern': ['Name of the collage?', 'What is the collage name?', 'Full name of the collage'],
            'response': ['The Collage name is Adamas University', 'The name is Adamas University',
                        'It's Adamas University']
            },

            {'tag':'t2',
            'pattern': ['Who is the Chancellor?', 'What is the Chancellor name?',
                        'Adamas University Chancellor name?'],
            'response': ['Prof. Sumit Roy is chancellor of Adamas University',
                        'Adamas University chancellor name Prof. Sumit Roy']
            },
    ]
}
```

FIGURE 28.5   Data in Database.

28.5.3 USE OF ARTIFICIAL NEURAL NETWORK

The Artificial Neural Network is a Sequential model (Fig. 28.6). In the input layer, an embedding layer is used where vocabulary size is 10000, the dimension of the dense embedding is 20, and the length of input sequences is 20. In the hidden layer, the Dense Layers have been used. Now overcome overfitting, few neurons are dropped. The activation function used here is "**ReLU.**" In the output layer, the Dense Layer is used where the activation function is "**Softmax.**"

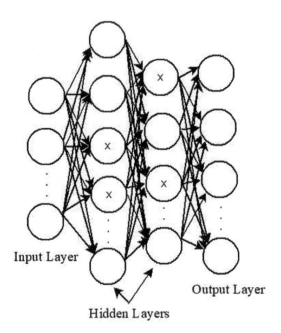

FIGURE 28.6   Artificial Neural Network Model.

28.5.4   *USER INTERFACE*

Users ask their queries, response to each of the queries is generated by the Chatbot. The responses are shown in the user interface or a dummy website (Fig. 28.7).

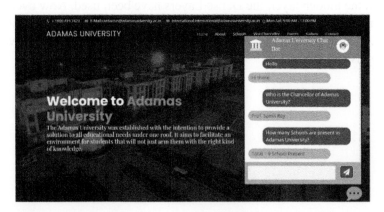

FIGURE 28.7   User Interface.

28.6 CONCLUSION

In this paper, the authors have focused mainly upon some selected papers that discuss the recent Chatbot design techniques within the past ten years, and based on the survey, the authors of this paper have implemented an educational-based interactive automated agent for Campus Environment (i.e., for Adamas University). Taking into consideration the different techniques used, Chatbots improved by using a variety of methods and approaches.

In future works, the authors would plan to add a speech recognition feature through which students can ask their queries verbally and get the answers from the Chatbot, adding a capability for the Chatbot to perform analytics user's sentiment based on which the bot can be retrained on human emotions so that more empathy can be added to the Chatbot, image option from which Chatbot can response as a place name or people name, etc to the user.

ACKNOWLEDGMENT

The authors would like to convey their heartiest thanks to Dr. Abhishek Roy, Adamas University for his constant support and also to the reviewers for their comments and insight.

KEYWORDS

- **Chatbot**
- **question answering**
- **natural language processing**
- **information retrieval**

REFERENCES

1. Singh, R.; Paste, M.; Shinde, N.; Patel, H.; Mishra, N. In *Chatbot using Tensor Flow for Small Businesses*, Second International Conference on Inventive Communication and Computational Technologies, 2018, doi:10.1109/icicct.2018.847299
2. Mathew, R. B.; Varghese, S.; Joy, S. E.; Alex, S. S. In *Chatbot for Disease Prediction and Treatment Recommendation using Machine Learning*, 3rd International Conference on Trends in Electronics and Informatics, 2019, doi:10.1109/icoei.2019.8862707

3. Kulkarni, C. S.; Bhavsar, A. U.; Pingale, S. R.; Kumbhar, S. S. BANK CHAT BOT—An Intelligent Assistant System using NLP and Machine Learning. *Int. Res. J. Eng. Technol.* **2017,** *4* (5), 2374–2377.

4. Shawar, B. A.; Atwell, E. S. Using Corpora in Machine-Learning Chatbot Systems. *Int. J. Corpus Linguist.* **2005,** *10* (4), 489–516.

5. Yan, M.; Castro, P.; Cheng, P.; Ishakian, V. In *Building a Chatbot with Serverless Computing*, Proceedings of the 1st International Workshop on Mashups of Things and APIs, 2016, doi:10.1145/3007203.3007217

6. Baby, C. J.; Khan, F. A.; Swathi, J. N. In *Home Automation using IoT and a Chatbot using Natural Language Processing*, 2017 Innovations in Power and Advanced Computing Technologies (i-PACT), 2017, doi:10.1109/ipact.2017.8245185

7. Chiu, P.; Chang, J.; Lee, M.; Chen, C.; Lee, D. Enabling Intelligent Environment by the Design of Emotionally Aware Virtual Assistant: A Case of Smart Campus. *IEEE Access* **2020,** *8*, 62032–62041.

8. Huang, J.; Zhou, M.; Yang, D. Extracting Chatbot Knowledge from Online Discussion Forums. *IJCAI* **2007,** *7*, 423–428.

9. Heller, B.; Proctor, M.; Mah, D.; Jewell, L.; Cheung, B. Freudbot: An investigation of Chatbot Technology in Distance Education. In *EdMedia+ Innovate Learning; Association for the Advancement of Computing in Education*, 2005; pp. 3913–3918.

10. Jia, J. The Study of the Application of a Keywords-based Chatbot System on the Teaching of Foreign Languages, 2003, arXiv:cs/0310018.

11. Dahiya, M. A Tool of Conversation: Chatbot. *Int. J. Comput. Sci. Eng.* **2017,** *5* (5), 158–161.

12. Ranoliya, B. R.; Raghuwanshi, N.; Singh, S. In *Chatbot for University Related Faqs*, International Conference on Advances in Computing, Communications and Informatics, 2017, doi:10.1109/icacci.2017.8126057

13. Xu, A.; Liu, Z.; Guo, Y.; Sinha, V.; Akkiraju, R. In *A New Chatbot for Customer Service on Social Media*, Proceedings of the CHI Conference on Human Factors in Computing Systems, 2017, doi:10.1145/3025453.3025496

14. Abdul-Kader, S. A.; Woods, J. Survey on Chatbot Design Techniques in Speech Conversation Systems. *Int. J. Adv. Comput. Sci. Appl.* **2015,** *6* (7) doi:10.14569/ijacsa.2015.060712

15. Serban, I. V.; Sankar, C.; Germain, M.; Zhang, S.; Lin, Z.; Subramanian, S.; Kim, T.; Pieper, M.; Chandar, S.; et al. A Deep Reinforcement Learning Chatbot, 2017, arXiv:1709.02349.

16. Setiaji, B.; Wibowo F. W. In *Chatbot using a Knowledge in Database: Human-to-Machine Conversation Modeling*, 7th International Conference on Intelligent Systems, Modelling and Simulation, 2016, doi:10.1109/isms.2016.53

17. Rahman, A. M.; Mamun, A. A.; Islam, A. In *Programming Challenges of Chatbot: Current and Future Prospective*, IEEE Region 10 Humanitarian Technology Conference, 2017, doi:10.1109/r10-htc.2017.8288910

18. Ilievski, V.; Musat, C.; Hossman, A.; Baeriswyl, M. In *Goal-Oriented Chatbot Dialog Management Bootstrapping with Transfer Learning*, Proceedings of the Twenty-Seventh International Joint Conference on Artificial Intelligence, 2018, doi:10.24963/ijcai.2018/572

19. Deka, M. N.; Kumar, K. A.; Christy, A. Chatbot using Data Sciences for Educational Institutions. No. 3303. EasyChair, 2020.

20. Mondal, A.; Dey, M.; Das, D.; Nagpal, S.; Garda, K. In *Chatbot: An Automated Conversation System for the Educational Domain*, International Joint Symposium on Artificial Intelligence and Natural Language Processing, 2018, doi:10.1109/isai-nlp.2018.8692927

21. Carlander-Reuterfelt, D.; Carrera, A.; Iglesias, C. A.; Araque, O.; Sanchez Rada, J. F.; Munoz, S. JAICOB: A Data Science Chatbot. *IEEE Access* **2020,** *8*, 180672–180680. doi:10.1109/access.2020.3024795

22. Kowsher, M.; Tithi, F. S.; Ashraful Alam, M.; Huda, M. N.; Md Moheuddin, M.; Rosul, M. G. In *Doly: Bengali Chatbot for Bengali Education*, 1st International Conference on Advances in Science, Engineering and Robotics Technology, 2019, doi:10.1109/icasert.2019.8934592

23. Patel, N. P.; Parikh, D. R.; Patel, D. A.; Patel, R. R. In *AI and Web-Based HUMAN-LIKE Interactive UNIVERSITY Chatbot (unibot)*, 3rd International Conference on Electronics, Communication and Aerospace Technology, 2019, doi:10.1109/iceca.2019.8822176

24. Carranza, K. A.; Manalili, J.; Bugtai, N. T.; Baldovino, R. G. In *Expression Tracking with Opencv Deep Learning for a Development of Emotionally Aware Chatbots*, 7th International Conference on Robot Intelligence Technology and Applications, 2019, doi:10.1109/ritapp.2019.8932852

25. Sreelakshmi, A.; Abhinaya, S.; Nair, A.; Jaya Nirmala, S. In *A Question Answering and Quiz Generation Chatbot for Education*, Grace Hopper Celebration, India, 2019, doi:10.1109/ghci47972.2019.9071832

CHAPTER 29

Issues in Retrieving Research Data from Open Source Software Projects: A Case Study

JASWINDER SINGH[1], ANU GUPTA[1], and PREET KANWAL[2]

[1]*Department of Computer Science and Applications, Panjab University, Chandigarh, India*

[2]*Department of Computer Science, SGGS College, Chandigarh, India*

ABSTRACT

To study and analyze the open source software development process, software engineering researchers need to deeply explore the publicly available software development data. The research data available from open source software projects, also called public software repositories, includes data from version control history, bug reports, feature requests, and discussions among projects' community members. Various existing code-hosting sites built on the top of distributed version control management systems offer various features for accelerating open source software development and promoting collaboration among developers. Although the open source software data is publicly available, yet it is a challenging task to extract meaningful data from the public repositories spread over a wide range of application areas. The present study takes GitHub, an online platform for software hosting, as a case study to identify the issues that arise at various   levels of the data extraction process for performing empirical research on open source

Computational Intelligence in Analytics and Information Systems, Volume 2: Advances in Digital Transformation, Selected Papers from CIAIS-2021. Parneeta Dhaliwal, PhD, Manpreet Kaur, PhD, Hardeo Kumar Thakur, PhD, Rajeev Kumar Arya, and Joan Lu (Eds.)

software projects. The interface provided by GitHub for automated retrieval of data as well as manual inspection has been applied on the test case repository to understand the issues in the data extraction process. A total of nine issues related to data retrieval for conducting a study of open source software projects have been identified.

29.1   INTRODUCTION

Open Source Software (OSS) follows a distributed development model in which participants all over the world contribute voluntarily over the Internet. Origin of cloud-based project-hosting sites such as SourceForge, GitHub, Bitbucket has facilitated this development process to a great extent. OSS projects, termed as public software repositories on these sites, contain an abundance of information regarding the software evolution. Software source code, version control data, bug reports, and discussions regarding the software development are generally warehoused in these public repositories. Software engineering researchers can freely access this data to analyze and uncover various aspects of OSS development.[1] Even an entirely new area of research known as "Mining Software Repositories" has emerged as a result of public availability of OSS development data.

Among various project-hosting sites, GitHub has emerged as the most widely used software development platform, with over 50 million registered users and 100 million repositories, covering a wide range of application domains and programming languages.[2] GitHub uses Git for version control which is a distributed version control system (DVCS). Fork and pull development model, modern web user interface (UI), and emphasis on social networking enabled GitHub to quickly surpass the much older and established project-hosting platforms such as SourceForge, in size and popularity.[3]

Software version control data is used by researchers to reconstruct the software development process of successful projects to replicate the same into newer projects for their effective growth.[4,5] Although public code-hosting sites have given researchers an opportunity to study the software evolution, still there are certain issues faced by researchers while retrieving data of interest from public software repositories. The present study focuses on GitHub as a case study to highlight various challenges faced by researchers while retrieving research data from GitHub public repositories for studying the OSS development process.

The remaining paper is organized as follows. Section 29.2 describes the literature review. Section 29.3 elaborates various issues faced by researchers while extracting data from GitHub. Section 29.4 concludes the paper and presents the future scope for this research work.

29.2 LITERATURE REVIEW

In the past, researchers have used publicly available OSS development data to reconstruct the software development process, guide project developers on various issues, predict bugs, and examine collaboration among the project community members.[6-8] GitHub, being the largest code-hosting site, has been of primary interest to the research community in recent years as it enables them to access historic data about an OSS project and its evolution through its official application programming interface (API). Onoue et al. have collected data from GitHub API to study the characteristics of developers by investigating the events generated by each developer.[9] By using data from software repositories hosted on GitHub, Ruscio et al. have proposed a workflow and tool chain to support the specification of custom quality models, which can guide automated analysis of open source software.[10] Kochhar et al. have examined over 300 large GitHub open source projects, to measure the code coverage of their associated test cases and to analyze correlations between code coverage and relevant software metrics such as lines of code, cyclomatic complexity, and number of developers.[11]

A few studies have identified potential risks and suggested some strategies to avoid such risks while extracting GitHub's data for research purposes. Bird et al. have examined various pros and cons of mining data from Git-based software projects for research.[4] They found that although DVCS provides new and useful data for improved comprehension of the software development process, yet some pitfalls associated with mining Git data remain. Kalliamvakou et al. have discovered thirteen perils and prevention mechanisms while pulling out the data from GitHub.[12] They revealed that 40% of all the pull requests did not appear as merged even though they are. Moreover, the majority of the projects on GitHub either are personal (owned and managed by a single individual) or have been completely inactive for a long time.

As the number of repositories and registered users on GitHub are in millions, automatic analysis of software repositories and developer communities is very much essential. The present study distinguishes itself from previous works in the fact that it identifies the challenges encountered while fetching data automatically from GitHub API in a software application.

29.3   DATA RETRIEVAL ISSUES

The presence of an enormous number of software projects and registered users on GitHub generates the need for automatic data fetching and analysis. While using GitHub API programmatically in a software application for extracting data related to an OSS project, certain difficulties are faced by the researchers. These difficulties have been elaborated in this section.

29.3.1   GITHUB AS FREE STORAGE

GitHub is a software project-hosting company that allows users to create a software repository for free or under a paid subscription as per the requirement. It provides all the distributed version control features of Git, added with its own features for effective software development. Pertaining to the extremely large number of repositories and registered users on GitHub, it has been a potential study subject for software engineering researchers to study software development. GitHub repositories are meant to contain software development projects, but it has been observed that many repositories on GitHub contain data such as text files, tutorials, homework assignments, images or simply backup of a personal computer that can be classified   as non-software resources. Kalliamvakou et al. found that 63.4% of a total sample of 434 repositories contain software development activity and rest of the repositories were being used for storage or academic purposes.[12] GitHub provides no information regarding the contents of a repository, that is, whether it is a software project or personal data of a user. Given the large volume of projects hosted on GitHub, it becomes difficult to select a sample   for a research study based on manual investigation. Moreover, it is challenging to distinguish a software project from a non-software repository using automated tools. Substantial quantities of such non-software project repositories in a random sample of research data may lead researchers to end up with impractical and potentially incorrect conclusions.

29.3.2 RESTRICTED ACCESS RATE

To comprehensively study and analyze the open source software development process and derive various software evolution patterns from this analysis, software engineering researchers need to download complete software development information. The information can be in the form of source code, commits, bug reports, feature requests, discussions among project community members, etc. GitHub provides an application programming interface (API) through which data related to OSS projects and be downloaded programmatically. In order to maintain the quality of service fulfilling the data access requests, GitHub distinguishes between authenticated and unauthenticated API requests. An unauthenticated request is one in which the user does not provide their GitHub credentials and is allowed only 60 API requests per hour for data fetching. In an authenticated request the user provides proper identification credentials and is allowed to create a maximum of 5000 API requests per hour. The samples for illustration purposes of unauthenticated and authenticated requests are shown in Figures 29.1 and 29.2, respectively. Considering millions of OSS projects hosted on GitHub, restrictions on API access create a hindrance for software engineering researchers.

```
curl -i https://api.github.com/users/octocat
HTTP/1.1 200 OK
Date: Sun, 13 Dec 2020 11:43:56 GMT
Content-Type: application/json; charset=utf-8
Content-Length: 1298
Server: 200 OK
X-RateLimit-Limit: 60
X-RateLimit-Remaining: 58
X-RateLimit-Reset: 1581248455
```

FIGURE 29.1 Sample of unauthenticated GitHub API request.

```
curl -i https://api.github.com/users/whatever?client_id=***&client_secret=***
HTTP/1.1 200 OK
Date: Sun, 13 Dec 2020 10:43:27 GMT
Content-Type: application/json; charset=utf-8
Content-Length: 1350
Server: GitHub.com
Status: 200 OK
X-RateLimit-Limit: 5000
X-RateLimit-Remaining: 4966
X-RateLimit-Reset: 1581248455
```

FIGURE 29.2 Sample of authenticated GitHub API request.

29.3.3 GITHUB PAGINATION

Registered GitHub users can contribute to an OSS project in the form of source code, bug reports, and feature requests, etc. GitHub follows a pull request-based model in which potential changes to the source code are reported to project maintainers by creating a pull request on the software repository.[13] Source code changes are then reviewed among project community members and, if approved, are merged into the standard code base of the software project in the form of version control commits. GitHub provides its own bug tracking system where users can report bugs as well as post new feature requests that are collectively called issues.

It has been observed that repositories hosted on GitHub can have hundreds or even thousands of commits, issues, pull requests, and other resources associated with it. GitHub API enables users to access these resources through different API endpoints in the form of web universal resource locators (URL's). The result of these API requests is an array containing JavaScript Object Notation (JSON) objects corresponding to each commit, issue, or pull request, etc. The API request that returns an array with multiple items (commits, issues, or pull requests, etc.) returns data in pages with a maximum of 30 items returned per page by default. For the next 30 items, a new URL has to be constructed and an API request has to be sent again. Depending upon the size of the project/repository, the total number of items associated with it may be very large in number. The constraints on pagination combined with the restricted API access as explained in Section 29.3.2 make the data extraction a slow and tedious process for researchers who need to extract complete data pertaining to any repository.

One of the important GitHub APIs, named Events API, reports all the events related to an OSS project. Some of the important events are source code commits, issue or pull request creation, comments made to a commit or issue, project starring or subscription, and fork creation. The Events API allow a maximum of 10 pages having 30 items per page to be accessed, thereby allowing a researcher to extract a maximum of 300 events only. Another restriction permits extraction of only those events which have been created in the last 90 days from the date of access even if the total number of events is less than 300. For studies which need the analysis of a complete set of commits, issues, pull requests and other events it becomes difficult to reproduce the software evolution process and draw substantive conclusions from the research study.

29.3.4   LINK HEADER

Hypertext Transfer Protocol Secure (HTTPS) is used to access data from GitHub API. HTTPS headers can be used with the API request URL to transmit and fetch additional information for a resource. For various resources such as commits, issues, and pull requests, data is provided by GitHub as an array of 30 items per page of output. For fetching all the data pages one by one, GitHub recommends using the Link header provided with the previous data page, that is, for the second page, a researcher needs to use the Link header value provided with the first page and so on, rather than manually constructing a URL with the required page number. This is recommended to avoid any conflict with future upgrades of the API. The general format of the Link header is shown in   Figure 29.3.

Link:

<https://api.github.com/user/repos?page=3&per_page=100>;rel="next",

<https://api.github.com/user/repos?page=50&per_page=100>; rel="last"

FIGURE 29.3   General format of HTTPS link header used in GitHub API.

Here, in the Link header, *rel* represents the relation of the additional data pages with the current URL. Possible *rel* values with their description are shown in Figure 29.4.

Name	Description
Next	The link relation for the immediate next page of results.
Last	The link relation for the last page of results.
First	The link relation for the first page of results.
Prev	The link relation for the immediate previous page of results.

FIGURE 29.4   Possible *rel* values for link header.

Next, commits data of reporeapers/reaper repository, hosted on GitHub, was fetched. The Link header obtained with the first page of the commits data is shown in Figure 29.5.

Link:

<https://api.github.com/repositories/31824415/commits?page=2>;rel="next,

<https://api.github.com/repositories/31824415/commits?page=12>;rel="last"

FIGURE 29.5 Link header obtained with first page of commits data of reporeapers/reaper repository.

It clearly indicates that there are a total of 12 pages of commits data. Moving further, data from the last page was fetched by using the URL as shown in Figure 29.6. The Link header obtained with this last page is shown in Figure 29.7.

https://api.github.com/repositories/31824415/commits?page=12

FIGURE 29.6 URL for fetching details of last page of commits of reporeapers/reaper repository.

Link:

<https://api.github.com/repositories/31824415/commits?page=13>;rel="next",

<https://api.github.com/repositories/31824415/commits?page=12>;rel="last"

<https://api.github.com/repositories/31824415/commits?page=1>;rel="first"

<https://api.github.com/repositories/31824415/commits?page=11>;rel="previous"

FIGURE 29.7 Link header obtained with last page of commits of reporeapers/reaper repository.

The Link header obtained with the last page of commits of reporeapers/reaper repository (Figure 29.7) shows *Page 13* as the next page of data although the repository has only 12 pages of commits data. When the URL for the nonexistent *Page 13* of commits data (Figure 29.8) was fed to the GitHub API, HTTPS status code 200 (meaning "No Error") was obtained. The Link header fetched with the page is shown in Figure 29.9.

https://api.github.com/repositories/31824415/commits?page=13

FIGURE 29.8 URL for page 13 of commits data of reporeapers/reaper repository.

Link:

<https://api.github.com/repositories/31824415/commits?page=1>;rel="first",

<https://api.github.com/repositories/31824415/commits?page=12>;rel="prev"

FIGURE 29.9   Link header obtained with nonexistent page 13 of reporeapers/reaper repository.

Thus, GitHub API returning address of a nonexistent page in the Link header can affect the results of applications that rely on the Link header for automatically accessing the data from all the pages.

29.3.5   MULTIPLE ROOT COMMITS

Version control system (VCS), also called revision control system, is a software application that is used to track changes to source code files. VCS is the backbone of OSS development. Modifications to the source code are added to the code repository in the form of a commit that saves the details of changed source code lines, timestamps, author/committer information and a link to the previous commit(s). Commits are arranged in a hierarchical manner so that the previous versions of the software can be retrieved easily. The first commit made to a software repository is called the root commit of the repository. A single-root commit is quite helpful in automatic research analysis of a software repository as it plays an important role in the following activities:

- Counting the total number of commits in a repository
- Computing the age of repository
- Finding details about authors and committers of the repository
- Tracing source code changes back to root commit to estimate the reliability, maintainability, etc.

Git, the primary VCS of GitHub, permits merging any number of different code bases into a single repository, leading to independent development of branches that do not share commit history, which ultimately produces multiple root commits. The official Git repository hosted on GitHub itself has 7 root commits. The presence of multiple root commits in software repositories makes the automatic analysis a difficult and challenging task for researchers.

29.3.6 AUTHOR AND COMMITTER

Git efficiently tracks modifications in the source code repository made by multiple developers. GitHub users, instead of making changes to a software project on GitHub's web interface, may clone a software repository on their local machines and then apply modifications to the source code through the Git command line. The changes can then be patched to the parent repository by the same user or any other project member having writable access to the repository. In Git terminology, the author is the original programmer who made the changes and the committer is the project member who pushed the code to the parent repository. Author as well as committer name and email_id can be set in the locally installed Git instance which also reflects in the Git commit object.

Author and committer identification is of utmost importance for a researcher exploring an OSS project as it assists in predicting the quality of the developer community working on the project. Researchers, working on GitHub repositories, extract author and committer information for individual commits through the GitHub Commits API, which tries to match the email provided in the local Git instance with the email_ids of registered users on GitHub. If there is a successful match, then GitHub provides complete information about the user; otherwise, it keeps the author_name and author_email fields as NULL in the API output. It may also happen that an email_id stored in the local Git instance may match to a completely different user on GitHub as Git performs no verifications while setting an email_id. Tracing the identity of author and committers becomes a challenging task in such cases where:

- GitHub API output provides no information of author and/or committer
- Multiple email_ids exist for the same author/committer

29.3.7 EXTERNAL BUG-TRACKING SYSTEMS

Bug tracking is an integrated part of OSS development. Bug-tracking systems, also called issue-tracking systems, allow users to report bugs encountered in the OSS. Bug trackers also provide the facility to request new features in the OSS project. GitHub provides its own bug-tracking system that allows users to report issues, label them with appropriate nouns, create milestones for their resolution, and assign users to manage these issues. Complete information about the issues can be extracted from the GitHub Issues API. Many OSS projects on GitHub are using external bug-tracking systems such as Bugzilla and Jira instead of its in-built issue tracker to manage bugs and feature requests associated with OSS projects. The data representation formats of these external bug-tracking systems do not necessarily match with GitHub's data schema. Hence, it becomes difficult to analyze such software repositories by mapping the issues (bugs and feature requests) with corresponding source code commits.

29.3.8   CATEGORIZATION OF ISSUES ON GITHUB

Tasks reported on a bug tracker can each be of a different priority and severity. Bug trackers provide different ways to highlight the threat of a task. The severity of a task can be low, medium, high, critical, or catastrophic. GitHub's inbuilt issue tracker enables the user to assign labels to issues in order to classify, prioritize, and manage issues.[14] Some of the best uses for GitHub labels are to assign priority of the issue, severity of the issue, deadline for the issue resolution or setting it as duplicate. In addition to some generic in-built labels, GitHub provides the facility to create new custom labels at the repository level that can be given any random name. These randomly named custom labels prove to be useful when dealing with a single software repository. However, it becomes cumbersome to uniformly categorize the customized labels when a large number of repositories are to be analyzed for research purposes. Absence of a homogeneous categorization of issues further leads to problems in formulating common hypotheses for the analysis of a large sample of software repositories.

29.3.9   REOPENED ISSUES

In OSS development, issue tracking and management is a vital component of the software development process. Issue-tracking systems are used to keep track of tasks, enhancements, and bugs related to a project. Whenever an issue is reported by someone, it is filtered, prioritized, and assigned to a developer for its resolution as it is a crucial element for the long-term stability of the project. All the issues that have been addressed and resolved by the developers are marked as closed. However, in exceptional cases, a previously closed issue may need to be reopened due to some reason associated with project development. Issue reopening is a deviation from the ideal software development behavior and is of particular interest to the software researchers.[1] Once resolved, an issue must not be reopened in a good quality software project. To avoid issue reopening in the future, the causes for the same must be carefully identified and analyzed.

GitHub's indigenous issue tracker provides the facility to reopen issues that have been previously closed. The state for both the originally opened and reopened issues is described as "open" in GitHub Issues API output. Moreover, the API output, which identifies the user who closed the issue, has fields "closed_by" and "closed_at" filled with NULL values for both the originally opened and the reopened issues, making it almost impossible to distinguish reopened issues from the issues that have never been closed. The nonidentification of reopened issues leads to difficulty in ascertaining the reasons for issue reopening and the areas of source code in software repositories for which issues have been reopened.

29.4   CONCLUSION

In this empirical study, a critical analysis of the publicly available data coming from GitHub (taken as a case study) has been made. Evidence has been presented in the current research work that automatic data extraction from GitHub is quite challenging. GitHub being used as a storage for personal content is one of the biggest threats to validity for any research using it as a primary data source. Restricted access on data fetching and pagination are the restrictions that GitHub has imposed to maintain the quality of service of its API. Link header is an issue that GitHub needs to address at its earliest so that software applications can use the links unambiguously. Multiple root commits and resolution of author and committer are the issues related to Git, the DVCS GitHub is using for version control. The last three data-fetching issues are related to bug tracking, whereby it has been found that software repositories using external bug trackers are hard to analyze due to the lack of uniformity among bug trackers. Evaluation of repositories using GitHub's in-built issue tracker is also quite challenging because of nonhomogeneous categorization of issues and lack of identification of reopened issues. An informed researcher, using GitHub as a source of data, must take into account these issues for performing a quality research on OSS projects. As a future scope of this research study, measures will be devised to overcome the issues identified in automatic data extraction to minimize the validity threats in research analysis of GitHub repositories.

KEYWORDS

- **open source software**
- **Git**
- **GitHub**
- **data retrieval issues**

REFERENCES

1. Gousios, G.; Spinellis, D. In *Mining Software Engineering Data from GitHub*, IEEE/ACM 39th International Conference on Software Engineering Companion (ICSE-C), May, 2017, IEEE; pp. 501–50.
2. GitHub About Page [Online]. https://github.com/about (accessed Nov 10, 2020).
3. Gousios, G.; Vasilescu, B.; Serebrenik, A.; Zaidman, A. In *Lean GHTorrent: GitHub Data on Demand*, Proceedings of the 11th Working Conference on Mining Software Repositories, May, 2014; pp. 384–387.
4. Bird, C.; Rigby, P. C.; Barr, E. T.; Hamilton, D. J.; German, D. M.; Devanbu, P. In *The Promises and Perils of Mining Git*, 6th IEEE International Working Conference on Mining Software Repositories, IEEE, May, 2009; pp. 1–10.
5. Gousios, G. In *The GHTorent Dataset and Tool Suite*, 10th Working Conference on Mining Software Repositories (MSR), IEEE, May, 2013; pp. 233–236.
6. Zimmermann, T.; Zeller, A.; Weissgerber, P.; Diehl, S. Mining version Histories to Guide Software Changes. *IEEE Trans. Soft. Eng.* **2005,** *31* (6), 429–445.
7. Ahmed, I.; Ghorashi, S.; Jensen, C. In *An Exploration of Code Quality in FOSS Projects*, IFIP International Conference on Open Source Systems, Springer: Berlin, Heidelberg, May, 2014; pp. 181–190.
8. Blincoe, K.; Sheoran, J.; Goggins, S.; Petakovic, E.; Damian, D. Understanding the Popular Users: Following, Affiliation Influence and Leadership on GitHub. *Inform. Soft. Technol.* **2016,** *70*, 30–39.
9. Onoue, S.; Hata, H.; Matsumoto, K. I. In *A Study of the Characteristics of Developers' Activities in GitHub*, 20th Asia-Pacific Software Engineering Conference (APSEC), IEEE, December, 2013; Vol. 2, pp. 7–12.
10. Di Ruscio, D.; Kolovos, D. S.; Korkontzelos, Y.; Matragkas, N.; Vinju, J. In *Supporting Custom Quality Models to Analyse and Compare Open-Source Software*, 10th International Conference on the Quality of Information and Communications Technology (QUATIC), IEEE, September, 2016; pp. 94–99.
11. Kochhar, P. S.; Thung, F.; Lo, D.; Lawall, J. In *An Empirical Study on the Adequacy of Testing in Open Source Projects*, 21st Asia-Pacific Software Engineering Conference, IEEE, December, 2014; Vol. 1, pp. 215–222.
12. Kalliamvakou, E.; Gousios, G.; Blincoe, K.; Singer, L.; German, D. M.; Damian, D. An In-Depth Study of the Promises and Perils of Mining GitHub. *Emp. Soft. Eng.* **2016,** *21* (5), 2035–2071.

13. Gousios, G.; Pinzger, M.; Deursen, A. V. In *An Exploratory Study of the Pull-based Software Development Model*, Proceedings of the 36th International Conference on Software Engineering, May, 2014; pp. 345–355.

14. Izquierdo, J. L. C.; Cosentino, V.; Rolandi, B.; Bergel, A.; Cabot, J. In *GiLA: GitHub label Analyzer*, IEEE 22nd International Conference on Software Analysis, Evolution, and Reengineering (SANER), IEEE, March 21, 2015; pp. 479–483.

CHAPTER 30

Proposed Model for Data Warehouse Requirement Engineering

HANU BHARDWAJ and JYOTI PRUTHI

Department of Computer Science & Technology, Manav Rachna University, Faridabad, India

ABSTRACT

The major focus and objective of data warehouse is to support in decision-making based on different kinds of available data and information. Requirement engineering in data warehouse plays a vital role and has gained importance over time. Requirement engineering is the process of identifying the need of all stakeholders and supporting those needs by a model. In this paper, we focus on former stage for data warehouse requirements engineering, that is, an "early information" part wherein relevant information for decision-making is discovered. Early information data warehouse requirements engineering starts with targets defined as pairs of the form <A, I>, wherein A is an organizational aspect and I is a business indicator's set. Targets are organized in a target hierarchy. This hierarchy is a complete specification of what is to be achieved by a top level target. We associate targets with choice sets so that alternative ways of target achievement can be represented. These alternatives form their own hierarchy. Finally, information relevant to selection of each alternative is discovered through Ends, Means, Key Success Factor, and Outcome Feedback analysis techniques. These techniques determine early information that is to be subsequently processed in the "late information"

Computational Intelligence in Analytics and Information Systems, Volume 2: Advances in Digital Transformation, Selected Papers from CIAIS-2021. Parneeta Dhaliwal, PhD, Manpreet Kaur, PhD, Hardeo Kumar Thakur, PhD, Rajeev Kumar Arya, and Joan Lu (Eds.)

requirements engineering stage. Appropriate techniques need to be identified for the elicitation of targets, sub-targets, choice sets etc.

30.1   INTRODUCTION

Requirements engineering in software engineering is the discipline concerned with understanding and documenting software requirements.[8] Requirements need to be gathered through an elicitation process, before they can be analyzed or modeled. Thus the requirements engineering process starts with requirements elicitation, which is followed by requirements analysis and specification. Elicitation of requirements is a process through which clients and developers discuss, review, and understand the needs of the clients and the constraints on the software.[4] The common techniques used for requirements elicitation, as listed in BABoK (Business Analyst Body of Knowledge), are interviews, questionnaires, brainstorming, prototyping/modeling, meeting focus groups, inspecting documents, observations, etc.

Data warehouses[2,5] can be applicable in different domains for assisting management in planning business processes, evaluation of performance of business processes, and support in making decisions in business processes. DW's main objective is to help in making decisions after analyzing distributed and heterogeneous information.

There is a significant difference in analyzing requirements for data warehouse systems as compared to analyzing requirements for traditional information systems. Difference lies in the nature of the problem addressed by the two kinds of systems itself. Traditional systems are "transaction" or "function" oriented and naturally, therefore, there is a need to discover and specify functions for the system to-be. On the other hand, in data warehouses, no "functions" are implemented. Rather, a collection of data that shall support the decision-making capability is to be identified. Therefore, the requirements engineering problem here is to find a way to identify this information and to structure it appropriately.

In its early years, data warehouse development was centered on the design problem. Approach followed by Bill Inmon for data warehouse is top-down which starts with the design of normalized data model. This is followed by the design of dimensional data marts centered around specific business processes or departments. The top-down approach has the disadvantage of representing a large project with a wide scope. Also it involves a significant up-front cost for the implementation of data warehouse, and there is a substantial time lag between the start of the project till the point where initial benefits can be experienced by the end users. This top-down approach is unresponsive and inflexible to varying needs of the departments at the time of implementation.

Bottom-up approach for designing a data warehouse has been given by Ralph Kimball. In this approach, creation of data marts is done first for providing reports and analysis for specific business processes, although the bottom-up approach used in Kimball methodology is the outcome of business-oriented top-down analysis of the relevant business processes to be considered for modeling.

30.2 PROPOSED PROBLEM

We have observed that the existing problem of requirements engineering in data warehouse is to define the information of a data warehouse to support the decision-making task at hand.

So we propose to partition this task into two parts:

a) "early information," wherein relevant information for decision-making is discovered.
b) "late," wherein the structuring of the information discovered is done as facts and dimensions.

Our focus will be on the former, that is, devising a way to elicit information that will go into the data warehouse for supporting in making decisions.

30.3 LITERATURE REVIEW

Requirements Engineering for data warehouses is gaining significance over the last few years. For data warehouse development, three life cycles have been referred,[9,10] which are driven by database schema, entity relationship diagram, and goals.

The life cycle discussed by Golfarelli starts with the development of database schema. It is based on the assumption that information contents of the data warehouse system are most likely defined by the contents of the data in operational databases. The idea behind designing the data warehouse follows the approach of exploring each relation of the database manually and makes a decision to adopt the same as fact/dimension in data warehouse. Relational databases do not support decision-making because they are designed for routine transactions. Also only the data existing in the database is considered, ignoring the data from external sources, which results in limited decision-making capability of the data warehouse constructed.

Now consider the life cycle that is based on entity relationship diagram (ERD) as proposed by Hüseman in.[7] The source of constructing ERD is either the relational databases or the operational systems. The limitation of considering only the ERD information and ignoring the information from external or internal sources is faced in this approach. And, moreover, this approach is not appropriate for handling complicated and random queries, which is the lifeline of data warehouses. ERD results in extremely normalized relations, which does not lead to a good data warehouse design that can handle intuitive queries. Kimball also stated "Entity relation models cannot be used as the basis for enterprise data warehouses," which discourages the use of ERD for data warehouse development.

Boehnlein, Golfarelli in[2] discuss the third approach of designing DW that is based on the goals of the organization and stakeholders involved. Horkoff in[6] also states that "goal modeling is not yet widely used in practice," although it has been applicable in case studies. Rolland in[12] discusses about the factors that stand in the way of adopting techniques based on goals: "(a) domain experts find the notion of a goal to be fuzzy which makes it difficult to deal with it, and (b) goal reduction is not a straightforward process." Thus, the similar issues are faced in requirement engineering for data warehouses as well.

30.4   PROPOSED OBJECTIVE

Our proposal here is directly related to determining the information that shall be stored in the data warehouse. The outcome of our requirements engineering step is not the multidimensional schema but early information that is unstructured. It identifies at a top level the information that is needed and is to be structured in subsequent stages.

30.5   PROPOSED METHODOLOGY

We trace the requirements engineering process and the various steps comprising the process are as shown in Figure 30.1:

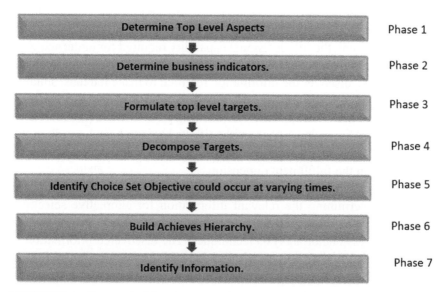

FIGURE 30.1 Steps comprising the process for proposed approach.

Our proposal for early information requirements engineering starts off by determining targets that organizations want to achieve. We define target as a pair, <A, I> where A is an organizational aspect and I is a set of business indicators. An aspect represents a work area, work unit, service, or quality in an organization. Business indicators are measures/metrics of aspect performance.[11]

The notion of target hierarchy is proposed which involves target reduction. This can be done by following either the aspect-driven or the indicator-driven approach.[1,3] In the former, sub-aspects of a top-level target are determined and their business indicators are found to form sub-targets. In the latter, sub-business indicators that go into computing the top-level business indicators are determined, their aspects found, and sub-targets formulated. Thus, we have a relatively clear basis for guiding target reduction as compared to goal reduction. We refer the target hierarchy as a relevance hierarchy also.

Although target hierarchies identify what the organization wants to achieve, decision-making is to be done to indeed achieve targets. Now we consider the second step of our "early information" requirements engineering stage. In this case, we associate choice sets with targets. We define a choice set as a pair <CSO, O> where CSO is the choice set objective and O is the set of alternatives for meeting the CSO. And similar to target reduction, we have choice set reduction. Each sub-choice set is associated with the target that it affects. This hierarchy is referred to as fulfillment hierarchy.

At this moment, the full decisional capability required for target achievement is known. Now, in the last stage of early information requirements engineering, we discover the information required to make the most suitable selections from choice sets.

We observe that indicators are the "sticking glue" between the relevance and fulfillment dimensions: (i) they identify "what is to be achieved" in the relevance hierarchy and (ii) can be used as a basis for defining "how it is to be achieved" in the fulfillment dimension.

Once choice sets have been discovered in the fulfillment dimension, the issue is of determining the relevant information for alternative selection. This information is discovered through Ends, Means, Outcome Feedback, and Key Success Factor analysis techniques. The discovered information is "early," abstract, fuzzy, and unstructured. It is to be converted into facts and dimensions in subsequent stages using the techniques spelled out in.[9] The proposed model as shown in Figure 30.2.

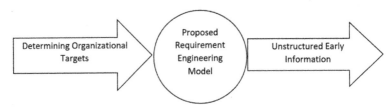

FIGURE 30.2   Input and expected outcome—proposed model.

KEYWORDS

- **data warehouse**
- **requirement engineering**
- **business intelligence**
- **business modeling**

30.6   CONCLUSION

The outcome of this proposed work shall be to propose a reliable method of gathering requirements for a data warehouse. It is hoped that the research investigations reported and suggestions made thereof would be very useful to the industry engaged in building data warehouses.

REFERENCES

1. Barone, D.; Jiang, L.; Amyot, D.; Mylopoulos, J. Composite Indicators for Business Intelligence. In *Conceptual Modeling—ER 2011. ER 2011. Lecture Notes in Computer Science*; Jeusfeld, M., Delcambre, L., Ling, T. W., Eds.; Vol. 6998; Springer: Berlin, Heidelberg, 2011; pp. 448–458.
2. Boehnlein, M.; Ulbrichvom Ende, A. In *Deriving Initial Data Warehouse Structures from the Conceptual Data Models of the Underlying Operational Information Systems*, Proceedings of Workshop on Data Warehousing and OLAP (DOPLAP), Kansas City, MO, USA; 1999.
3. Frank, U.; Heise, D.; Kattenstroth, H.; Schauer, H. Designing and Utilizing Indicator Systems Within Enterprise Models—Outline of a Method; *MobIS*, pp. 89–105; 2008.
4. Goguen, J. A.; Linde, C. In *Techniques for Requirements Elicitation*, Proceedings of the International Symposium on Requirements Engineering, Colorado Springs, CO, April 18–22, 1993; IEEE Computer Society Press: Los Alamitos, CA, 1993.
5. Golfarelli, M.; Maio, D.; Rizzi, S. The Dimensional Fact Model: A Conceptual Model for Data Warehouses. *Int. J. Coop. Inf. Syst.* **1998**, *7* (2–3), 215–247.
6. Horkoff, J.; Yu, E. Comparison and Evaluation of Goal-oriented Satisfaction Analysis Techniques, *Requirements Eng.* **2013**, *18*, 199–222.
7. Hüsemann, B.; Lechtenbörger, J.; Vossen, G. In *Conceptual Data Warehouse Design*, Proceedings of the International Workshop on Design and Management of Data Warehouses (DMDW 2000), Stockholm, Sweden, 2000; pp. 5–6.
8. Prakash, N.; Singh, Y.; Gosain, A. Informational Scenarios for Data Warehouse Requirements Specification. In *Conceptual Modeling-ER'2004*; Atzeni, P., Chu, W., Zhou, S., Ling, T. K., Eds.; LNCS 3288, Springer, pp. 205–216; 2004.
9. Prakash, N.; Gosain A. An Approach to Engineering the Requirements of Data Warehouses. *Requirements Eng. J.* **2008**, *13* (1), 49–72.
10. Prakash, N.; Prakash, D.; Sharma, Y. K. *Towards Better Fitting Data Warehouse Systems*; Persson, A., Stirna, J., Eds.; PoEM 2009, LNBIP 39, 2009; pp. 130–144.
11. Prakash, N.; Bhardwaj, H. Early Information Requirements Engineering for Target Driven Data Warehouse Development, In *The Practice of Enterprise Modeling. PoEM 2012. Lecture Notes in Business Information Processing*; Sandkuhl, K., Seigerroth, U., Stirna, J., Eds.; Vol. 134; Springer: Berlin, Heidelberg, 2012; pp. 188–202.
12. Rolland, C. In *Reasoning with Goals to Engineer Requirements*, International Conference on Enterprise Information Systems, France, 2003.

CHAPTER 31

Random Cloudlet Priority Scheduling: An Enhanced Approach

SUMIT BANSAL[1], HIMANSHU AGARWAL[2], and MAYANK AGARWAL[1]

[1]*Gurukula Kangri (Deemed to be University), Computer Science & Engineering Department, Haridwar, Uttrakhand, India*

[2]*Computer Science & Engineering Department, Punjabi University, Patiala, Punjab, India*

ABSTRACT

In this fast-growing world, everything needs to be done quickly and at the earliest. The cloud computing is a technology that makes the globalization easier by managing the tasks at various levels and dividing the whole process into very small parts to maximize the output. A very essential component is scheduling because prioritizing the task in an orderly fashion is more important than completing the task haphazardly. In this research paper we tried to devise a new algorithm in the scheduling and introduced it in this paper with the name of Random Priority Scheduling Algorithm (RPSA) that focuses on the drawbacks of starvation and cost. Starvation is defined as too much accomplishment of high-priority task on a regular basis and overlooking of low-priority task resulting in disuse of cloudlet servers in inadequate proportion. In this experiment an attention to makespan has also been given to make the process efficient in various parameters.

Computational Intelligence in Analytics and Information Systems, Volume 2: Advances in Digital Transformation, Selected Papers from CIAIS-2021. Parneeta Dhaliwal, PhD, Manpreet Kaur, PhD, Hardeo Kumar Thakur, PhD, Rajeev Kumar Arya, and Joan Lu (Eds.)

31.1 INTRODUCTION

Cloud computing (CC) is next-generation computing and software technology that basically provides a higher and better level of computing experience to the user. The user could use advanced software and compilation technology at the same site (anywhere in the world), with the same hardware, with minimal resource consumption of the user, at a minimal cost in a short time. CC provides the user with characteristically three interfaces that decrease the need of purchasing them separately and also provides efficient coordination between them, so that the user gets the best ever experience of computing technology.[1,3] Cloud computing can provide its services at various levels by following different types of deployment models which include public cloud, community cloud, private cloud, and hybrid cloud. Cloud computing becomes an integral part because of its high qualities and better efficiency. It increases the scope of improvement in various values like that of cost of technology, completion and execution time, power consumption reduction, better resource utilization, makespan and response time, etc. Even after so much growth in this field, there is large scope left in maintaining few items such as load balancing, virtualization, fault tolerance, and newer scheduling programmes.[2,20] Devising an algorithm for scheduling carries two main functions: allotting the task/ cloudlet to the virtual machine by applying the formula devised in the algorithm and submitting the cloudlet to the cloud computing server for the completion of the task. While forming an algorithm, few things have to be kept in mind that the parameters such as bandwidth, load balancing, price of the service, priority vector, makespan, and comparison matrix should be checked and compared for the assessment of the new method and its efficiency.[10,17]

The proposed work in this paper has been experimented and simulated on a simulated tool known as CloudSim Toolkit. The comparisons between the various parameters describing the efficiency of existing algorithms and Random Priority Based Scheduling Algorithm have been shown in the form of graphs. We have proposed a new algorithm random priority scheduling algorithm (RPSA), which works by the pattern that the tasks are allotted the priority, but also they are scheduled randomly so as to make sure that none of the tasks whether it is high or low priority gets delayed. The results collected after applying on a simulator tool are compared with the pre-existing algos such as CM-eFCFS, SJF, RR, Min-Min and are displayed in the form of graphs and tables in this paper. The results show clearly that the newer algorithm developed Random Priority Scheduling Algorithm (RPSA) is better than the existing ones. The main priority and focus of this paper are kept on: (a) Devising an algorithm for solving the problem of starvation that is not solved by any of the pre-existing algorithms. (b) Formulation of an algorithm for better efficiency, scalability, time management, and quality of work.

Neelam et al.[16] introduced a scheduling algorithm CM-eFCFS, which is a confined cloud migration (CM)-based scheduling algorithm. The aim of the algorithm is to minimize the cost, resource utilization, and makespan. This paper presents the migration of cloudlets from one to another free cloudlet, and thus 99.8% resource utilization is achieved. Krishnaveni and Prakash[9] introduced a new efficient algorithm Execution Time Based Sufferage Algorithm (ETSA) that works more efficiently to improve the parameters such as makespan and resource utilization. In their work, the authors try to schedule the number of tasks to improve the overall efficiency of the algorithm. Malleswari and Vadivu[11] have proposed an approach a deduplication approach for a live virtual machine for effective overloading and underloading policies for VM migration. The rolling Karp algorithm is used in this process to enhance the security effectiveness. The reduction in this space size is dependent in this manner on implementation of the existing deduplication techniques fixed length, variable length block deduplication techniques and compared with proposed adaptive deduplication techniques. Fikru and Abebe[5] have proposed a approach namely the approach VM placement algorithm Modified Best-Fit Decreasing (MBFD) is based on a heuristic that handles only minimizing the number of servers. The heuristic is not only less energy efficient but also increases Service Level Agreement (SLA) violation and consequently causes more VM migrations. Somula and Sasikala[19] proposed an algorithm named honey bee, inspired by cloud-lets selection for resource allocation and resource-intensive applications from users. This algorithm not only selects low loaded cloudlet but also performs load balancing among cloudlets, which reduces the waiting time, user offloading task in queue. Mazumder et al.[12] have proposed a dynamic allocation algorithm that allocates the type of task in cloud computing for efficient computing. By making use of this algorithm makespan has been reduced than the min–min algorithm and also the average waiting time is reduced by 46.7% than the max–min algorithm. Hung et al.[7] proposed the MMSIA algorithm to improve the max–min scheduling algorithm by using the "Learned Learning" machine learning. Because of this the processing time in the cloud data center has been reduced, which implies that this algorithm has improved cloud performance and enabled faster excess to cloud services for users. Gravitational Search Algorithm (GSA) and Non-Dominated Sorting Genetic Algorithm-II (NSGA-II) have been presented by Ketaki et al.,[8] concentering on the new approach Hybrid multi-Heuristic algorithm (HH), which works on three objectives: execution cost, response time, and energy consumption. This algorithm's aim is to achieve minimum response time and execution time. A priority-based process scheduling algorithm has been proposed by Misbahul et al.[13] in cloud computing developed by using block-based Queue. The aim of this article that uses preemptive part is to calculate the energy consumption and reduce starvation of process based on their burst time and lead time. To evaluate inline works scheduling algorithms have been presented by Durgesh et al.,[4] which prepares its execution order. Keeping in mind the targeted role new jobs are evaluated by this algorithm with this cost of execution being minimized and completion time is also reduced. Greedy approach has been used to schedule the task and to select the resource in this paper.

31.2   SYSTEM MODEL AND COMPONENTS

The system model represents the components of the process and its hardware and software parts. It can be shown in the form of a flow chart or a diagram to make it easy to understand as well as to design it in a real scenario. It consists of cloudlets represented by C_1, C_2, and C_3 at one end which are assigned to their specific virtual machines labeled as Vm_1, Vm_2, and Vm_3 at the other end. Each of the tasks assigned runs independently and in a parallel fashion making it possible to do more than one task at the same time. The proposed system model is tried and tested at a simulation device known as CloudSim Tool. This toolkit provides nearly real-time situations and configurations so as to make the results comparable and applicable in real time.[14] The components of the model are divided into two parts: first of which consists of operating system, virtual machine, and its monitor, time zone etc. and these are known as data center characteristics shown in Figure 31.1. Few other requirements such as Random Access Memory (RAM), Storage, Bandwidth, Process elements, and Schedular are known as Host characteristics. The initial most step in this system is of cloudlet that is characterized by size of the input file, length, number of processing elements to be required for its completion. The system model also is characterized by Virtual Machine (VM) Characteristics that include RAM, schedular, bandwidth, storage etc.; the process in the model is based on the datacenter broker method with subparts such as VM creation, submission, and distraction.[6]

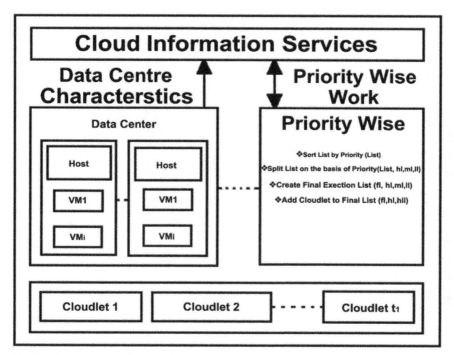

FIGURE 31.1 Proposed scheduling approach.

31.2.1 FLOW CHART DESCRIPTION FOR PROPOSED APPROACH

In Figure 31.2 the steps of the proposed algorithm have been shown; it starts when the user sends a request for some task and then the computing system calculates the time needed by the VM for being ready. Then cloud checks again for the cloudlet list, if the list is found empty then the process ends. If the cloudlet list has some task remaining, then first it gets selected and then its execution and completion time are calculated. After that it is assigned to a VM given by a higher priority and ready time of the VM is updated again for the next task. After the task is over the process ends.

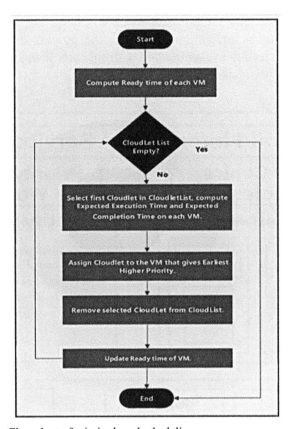

FIGURE 31.2   Flow chart of priority-based scheduling.

31.2.1.1   *ALGORITHM OF RANDOM SCHEDULING PRIORITY ALGORITHM (RSPA)*

Set priority randomly to the cloudlet as—High, Medium, Low

1. Make 4 ArrayList for storing different cloudlets
    (a) FinalList for storing all cloudlets in priority order
    (b) HighList for storing all cloudlets of high priority
    (c) MediumList for storing all cloudlets of medium priority
    (d) LowList for storing all cloudlets of low priority
2. Assign priority to cloudlet as
    HighPriority cloudlet =0,

MediumPriority cloudlet =1,

LowPriority cloudlet =2

3. Add all cloudlets in their respective list

4. Add all cloudlets from different lists in an order such that it cannot create a problem of starvation.

   First we add 2 high-priority cloudlets, then 1 medium-priority cloudlet and after 2 medium-priority cloudlet we add 1 low-priority cloudlet in FinalList.

5. We execute it in the same order.

This will not create a problem of starvation and execute in their respective priority.

31.2.2 *CLOUDLET ORDER WITH RANDOM PRIORITY*

Cloud computing is a platform provided for the conversion of a simpler form of data into a complex and concise application via intelligent software. To determine the sequence of sending the data and related task to the cloud software the process followed is known as scheduling. It makes the approach very simple by arranging them in an order on the basis of some parameters and already-decided manner.[15,18] This arrangement is based on a preliminary requirement known as algorithm. The algorithm provides a basic structure for arranging the jobs to be done according to the requirement of the developer. The algorithm developer puts a parameter like priority on the basis of resource, application, time, etc. When the parameter is set then the algorithm is developed for describing it further and applying it to the tasks. The commonly used parameters are on the basis of priority and urgency of the task to be done. The major drawback of this technique is that the lower priority tasks get overlooked and neglected but to overcome this problem we have tried to put on a new algorithm to be known as Random Scheduling Priority Algorithm. The quality of this algorithm is that it maintains the priority of the jobs that was maintained by the older algorithms, but at the same time it does not compromise in the completion of lesser priority task by keeping the scheduling process to be random also. The picking up of lower and higher priority tasks is completely random, but the number of each of them to be picked up at the same time is constant and depends upon the availability of the number of virtual machines and the count set on the algorithm parameters is shown in Figure 31.3.

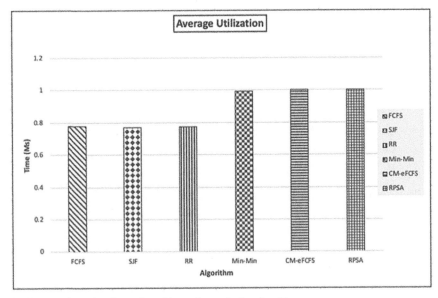

FIGURE 31.3   Cloudlet order with random priority algorithm.

The biggest advantage of Random Priority Scheduling Algorithm (RPSA) is that it is very simple to apply because of being a random selector of tasks and it also maintains the integrity of the cloud computing system by keeping the choices on priority bases also. It checks the overloading of a single virtual machine and underworking of another virtual machine and provides the much necessary balance between the various machines.

31.3   RESULTS AND DISCUSSION

31.3.1   *IMPLEMENTATION*

After the proposition of the theoretical framework of our new algorithm it is tried and tested upon a tool known as CloudSim. This tool provides a simulated environment for the application of the new algorithm Random priority scheduling algorithm (RPSA). Table 31.1 shows the parameters and configurations of the simulator tool that includes RAM, Bandwidth, MIPS, System Architecture, Operating System, Size, No. of Processing Elements, Storage, Virtual Machine Monitor, etc.

TABLE 31.1 Cloud Configuration Explanation.

Tool configuration	No. of VM = 2	No. of VM = 4	No. of VM = 8
Operating system:	Linux	Linux	Linux
System architecture:	X86	X86	X86
VMM:	Xen	Xen	Xen
VM explanation			
Size (amount of storage):	10000 (MB)	10000 (MB)	10000 (MB)
MIPS:	1000	1000	1000
Bandwidth	1000	1000	1000
RAM:	512	512	512
File size	300	300	300
Host explanation			
RAM:	2048 (MB)	2048 (MB)	4096 (MB)
Bandwidth:	10000	10000	10000
Cloudlet length	600	800	1000
No. of PE:	2	4	8
Storage:	1000000	1000000	1000000

After the implementation of the algorithm on the simulator tool the results were obtained and compared with the existing algorithm such as CM-eFCFS, RR, SJF, and Min-Min. The comparison between the newer and older algorithms will establish the supremacy of one over the another. There are many ways to detect the efficiency of a particular algorithm, when applied in a particular setting some of which are:

Cost: It is the first and foremost factor deciding the algorithm's performance because it should be cost effective; otherwise, the motive for a newer technology will be defeated. Also, the user is most concerned about the cost of the task rather than about the priority.

$$\text{Processing Cost} = \sum_{j=1}^{m} \text{Cos} t * EVMj \qquad (31.1)$$

Resource utilization: The availability of the server and virtual machines and the time for which they are working are significant; if the virtual machine is idle for too much time then the resource utilization is poor and wastage is more.

$$\text{Average Utilization} = \frac{\sum j / VMs\, CTj}{Makespan * Number\, of\, VMs} \qquad (31.2)$$

Execution Time (ET): The time taken for the fulfilment of cloudlet after getting recruited according to the algorithm on the cloud computing software. It does not include the time taken to get the priority to the task and the idle waiting time of task before getting recruited. It helps in defining the efficiency of working machines (Virtual Machines).

Completion Time (CT): The time difference between the assigning of the task to a particular virtual machine to till the end of complete execution and production of results.

Makespan: The time elapsed from the beginning of process that is coming of the task to get performed to till the entire accomplishment of the job. It is the longest time interval among all the time parameters.

$$\text{Makespan} = \max\left(CTj\right)j \;\; \in VMs \qquad (31.3)$$

It is favorable for an algorithm to have a smaller makespan to prove its efficiency and time-saving quality.[21]

31.3.2   COMPARISON OF MAKESPAN

A mathematical formulation is used to calculate the makespan that is given in eq 31.3 and Graphs 31.1 and 31.2 show the different ranges of makespan on different numbers of cloudlets working on four Virtual machines.

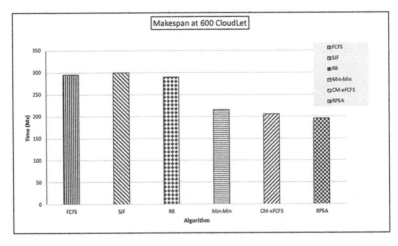

GRAPH 31.1   Makespan values at Cloudlet 600.

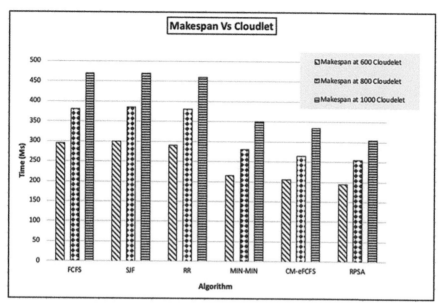

GRAPH 31.2   Makespan values at different cloudlets.

After seeing the compared data, it has been concluded that RSPA is very much efficient in utilizing the time over the other previous existing algorithms.

31.3.3   COMPARISON OF UTILIZATION

Resource utilization is defined as the maximum usage of the available resources so as to get maximum output in the minimum resources. It is calculated by using the mathematical formulation as described in eq 31.2. For reducing the cost of the process, it is required to diminish the wastage of resources and increase high yield out of minimum resources.

It also signifies the efficiency of the setup and the process. In the comparison Graph 31.3 shown earlier, we have compared RSPA with the previous existing algorithms such as Min-min, FCFS, RR, and CM-eFCFS. On the comparison it is found that the process used by our algorithm is very efficient and there is very minimal wastage of resources when compared to older algorithms.

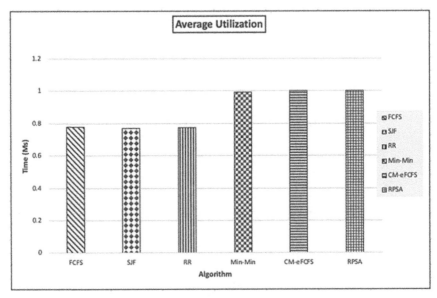

GRAPH 31.3   Average utilization of resources at different algorithms.

31.4   CONCLUSION

Since the ever-rising demand for a more efficient computing system is raising the bars of technology, newer algorithms would be needed to meet them. By keeping this in mind we have proposed an algorithm called Random Priority Based Scheduling Algorithm that provides a better result when compared to the existing algorithm including CM-eFCFS, Min-Min, SJFS, and RR. In earlier developed algorithms the major technique was making the schedule on the basis of priority due to which the lower priority tasks may get left out. But, in Random Scheduling Priority Algorithm (RSPA) the lower priority task has also been given importance without compromising the resources requirement of the high priority tasks. It not only focuses on the problem of starvation but also gets significant improvements in makespan time, average utilization etc. In this research, the makespan of the algorithm is 193.23 which is lower than the value of 209.19 of the existing algorithms. It is a significant number and our algorithm has shown great improvement over the others. With comparison of other algorithms, it is observed that our approach uses minimal resources of wastage. The cost for this algorithm is slightly on the higher side and it can be improved on further efforts. So, after the analyses of various algorithms such as CM-eFCFS, RR, SJF, and min–min, it is safe to conclude that the proposed algorithm Random Scheduling Priority Algorithm is better in all the parameters and can be used for future cloud computing purposes.

KEYWORDS

- **cloudlet**
- **cloud computing**
- **VM migration**
- **utilization**
- **cost**
- **resource utilization**

REFERENCES

1. AlShayeji, M. H.; Samrajesh, M. D. Energy Efficient Virtual Machine Migration Algorithm. *J. Eng. Res.* **2017,** *5* (2), 19–42.
2. Amalarethinam, I. G.; Leena, H. M. In *Enhanced RSA Algorithm with Varying Key Sizes for Data Security in Cloud*, 2017 World Congress on Computing and Communication Technologies, 2017; pp. 172–175.
3. Chen, W.; Xie, G.; Li, R.; Bai, Y.; Fan, C.; Li, K. Efficient Task Scheduling for Budget Constrained Parallel Applications on Heterogeneous Cloud Computing Systems. *Future Gener. Comput. Syst.* **2017,** *74* (C), 1–11.
4. Durgesh, N. J.; Gill, S. K.; Sharma, P.; Singh, V. P. Optimization of Task Scheduling and Cloudlets Cost Scheduling Algorithms on Cloud Using Cloud Simulator. *Int. J. Adv. Stud. Sci. Res.* **2019,** *4* (2).
5. Feleke, F.; Abebe, S. L. Energy-aware VM Placement Algorithms for the OpenStack Neat Consolidation Framework. *J. Cloud Comput.* **2019,** *8* (1), 1–14.
6. Haque, M.; Islam, R.; Kabir, M. R.; Nur, F. N.; Moon, N. N. A Priority-based Process Scheduling Algorithm in Cloud Computing. In *Emerging Technologies in Data Mining and Information Security*; Vol. 755; Springer: Singapore, 2019; pp. 239–248.
7. Hung, T. C.; Hieu, L. N.; Hy, P. T.; Phi, N. X. MMSIA: In *Improved Max-Min Scheduling Algorithm for Load Balancing on Cloud Computing*, Proceedings of the 3rd International Conference on Machine Learning and Soft Computing, 2019; pp. 60–64.
8. Ketaki, G.; Gandhi, M.; Patil, S. H. Multiobjective Virtual Machine Selection for Task Scheduling in Cloud Computing. In *Computational Intelligence: Theories, Applications and Future Directions-Volume I*; Springer: Singapore, 2019; pp. 319–331.
9. Krishnaveni, H.; Prakash, V. S. J. Execution Time based Sufferage Algorithm for Static Task Scheduling in Cloud. In *Advances in Big Data and Cloud Computing*; Springer: Singapore, 2019; pp. 61–70.

10. Kumar, D.; Jaiswal, N.; Gill, S. K.; Sharma, P.; Singh, V. P. Optimization of Task Scheduling and Cloudlets Cost Scheduling Algorithms on Cloud Using Cloud Simulator. *Int. J. Adv. Stud. Sci. Res.* **2019,** *4* (2).

11. Malleswari, T. Y. J.; Vadivu, G. Adaptive Deduplication of Virtual Machine Images using AKKA Stream to Accelerate Live Migration Process in Cloud Environment. *J. Cloud Comput.* **2019,** *8* (1), 1–12.

12. Mazumder, A. M. R.; Uddin, K. A.; Arbe, N.; Jahan, L.; Whaiduzzaman, M. In *Dynamic Task Scheduling Algorithms in Cloud Computing*, 2019 3rd International Conference on Electronics, Communication and Aerospace Technology (ICECA), IEEE, 2019; pp. 1280–1286.

13. Misbahul, R. I., Kabir, M. R.; Nur, F. N.; Moon, N. N. A Priority-based Process Scheduling Algorithm in Cloud Computing. In *Emerging Technologies in Data Mining and Information Security*; Springer: Singapore, 2019; pp. 239–248.

14. Moges, F. F.; Abebe, S. L. Energy-aware VM Placement Algorithms for the OpenStack Neat Consolidation Framework. *J. Cloud Comput.* **2019,** *8* (1), 1–14.

15. Naik, K.; Gandhi, G. M.; Patil, S. H. Multiobjective Virtual Machine Selection for Task Scheduling in Cloud Computing. In *Computational Intelligence: Theories, Applications and Future Directions-Volume I*; Springer: Singapore, 2019; pp. 319–331.

16. Panwar, N.; Negi, S.; Rauthan, M. S.; Aggarwal, M.; Jain, P. An Enhanced Scheduling Approach with Cloudlet Migrations for Resource Intensive Applications. *J. Eng. Sci. Technol.* **2018,** *13* (8), 2299–2317.

17. Razzaq, S.; Wahid, A.; Khan, F.; Amin Ul, N.; Shah, M. A.; Akhunzada, A.; Ali, I. Scheduling Algorithms for High-Performance Computing: An Application Perspective of fog Computing. In *Recent Trends and Advances in Wireless and IoT-enabled Networks*; Springer: Cham, 2019; pp. 107–117.

18. Rizwana S.; Sasikumar M. Data Classification for Achieving Security in Cloud Computing. *J. Procedia Comput. Sci.* **2015,** *45*, 493–498.

19. Somula, R.; Sasikala, R. A Honey Bee Inspired Cloudlet Selection for Resource Allocation. In *Smart Intelligent Computing and Applications*; Springer: Singapore, 2019; pp. 335–343.

20. Tari, Z.; Yi, X. Security and Privacy in Cloud Computing: Vision, Trends, and Challenges. *IEEE J. Cloud Comput.* **2015,** *2* (2), 30–38.

21. Zhou, Z.; Li, F.; Zhu, H.; Xie, H.; Abawajy, J. H.; Chowdhury, M. U. An Improved Genetic Algorithm using Greedy Strategy Toward Task Scheduling Optimization in Cloud Environments. *Neural Comput. Applic.* **2020,** *32*, 1531–1541.

CHAPTER 32

RAFI: Parallel Dynamic Test-Suite Reduction for Software

NAJNEEN, MANISH KUMAR MUKHIJA, and SATISH KUMAR

Department of Computer Science, Arya Inst. of Engg. & Tech., Jaipur, Rajasthan, India

ABSTRACT

A pattern in programming testing diminishes the size of a test suite while protecting its general quality. For programming, test cases and a bunch of requirements are given. Each test case is covering a few requirements. In this paper, we will probably discover the technique for test-suite reduction to compute the subset of test cases covering every one of the requirements. While this issue has acquired huge consideration, it is as yet hard to track down the littlest subset of test cases and generally utilized strategies to tackle this issue with inexact arrangements. In this paper, we will likely track down the technique for test-suite reduction to find the subset of test cases that are covering every one of the requirements across renditions. There are as of now existing greedy algorithms and exponential-time algorithms to discover the TRS in a rendition explicit and across adaptations. We proposed another similar greedy heuristic technique RAFI to discover negligible test sets across forms. Our methodology shows that: (i) RAFI is a lot quicker than the exponential-time method and roughly multiple times quicker than the traditional greedy technique. (ii) RAFI strategy generally accomplishes a similar decrease rate contrasted with the traditional greedy method.

Computational Intelligence in Analytics and Information Systems, Volume 2: Advances in Digital Transformation, Selected Papers from CIAIS-2021. Parneeta Dhaliwal, PhD, Manpreet Kaur, PhD, Hardeo Kumar Thakur, PhD, Rajeev Kumar Arya, and Joan Lu (Eds.)

32.1   INTRODUCTION

We can testify that software products' quality is a massive problem for the software industry, and software failure is a significant loss for a software company. Software testing is an essential technique for software quality solace, and it is a challenging but necessary process of growth of information. If we increase software size, we increase the quantity of test cases, and automatically cost will be increased. If we design software test cases, then we have to fulfill the demand of the software quality. So a cardinal set of the test cases is redundant. We are selecting a minimum cardinal subset for selecting a test case of requirements. Test suite reduction (TSR)[3–5] can solve the condition's problem and decrease the activity load, automatically reducing software testing costs. The TSR technique[6–8] goes under regression testing.[1,2] This paper can satisfy how we select a base number of test cases and satisfy every one of the prerequisites. It is the key to the topic of test case reduction.

Next, every software has some defect, less feature, and some BUGs. So we are releasing the new version of the programming with a BUG fix or an additional feature. Before releasing the feature again, we have to test our software for quality and correctness purposes. For this reason, the normal way is to refind the minimal test set to execute our software. Then it will become more costly to find the reduced test set again. In this paper, we propose a RAFI method to find the reduced test set across the versions by using the information of added features and the previous version's reduced test set. Now we will understand what the test suite reduction problem is. We will define the test suite reduction problem[10,11] as follows:

1. If T = {r1, r2, r3, r4, r5,........rn} are the requirements of the software.
2. If R = {t1, t2, t3, t4, t5, ...tn} are the test cases of software.
3. If S = {(t,r)} S is the connection between requirements and the test cases.

Some test cases cover each requirement, and each test case will cover some requirements. In the example (see Fig. 32.1), * indicates that there is a connection between the corresponding requirement and the test case.[9] The above notation can be said to be the array representation of the coverage graph. Coverage graph is the graph that will show the relationship between the test cases and the requirements. We can also represent this relation by bipartite graphs.[11–13]

	r1	r2	r3	r4	r5	r6	r7	r8
t1	*		*			*		
t2		*		*	*			*
t3		*	*			*		
t4			*		*		*	
t5		*		*	*		*	

FIGURE 32.1 Test cases cover the requirements. *There is a connection between the corresponding requirement and the test case.

In Figure 32.1, there are a lot of test sets that are covering all the requirements, for example, {t1, t2, t4, t5}, {t1, t2, t4}, etc. But we observe that the second subset is minimal than the first one. So we can say that subset {t1, t2, t4} is the minimal subset covering all the requirements. In this t1 is covering {r1,r3}, t2 is covering {r2, r4, r5, r8}, and t3 is covering {r3, r5, r7}. We can say that {t1, t2, t4} covers all the requirements and the reduced test set. There are many approaches for TSR, some are exponential, and some are polynomial-time approaches.

32.2 BACKGROUND AND RELATED WORK

This section discussed some existing methods of implementing Test Suite Reduction techniques, which we can use to find the reduced test set in a particular version or across the versions. Some of the techniques are the Exponential and polynomial-time algorithms.

32.2.1 *EXPONENTIAL TIME ALGORITHMS*

There are several algorithms for Test Suite reduction whose time complexity is exponential, which gives the exact, and the Flower method is one method.

32.2.1.1 *FLOWER METHOD*

The flower method[14] comes under the exact approach. We can get the optimal solution by using this method. In this method, we solve a problem as a flow network[15] and use the Ford Fulkerson algorithm.[15] The Flower technique addresses a network of flow where each edge has a limit. Likewise, given two vertices, source S and sink D, in the graph, discover the greatest conceivable stream from S to D. Stream tense does not surpass the given limit of the edge. Inflow is equivalent to outflow for each vertex aside from S to D. Time complexity of this algorithm is exponential and equal to $O((2^\wedge|\text{test cases}|)*\text{edges} * |\text{requirements}|)$, which seems an exponential time approach. The Flower method is an integer linear programming (ILP) method.[16,17]

32.2.2   POLYNOMIAL-TIME ALGORITHMS

There are several algorithms for Test Suite reduction whose time complexity is polynomial, which give approximate results. The traditional greedy method is one of the methods.

32.2.2.1   TRADITIONAL GREEDY METHOD

Traditional greedy[18] is a heuristic approach to find the reduced test set that covers all requirements. We will not get the exact result that we are expecting, but we can get the approximate solution for this. This approach iteratively selects a test case that will cover all the maximum number of remaining requirements. We performed this iteratively until all requirements are not covered. A traditional Greedy method is a heuristic approach, so time complexity is polynomial. Its time complexity depends on the quantity of requirements, the quantity of test cases, and the relationship between the test case and requirements. The basic Greedy method time complexity is $O(r * t * \text{minimum}(r, t))$, where t is the quantity of test cases, and r is the quantity of requirements.

32.2.2.2   HGS (HARROLD GUPTA SOFFA)

In HGS,[19] we create a group of requirements covered by one of the test cases. Then we find a group of requirements for each test case. HGS selects the test cases that satisfy the sets. The RTS contains the selected test cases.

32.2.2.3 2OPT (2-OPTIMAL)

2OPT[20] approach is similar to traditional greedy. In this approach, iteratively select two test cases that are covering the maximum number of requirements. We performed this iteration until all the requirements were covered.

32.2.2.4 GE

In GE[21] we select the test cases covering the requirements whose cardinality is one. The remainder of the interaction is something very similar to the traditional greedy method for finding the reduced test set.

32.2.2.5 GRE

In GRE[21] we removed the redundant test cases. Redundant test cases are those test cases that satisfy the requirements which are already covered by other test cases. The next step is similar to the traditional greedy method to find the reduced test set.

32.3 OUR APPROACH: RAFI SEQUENTIAL METHOD

In every software, new versions are released. So before releasing the new version of the software, it must pass all the test cases for quality purposes. Due to the new version of the software, our old coverage got changed. Some edges can be added or deleted. If the edges are added, then we can say that some test cases are now covering more requirements, and if the edges got deleted, then we can say that some tests are not covering requirements that they previously covered. Now we have to find the reduced test set in the new coverage graph. This section implemented the RAFI method to find the reduced test set in the new coverage graph. In the RAFI method, we are using some information, and that information is 1) a reduced test set of the old coverage graph, 2) edges that were modified (added and deleted).

There are two types of edge modifications in the old coverage graph.

1. Edge deletion
2. Edge addition

We will see how we are handling the edge modification to find the reduced test set and how we are taking advantage of the old reduced test set.

32.3.1   HANDEL EDGE DELETION

Two types of edge deletion are possible

1. Deleted edge belongs to the old reduced test set
2. Deleted edge that does not belong to the old reduced test set

32.3.1.1   Deleted Edge Belongs to the Old Reduced Test Set

The graph in Figure 32.2 shows an example of edge deletion, which belongs to the old reduced test set. When we ran the old coverage graph in a traditional greedy method, we found that the reduced test set was {t1, t2}. After the deletion of the edge {t1, r1} we found that t1 belongs to the old reduced test set, and the old reduced test set now uncovers r1, so we have to cover r1. First, we will check whether the current old reduced test set covers r1 or not. The example below r1 is not covered by any selected test case {t1, t2}, so we will add test cases from the test set that will cover the requirement r1 because t3 covers the r1 requirement, the t3 is added to the old reduced test case. Now the reduced test case will become {t1, t2, and t3}. Now we try to optimize the reduced test set. We had added the t3 test case because t1 is not covering r1, so we try to cover all requirements without the t1 test case in the new reduced test set. In this case, we can cover all the requirements by {t2, t3}. The new reduced test set will be {t2 and t3}.

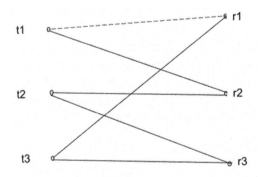

FIGURE 32.2   New coverage graph after the deletion of the edge {t1, r1}.

32.3.1.2 DELETED EDGE DOES NOT BELONG TO THE OLD REDUCED TEST SET

The graph in Figure 32.3 shows an example of edge deletion, which does not belong to the old reduced test set. When we ran the old coverage graph in a traditional greedy method, we found that the reduced test set was {t1, t2}. Now we deleted the edge {t3, r1}. We know that t1 does not belong to the old reduced test set. We found that r1 still got covered by the old reduced test set, so nothing will be affected. The new reduced test set will be {t2 and t3} as the old decreased test set.

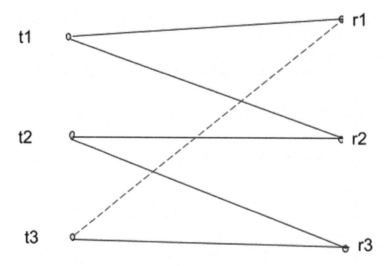

FIGURE 32.3   New coverage graph after the deletion of the edge {t3, r1}.

Algorithm
1. Reduced test set as ReducedSet;
2. Delete the edge as DeletedEdge;
3. delete DeletedEdge from CoverageGraph;
4. if DeletedEdge belongs in TestCase(t1), which is in ReducedSet then
5. nothing to do for DeletedEdge;
6. else if DeletedEdge belongs in Requirement(r1), which is covered by TestCase(ti) which is in ReducedSet then
7. nothing to do for DeletedEdge;
8. else

9.   Add one TestCases that satisfy that Requirement(r1);
10. end
11. if all requirements that covered by TestCase(t1) can be covered by ReducedSet - { TestCase(t1) } then
12. ReducedSet = ReducedSet - { TestCase(t1) };
13. end
14. end
15. return Reduced test set as ReducedSet;

Line 1: In the ReducedSet set, we will store the final reduced test set. Line 2 DeletedEdge, we store the test case and the requirement relationship. Lines 4–5: If the deleted edge does not belong to the reduced test set, we will do nothing. Lines 6–7: If the deleted edge belongs to the reduced test set and r1 is still covered by another test case that belongs to the reduced test set. We will do nothing. Line 9: If not, then we will add the test case that covered r1. Lines 11–12: If all requirements that t1 covers get covered by the current reduced test set except t1, we can remove t1 from the reduced test set. Line 15: Return reduced test set.

32.3.2   HANDEL EDGE ADDITION

Two types of edge addition are possible:

1.   Added edge belongs to the old reduced test set.
2.   Added edge does not belong to the old reduced test set.

32.3.2.1   ADDED EDGE BELONGS TO THE OLD REDUCED TEST SET

The graph in Figure 32.4 shows an example of edge addition that belongs to the old reduced test set. When we ran the old coverage graph in a traditional greedy method, we found that the reduced test set was {t1, t2}. After adding the edge {t2, r1}, we found that t2 belongs to the old reduced test set, and r1 is now covered by the other test case, which belongs to the old reduced test set. Therefore, we try to optimize the reduced test set. For this, we will check the cardinality of the test case, which was covering r1. If that cardinality is one, then we can remove that test case from the old RTS. In the below example, the cardinality of t1 is one, so we will remove t1 from the old reduced test set. In this case, we can cover all the requirements by {t3} only. So the new reduced test set will be {t3}.

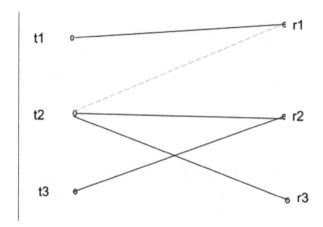

FIGURE 32.4 New coverage graph after adding the edge {t2, r1}.

32.3.2.2 ADDED EDGE DOES NOT BELONG TO THE OLD REDUCED TEST SET

The graph in Figure 32.5 shows an example of edge addition that does not belong to the old reduced test set. When we ran the old coverage graph in a traditional greedy method, we found that the reduced test was {t1, t2}. Now we added the edge {t3, r2}. We know that t3 does not belong to the old reduced test set. We found that r1 is not covered by another test case that belongs to the old reduced test set, so nothing will be affected. The new reduced test set will be {t2 and t3} as the old reduced test set.

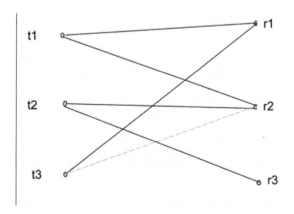

FIGURE 32.5 New coverage graph after adding the edge {t3, r2}.

Algorithm

1. Reduced testSet as ReducedSet;
2. Add edge as AddEdge(e1);
3. Add AddEdge(e1) (connected by Requirement(r1) and TestCase(t1)) in CoverageGraph;
4. if AddEdge(e1) belongs to TestCase(t1) which is not in Reduced_Set then
5. do nothing for AddEdge(e1);
6. else
7. if degree of TestCase(ti) is one and AddEdge(e1) belongs to Requirement(r1) that is covered by ReducedSet - { TestCase(ti) } then
8. ReducedSet = ReducedSet - { TestCase(ti) }
9. else
10. do nothing for AddEdge(e1);
11. end
12. end
13. return Reduced testSet as ReducedSet;

Line1: In the ReducedSet set, we will store the final reduced test set. Line 2 AddedEdge, we store the test case and the requirement relationship. Lines 4–5: If the added edge does not belong to the reduced test set, we will do nothing. Lines 7–8: If the added edge belongs to the reduced test set and the test case's cardinality, which covered the old reduced test set requirement, is one, then we will remove that test case. Line 13: Returns a reduced test set.

32.4   EXPERIMENT EVALUATION, RESULT, AND ANALYSIS

This research work evaluated Flower Method, the traditional greedy sequential method, the traditional greedy parallel method, and the parallel RAFI method. We evaluated different factors in different benchmarks.

RQ1: Which method is time-efficient—the Traditional greedy method or the Flower method?.

RQ2: What amount would we be able to diminish the size of the test suite?

RQ3: Is the RAFI method more time-efficient to find the reduced test set compared with traditional greedy across versions?

RQ4: Is the RAFI method efficient in terms of reduction compared with traditional greedy across versions?

32.4.1 EXPERIMENT SUBJECT

In this, we will evaluate our experiment in the set of standard benchmarks (SIR). In this, there are a total of eight benchmarks, namely, tcas, totinfo, schedule, printtokens, printtokens2, replace, schedule2, space. From the benchmarks in Table 32.1, we can say that the requirements are between 58 and 1515. Total test cases are between 1052 and 13585. The total numbers of edges are between 12825 and 5713638. We will run our Flower method, traditional greedy method, both sequential and parallel, in these standard benchmarks. We can see the properties of each benchmark from Table 32.1.

TABLE 32.1 Standard Benchmarks.

Sr. No.	Benchmark	Test cases	Requirements	Edges
1	Totinfo	1052	132	88682
2	Tcas	1608	58	39413
3	Space	13585	1514	5713638
4	schedule2	2710	125	258929
5	schedule	2650	100	203000
6	replace	5542	229	628464
7	printtokens2	4115	200	12825
8	printtokens	4130	157	344020

32.4.2 EXPERIMENT SETUP

Our aim is to: (1) Find the minimal test suite to such an extent that it can cover every one of the requirements. (2) Find the time taken to compute the minimal test suite for Flower, Traditional greedy sequential. (3) Speed up for RAFI when we vary the number of threads. (4) Speed up for RAFI when we vary the percentage of adding edges. (5) Reduce rate for RAFI when we vary the percentage of adding edges. (6) Speed up for RAFI when we vary dynamic changes in edges. (7) Reduce rate for RAFI when we vary dynamic changes in edges. We will run all our implemented methods in the standard benchmarks (SIR). For evaluating the RAFI method, there are three parameters on which the performance can be varied. The parameters are

1. The number of threads on which we ran the RAFI.
2. Structural change in the old coverage graph means the percentage edges that were modified.
3. In edge modification, what is the percentage of added edges, and what is the percentage of the remaining edges deleted?

We will evaluate the RAFI method for these parameters. We will fix two parameters and will vary the remaining one parameter.

The operating system we are using on our machine is Linux version 4.4.0-159-generic, Operating System Type: 64-bit processor, RAM: 4 GB, and Processor: Intel 2.60GHz*4.

32.4.3 RESULT AND ANALYSIS

In this section, we will explore the result of the Flower method, and the traditional greedy sequential method for finding the reduced test set, and the RAFI parallel method for finding the reduced test set in the modified coverage graph.

32.4.3.1 TIME EFFICIENT

We ran Flower and traditional greedy methods to find the minimal test set to cover all the requirements. We ran our experiment on the benchmarks given in Table 32.1. We found the time complexity of the Flower method to be exponential. Therefore, it took exponential time and failed to find the reduced test set in a reasonable time. On the other hand, the traditional greedy method is a polynomial-time algorithm. So we were able to find the reduced test set in a few milliseconds. Hence, we can say that the traditional greedy algorithm can find the reduced test set in a reasonable time while the Flower method fails to do this. Figure 32.6 shows how much the greedy strategy is taking to track down the decreased test set for various benchmarks.

32.4.3.2 REDUCED SIZE OF THE TEST SET

We ran our traditional greedy method for different benchmarks and found how much they reduced the test set to find the reduced test set to cover all the requirements. Figure 32.7 shows the reduced set size of all benchmarks that we are using for the evaluation.

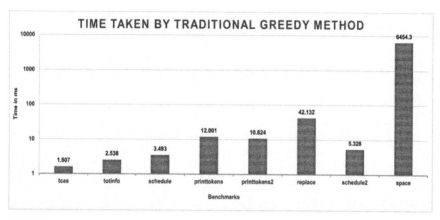

FIGURE 32.6 Time taken by the traditional greedy method to find the test cases' reduced set size for different benchmarks.

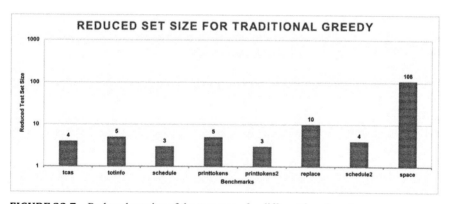

FIGURE 32.7 Reduced set size of the test cases for different benchmarks.

32.4.3.3 *RATE OF SPEEDUP WHEN WE VARY THE NUMBER OF THREADS*

We will vary the number of threads from 1 to 8. The percentage of dynamic changes in edges will be fixed that is 10%, and fixed 25% of edges added and 75% deleted. We calculated the speedup, the ratio of time taken by Greedy, and the time taken by RAFI. We obtained the maximum speedup when the number of threads is 4.

From these two graphs in Figure 32.8, we can consider that to increase the quantity of threads, we are getting speedup, but after a certain time, speedup got reduced. Because when the number of threads was increased, most of the time was being wasted in scheduling the thread instead of doing the required work.

32.4.3.4 *RATE OF SPEEDUP WHEN WE VARY THE PERCENTAGE OF ADDING EDGES*

We will vary the percentage of edge addition from 0% to 100%, and the rest will be edge deletion. We fixed the number of threads to 4 and fixed the percentage dynamic change to 1%. We calculated the speedup, which is the ratio of time taken by Greedy and time taken by RAFI. We found the maximum speed of 489 for schedule 2 benchmarks. The maximum speedup we got when the percentage of adding edges was 100%. From these two graphs in Figure 32.9, we can see that as we are increasing the percentage of edge addition, then speed was increased except in the tcas benchmark.

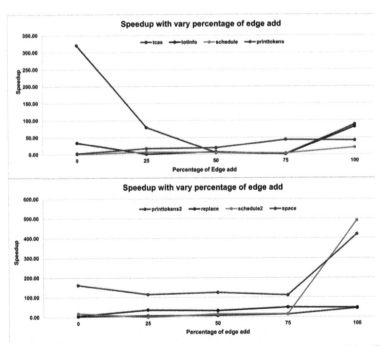

FIGURE 32.8 Speedup of the RAFI method compares traditional greedy parallel to find the reduced set size of the test cases for different benchmarks.

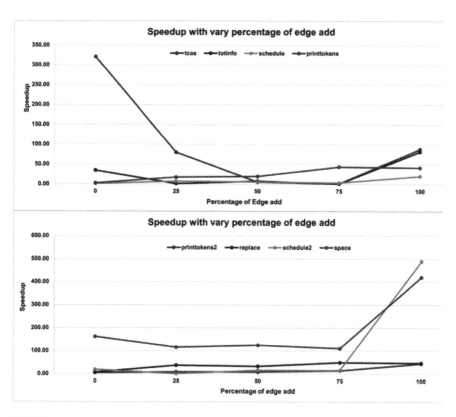

FIGURE 32.9 Speedup of the RAFI method compares traditional greedy parallel to find the reduced set size of the test cases for different benchmarks.

32.4.3.5   REDUCTION RATE WHEN WE VARY THE PERCENTAGE OF ADDING EDGES

In this, we evaluated the normalized reduced set size for the above three parameters. We calculated the reduction rate, which is the ratio of reduced test set size of traditional Greedy and reduced set size of RAFI method.

From these two graphs in Figure 32.10, we can see that the reduction rate varies from 0.52 to 1. Still, there is a possibility that we can get a reduction rate greater than one. The maximum speedup of reduction rate we are getting when the percentage of adding edges is 0% and deleting edges is 100%.

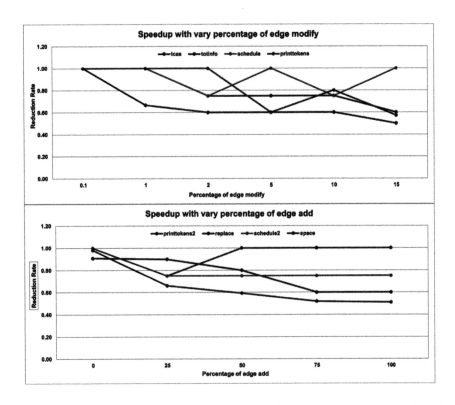

FIGURE 32.10 Reduction rate of the RAFI method with a comparison of traditional greedy parallel for different benchmarks.

32.4.3.6 *RATE OF SPEEDUP WHEN WE VARY DYNAMIC CHANGES IN EDGES*

In this, we will vary the percentage of dynamic changes in edges from 0.1 to 15%. We fixed the number of threads to 4 and fixed the 25% of edges added and 75% deleted. We calculated the speedup, which is the ratio of time taken by Greedy and time taken by RAFI. We obtained the maximum speedup when the dynamic changes were 0.1%.

From these two graphs in Figure 32.11, we can see the maximum speedup we get for benchmark tcas, equal to 1590, and the maximum speedup when the percentage of dynamic changes is 0.1%.

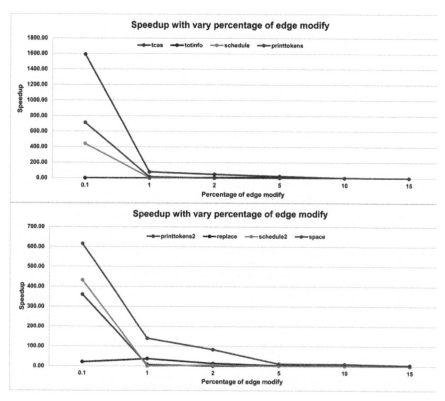

FIGURE 32.11 Speedup of the RAFI method compares traditional greedy parallel to find the reduced set size of the test cases for different benchmarks.

32.4.3.7 *REDUCTION RATE WHEN WE VARY DYNAMIC CHANGES IN EDGES*

In this, we evaluated the normalized reduced set size for the above three parameters. We calculated the reduction rate, which is the ratio of reduced test set size of traditional Greedy and reduced set size of RAFI method.

From these two graphs in Figure 32.12, we can see that the reduction rate varies from 0.34 to 1. Still, there is a possibility that we can get a reduction rate greater than one. The maximum speedup of the reduction rate was obtained when the percentage of dynamic changes is 0.1%.

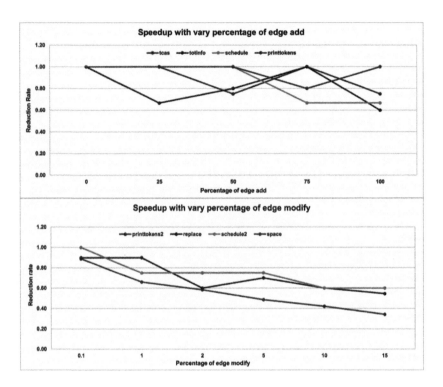

FIGURE 32.12   Reduction rate of the RAFI method with the comparison of traditional greedy parallel for different benchmarks.

32.5   CONCLUSION AND FUTURE WORK

Given a set of test cases and the software requirement, we aimed to find the reduced test set, such that it covers all the requirements. We implemented some existing exponential methods such as Flower and some polynomial methods such as the Traditional greedy method. We ran these methods in some standard benchmarks (SIR) and found that the traditional greedy method can find the reduced test set reasonably, but the Flower method failed to do this in a reasonable time. Further, we found that the traditional greedy method can reduce the test setup to 0.07%. Further, we implemented the RAFI method to find the reduced test set in the modified coverage graph. We aimed to find the reduced test set using the old reduced test set and edges modified to cover all the requirements. We ran the RAFI method, and for comparison, we ran the Traditional greedy method. We found that RAFI gives a reduced test set in very little time compared to Traditional Greedy. We got speedup up to 1590X. The reduction rate varies from 0.38 to 1 for the RAFI method.

We can test different data structures such as trees and adjacency lists to store the graph to reduce memory access and space in future work. Further, adding the notion of test case execution time, suppose edges are weighted. Here, weighted means that some test cases may take longer to execute. Then, in this situation, how will the reduced test set be found? Because if test cases are weighted, then there is a possibility that the reduced test set whose cardinality is more can give better results.

KEYWORDS

- **software testing**
- **test-suite**
- **greedy approach**
- **test set**

REFERENCES

1. Lin, C.-T.; Tang, K.-W.; Wang, J.-S.; Kapfhammer, G. M. Empirically Evaluating Greedy-based Test Suite Reduction Methods at Different Levels of Test Suite Complexity. *Sci. Comput. Progr.* **2017,** *150,* 1–25.
2. Kapfhammer, G. M. Regression Testing. In *Encyclopedia of Software Engineering Three-Volume Set (Print)*; Auerbach Publications, 2010; pp. 893–915.
3. Rothermel, G.; Harrold, M. J. A Safe, Efficient Regression Test Selection Technique. *ACM Transac. Soft. Eng. Methodol.* **1997,** *6* (2), 173–210.
4. Rothermel, G.; et al. In *An Empirical Study of the Effects of Minimization on the Fault Detection Capabilities of Test Suites*, Proceedings. International Conference on Software Maintenance (Cat. No. 98CB36272), IEEE; 1998.
5. Wong, W. E.; et al. Effect of Test Set Minimization on Fault Detection Effectiveness. *Softw.: Pract. Exp.* **1998,** *28* (4), 347–369.
6. Gligoric, M.; Eloussi, L.; Marinov, D. In *Practical Regression Test Selection with Dynamic File Dependencies*, Proceedings of the 2015 International Symposium on Software Testing and Analysis; 2015.
7. Marchetto, A.; et al. A Multi-Objective Technique to Prioritize Test Cases. *IEEE Trans. Softw. Eng.* **2015,** *42* (10), 918–940.
8. Wong, W. E.; et al. Effect of Test Set Minimization on Fault Detection Effectiveness. *Softw.: Pract. Exp.* **1998,** *28* (4), 347–369.

9. Zhang, L.; et al. In *An Empirical Study of Junit Test-Suite Reduction*, IEEE 22nd International Symposium on Software Reliability Engineering, IEEE; 2011.

10. Lin, J.-W.; Huang, C.-Y. Analysis of Test Suite Reduction with Enhanced Tie-Breaking Techniques. *Inform. Soft. Technol.* **2009**, *51* (4), 679–690.

11. Jeffrey, D.; Gupta, N. Improving Fault Detection Capability by Selectively Retaining Test Cases during Test Suite Reduction. *IEEE Trans. Softw. Eng.* **2007**, *33* (2), 108–123.

12. Qu, X.; Cohen, M. B.; Rothermel, G. In *Configuration-Aware Regression Testing: An Empirical Study of Sampling and Prioritization*, Proceedings of the 2008 International Symposium on Software Testing and Analysis, 2008.

13. Jeffrey, D.; Gupta, N. In *Test Suite Reduction with Selective Redundancy*, 21st IEEE International Conference on Software Maintenance (ICSM'05), IEEE; 2005.

14. Gotlieb, A.; Marijan, D. In *FLOWER: Optimal Test Suite Reduction as a Network Maximum Flow*, Proceedings of the 2014 International Symposium on Software Testing and Analysis; 2014.

15. Cormen, T. H.; Leiserson, C. E.; Rivest, R. L.; Stein, C. *Introduction to Algorithms*; MIT press; 2009.

16. Black, J.; Melachrinoudis, E.; Kaeli, D. In *Bi-Criteria Models for All-Uses Test Suite Reduction*, Proceedings of 26th International Conference on Software Engineering, IEEE; 2004.

17. Chen, Z.; Zhang, X.; Xu, B. A Degraded ILP Approach for Test Suite Reduction. In *SEKE*, 2008; pp. 494–499.

18. Li, Z.; Harman, M.; Hierons, R. M. Search Algorithms for Regression Test Case Prioritization. *IEEE Trans. Softw. Eng.* **2007**, *33* (4), 225–237.

19. Harrold, M. J.; Gupta, R.; Soffa, M. L. A Methodology for Controlling the Size of a Test Suite. *ACM Trans. Softw. Eng. Methodol.* **1993**, *2* (3), 270–285.

20. Smith, A. M.; Kapfhammer, G. M. In *An Empirical Study of Incorporating Cost into Test Suite Reduction and Prioritization*, Proceedings of the 2009 ACM Symposium on Applied Computing, 2009; pp. 461–467.

21. Chen, T. Y.; Lau, M. F. On the Divide-and-Conquer Approach Towards Test Suite Reduction. *Inform. Sci.* **2003**, *152*, 89–119.

CHAPTER 33

Security Optimization Through Programmability and Flexibility in Software-Defined Networking: A Novel Approach

PRADEEP KUMAR SHARMA and S. S TYAGI

Department of Computer Engineering, MR International Institute of Research and Studies, Faridabad, Haryana, India

ABSTRACT

Network security management and configuration have always been a daunting task for network professionals and it require lots of manual intervention by typing the commands through Command Line Interfaces using terminal programs which leads to several misconfiguration and security issues as the number of devices increases in the traditional network. As a result network automation and programmability are necessary requirements for securing and managing the network. Traditional automation techniques and configuration methods are not able to provide a complete common solution due to architectural bottleneck in traditional network where software and hardware are tightly coupled within the devices and there is no scope for programmability and automation. Software-Defined Networking (SDN) is a new technology that redefines the network architecture and decouples the software logic from the devices to a central place and provides an API for programmability, innovation, and automation. In this chapter, we present an

Computational Intelligence in Analytics and Information Systems, Volume 2: Advances in Digital Transformation, Selected Papers from CIAIS-2021. Parneeta Dhaliwal, PhD, Manpreet Kaur, PhD, Hardeo Kumar Thakur, PhD, Rajeev Kumar Arya, and Joan Lu (Eds.)

SDN-based framework to show how the SDN can provide improvised auto-mation and optimized security through programmability at northbound API and centralized control for policy enforcement. We discuss about possible automation techniques in traditional networks and their limitations. An SDN framework for network application development has been constructed with result and analysis. For evaluation and experiments we are using mininet, a network emulator, and Ryu as a controller. The network engineers and researchers who want to scale their network with optimized security func-tions provided by the SDN can be benefited from this work.

33.1   INTRODUCTION

Security is ubiquitous. In this era of digital transformation we are all surrounded by digital information such as e-commerce, electronic trans-actions and even organizations are making their whole processes online through ERP systems and this needs to be protected. As a result, the volume of digital data and the number of ICT devices that deal with this data are increasing day by day and with the advent of Big Data, Internet of Things (IoT), cloud computing, and mobile devices the need for automated security systems has grown very rapidly. In the present scenario data is new currency and there is a need for some dynamic security solutions for securing this increasing size of digital data. Traditional ways of security where security is applied at the edge, for example, firewall are not enough for protecting the enterprise data. These conventional security systems require lots of manual interventions and configurations are done through CLI by typing commands that may lead to several misconfigurations and security errors. Most of the security solutions are proprietary which have vendor owned software and hardware with specific predefined way of configuration and management. Engineers interact with these devices through CLI mode typing commands and output of these commands is designed to fit for a human in mind. This output cannot be used by a machine to do the further processes. Hence, there is no scope of innovation, automation, and programmability for the network engineers who want to scale their network as per the changing demands. Over the past few years the only change in managing the network devices is to use the SSH in place of CLI. There is a need to develop a common programmability-based solution for the interaction and configuration of the devices and this may result in complete automated security solutions suitable for the current technology demands.[1]

Software-Defined Networking (SDN) is a new technique that can fulfill the above-said requirement by providing better management and policy configuration through centralized controller and programmability at Northbound API.[2] SDN provide a great visibility and complete control of network which give new ways for security optimization in these networks. The remaining paper has been organized in the following manner. In the second section we will discuss about the traditional networks architecture and their limitations, Section three describes the related work. Section four introduces our security architecture based on SDN, which shows how the security functions can be optimized in SDN. Section five is dedicated to development and implementation of security system in SDN. Section six presents the advanced analysis and further enhancement followed by conclusion in Section seven with promising research directions.

33.2 TRADITIONAL NETWORK AND LIMITATIONS

The present computer network containing various devices such as switches, routers, gateways, firewalls, load balancers, and different application-specific devices like RADIUS etc. has become so complex and overly distributed that dynamic changes in the network policies are very difficult to apply. By the advancement of web, there is so much online traffic being produced now, data scientists gauge that the computerized world duplicates in size in every two-year passage, there are not sufficient individuals to examine all the alarms. Rules-based frameworks and solutions are complex and it is not easy to configure, monitor, and manage them. Mainly these do not function good enough to justify the exertion needed to keep them current. The solution is automation,[3] where the output of one system or aspect should be the input for another analysis in a software system. Unfortunately, it is very difficult to find in a traditional network due to closed box devices concept, CLI approach to configure the network which provides the output as per human operator. Different vendors have different CLI in which one command may generate different outputs in different systems. The only solution is that we need to communicate in a standard programming language with the network equipment. This shows the way to acquire automation.[4] In this section we will discuss the low-level ways to configure directly to the traditional network equipment. Python has two good libraries Pexpect and Paramiko that can be used to manage the legacy routers and switches. Pexpect is a completely python-based project and comprises many child applications, directing these and reverting in the same way as per expected output. For example, if we want to telnet a router having ip address 172.16.1.20 then we can do this by the below-mentioned pexpect program.[5]

Pexpect generated a child process and controlled it in an interactive manner. There are two main functions as we can see in the above example, expect() and sendline(). The sendline() is like you are squeezing the Enter on keyboard when you Telnet a network device manually and press enter in the end. From the device perspective it is like we are typing the command from a terminal program.

```
>>> import pexpect
>>> child = pexpect.spawn('telnet 172.16.1.20')
>>> child.expect('Username')
0
>>> child.sendline('ciscoR6')
6
>>> child.expect('Password')
0
>>> child.sendline('manavrachna')
```

The router takes it as it is communicating with human being who is typing the commands. But downside of the pexpect program is that it does not provide a structured data, that is, it can be interpreted by a human eye but not by the computer as a program. Paramiko is also a python library to interact with devices. Both these libraries provide a simulated environment of user typing command in front of a computer. This works fine up to a point but does not provide programmability. The answer is the application programming interface (API). An API is a collection of tools and methods that are required when we design computer software. It is a set of standard rules how the different components of application will communicate with one another to ensure the functioning of software system. A good API provides an environment where a developer can easily find the required components for software development. Traditional networks are unable to provide an API-based network configuration and programmability due to closed box proprietary network devices concept.[6] SNMP, NETCONF, and YANG try to simplify the things, but none of the above technique gives a complete common solution with traditional network architecture and proprietary device concept. Software Defined Networking is a technology that decouples logical control from devices and provides an API for network control and configuration through programming. Traditional network are unable to provide an API based network configuration and programmability due to closed box proprietary network devices concept as shown in Figure 33.1a which represents legacy switch architecture.[6] Figure 33.1b shows the openflow switch where control and data plane been decoupled and communication of data plane and control plane is done through an API.

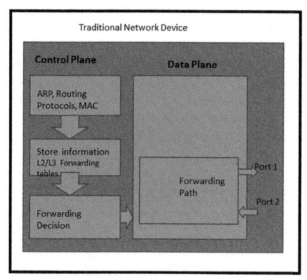

FIGURE 33.1A Legacy switch.

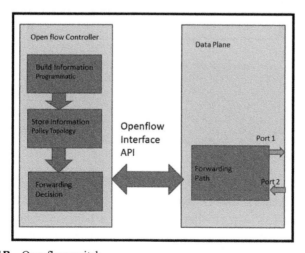

FIGURE 33.1B Openflow switch.

33.3   SDN HISTORY AND PRESENT STATUS

SDN foundations were started by a Ph.D. student named Martin Casado in his research thesis in Stanford University. He proposed a security architecture for enterprise network (SANE) which advocates security at a central place instead of an edge that is prevalent in traditional networks. It provides a unified control over the network and security can be checked at each point in the network as required.

The term Software Defined Networking comes from OpenFlow project (ACM SIGCOMM 2008). In 2009 Stanford developed OpenFlow V1.0.0 specs and Martin Casado again took part in this venture and cofounds Nicira in June 2009. Open Networking Foundation (ONF) was constituted by a group of organization and researchers on March 2011 and they commenced their first open networking seminar on Oct 2011. Several organizations Juniper, Cisco announced to support the venture.

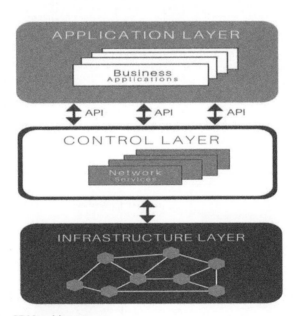

FIGURE 33.2   SDN architecture.

SDN is a concept that decouples control or logic from the devices to a central place called controller. The network behavior can be controlled from controller through the various applications in northbound API. The communication of network devices is coordinated by the controller through a southbound protocol, for example, openflow.[7] The architecture of SDN is shown in Figure 33.2. By this arrangement the trend of proprietary hardware-based network devices can be discontinued. We may use vendor-specific southbound API and hardware, but we may use software or network applications of our choice in northbound API to control and manage the network. This is how we can program the network and it is called programmability in SDN which is not possible in a conventional network due to proprietary devices. Several business giants have captured the SDN wave and started their SDN solution in production.

CISCO has provided CISCO API and ACI for its data center solutions. Nexus (NX-API) is a CISCO product line that permits the administrator to communicate with the network devices through a variety of transports HTTP, SSH, and HTTPS.[8] Juniper is also using SDN in its corporate networking solution and uses Network Configuration Protocol (NETCONF). It is an IETF effort and was first published in 2006 as RFC 4741 and its updated version was revised in RFC 6241. Most of the Juniper devices support NETCONF. NETCONF uses Extensible Markup Language (XML) for data encoding. Juniper is working on Extensible Messaging and Presence Protocol (XMPP) as a southbound API for its contrail SDN products. Arista Networks also provide an API-supported solution for data center equipment. It moves a rundown of show or config commands over HTTP or HTTPS and reactions back in JSON. A significant differentiation is that it is a Remote Procedure Call (RPC) and JSON-RPC, rather than the REST API. Meanwhile, all of these SDN-inspired solutions are proprietary and enhance the flexibility of their existing hardware or some SDN-specific hardware having their own southbound and northbound API. But if we think about the open source SDN framework than open flow comes in mind first.

33.3.1 SDN AND OPENFLOW

Openflow is an innovation that is layered above of the Transmission Control Protocol (TCP) that isolates the control from the devices to a central place called controller.

It works as an interface between the controller and devices and governs the communication of control path and data path which has been separated in the SDN switch. The work flow diagram of openflow is shown in Figure 33.3.

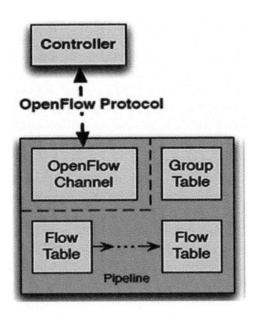

FIGURE 33.3   Openflow work flow.

When host A wants to communicate to host B, it sends a data packet to the switch. The switch looks for a matching entry in its flow table, if there is a match then communication takes place. If there is no match the packet is sent to the controller, the controller asks the switch to broadcast the packet, then a matching attribute is found at a port where host B is connected. Switch updates its flow table and host A is communicated the location of host B through the controller and further communication takes place without the intervention of controller. By this way we have complete control of data forwarding in switches. But, another hardware device like routers, firewalls, and other traditional devices may be transformed to the network applications or software that can work in coordination with the controller. This introduces the term programmability in SDN and further provides the flexibility for automation goals.

Figure 33.4 shows that all the open flow switches are there in the data plane which forwards the data as per the instructions from the controller. All the controlling part like switching, routing, and security is done by the various applications in the application plane. The communication of application plane and controller is enabled by northbound API, for example, REST API. This provides a standard programmability approach to control the overall network through applications rather than proprietary, device-specific command base approach in legacy networks. This arrangement proffers many challenges and innovations in the field of security in SDN. Securing the SDN, that is, SDN controller is a challenge and the authors are providing various solutions and research articles in area.[9] But one of the most interesting areas is how we have been benefited by SDN in providing the various security services such as firewall, network monitoring, intrusion detection, and anomaly detection. With programmability in hand, it will be much possible for researchers and network engineers to implement, if they have some new and innovative ideas and algorithms.[10] If network devices will be configured and controlled by the standard programming languages, then we are no more far away from network automation that contains very few or no manual intervention in network processes.

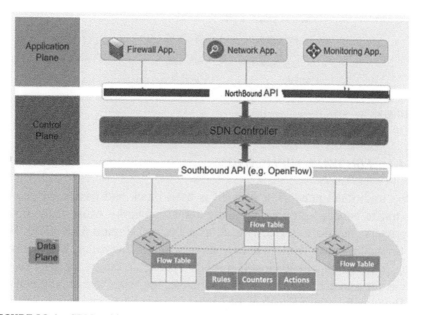

FIGURE 33.4 SDN architecture.

33.4 SECURITY OPTIMIZATION IN SDN

This section is dedicated to how the various security functions work in SDN. We will discuss how these security terminologies such as firewall, IDS, and IPS have been benefitted with SDN architecture and what the challenges are.[11]

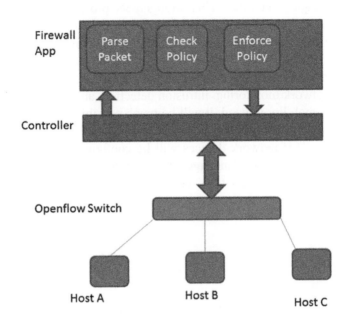

FIGURE 33.5   SDN firewall application.

33.4.1   *FIREWALL APPLICATION*

In the traditional network a firewall is used block and passes the respective traffic between the internal and external networks. Most of the time a proprietary hardware device is used as a firewall. Figure 33.5 shows how the firewall app can work in coordination with the controller. When Host A wants to communicate to Host B it sends a packet to the switch. The switch checks for a matching entry in its flow table, but when a matching entry is not found in the flow table then the packet is forwarded to the controller. The controller sends the packet to firewall application for policy check. First, it parses the packet and checks if it matches with any policy specified in firewall, as firewall has a policy to block traffic from A to B (A-->B: Block). The application enforces a rule through the controller to drop the packet and the controller installs a flow rule in the switch flow table to drop all the incoming traffic from Host A to Host B. This is how we can block and allow flow in openflow through a firewall application. It means through this firewall app a switch can work like a firewall, that is, technology allows us to decide the functions of a switch. As a result additional security devices are not required as security services can be enabled within the devices. In the traditional network another problem is the placement of firewall optimized coverage of security services has been nullified as any device in the network can be turned into a firewall. We can also think of as a distributed firewall that will be very helpful for detecting internal threats but difficult to implement as there are many challenges such as policy conflict and controller performance.[12]

33.4.2 INTRUSION DETECTION

Intrusion detection is another security function that is used to detect known security threats. Basically, threat detection is applied on passive traffic despite active traffic. That is the traffic which threat detection application wants to monitor should be mirrored and forwarded to original destination and Network Threat Detection Application. Signature-based threat detection can be implemented through Network Threat detection Application. When a packet reaches at a controller it sends it to the original destination as well as threat detection app that parses the packet and compares with an available threat pattern if it found a matching alert is generated through the controller. An additional interface is used between control plane and data plane for collecting the full payload information of incoming traffic as this cannot be sent through the openflow channel.[13]

33.4.3 ANOMALY DETECTION

Network anomaly detection techniques are used to detect unknown threats. Most of the time it includes network scans and distributed denial of service threats. It is being present here how the anomaly detection works in SDN.[14] As we know that anomaly detection algorithms are applied to the data collected from different ports in the network and for that we need to manually measure the network statistics through hardware or software by monitoring all packets. But in SDN there is no need to do extra arrangement for data collection as this network statistics data can be easily retrieved from the data plane through the controller. An anomaly detection application is shown in Figure 33.6. The flow collector module requests the controller for network statistics data. The controller sends the request to switches in data plane. The data plane sends the related network information to the flow collector through the controller. The collector sends the data to the analyzer and it inspects the data through anomaly detection and network scan algorithm. The application takes the decision of a detection-based detection algorithm and it raises alert for detection.

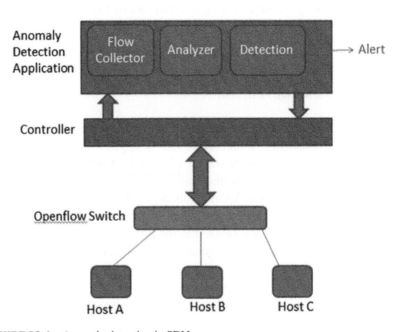

FIGURE 33.6   Anomaly detection in SDN.

33.5   DESIGN AND IMPLEMENTATION OF SECURITY FUNCTIONS IN SDN

In this section, we present the basic building blocks and require an algorithm to design an application on SDN for performing different networking functions, for example, routing, firewall, load balancer, and switching. First, we will focus on basic steps and algorithm for designing an application as per controller and data plane communication.

33.5.1   APPLICATION DESIGN

Python language is used to develop the network applications based on Ryu controller. Ryu is a components-based controller that has various modules for application design and control. In our virtual image at home/ubuntu/ryu it has various folders app, base, and ofproto. App folder can contain various applications such as firewall, router, and load balancer. Base folder contains App_manager that helps to run the different applications and prepares framework and datapath for running the application. Ofproto deals with openflow version-related queries and matching capabilities. For designing an SDN application we need to collect and understand the initial requirements and the booting process of SDN network framework.

- In the first step switch boots up and contacts the controller for openflow version-related queries and checks its capabilities.
- The controller installs Packet In function and table miss function and prepares itself for queries from switch.
- When receiving Packet In, the controller learns the source MAC and mentions the MAC and port information in the flow table. It checks for the destination MAC address if it is available in flow tables, it uses Packet Out function on the port and installs the flow and stores the same for future uses.
- If the destination MAC address is not available in the flow table, that is, a table misses then the controller uses packet out function to broadcast the packet to all ports.

```
1   from ryu.base import app_manager
2   from ryu.controller import ofp_event
3   from ryu.controller.handler import CONFIG_DISPATCHER, MAIN_DISPATCHER
4   from ryu.controller.handler import set_ev_cls
5   from ryu.ofproto import ofproto_v1_3, ofproto_v1_0
6   class SimpleSwitch(app_manager.RyuApp):
7   OFP_VERSIONS = [ofproto_v1_0.OFP_VERSION]
8   def __init__(self, *args, **kwargs):
9   super(SimpleSwitch, self).__init__(*args, **kwargs)
10  self.mac_to_port = {}
11  @set_ev_cls(ofp_event.EventOFPSwitchFeatures, CONFIG_DISPATCHER)
12  def switch_features_handler(self, ev):
13  print("ev message: ", ev.msg)
14  datapath = ev.msg.datapath
15  print("datapath: ", datapath)
16  ofproto = datapath.ofproto
17  print("ofprotocol: ", ofproto)
18  parser = datapath.ofproto_parser
19  print("parser: ", parser)
```

FIGURE 33.7 Basic code architecture.

The above code, presented in Figure 33.7, is a simple representation of the different functions required to develop a full functional network application. In this code, first, we have changed the openflow version from 1.3 to version

1. We printed output of various variables ev, datapath, ofproto, and parser. The above code is a complete application that does not do much, except showing the switch version and the output of the above print functions. But this application is a road to Ryu application development and provides the all the foundation steps to understand the ryu code architecture. If we study Ryu code we see it has different components of software as a whole. By using the ryu controller framework we can design and deploy customized security application. With programmability approach in SDN we can have our own security application in the ryu app folder and program it as per network demands and configure it through standard API. Traditional security solutions, the vendor-specific, for example, fortigate and Cisco, they have their own proprietary code and configuration methods that are fixed and cannot be customized as per demands. There are some open source firewalls such as pfsense and opensense that are good and open source, but they also have their own configuration scripts architecture to control the traffic. There is no standard configuration pattern to communicate and configure these devices. In SDN we can develop a security application in the standard programming language and communicate and configure the same in standard API, for example, RESTful API.[15]

33.5.2   RESULTS AND DISCUSSION

For testing and analysis we will develop a network topology in mininet with 3 hosts h1, h2, and h3 and one switch s1. We are using RYU as a controller. Figure 33.8 shows mininet window as network topology.

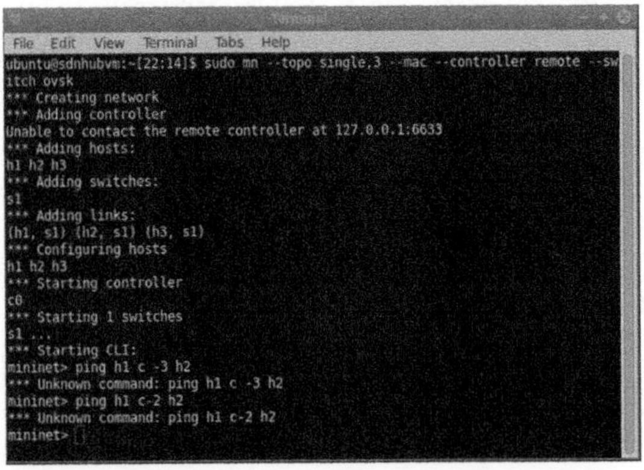

FIGURE 33.8   Single switch topology in mininet.

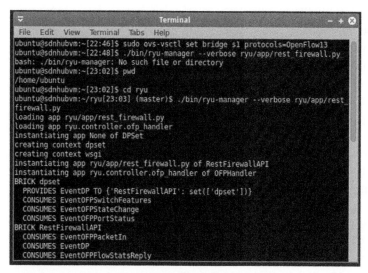

FIGURE 33.9A   Security firewall application with Ryu controller.

FIGURE 33.9B   Application joined as a firewall.

Now we will invoke the firewall application and configure the same through standard API, that is, REST API. In Figure 33.9a, first, we changed the openflow version from version 1.0 to 1.3; then we run the firewall application. The whole process has been shown in Figures 33.9a and 33.9b.

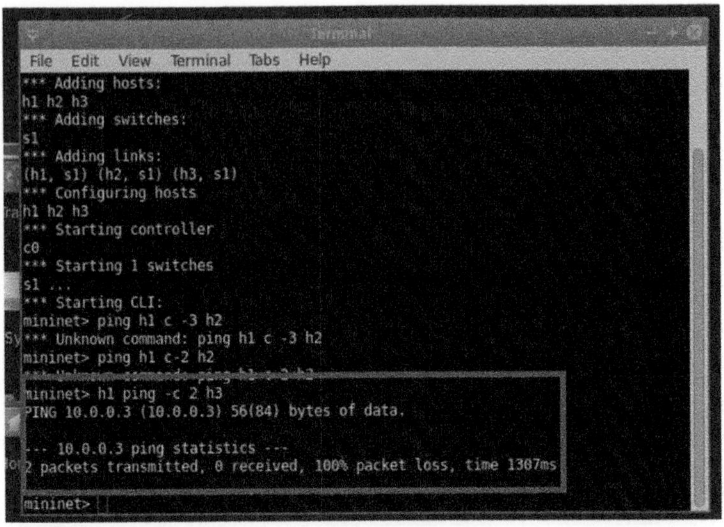

FIGURE 33.10   Ping status when the firewall is running.

In Figure 33.12 we have configured the firewall. First, we get the status of the firewall module through curl -X GET http://localhost:8080/firewall/ module/status. By default switch is disabled, we need to enable the same through curl -X PUT http://localhost:8080/firewall/ module/ enable/ 0000000000000001. Now the switch is enabled.

FIGURE 33.11   Traffic blocked status at firewall screen.

FIGURE 33.12 Configuring firewall with cURL REST API and adding the rule.

Figure 33.10 shows the status of ping reply, when we ping from h1 to h3, it shows 100% packet loss as firewall app is running; there is no by default communication. This can also be seen in Figure 33.11 firewall screenshot. Now we need to create a rule in firewall to establish communication between h1 and h3. This can be done through curl -X POST -d '{"nw_src": "10.0.0.1", "nw_proto": "ICMP"}'http://localhost:8080/firewall/rules/0000000000000001

curl-X POST -d '{"nw_src": "10.0.0.3", "nw_proto": "ICMP"}'http://localhost:8080/firewall/rules/0000000000000001.

FIGURE 33.13 Getting the output through API after adding the rule.

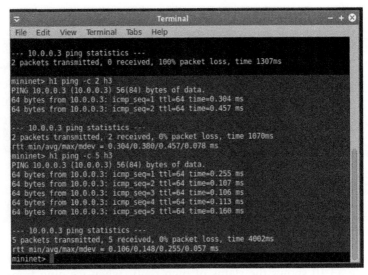

FIGURE 33.14   Ping success after adding the rule.

We can also check the result of the above configuration through API. curl -X GET http://localhost:8080/firewall/rules/0000000000000001. The output of the above commands can be seen in Figures 33.12 and 33.13, respectively. After adding the rule we can check the status of ping from h1 to h3 and there we can ping successfully as shown in Figure 33.14.

33.6   CONCLUSION AND FUTURE WORK

Software-defined networking has compelled the networking giants to redesign their networking solutions and to provide the customers an API-based system to configure and manage the devices. But still they are providing their own proprietary devices with their own proprietary software which are very costly as a whole. But we consider SDN as a solution where organizations sell their proprietary data plane devices without software and we may use the software application and controllers by our own choices or even manage the devices by an API. In academia and corporate world, openflow is a good solution where we can implement the SDN easily. There are many organizations that are selling their data plane devices supported by openflow. In this paper, we have shown how the SDN has provided a platform to configure the network in more innovative ways while traditional networks have limitations due to their closed box device architecture. We have compared the traditional networking with SDN functions such as programmability, flexibility, and a centralized view of network and controlling the traffic through the networking applications. Again, we provided the analysis of different security operations in SDN and it has been explored how the SDN can optimize the security functions with innovative ways to design and deploy customized security applications through programmability in northbound API, for example, REST. We have implemented an application as a firewall with the Ryu controller. We also explored the code architecture of the Ryu controller with algorithm to design an SDN application. Moreover, we have also shown the configuration of firewall through REST API, that is, a standard way to communicate with networking devices. With all possibilities and opportunities in hands to implement complete automation in future network services, we believe that SDN as a whole is proved to be a paradigm shift from the traditional way of networking to the SDN world. Here, we have implemented the basic features of a firewall. This work can be explored as a future work to provide more complex security features if you have a new idea for firewall designing.

KEYWORDS

- **software-defined networking**
- **control plane**
- **data plane**
- **openflow**
- **programmability**
- **automation**

REFERENCES

1. ONF. Software-Defined Networking: The New Norm for Networks. White Paper [Online]. https://www.opennetworking.org
2. Ali, S. T.; Sivaraman, V.; Radford, A.; Jha, S. A Survey of Securing Networks using SDN. *IEEE Trans. Reliab.* **2015,** *64* (3), 1086–1097.
3. Ahmed, K.; Nafi, N. S.; Blech, J. O.; Gregory, M. A.; Schmidt, H. In *Software Defined Industry Automation Networks*, 27th International Telecommunication Networks and Applications Conference (ITNAC); 2017.

4. Pham, M.; Hoang, D. B. In *SDN Applications—The Intent-based Northbound Interface Realisation for Extended Applications*, IEEE NetSoft Conference and Workshops *(NetSoft)*, 2016; pp. 372–377.

5. https://pexpect.readthedocs.io/en/stable/

6. Li, L.; Chou, W.; Zhou, W; Luo, M. Design Patterns and Extensibility of REST API for Networking Applications. *IEEE Trans. Netw. Service Manag.* **2016**, *13* (1), 154–167.

7. McKeown, N.; Anderson, T.; Balakrishnan, H.; Parulkar, G.; Peterson, L.; Rexford, J.; Shenker, S.; Turner, J. OpenFlow: Enabling Innovation in Campus Networks. *ACM SIGCOMM Comput. Commun. Rev.* **2008**, *38* (2), 69–74.

8. https://www.cisco.com/c/en/us/td/docs/switches/datacenter/nexus9000/sw/6x/ programmability/guide/b_Cisco_Nexus_9000_Series_NXOS_Programmability_ Guide/b_Cisco_Nexus_9000_Series_NXOS_Programmability_Configuration_Guide_ chapter_0101.pdf

9. Nam, K.; Kim, K. In *A Study on SDN Security Enhancement using Open Source IDS/ IPS Suricata*, International Conference on Information and Communication Technology Convergence (ICTC), 2018; pp. 1124–1126.

10. Ibdah, D.; Kanani, M.; Lachtar, N.; Allan, N.; Al-Duwairi, B. In *On the Security of SDN-Enabled Smartgrid Systems*, International Conference on Electrical and Computing Technologies and Applications (ICECTA), IEEE; 2017.

11. Zhao, Z.; Doupé, A.; Ahn, G.-J.; Kyung, S.; Han, W.; Tiwari, N.; Dixit, V. H. In *HoneyProxy: Design and Implementation of Next-Generation Honeynet via SDN*, IEEE Conference on Communications and Network Security (CNS), 2017.

12. Sharma, P. K.; Tyagi, S. S. Improving Security through Software Defined Networking (SDN): An SDN based Model. *IJRTE* **2019**, *8* (4), 295–300.

13. Ezekiel, S.; Divakaran, D. M.; Gurusamy, M. In *Dynamic Attack Mitigation using SDN*, 27th International telecommunication networks and applications conference (ITNAC), IEEE; 2017.

14. Mehdi S. A.; Khalid J.; Khayam S. A. Revisiting Traffic Anomaly Detection using Software Defined Networking. In *Recent Advances in Intrusion Detection*; Springer, 2011; pp. 161–180.

15. Sharma, P. K.; Tyagi, S. S. Strengthening Network Security: An SDN (Software Defined Networking) Approach. *Int. J. Electr. Electron. Comput. Sci. Eng.* **2018**.

CHAPTER 34

Test Case Optimization Using Genetic Algorithm

NEERU AHUJA and PRADEEP KUMAR BHATIA

Department of Computer Science and Engineering, Guru Jambheshwar University of Science and Technology, Hisar, India

ABSTRACT

The assurance of software quality needs optimization of test data that consumes a lot of time and cost. Test case optimization is a technique that optimizes test cases by prioritizing and reducing the test case according to criteria. In the present work genetic algorithm (GA)-based testing is used that reduces the test cases. The proposed approach implemented path testing that traverses the most critical path of the program considering it as the maximum. Weights are assigned to paths that play a major role in GA and improve testing efficiency. Some graphical results have also been provided by implementing GA.

34.1 INTRODUCTION

In the present situation of the world, the role of software is very important even in life and security systems. Testing of software determines whether the software is either meeting or not those requirements for which it has been developed. While testing the software it is the responsibility of a

Computational Intelligence in Analytics and Information Systems, Volume 2: Advances in Digital Transformation, Selected Papers from CIAIS-2021. Parneeta Dhaliwal, PhD, Manpreet Kaur, PhD, Hardeo Kumar Thakur, PhD, Rajeev Kumar Arya, and Joan Lu (Eds.)

programmer to test all the inputs whether it is valid or not. But practically it is impossible for huge combinations of test cases. A number of test cases are being required that take minimum time or cost for running. So testing needs perfect planning for the implementation of the test activities that consist of designing test cases, implementing test cases and give a description of the result.[3] Test suite minimization is one of the ways that find duplicate test cases and remove them. To determine the duplicity in any test case, a number of criteria can be used such as path coverage, statement coverage, and condition coverage.[13]

All of these cover under structural testing. Structural testing is one of its better alternatives that involve unit testing. The developers carry out testing of each unit on the basis of source code of present software. Path testing being an important part of structural testing covers as much as about 60–70% of shortcomings present in the software under test.

Several researchers have come up with a number of techniques for the optimization of the given problem. Genetic algorithm (GA) is one such heuristic algorithm used for optimization. GA can be used for single- and multiobjective optimization. This paper investigated an approach that is executed on structural testing (CFG) to find out the path.

34.2 STATE OF THE ART

Mishra et al.[11] proposed a technique Real coded genetic algorithm for path coverage (RCGAPC) to optimize test data to test critical paths (2018). They use a one-to-one injective mapping scheme. They applied an average crossover and a Gaussian mutation operator. They have chosen the GCD, triangle classifier problem in their case study and found that their technique achieves 100 percent path coverage.

Rajappa et al.[14] presented an approach that is based on the graph theory that decides the complete automata of state transition for the system to be tested (2008). They used the maximum clique algorithm and approximation algorithm for creating the fitness function. They also defined that the technique will be more accurate in case of network testing and system testing.

Babamir et al.[3] investigated GA-based testers that used an IP-based fitness function and stopping criterion (2010). Their technique identified infeasible independent paths and reduced time from $2n$ to n. But using input as IP is also a disadvantage since if an input is calculated wrongly then results will differ.

Garg et al.[5] used the extended level branch fitness function with simple GA and hybrid GA for path testing (2015). Khan et al.[9] implemented GA and mutation analysis to optimize software testing efficiency (2016). Their approach covers 100% path coverage and boundary coverage. Some authors used the 80–20 rule for assigning weight in the fitness function that they used.[16]

34.3 GENETIC ALGORITHM

GA is a practical and a heuristic search-based technique that is used for solving optimization problems. It produces high-quality data automatically and can solve even the very complex problems. The basic idea behind GA is to retain a population of chromosomes with a higher fitness value. This population evolves over time via a consecutive iteration process of competitions and controlled variation. Every state of population is known as a generation. The fitness value of each chromosome can be calculated using GA that indicates the quality of solution. For optimizing a given problem the optimum value of the fitness function has to be reported. Depending upon the optimization value of the fitness function, the chromosomes can be selected through any one of the selection operators such as roulette wheel. After that the crossover and mutation operator produce the new chromosomes. These five steps are explained below and a graphical representation is shown in Figure 34.1.

34.3.1 INITIAL POPULATION

GA begins with a set of solutions that can be initialized randomly called population. Every solution in the population is called a chromosome.

34.3.2 FITNESS

It is an objective function that is used to optimize a value according to the problem. The whole GA revolves around the fitness function.

34.3.3 SELECTION

In this step, we select two chromosomes from the mating pool to produce new offspring for the selection process in which a number of techniques are available.

34.3.4   CROSSOVER

This step selects to parent and produce two children. It is also called recombination crossover operator, which has a probability between zero and one, and which is defined as pc. Crossover has also many types such as a single-point crossover, multipoint crossover, and uniform crossover.

34.3.5   MUTATION

The next step creation for a new generation is mutation. In mutation, one or more bits are flipped. The probability of mutation is between 0 and 1 and denoted by pm.

34.4   PATH TESTING

It is a collection of testing techniques that select the test path from the program judiciously. It involves the generation of such sets of paths that cover almost all of the program and to find out the set of test cases that perform each path in the program. Path testing consists of a number of techniques and CFG is one of those techniques.

34.4.1   STEPS INVOLVED IN PATH TESTING

1. Draw CFG to find out different program paths.
2. Use metric to come across the number of independent paths.
3. Discover the set of paths.
4. Create the test case to check each path.

34.5   PROPOSED APPROACH

The design of path testing is such that it covers the execution of all the linearly independent paths of a program at least once. The CFG gives the linearly independent path of the program. An independent path is a path in the course of a DD path graph that introduces at least a new set of processing statements or new conditions.[7] While applying the approach we have to consider that all paths should be covered in minimum time.[4]

In the proposed method, the source code has been converted into weighted CFG that can be defined as an input. The weight has been assigned on the basis of the 80–20 rule. The 80% weight has been assigned to the most critical paths that cover looping and branching path whereas 20% to the simple path. Figure 34.2 describes the pseudo code of the proposed approach.

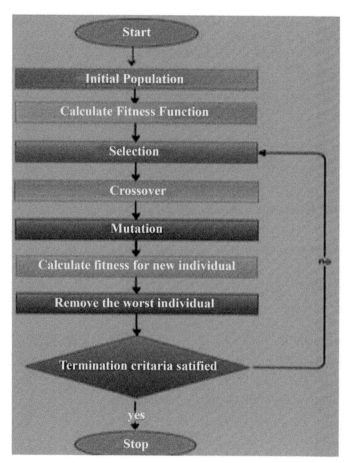

FIGURE 34.1 Steps of genetic algorithm.

1. Initialize the random population of test suite
2. Calculate the fitness function according to weight assign to each edge (i.e. sum of path of given input)
3. Iteration = 1
4. while (! = Termination criteria) do

5. Apply roulette wheel selection operator (calculating probability and cumulative probability)
6. Apply single point crossover
7. Apply mutation operator

1.	Initialize the random population of test suite
2.	Calculate the fitness function according to weight assign to each edge (i.e. sum of path of given input)
3.	Iteration=1
4.	while (!= Termination criteria) do
5.	Apply roulette wheel selection operator (calculating probability and cumulative probability)
6.	Apply single point crossover
7.	Apply mutation operator
8.	Calculate fitness function for newly added test suites
9.	Discard the worst fit test suites with new test suite
10.	iteration = iteration +1
11	end while

FIGURE 34.2   Pseudo code of proposed approach.

The proposed approach may be summarized as follows:

- **Initialization**

Initial population is randomly initialized.

- **Fitness function**

It is the objective function and can be calculated according to weight assigned to each edge in the path of the test case. Maximum weights are assigned to critical paths such as branches and loops.

$$F(x) = \Sigma_{(j=1)}^{n} w_j \qquad (34.1)$$

w_j is the weight of the jth edge of a particular path and n is the size of the population.

- **Selection**

The selection has been made on the basis of the roulette wheel method. Roulette wheel is a random operator. Fittest individuals have higher probability of being selected in the succeeding generation. The probability can be calculated by dividing the fitness function with the sum of fitness functions.

$$Pi = fi / \sum\nolimits_{i=1}^{n} fi \qquad (34.2)$$

The individuals that carry the highest fitness values are selected for the next generation.[2] After that cumulative process is calculated and can be defined as eq 34.3.

$$Ck = \sum\nolimits_{k=1}^{m} P_k \qquad (34.3)$$

- **Crossover**

After selecting the two individuals by roulette wheel, single-point crossover is used to produce two children. For crossover .8 pc is applied where pc is crossover rate.

- **Mutation**

Last but not the least, the mutation operator has been applied to convert some bits from 0 to 1 or conversely. This process executes when GA generates a random number in the interval [0, 1] and $r < $ pm, where r is a random number and pm is the mutation rate.

34.6 EXPERIMENTAL STUDIES

34.6.1 SELECTION OF PROGRAM

For implementing the proposed approach, we have chosen the program of sum of n natural numbers. A brief description of the program and CFG is given in Figure 34.3.

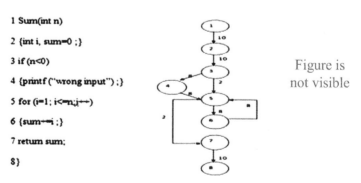

FIGURE 34.3 Program and CFG of case study.

34.6.2   RESULT AND DISCUSSION

We have randomly initialized the population and taken different population sizes 20, 150, and 200 to check the impact on the fitness function when the generation size is the same as shown in Figure 34.4. The fitness function is calculated using eq 34.1 and probability and cumulative probability are calculated with the help of eqs 34.2 and 34.3.

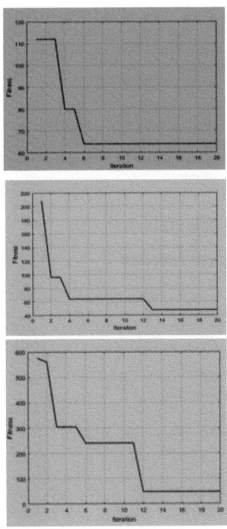

FIGURE 34.4   (a) Pop size 20, (b) pop size 150, (c) pop size 200.

The whole process of GA is performed for 20 generations and the results for iterations 1, 2, 10, and 20 are displayed in Table 34.1. It is evident from Table 34.1 that the test cases are minimized in iteration 20 as compared to iteration 1 and the fitness function with respect to cost is reduced significantly.

TABLE 34.1 Best and Worst Fitness Value.

Iteration	Best fitness	Worst fitness
1	320	2304
2	96	1024
10	64	320
20	48	206

When the population size is 150 and 200 it does not show much variation. If we change the generation size significantly, its impact is different as shown in Figure 34.5. The fitness function of GA has been found to be more effective when the size of population as well as that of generations is significantly large enough.

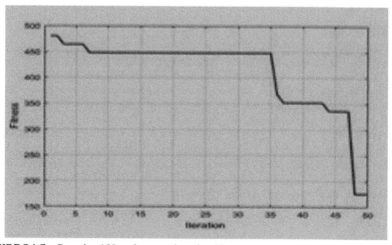

FIGURE 34.5 Pop size 150 and generation size 50.

34.7 CONCLUSIONS

For improving the efficiency, computation time and cost of a software unnecessary test case have to be removed. GA is one such algorithm that is often used to solve the problems related to optimization. In this paper, we have used GA to discover critical paths for the improvement in software testing and saved the computation cost. We have shown in experiments, a reduced fitness value in iterations 2, 20 as compared to iteration 1 as shown in Table 34.1. From the results we conclude that applying GA in finding the critical path in testing leads to the improvement in the efficiency as well as the cost. Keeping these results in view we will apply this approach to large test suites for future work.

KEYWORDS

- **genetic algorithm**
- **path testing**
- **software testing**
- **test cases**
- **optimization**

REFERENCES

1. Aggarwal, K.; Singh, Y. *Software Engineering Programs Documentation, Operating Procedures*; 2nd ed.; New Age International Publishers, Revised, 2005.
2. Bhawna, K. G.; Bhatia, P. K. Software Test Case Reduction using Genetic Algorithm: A Modified Approach. *Int. J. Innov. Sci. Eng. Technol.* **2016,** *3* (5), 349–354.
3. Babamir, F. S.; Hatamizadeh, A.; Babamir, S. M.; Dabbaghian, M.; Norouzi, A. In *Application of Genetic Algorithm in Automatic Software Testing*, Networked Digital Technologies. NDT 2010. Communications in Computer and Information Science; Zavoral, F., Yaghob, J., Pichappan, P., El-Qawasmeh, E., Eds.; Springer: Berlin, Heidelberg. 2010; Vol. 88; pp. 545–552. https://doi.org/10.1007/978-3-642-14306-9_54
4. Dasoriya, R.; Dashoriya, R. In *Use of Optimized Genetic Algorithm for SoftwarTesting*, IEEE International Students' Conference on Electrical, Electronics and Computer Science (SCEECS), Bhopal, 2018; pp. 1–5. doi: 10.1109/SCEECS.2018.8546957.
5. Garg, D.; Garg, P. Basis Path Testing using SGA & HGA with ExLB Fitness Function. *Procedia Comput. Sci.* **2015,** *70*, 593–602.
6. Khan, S.; Nadeem, A.; Awais, A. In *TestFilter: A Statement-Coverage based Test Case Reduction Technique*, IEEE International Multitopic Conference, 2006. https://doi.org/10.1109/inmic.2006.358177
7. Kim, T. H.; Srivastava, P. R. Application of Genetic Algorithm in Software Testing. *Int. J. Softw. Eng. Appl.* **2009,** *3* (4), 87–96.
8. Kumar, G.; Bhatia, P. Software Testing Optimization Through Test Suite Reduction using Fuzzy Clustering. *CSI Trans. ICT* **2013,** *1* (3), 253–260.

9. Khan, R.; Amjad M. In *Optimize the Software Testing Efficiency using Genetic Algorithm and Mutation Analysis*, 3rd International Conference on Computing for Sustainable Global Development (INDIACom), New Delhi, 2016; pp. 1174–1176.

10. Mittal, S.; Sangwan, O. Prioritizing Test Cases for Regression Techniques using Metaheuristic Techniques. *J. Inform. Optim. Sci.* **2017,** *39* (1), 39–51.

11. Mishra, D.; Mishra, R.; Das, K.; Acharya, A. Test Case Generation and Optimization for Critical Path Testing Using Genetic Algorithm. In *Adv. Intelligent Systems And Computing*, 2018, pp. 67–80.

12. Mohanty, S.; Mohapatra, S. K.; Meko, S. F. Ant Colony Optimization (ACO-Min) Algorithm for Test Suite Minimization. In *Progress in Computing, Analytics and Networking. Advances in Intelligent Systems and Computing*; Das, H., Pattnaik, P., Rautaray, S., Li, K. C., Eds.; Vol. 1119; Springer: Singapore, 2020.

13. Noemmer, R.; Haas, R. An Evaluation of Test Suite Minimization Techniques. Software Quality: Quality Intelligence, In *Software and Systems Engineering*, 2019; pp. 51–66. https://doi.org/10.1007/978-3-030-35510-4_4

14. Rajappa, V.; Biradar, A.; Panda, S. In *Efficient Software Test Case Generation using Genetic Algorithm based Graph Theory*, First International Conference on Emerging Trends in Engineering and Technology, 2008.

15. Rao, K. K.; Raju, G.; Nagaraj, S. Optimizing the Software Testing Efficiency by using a Genetic Algorithm. *ACM SIGSOFT Softw. Eng. Notes* **2013,** *38* (3), 1–5.

16. Reena, B. P. K. In *Test Case Minimization in COTS Methodology Using Genetic Algorithm: A Modified Approach*, Proceedings of ICETIT 2019. Lecture Notes in Electrical Engineering; Singh, P., Panigrahi, B., Suryadevara., N., Sharma S., Singh A., Eds.; Vol. 605; Springer: Cham, 2020.

17. Ma, X.-Y.; Ha, Z.-F.; Sheng, B.-K.; Ye, C.-Q. In *A Genetic Algorithm for Test-Suite Reduction*, IEEE International Conference on Systems, Man and Cybernetics, 2005.

18. Yamuc, A.; Cingiz, M. O.; Biricik, G.; Kalipsiz, O. In *Solving Test Suite Reduction Problem using Greedy and Genetic Algorithms*, 9th International Conference on Electronics, Computers and Artificial Intelligence (ECAI), 2017.

19. Zhong, H.; Zhang, L.; Mei, H. An Experimental Study of Four Typical Test Suite Reduction Techniques. *Inform. Softw. Technol.* **2008,** *50* (6), 534–546.

Index

Printed and bound by CPI Group (UK) Ltd, Croydon, CR0 4YY

23/10/2024

01777693-0013